Budgeting
Politics and Power

CAROL W. LEWIS
University of Connecticut

W. BARTLEY HILDRETH
Georgia State University

New York   Oxford
OXFORD UNIVERSITY PRESS
2011

Oxford University Press, Inc., publishes works that further Oxford University's
objective of excellence in research, scholarship, and education.

Oxford   New York
Auckland   Cape Town   Dar es Salaam   Hong Kong   Karachi
Kuala Lumpur   Madrid   Melbourne   Mexico City   Nairobi
New Delhi   Shanghai   Taipei   Toronto

With offices in
Argentina   Austria   Brazil   Chile   Czech Republic   France   Greece
Guatemala   Hungary   Italy   Japan   Poland   Portugal   Singapore
South Korea   Switzerland   Thailand   Turkey   Ukraine   Vietnam

Copyright © 2011 by Oxford University Press, Inc.

Published by Oxford University Press, Inc.
198 Madison Avenue, New York, New York 10016
http://www.oup.com

Oxford is a registered trademark of Oxford University Press

ISBN   978-0-19-538745-2 (paper)

Printing number: 9 8 7 6 5 4 3 2 1

Printed in the United States of America
on acid-free paper

This book is dedicated to our spouses,
Saul H. Nesselroth and Rhonda N. Hildreth

BRIEF CONTENTS

CONTENTS

BOXES, FIGURES, AND TABLES

⚛

BOXES

FIGURES

TABLES

WEB SITE RESOURCES

1. Advocacy Politics in Budgeting (Exercise)
2. Analyzing the Costs of Public Programs
3. Bouncing off the Base in Government Budgeting
4. Budget Formats
5. California Dreamin': Tools of Direct Democracy
6. Capital Planning Principles
7. Chronology of Federal Budgeting, 1789–2008
8. Citizen's Guide to Budgeting in Alexandria, Virginia
9. Cutbacks and Priorities (Exercise)
10. Fairness and the Federal Income Tax
11. Fiscal Year
12. Further Resources
13. Health Care Basics and the Budget
14. How Budgets Interact with Economic Conditions (Exercise)
15. How to Read Highlights of the Federal Budget (with self-test)
16. How War Affects the Formal Federal Budget Process
17. Information Is Power (Case Study)
18. Internet Resources by Topic
19. Journals for Further Reading
20. Opinion Polls in a Democracy (Exercise)
21. Paradox of Efficiency (Case Study)
22. The Politics of Redistribution and Resentment (Exercise)
23. Portland's Budget Process
24. Power Grab or Neutral Reform? (Case Study)
25. Public Spending Helps Define Us and Our Future: The Story of Hurricane Katrina
26. Resources on Different Approaches to Fairness and Participatory Budgeting in Developing Democracies

PREFACE

A NOTE OF APPRECIATION AND WELCOME

By writing this book, we discovered how much fun it is to live in our students' world. Then we realized that actually we are living in our students' world; our own loses its color and passion without a sense of the future. The future is you, the reader, who will make your mark as surely as an astronaut left a footprint on the moon.

We also came to appreciate the wisdom of the American public. Voters and taxpayers may not always know all the facts or understand all the details, but somehow they eventually see the big picture with breathtaking insight. We relearned the value of democratic institutions and fragmented authority. Through this lesson, we rediscovered the soul of the politics of budgeting: More, much more, is at stake than efficiency. In the public sector, when at its best, money chases problems and priorities, not profits.

Many threads of our thinking came together as we worked on this book. We are grateful for the political community in which we live. We are grateful, too, to the professional community in which we work.

Admitting that few, if any, intellectual undertakings today occur in a vacuum, we admiringly draw upon the work, insights, and experiences of innumerable colleagues in academia, research organizations, public opinion firms, professional associations, budget offices, and firms throughout the United States and in other countries. We build upon the insights of theorists on democracy and politics, which have been topics of discussion for thousands of years.

Many agencies, organizations, and individuals provided materials and were generous with information and reprint permission. We are indebted in particular to the Council of State Governments; National Conference of State Legislatures and Peggy Kerns; National Association of State Budget Officers; Government Finance Officers Association; Roper Center for Public Opinion Research, University of Connecticut and Lois Timms-Ferrara; National League of Cities; states of California, Connecticut, Kansas, Massachusetts, Minnesota, and Texas and their departments; cities of Alexandria, Arlington, Boston, Minneapolis, Oklahoma City, Portland, and Raleigh; Broward County, Florida and the County of Sedgwick, Kansas; Center on Budget and Policy Priorities; Public Agenda; Program on International Policy Attitudes; American Numismatic Association; American National Election Studies; Tax Foundation; Governmental Accounting Standards Board; Peter G. Peterson Foundation; Harris Poll; U.S. Treasury; Federal Reserve; Government Accountability Office; Cato Institute; Heritage Foundation; United Nations; Organisation for Economic Co-operation and Development (OECD); and others. We appreciate the contributions of many individuals including John Books, Ann Hess Braga, Christopher Chantrill, Paul Epstein, Laura Gilbert, Joel R. Glucksman, Nigel Holmes and *American History*, Barbara Menard, Zhang Mengzhong, Douglas Morgan, and Todd Sandler for their support and assistance. Special recognition is due Representative Denise Merrill, majority leader in Connecticut's House, for the case she wrote for this book. Graduate students in political science at the University of Connecticut, Zsolt Nyiri, Chris Andrews, Iain R Bolton, Joshua Stapel, Daniel Tagliarina, Aaron Paterson, and especially Joseph Mello, put in the time and attention needed to make this book possible, as did Michael Woodrum, the George Van Riper Endowed Fellow in Public Finance, and Clifford H. Paxson, both at Wichita State University.

There are simply too many contributing public interest groups, think tanks, associations, firms, nonprofits, governments, and people to list each one here. We are indebted to you all, and we thank you. Please accept the citation or credit line as our thank you.

We are grateful to our students who, unfamiliar with the subject, ask pointed and important questions. We also think of the experienced practitioners and professional budgeters we have met over the years in training programs, conferences, and public agencies, who taught us a thing or two...and more. We also thank the class in the politics of budgeting course at the University of Connecticut whose students beta-tested many of our chapters in 2008.

In addition, we would like to thank the following reviewers for their comments: Cheryl A. Brown, Marshall University; Sebahattin Gultekin, University of North Texas; Boris Morozov, University of Nebraska at Omaha; Catherine C. Reese, Arkansas State University; Bernard Rowan, Chicago State University; Greg Streib, Georgia State University; Joseph Wert, Indiana University Southeast; and Zhirong Jerry Zhao, University of Minnesota. We appreciatively acknowledge Jennifer Carpenter and the team at Oxford University Press for their commitment to this book. We are grateful to India Gray for the care she took with our manuscript.

Even so long a list of credits would be incomplete without this very special salute. We extend a heartfelt thanks to our spouses and families. We are thankful for their patience, support, and understanding throughout this project.

A Different Take on the Subject

There are other books on budgeting, but this one is different in several important ways. We bring to the collaboration different backgrounds, academic specialties, and political viewpoints. What we share is a fascination with the subject and a commitment to democracy. Coming to terms with each other's views and values was an exercise in democratic dialogue. We learned again and again to appreciate the worth of the process and each others' insights.

We dedicated ourselves from the start to an inclusive, balanced perspective. So if readers are searching for an ideological or partisan book, this is not it. Our intent is to be scrupulously nonpartisan and nonideological. Our overarching theme is budgeting in a democracy and derivative themes are accountability, transparency, responsiveness, and participation. We try to present different arguments and political perspectives on budget controversies, just as we debated the issues during our writing. Each chapter includes material on ethics, along with comparative and historical material.

We also share the belief that budgeting is too important to our democracy to exclude citizens and to be left only to experts and public officials. Often, budgeting is seen as a technical, boring subject, but we see it and try to present it as something very different. We use humor, a touch of popular culture, examples, and case studies to encourage readers to connect with the subject, become engaged, and even to participate in the politics of budgeting.

People and organizations produce and post videos on the Internet to make a point. Many videos are advocacy pieces, arguing from emotion or humor to advance a particular viewpoint. Often they are partisan or ideological and sometimes the argument is inaccurate or misleading. Because different types of communication support different learning styles, we include on our Web site many links to videos that illustrate our themes. The videos are examples of political communication that reflects political perspectives; they are not statements of our points of view. We also include links to nonpartisan and analytic videos where possible. Here we issue a fair warning: some of the links may take readers to sites open to uncensored comments posted by viewers or show links to other videos; these comments or related links may contain material objectionable to some readers. We regret this. We tried to avoid objectionable material when making our selections, but Web sites develop and change.

Humor cheers us on by giving us confidence to explore new topics: Yes! I can do this. Rather than make a serious matter seem trivial, a chuckle or a smile promotes trust and dialogue. Humorous cartoons, illustrations, and videos may broaden our perspective by presenting new ones. They certainly are useful hooks on which our memory can hang important ideas. They also allow a breather for readers laboring over new material.

This book is about how to, as well as about why and so what. We assume that you, our reader, is a muggle where budgetary politics is concerned, but we are eager to help you change your status. In the world of Harry Potter, a muggle is an ordinary person without magical powers; the word is now used to mean someone unskilled or a novice. Our goal is to give you the skills and tools you need to work through the political challenges and controversies for yourself. This is why we organize the chapters around key questions. Although we answer them as best we can, we know the answers are really up to you and other voters, taxpayers, and decision makers.

To help you develop your answers, we recommend additional reading and research tools. We offer supplemental resources on our companion Web site, such as chronologies, an inventory of Web resources, some more technical material, and primers on reading federal and state budget documents, so that you can access and understand the decisions for which you hold decision makers accountable. An overview of local budget documents and a glossary, both included in this book, are designed to help you avoid being cut off from political access and influence by some technically savvy players who use technical jargon to protect their power.

Readers who wish to dig deeper can find on our Web site some more advanced or technical material, such as different budget formats and instructions on how to use the Consumer Price Index. The case studies that end each chapter and the many exercises, applications, and links to videos and Internet resources throughout the book offer experience in budgetary politics and problem solving. (All the cases, but one, concern state and local budgeting; the exception focuses on federal and state budgeting.) This active learning, we believe, is the most meaningful and lasting learning there is.

We take a broad view of the subject. We meld theory and practice and draw on different academic disciplines, including political science, public administration, public policy, economics, psychology, demography, and history. We draw on the history and experiences of other countries to provide rich detail and a context that gives a sense of where we fit in and the direction in which we are heading. We enthusiastically chew on the ethical dimensions of the politics of budgeting. After all, budgeting is the core decision-making process in which Americans make public policy and set public priorities. An overlay of ethical considerations ideally helps decision makers select budget priorities and understand political responses. It surely helps readers and analysts clarify the issues and interests at stake.

Organization and Learning Style

Facing the inescapable trade-off between depth and breadth, all authors make choices. We prefer to highlight the main themes and central questions, so that the book's detail and length do not overwhelm our readers. As social scientists, we are more interested in patterns than personalities, but we recognize the impact of both. We understand the importance of institutions and formal rules, but organize the book nontraditionally, around ideas and problems that are meaningful to our readers. Rather than take the usual institutional perspective that organizes by branch of government (executive, legislative, judiciary) and by level of government (treating federal, state, and local levels of government separately), we bundle theory and practice into packages of issues and questions relevant to citizens, voters, taxpayers, and leaders in a democracy. The questions around which the chapters are organized and the review questions at each chapter's end import into this book our classroom experience with the Socratic method of teaching and learning. We use real-life examples to bring the ideas and issues home and give them life.

Some topics, such as fiscal federalism and budget reform, customarily are treated separately in books about budgeting. Other topics, such as separation of powers and electoral politics, are usual in books about democracy. In this book about budgeting in a democracy, we incorporate these topics in chapters organized around political ideas, questions, and challenges that the politics of budgeting provokes. For example, we examine the ideas of balance and sustainability before the details of spending and revenue because the underlying ideas and political factors give meaning to the details. Debt and unfunded obligations are treated in several chapters, depending upon the particular aspect under our microscope.

This book has ten chapters, a glossary, an appendix, and a supporting Web site. The chapters include a case study and conclude with a thumbnail or summary, a list of supporting Web site resources, and questions for discussion and review. The appendix on the federal budget process hits the high points of what many political observers find is a very complicated process. The glossary includes terms useful in the politics of budgeting.

Chapter 1 presents the main themes of accountability, participation, transparency, and responsiveness. Chapter 1 lays out the dominant values in budgetary politics and the obligations of citizenship and political leadership. The chapter also explains why budgeting is political, how it relates to democracy, and what the *public* in public sector means.

Chapter 2 examines direct and indirect public participation in budgetary politics and the role of public opinion, voting, and ideology. It considers the responsiveness of public leaders' to citizens' views about budgeting.

Chapter 3 examines crucial political issues in a democracy—fairness, performance, and trust—and how they affect one other and the politics of budgeting.

Chapter 4, emphasizing the appropriations process, describes how formal and informal processes produce operating budgets. Because Chapter 4 traces the budget process through the stages of the executive model of budgeting, it offers more of an institutional perspective than the other chapters.

Chapter 5 focuses on balance as a core goal in budgeting—how it is achieved, and what happens when the goal is not reached. The chapter explains how public organizations move from scarcity (Chapter 1) and participant claims and demands (Chapters 2 and 3), through the political process (Chapter 4), to the desired goal of budget balance. Key topics include deficits and structural deficits, closing the gap, and debt.

Chapter 6 analyzes the politics and processes of spending public resources.

Chapter 7 looks at revenue as a means of financing public policy and at the policy preferences and political implications of different revenue choices.

Chapter 8 considers capital budgeting, its processes and policies.

Chapter 9 is the practical application of many of the ideas introduced in earlier chapters. This primer on reading a local budget takes readers to the core political and financial concerns. The chapter concludes with two applications.

Chapter 10, our concluding chapter, evaluates how well or poorly the politics of budgeting addresses democratic concerns and policy needs. Has accountability increased? Is the process more open in meaningful ways? What big problems urgently demand the attention of citizens, voters, taxpayers, and decision makers? The chapter is less of a conclusion and more of a summing up because, in a dynamic democracy, the politics of budgeting produces temporary settlements and provisional answers to our questions. The chapter ends with overarching questions (a baker's dozen) aimed at helping readers draw together the main threads woven throughout the book.

We welcome you to the challenging and sometimes raucous world of budgetary politics. We hope you enjoy reading this book as much as we enjoyed writing it.

About the Authors

Carol W. Lewis (Ph.D., Princeton University; B.A., Cornell University) is a professor of political science at the University of Connecticut. Her research interests are public budgeting and finance and public sector ethics. She has lectured throughout the United States and internationally, including most recently in South Africa, England, China, Israel, and Singapore. She has written and edited books and has published scholarly articles in *Public Administration Review, Municipal Finance Journal, Publius,* and other in journals. She served as an elected official on a board in her New England town. A scuba diver, she knows that buoyancy, balance, and taking deep breaths are important in diving, so she believes the sport is good training for the politics of budgeting.

W. Bartley Hildreth (Ph.D., University of Georgia; M.P.A., Auburn University; B.A., University of Alabama) is the Dean of the Andrew Young School of Policy Studies at Georgia State University in Atlanta. Before assuming the position in July 2009, he was the Regents Distinguished Professor of Public Finance in the finance faculty of the W. Frank Barton School of Business and the public administration faculty of the Hugo Wall School of Urban and Public Affairs at Wichita State University. His research interests are in tax policy, municipal securities, and public budgeting and finance. He received the Aaron B. Wildavsky Award for lifetime scholarly achievement in public budgeting and finance in 2008 from the Association for Budgeting and Financial Management. His experience includes service as a city's chief financial officer and as a member of the National Advisory Council on State and Local Budgeting.

Introduction

BUDGETING AND DEMOCRACY

Democracy is the worst form of government, except for all those other forms that have been tried from time to time.

BRITISH PRIME MINISTER SIR WINSTON CHURCHILL,
SPEAKING TO THE HOUSE OF COMMONS IN 1947

This book is about power and money in public life. It also is about politics, where we meet head-on a practical and inescapable problem: there is never enough money to satisfy every need and demand. Resources always fall short of demands, even in relatively rich countries. The hard reality of scarcity leads to competition over public resources. We call this competition over policies and priorities **politics**.

Politics is the use of power and authority to tackle shared problems in the face of scarcity and competing demands. In budgeting, we make the decisions about who gets, who pays, and who and what wins or loses. Power uses coercion to get people to do what they otherwise would not do; authority, on the other hand, uses voluntary cooperation and influence. The case studies in this book show how we use both power and authority in the politics of budgeting.

Cynics may protest that politics is all about how the wealthy and powerful capture personal benefits and special interests line their pockets. This, they would argue, defines the politics of budgeting. Idealists, on the other hand, may see budgeting as a struggle to meet a community's needs and demands, such as national defense, food inspection, safe bridges, clean water, or disaster relief. Where goods and services such as these are concerned, they expect justice and efficiency, but rule out pragmatic compromise and horse-trading.

Politics—competition over public policy and priorities through the use of power and authority.

The authors prefer skepticism to cynicism and optimism to idealism as attitudes more befitting citizens and scholars. Thinking of ourselves as realists, we see principles and interests at play, along with fairness and advantages, and give-and-take and conflict in the politics of budgeting. We sum up our view in the words of the nineteenth-century German politician Otto von Bismarck: "Politics is the art of the possible."

The political process includes formal institutions, rules and law, and elected leaders. It also includes informal influences, such as opinion polls, the media, and lobbyists. All the different elements and participants play a part. Participants are more or less powerful, more or less good-natured, and more or less skilled in political arts, but they all take the process as seriously as it deserves (see figure I.1).

Democracy

The political context of budgeting in the United States is democracy. It is a messy, noisy, dynamic system. These qualities are part of democracy's appeal. Although some reject democracy outright, a Nobel laureate in economics tells us that democracy is the most acceptable form of government around the world and is universally important (Sen, 1999, p. 45). World Public Opinion's 2008 survey of nineteen nations, accounting for 59 percent of the world's population, finds that the public in each country agrees with democratic principles. Using representative national samples conducted in fifty-two countries from 1981–2007, the World Values Survey shows that the scope of free choice in a society strongly affects people's happiness; democracy increases perceived freedom of choice.

Democracy's very qualities and varieties across time and countries make it difficult to define precisely. The many meanings of democracy drive our choice of four main themes: accountability, transparency, participation, and responsiveness.

Some definitions of democracy focus on meaningful citizen participation in decision making, either directly or through representatives. The politics of budgeting is a way to examine the public's influence on public policies and priorities and how leaders are more or less responsive to the public. The basic nuts and bolts

Figure I.1. Budgeting Is How We Make Decisions about Public Resources
Reproduced by permission of Grantland Enterprises.

of how budgeting works matters because only informed citizens can participate effectively. Conquering these basics is one route to political power.

Some definitions of democracy require a set of institutions and procedures, such as competitive elections. For this reason, electoral politics is a part of analyzing budgetary decision making and its products. For example, almost seventy years ago, Joseph Schumpeter wrote that democracy is the "institutional arrangement for arriving at political decisions in which individuals acquire the power to decide by means of a competitive struggle for the people's vote." (Schumpeter, 1943, p. 269) A more modern version says: "Modern political democracy is a system of governance in which rulers are held accountable for their actions in the public realm by citizens, acting indirectly through the competition and cooperation of their elected representatives" (Diamond and Plattner, 1996, p. 50).

Another view of democracy emphasizes political outcomes, such as equality or liberty. Political values are central to a serious discussion of the politics of budgeting in a democracy.

Many see modern democracy as holding leaders accountable for their actions to the citizens. The accountability and transparency that permit public scrutiny figure among the central concerns in budgetary politics.

The politics of budgeting tells us as citizens, taxpayers, and public leaders what problems we are tackling and how good a job we are doing. Effectiveness and performance count in public budgeting because decision makers are using someone else's money and public authority to confront real problems. This exposes the big problems we are solving, the problems we are ignoring, and the ones we are creating through the politics of budgeting.

Robert Dahl (1982, p. 11) specifies the rules and rights that define democracy:

1. Control over government decisions about policy that is constitutionally vested in elected officials.
2. Elected officials are chosen in frequent and fairly conducted elections in which coercion is comparatively uncommon.
3. Practically all adults have the right to run in the election of officials.
4. Practically all adults have the right to run for elective offices in the government.
5. Citizens have a right to express themselves without the danger of severe punishment on political matters broadly defined.
6. Citizens have a right to seek out alternative sources of information. Moreover, alternative sources of information exist and are protected by law.
7. Citizens also have the right to form relatively independent associations or organizations, including independent political parties and interest groups.

Politics
The politics of budgeting in the United States is shaped by its context: democracy and a relatively free market economy. The tensions that typify budgetary politics

reflect the tensions built into such a system of fragmented, often disjointed authority, decision making, and problem solving. Modern democracy blends the will of the people with individual liberty. Representative government sees politicians as reflecting the will of the people (the delegate role) while expecting politicians to make decisions based on judgment and conscience (the trustee role). **Separation of powers** depends on the three branches of government to work together or at least to quietly accept what the others are doing. Yet, each branch carefully guards its rights and privileges. Similarly, a federal structure of government, or **federalism**, requires all governments to work together to accomplish domestic policy, although their interests and muscle may be different or even opposed. Democratic government within an energetic free market economy requires cooperative interaction among government, nonprofit, and for-profit institutions and leaders, but the differences among them often set them at odds.

The players in budgetary politics—citizens, voters, taxpayers, and decision makers—cannot afford to forget for a minute that the subject is a serious one, with profound implications for the way the American society works and the ways in which it does not work so well. Public budgeting is about how the players use shared resources and which problems they put on the public agenda. The solutions affect all Americans now and in the future, as well as many others around the world. A failure now not only costs more to fix later on, but also leaves the bill for someone else to pay.

The many players have different notions about what it means to get it right, who should get, and who should pay. To get it right means, at the very least, that the players must face up to the many shared challenges and controversies: the deficit, tax and service inequalities, financing Medicare and Social Security, tax and spending limits, education funding, and more. There is no workbook solution or spreadsheet to handle these issues. That is the purpose of politics.

Politics today is complex and wide-ranging. Political challenges and controversies crop up at every level of government and in the interactions among interdependent governments, nonprofit agencies, and private entities. For this reason, *public* is broadly defined to include nongovernmental public organizations. Historical and comparative perspectives let us know that others face similar problems (see figure I.2), and that there are alternatives to the way the current generation of Americans is used to doing things. It is also efficient to learn from others' mistakes and successes.

The practice and promise of budgeting in a democracy stress the ethical dimensions of shared resources and public purposes. Americans share these concerns with many others around the world. Corruption—fraud, embezzlement, bribery, criminal conflict of interest, and more—is unethical and illegal (see figure I.3). Although public corruption in the United States is low compared to many other

---

Separation of Powers—each branch of government has its own set of powers, not to be infringed upon by another branch of government.

Federalism—the study or operation of different levels of government.

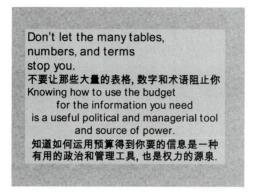

Figure I.2. A Comparative View Shows that We Share Some Problems
Translation courtesy of Professor Zhang Mengzhong.

countries, it remains a problem. More than 1,000 federal, state, and local government officials were convicted of public corruption under federal criminal statutes in 2006; in the twenty-year period from 1987 through 2006, more than 50,000 people were convicted of public fraud, an average of about 2,500 each year. This is a small number, considering that there are more than 89,500 units of government, each with many public officials. With a score of 7.2, the United States ranked 20th out of 179 countries on Transparency International's 2007 Corruption Perceptions Index. (The first index dates to 1998.) The score measures perceptions about the degree of corruption in a country and ranges from highly corrupt scored at zero to highly clean scored at ten.

The politics of budgeting raises many important ethical issues. Is pork (now called earmarks) legitimate or does it undercut the public interest? The idea of the public interest is about a community's mutual interests and shared concerns, often in contrast to an individual's interest or subgroup's special or private interests. A widely used definition comes from Walter Lippmann (1956, p. 40): "The public interest may be presumed to be what... [people] would choose if they saw clearly, thought rationally, acted disinterestedly and benevolently."

Does making a deal to get legislation passed mean compromising principles? Does the need for votes and campaign contributions *distort* the use of public resources or is it proper to use them to reward constituents and supporters? The public policies and priorities developed through the politics of budgeting sketch out the interaction between getting and using public resources on the one hand and fairness and trust on the other.

Decisions about budgets are decisions about today and tomorrow and have heavy moral content. The politics of budgeting spells out how promises are made but not funded and how the rising public debt pushes the cost of current policies and services off onto future generations who have no say in the matter. Budgetary politics draws attention to truth and full disclosure on the public record and in public policy debates. Players suspect that one or another of these issues interests

Figure I.3. Ethics Is Important in Budgeting

1. You scratch my back, and I'll scratch yours. (English)
2. A bribe. (Spanish)
3. Pot of wine; a bribe. (French)
4. To bribe. (Arabic)
5. To bribe. (Chinese)
6. Without oil, there's no driving. (Russian)
7. One hand washes the other. (Italian)
8. If you favour me, I'll favour you. (Turkish)
9. Isn't there another way out? (Portuguese)
10. Pay us all you have got. (Swahili)

Reproduced by permission. United Nations Office on Drugs and Crime. Photos: Ioulia Kondratovitch.

other players because democrats—with a small "d"—have been talking about them for a long, long time.

Ethics helps us answer central political questions: What is the right thing to do? Is public policy fair? How should we treat one other and how should we expect others to treat us? There is moral content in decisions about the budget. Many—if not most—observers and players recognize that the power to affect people's lives carries with it moral responsibilities. Also, efficiency may get shoved aside by moral urgencies, as the Web site resource Cutbacks and Priorities shows. Members of a public board in one city asked an ethicist to help them weigh the moral aspects of the choice in front of them in 2008: balance the budget or introduce a new and expensive—but needed—program to provide housing for homeless people with mental illnesses (Olson, 2009). Observers of the political scene expect to watch ethics play out in the politics of budgeting because budgeting is the core decision-making process in our shared or public life.

Theoretically Speaking

The authors opt to look at the subject in a descriptive way; rich enough in detail to encourage your appreciation of budgeting and your participation in its politics. We also want to present enough explanation so that the details form a meaningful whole, with identifiable patterns and predictable results that make participation worthwhile. To do this, it is not necessary (and probably counterproductive) to build a new grand theory of political life or budgeting. Instead, we draw on many useful theoretical approaches and insights from different social science disciplines. This book's analytic framework emphasizes six factors in decision making about budgets and in budgetary policies:

1. in a *political context* (electoral, partisan, institutional, other)
2. in *complex settings* (many different and more-or-less public and private organizations)
3. through repetitive, interactive *processes* (organizations and bureaucracies, multiple players, long-term relationships, agenda-setting, advocacy coalitions)
4. influenced by formal and informal *actors and personalities* (experience, style, role, reputation, trust)
5. bounded by internal and external *constraints* (law, regulation, rules, procedure, deadlines, timetables, norms, professional standards)
6. strongly influenced by the *external environment* (economic conditions, war, system shocks)

A focus on politics makes power and authority central concerns. The primary feature of the political context in the United States is representative democracy, meaning that the institutional settings, formal processes, rule of law, and other constraints on behavior influence what the process produces. The process produces *outputs*, such as tax and spending policies and lesser decisions about programs, along with their effects on who and what benefits and who pays. Making room for the impact of roles and individuals moves the analysis (or changes the level and unit of analysis) from patterns to people, but captures cognitive limits, hard-wired decision biases, cultural norms, and other social and psychological factors. The primary feature of the economic context in the United States is a competitive market economy and so the ideas of choice, private property, and economic rationality are also drawn into the picture. The complexity of the setting and interactions calls attention to ambiguity, risk, transaction costs, and unintended consequences.

We must turn to social science theory to understand how all these factors or variables interact. Only some theoretical grounding can help readers with the most important task: to understand *why* the politics of budgeting works the way it does and why the way it works matters. As Aaron Wildavsky famously put it in his 1964 classic *The Politics of the Budgetary Process*: "A theory which contains criteria for determining what ought to be in the budget is nothing less than a theory stating what government ought to do...Perhaps the 'study of budgeting' is just another expression for the 'study of politics'."

The study of budgeting and budgetary politics has been dominated by two major theories. Neither is enough to do the two things social scientists generally want from theory: (1) to adequately predict outputs and/or behavior, and (2) to permit hard testing in the real world (empirical validation). These two theories have different assumptions, methodologies, and factors that are considered key to the politics of budgeting.

One major theory is called *incrementalism*, with roots going back more than one-half century to Nobel laureate Herbert Simon's theory of "bounded rationality" or the "satisficing" that Charles Lindblom described as "muddling through." This idea developed as a reaction to the economic model of a single rational decision maker that Simon, Lindblom, and others found inadequate because (1) it did not describe the actual behavior of decision makers in organizational settings, and (2) it did not accurately predict outcomes from large-scale decision-making processes. The basic idea of incrementalism is that decision making in organizations is heavily affected by limits on time, resources, intelligence, and other factors. As a result of these constraints, decision makers choose the first acceptable and available solution. When consensus matters, as it does in this theory, then familiarity or comfort level is important and small changes from previous practices are more likely than are radical changes. Applying the idea specifically to budgeting, Aaron Wildavsky specified incrementalism's three components. The starting point for decision making is the *base*, usually defined as last year's appropriation. *Fair share* is the idea that decision makers expect the slice of the budget pie going to particular agencies or programs to stay about the same size in the short-term and that expecting stable allocations helps structure the competition over resources in any budget cycle. The third component is the *increment*—a small percentage change from the base—that is the budget output from each go-around in the budget process.

The theory of incrementalism has been criticized for (1) its irrelevance to federal budgeting dominated by automatic spending on entitlements and debt payments; (2) the failure to specify how small a change must be to qualify as an increment; (3) its failure to specify whether the theory applies to budget totals, agency totals, program totals, and so on, and the fact that many, many changes are buried in these totals; (4) its lack of questions that can be tested by accepted social science methods; and (5) its conservatism or bias toward stability. The first four criticisms are valid concerns, but the fifth confuses empirical theory (what actually happens) with normative theory (what should happen) and also overlooks the simple fact that small changes that compound over repeated budget cycles over time build into large-scale shifts in budgetary outcomes. Chapter 6 shows that, in spite of the criticism in the academic literature, incrementalism still dominates the way practitioners think about and practice budgeting.

The second dominant theory is rational choice theory and its variant, public choice theory. Importing the economic model of the rational actor into the political realm, this theory explains political behavior by the actor's self-interest. The theory assumes that actors pursue their interests or preferences rationally, in a way that is linked logically and efficiently to what they want to accomplish. Anthony Downs argued in *An Economic Theory of Democracy* (1957) that political activity is best explained by voters' self-interest. With its simplifying assumptions about human behavior, rational choice theory offers the advantage of cutting down the number of factors that must be considered. History and culture are irrelevant in this theory, as are ideology, partisanship, and noneconomic values. The theory is associated with the work of Nobel laureate Kenneth Arrow, Anthony Downs, James Buchanan, Gordon Tullock, Mancur Olson, and the winner of the 2009 Nobel Economics Prize, Elinor Ostrom.

This theory is criticized for several reasons. Some critics argue that budgetary politics is broader than the simple calculation and pursuit of material self-interest: there is more to political life than money. They point out that by ignoring important parts of political life—such as social factors—this theory is unable to predict important outputs from the budget process. That many of the arguments have not been tested in the real world is a problem that this theory shares with incrementalism.

Rational choice theory has contributed several significant insights into the politics of budgeting. Some rational choice theorists added political institutions as an explanatory variable. Institutions, they argue, help structure decision making, along with opportunities for building alliances and coalitions. According to rational choice theory, policy outputs are best explained by the assumption that actors try to "maximize their utility," meaning to get the most of what they want to get. Because political players rarely really know the probabilities or the utilities, attention shifts to ways of dealing with risk and uncertainty (cost-benefit analysis and risk assessment, for example). Our understanding of local government finance is indebted to the work of C. Tiebout published in 1956. The idea of **rent-seeking** shows special interest groups working to capture public resources (or transfer income). (Rent-seeking refers to actions to increase one's income or economic returns at others' expense, such as a special interest group trying to increase its economic returns at the expense of the community's overall good.) In his 1971 *Bureaucracy and Representative Government*, William Niskanen drew a picture of the budget-maximizing bureaucrat interested only in increasing the size of the budget.

Rational choice and incrementalism are not the only theories, but they are the broader and more common ones and suit the purposes of this text. The bookend choice seems to be between (1) incrementalism, a theory that describes decision

---

Rent-seeking—actions to increase one's income or economic returns at the expense of others, such as special interest group seeking to increase its members' income or economic returns at the expense of other taxpayers.

making but offers little in the way of predicting what the politics of budgeting will produce; and (2) rational choice theory, in which the simplifying assumptions of this rich theory do not seem to describe daily budgeting and the concrete problems of collective decision making when power is fragmented and deals must be cut. But why frame the situation as an either/or choice? This book's authors see the situation as theoretically wealthy, with different variables and explanations useful for different levels and units of analysis and different political activities. This book draws on multiple theoretical resources for a full, rich picture of the politics of budgeting. On top of these theoretical approaches, the authors add the overarching theory of democracy.

WEB SITE RESOURCES

- Cutbacks and Priorities

1

Follow the Money

This chapter answers five questions:

- What Is the Public Sector?
- Why Do We Need to Make Political Choices?
- Do the Choices Matter?
- How Does Democracy Affect Budgeting?
- What Is a *Good* Budget?

> It seems that money sings to just about everyone. Did you ever
> hear James Taylor's "Money Machine"? The musical *Cabaret*
> declares that money is important. ABBA sang about how much
> nicer the world is for someone with money. Fast forward a cou-
> ple of decades and, in "Gangsta's Paradise," Coolio raps about
> the relationship between money and power.

Budgeting is from the old French word *bougette*, meaning a little leather bag
or pouch the ruler's secretary carried to hold valuables to trade and perhaps a
scrap or two of handwritten paper about financial matters.

Budgets and financial papers today may run to thousands of pages and many
gigabytes. Are we making better decisions? How do we know? And why should
we care?

The **budget process** is how we make decisions about shared resources.
Budgeting is developing a plan for the way costs and benefits are to be temporarily
settled and distributed. Budgeting tells the story of political power and is the core
decision-making process in the public sector.

Budget Process—how choices are made about shared purposes and/or public resources
through the political process.

11

The budget is important to any organization. Public organizations are no exception. It is so important to government because the official budget is

1. a future-looking statement of government purposes, public policy, and shared values;
2. a legally enforceable plan of operations expressed in dollars and for a specified time period;
3. a way to assign financial, human (time, labor), and other resources (such as information) to selected uses through political processes for a specified time period;
4. a record of the accommodations and agreements, and wins and losses in the political process.

WHAT IS THE PUBLIC SECTOR?

There is no clear dividing line between what is public and what is private in today's complex and dynamic world. It is more realistic to think of different organizations, agencies, and activities as running the gamut from more or less public to or more or less private. Figure 1.1 shows that government agencies tend toward the far left of this range. Even so, not all governments are alike and government itself is complex. Table 1.1 outlines the many different governments in the United States, where less than one-half of the more than 89,500 governments are general purpose and provide a wide range of services.

The U.S. Constitution mentions only the states and the federal government; the many local governments are created by the fifty states. Yet, local budgeting is important politically for six key reasons:

1. the property tax, a mainstay of local government finance, is the least favorite tax;

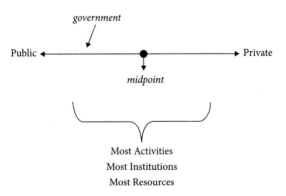

Figure 1.1. The Range of Possibilities

Reprinted with permission of John Wiley & Sons, Inc. Adapted from Lewis, Carol W. and Stuart C. Gilman, 2005. The Ethics Challenge in Public Service: A Problem-Solving Guide. San Francisco: Jossey-Bass.

Table 1.1. U.S. Governments by Type and Number, 2007

	1987	1997	2007
Total	**83,237**	**87,504**	**89,527**
Federal	1	1	1
State Governments	50	50	50
Local Governments	83,186	87,453	89,476
Counties	3,042	3,043	3,033
Municipal	19,200	19,372	19,492
Townships/Towns	16,691	16,629	16,519
School Districts	14,721	13,726	13,051
Special Districts	29,532	34,683	37,381

SOURCE: U.S. Census Bureau, 2009, table 410.

2. the public believes it gets the most for its tax dollars from local government;
3. the budgets of more than 13,000 school districts are tied directly to public education. The public tends to strongly support public spending on public education, which is probably viewed by many as the most important of all the services provided by state and local governments;
4. much of state aid is directed toward financing public education, and this means that the politics of local budgeting and the politics of state budgeting are entangled;
5. as "laboratories of democracy," the many local governments offer opportunities for political and administrative innovations to get started and tested;
6. citizens find it easier to participate in budgetary politics at the local level. It is simply more convenient and more comfortable to attend a meeting in town, to pigeonhole a council member at a neighbor's barbeque, or to pick up the phone and complain to the city manager than it is to "work the Hill" (meaning Capitol Hill, the site of the U.S. Congress) or to organize a statewide protest.

The public sector is broader than government alone. The nonprofit and philanthropic community tilts toward the public sector. Enjoying a privileged tax status, many nonprofit organizations also are partially publicly funded. Many nonprofit and philanthropic organizations are devoted to community services and purposes that serve the broad public interest. Government contracts finance the operations of many social service agencies, such as clinics and daycare centers. The **nonprofit** community in the United States includes organizations that the Internal Revenue Service (IRS) classifies as charitable nonprofit organizations and foundations. Charities, and many museums,

Nonprofit—an organization classified by the U.S. Internal Revenue Code as a religious, charitable, or educational in purpose; activities that directly support those purposes are not subject to federal income tax (and most state income tax laws also).

hospitals, and schools are on this list; health services represent almost one-half of all U.S. nonprofits.

Public charities, private foundations, religious congregations, and social-service/welfare agencies in the United States number about 1.5 million. Accounting for more than 7 percent of the U.S. economy, they have about 10 million employees working full time, with the number of employees doubling when volunteers are added. Almost one-third of these organizations' revenue comes from government. Another one-fifth of revenue comes from charitable contributions that are tax deductible under the federal tax code.

The many mixed activities and joint operations—such as contracts to buy and sell goods and services and government regulation of industries—mean that nonprofits, businesses, and governments work with each other. As a practical matter, most activities, most institutions, and most resources fall between the polar extremes of purely governmental and purely private. Because the public sector is so large and plays a growing role in modern society, how the public sector works, how it uses resources, and who pays and how much, in large part defines political power.

WHY DO WE NEED TO MAKE POLITICAL CHOICES?

The politics of budgeting is driven by scarcity. This scarcity forces a competition among alternative possibilities. Choices and trade-offs must be made. Once it enters the broad public forum, each alternative is a "good idea," at least in the opinion of its advocates. The obviously silly or strange alternatives are culled early in the budget process. (An objection to earmarks is that they take a shortcut and bypass the culling process.) Every good idea in this competition has its advocates and its opponents, who prefer another use of the resources. This is the point of figure 1.2: budgeting is the way we choose among good ideas.

Not a Brawl
For a society to thrive, the competition must not spiral out of control or tumble into all-out conflict. Down this path is violence or revolution. We accept

Figure 1.2. Budgeting Is the Competition among Good Ideas
Reproduced by permission of United Media. By Charles Schulz (1922–2000), Peanuts, originally published in 1980.

=== **BOX 1.1** ===

What Is the Federal Budget?

☑ A plan for how the Government spends your money
What activities are funded? How much does it spend for defense, national parks, the FBI, Medicare, and meat and fish inspection?

☑ A plan for how the Government pays for its activities;
How much revenue does it raise through different kinds of taxes—income taxes, excise taxes, and social insurance payroll taxes?

☑ A plan for Government borrowing or repayment of borrowing;
If revenues are greater than spending, the Government runs a surplus. When there is a surplus, the Government can reduce the national debt—money it owes to American and foreign investors.

☑ Something that affects the Nation's economy
Some types of spending on things like education and support for science and technology are done in the hope they will increase productivity and raise incomes in the future. Taxes, on the other hand, reduce incomes, leaving people with less money to spend.

☑ Something that is affected by the Nation's economy
When the economy is doing well, people earn more and unemployment is low. In this atmosphere, revenues increase and the surplus grows.

☑ A historical record
The budget reports on how the Government has spent money in the past, and how that spending was financed.

SOURCE: Office of Management and Budget (OMB), 2002, p. 1.

certain limits in order to tone down the competition and keep it within acceptable boundaries. Perhaps this is why it has been said, "A budget takes the fun out of money."

One limit on the competition is the public's and political leaders' accepting the fact that choices must be made (see box 1.1). When the need for choice is ignored, the system fails, and imbalance is the result. Many decision makers and citizens realize that people cannot have and do everything at the same time and that just any ol' choice is not good enough.

A second limit is that we agree it is important that these choices are made in a politically acceptable way, according to the rules spelled out in later chapters. Like other formal political processes, budgeting has timetables, deadlines, and routine ways of making choices. The law is one of the most important of these limits, and the Constitution is the heart and soul of the legal framework for budgeting.

Knowing that no loss is necessarily permanent is a third limit on competition. Certainly, it is easier to build upon an early win. Choices spin-off effects, of course, but the choices themselves are not made for all time. They are not set in concrete. Choices are made again and again, so that the future holds out a chance for reviving a rejected proposal and for a defeated political player.

Budgeting is a plan for spending money, but it is a short-term plan. It is often said in politics that the long-term is the next election and the short-term is the next budget. Most governments and nonprofits make budgets every year that are linked to a limited time frame (called the *fiscal period*, usually a twelve-month period termed the **fiscal year**; see Web site resource, Fiscal Year). The budget for the next round in the competition offers another chance. So do adjustments during the fiscal year to deal with new problems, such as a war or natural disaster. We accept that not everything and everyone can have it all and for all time.

Political Process

Budgeting is a political process for making choices among alternatives. Process matters. The process includes formal elements, such as laws that govern deadlines, rules that set limits, authority to spend and collect taxes, and majority votes. For example, the legislature must pass and the chief executive officer (the governor or mayor, for example) must sign the bill for a budget to become a law. The budgeting process also includes informal elements such as access, reputation, status, influence, favors, logrolling, lobbying, rumors, petty greed, and even sex.

The key is that we make our choices through a *political* process. Politics is often used as a negative label. President Ronald Reagan once quipped, "Politics is supposed to be the second oldest profession. I have come to realize that it bears a very close resemblance to the first."

We sum up the road from scarcity to budgetary politics this way:

(Scarcity $\Rightarrow$ Competition $\Rightarrow$ Limited Choice) = **Budgetary Politics**

DO THE CHOICES MATTER?

Who and what win and lose matter, and not just for advocates and opponents. These choices affect the society, the political system, and the citizens' life chances. Making this point, a state budget director slaps his hand down on the massive budget open in front of him and explains that "some people think that this book is all about numbers, about dollars...but they are wrong. It is about people, their dreams, and their opportunities." Budgets matter to government agencies and community organizations and to their leaders and employees. They matter to a society's quality of life.

Fiscal Year—the period designated by an organization for the beginning and ending of financial transactions for official budgeting and external financial reporting purposes; typically a twelve-month period.

Budgetary Politics—elements of the budget process that help to decide how much money is raised (revenues) and how the money gets spent (expenditures).

Guarantee

Most government programs and community services are funded largely or wholly through a budget and budget process. In government, it is illegal and improper to spend public resources in ways and amounts other than set out in law (see the Web site resource, The Paradox of Efficiency). The federal **Anti-Deficiency Act** that dates to 1906 currently requires government officials and employees to spend public funds only on the basis of law (the appropriation).

Using public resources without legal authority is not usually expected or tolerated. For many nonprofit agencies, grants are legally binding contracts, often with governments; watchdog agencies and public interest groups examine agencies' practices; and donors expect their money to go to programs as promised. As a result, for most activities in the public sector, if they are not in the budget, they are not going to happen. Guaranteed!

But this guarantee does not mean that if a program is in the budget it will happen or it will work. Effective and efficient financial and program performance is needed to move a program from the budget to making a difference.

Limits to Budgeting

No single process can serve every purpose, and no document can record everything going on. It is best to start by admitting that not everything that is important to people and society is included in a budget. A budget can include only those things that can be counted and valued in dollars. Yes, it is useful to count. Sometimes there is magic in numbers; ask anyone who has made it into a hall of fame by breaking a record. Still, numbers cannot capture everything or every value, and neither can dollars. Albert Einstein is said to have had a sign in his office that read, "Not everything that can be counted counts, and not everything that counts can be counted." Although our technical capability has increased since the days of the leather *bougette*, some important things still can't fit in the pouch. Even if you can put a dollar value on rebuilding something, is that the only value to the Statue of Liberty? Or just ask yourself, "What is the dollar value of democracy?"

HOW DOES DEMOCRACY AFFECT BUDGETING?

In a democracy, *how* we make choices is important because it is the process we use that makes decisions acceptable or legitimate to the citizens. This way, we can draw on authority rather than use raw power to go forward with the good ideas that win the competition. To really work, budgeting in a democracy depends on six key factors. Two are citizen responsibilities: public participation and public scrutiny. The public must voice political demands, vote, and watch their elected leaders.

Anti-Deficiency Act—law enacted in 1906 that requires a legal basis for any obligation by federal officials or employees for the federal government to spend any money.

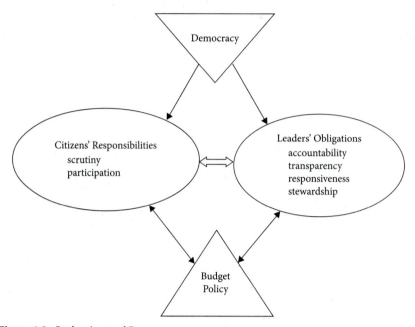

Figure 1.3. Budgeting and Democracy

To do these things, the public depends on political leaders to fulfill their four obligations: accountability, transparency, responsiveness, and stewardship. The case at the end of this chapter introduces these obligations. Figure 1.3 depicts the six political factors that are critical to budgeting in a democracy.

Accountability

More than a century ago, and well before he took the presidential oath of office, Woodrow W. Wilson wrote, "Power and strict accountability for its use are the essential constituents of good government." **Accountability** means answering *to someone* (such as the legislature, chief executive, or taxpayer) *for something* (such as a decision, a program, or mistake). The central way democracies hold public leaders accountable is through elections, but relatively few decision makers are elected to public office. Many decision makers, such as members of the president's cabinet or agency heads, are political appointees; other decision makers are hired as staff, such as the president's staff in the White House. Still others are civil servants and hired and promoted on the basis of merit without attention to their links to a political party. Public records (such as accounts), public disclosure, and the chain of command in organizations are some ways nonelected public servants are held accountable.

Accountability—answering to someone (such as the legislature, chief executive, or taxpayer) for something (such as a decision, a program, or mistake); democracies hold public officials and employees accountable through elections, public records (such as accounts) and disclosure, and the chain of command in organizations.

Accountability is central to public budgeting because the people who vote and pay are different from the decision makers in the legislatures, executive mansions, governmental bureaucracies, and nonprofit agencies. Accountability is so important to democratic politics and budgeting in particular that it finds a place in the Constitution (Article I, Section 9, Clause 7): "a regular Statement and Account of the Receipts and Expenditures of all public Money shall be published from time to time."

The Constitution gives us a framework built on separation of powers among different branches of government and a federal system with states that interact with one other and the federal government in Washington. Add to these the host of nonprofit and philanthropic organizations, **public interest groups**, and others. Now we have a picture of the public sector. It works in a crowded, disorderly institutional context. Authority is shared among many players, and choices can be made only through negotiation and compromise. Because no decision of any consequence is made by one political actor or institution, accountability is key.

Transparency

The essence of **transparency** is that (1) information is readily available and understandable or clear and (2) decision-making processes are regular, known, open, and participatory. It is not enough that reports are written. People must be able to get them, read them, and understand them if democracy is to have meaning. Political leaders have always understood this, which is why secrecy is central to authoritarian regimes. This is understood in democracies as well. For example, Thomas Jefferson believed, "Particulars on government expenditures and taxation should be plain and available to all if the oversight by the people is to be effective."

Never has information been as important a source of political power as it is today. (Surely this is the reason *google* has become a verb.) Information must be available to decision makers to frame public policy, to citizens to decide how to cast their votes, and to taxpayers and the broader financial world (see box 1.2). The number of governments and nonprofit agencies with their budgets and other documents posted on the Internet suggests the importance of transparency to encouraging citizen confidence and trust in a democracy. President Barack Obama echoes this sentiment in his 2009 video (see Web site video, "Recovery.gov").

Responsiveness

There is little point to making your voice heard if you think no one is listening or cares about what you want. The public's assessment of public leaders' and organizations' responsiveness to public opinion and public demands is critical

---

Public Interest Group—a collection of like-minded people organized together for political action that the group claims benefits the general public.

Transparency—information is readily available and understandable and decision-making processes are regular, known, open, and participatory.

BOX 1.2

Global Spotlight on Budget Transparency

Available, useful, and understandable information about budgeting is important to budgeting and politics around the world. Transparency supports public
accountability, democracy, good governance, economic development, and anti-
corruption efforts. Drawing its members from among the more economically developed countries, the Organisation for Economic Cooperation and Development
builds its approach to good governance on the foundation of transparency. The
United Nations' Economic Commission for Africa and the International Monetary
Fund stress the principles and practices of budgetary transparency for developing
countries. The Center for Budget Priorities' International Budget Project assesses
transparency in different countries.

In 2006, non-governmental organizations from fifty-nine countries developed
the Open Budget Index that rates countries on how open and understandable
their budgets are to citizens. Only five of the fifty-nine countries surveyed in 2008
provide "extensive" information in budget documents: France, New Zealand, South
Africa, United Kingdom, and the United States (Open Budget Initiative, 2009).

See Best Practices and International and Comparative Resources on the Web site resource,
🖥 Internet Resources.

---

to the public's recognition of legitimate authority and voluntary cooperation
with leaders' choices. Figure 1.4 shows how responsive Americans think the
federal government is: there is plenty of room for improvement. When asked
by the Pew Research Center in 2007, almost two-thirds of Americans dis-
agreed with the statement that "most elected officials care what people like
me think."

As the core decision-making political process, budgeting is one mechanism through which leaders and organizations respond to political demands.
Lobbying, examined in the next chapter, is evidence of this. The budget as a
plan of operations is also a plan of responsiveness. The public knows: follow the
money.

Stewardship and Efficiency

Citizens, taxpayers, and voters expect public leaders to look after public resources
when the leaders make choices in the political competition we call budgeting. As
stewards, public servants are expected to take special care and treat other people's money as...just that. This way, they safeguard the public's purse and future
choices and opportunities.

Stewardship calls for more than simply being efficient. Our founding documents such as the Declaration of Independence, and core political documents
such as the Gettysburg Address, do not talk about efficiency. Efficiency means
that there is a solid, positive link between what goes in and what comes out—the

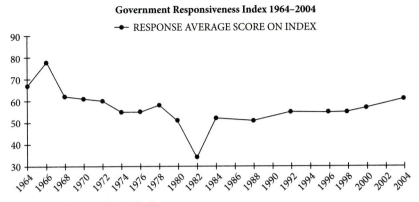

Figure 1.4. Is Anyone Listening?

The index combines data from two questions:

1. Over the years, how much attention do you feel the government pays to what the people think when it decides what to do—a good deal, some, or not much?
2. And how much do you feel that having elections makes the government pay attention to what the people think, a good deal, some or not much?

SOURCE: The American National Election Studies, 2005, Graph 5C.3.1.

operation or service is getting the most from the resources used. Efficiency calls to mind the opposite of wasteful spending or squandering resources. **Efficiency** relates the cost to the actual output or performance (and often is expressed in dollars per unit of output). Efficiency is only politically influential when it is absent or believed absent. (Chapters 3 and 10 discuss the widespread belief that the public sector wastes public resources and why this belief is politically important.) Efficiency is a narrow idea in the sense that it is about how something is done; it links cost and performance, but says nothing about *why* something is being done.

Efficiency is important, but so are other values, such as integrity, liberty, justice, and democracy. It is these other values that describe who we are and want to be. These values, along with efficiency, define **stewardship.** The steward juggles all of these values, plus keeps an eye on the future impact of today's decisions. Concerned with sustainability, the steward asks, "Can we keep on doing what we think is important enough to claim public resources today, or is today's path a dead end or a public version of a Ponzi scheme?" (The Securities and Exchange Commission [SEC] tells us that "the Ponzi scheme continues to work on the 'rob-Peter-to-pay-Paul' principle, as money from new investors is used to pay off earlier investors until the whole scheme collapses.")

Efficiency—relates the cost to the actual output or performance.

Stewardship—preserving the value of an asset over time; to safeguard the public's purse and also future choices and opportunities.

Table 1.2. What Is Important in Budgetary Politics?

VALUE	FOCUS	TYPE	CONCERNS AND QUESTIONS
Economy	inputs	economic	How little must we raise and spend?
Efficiency	outputs, performance	economic	What are we getting for the resources we use?
Effectiveness	outcomes, problem solving	social	What difference are we making?
Equity/ Fairness and Participation	justice, due process, inclusion, representation, public trust, intergenerational equity	political	Is procedure followed? Is law? Are processes and outcomes fair? Should we do this?
Accountability and Transparency	legal compliance, disclosure, public scrutiny, truth, and responsibility	political	Can we legally do this? Are records true, complete, open, and accessible? Are decisions open, traceable, declared, and understandable? Are leaders answerable for their decisions?
Responsiveness	public demands, public opinion	political	Are decision makers paying attention?
Liberty	individual freedom, choice	political	What are the proper role and size of government and other public budgets? Does the use of public resources add to or decrease individuals' freedom?
Sustainability	stewardship, future impact of today's decisions, unfunded promises, debt	fiscal	Are spending burdens pushed into the future? Does revenue policy reduce future capacity and possibilities? Can we meet financial and service obligations over the long haul? Are we looking forward?

What is important in budgetary politics? Go to your state's or city's budget, read the first few pages of the budget message, and show where the chief executive calls on specific values to explain the budget choices.

Often it falls to political leaders to redefine the goal or problem in order to build a consensus, reduce conflict, construct a win/win compromise, and move forward toward shared purposes. Table 1.2 lists the many answers to the question, "What is important in budgetary politics?" Laying these values over budget priorities can help decision making (see the Web site resource, Cutbacks and Priorities).

WHAT IS A *GOOD* BUDGET?

In political terms, a *good* budget performs five major tasks:

1. A good budget shows a reasonable, responsible, *balanced* relationship between spending on services to be delivered and willingness and ability to pay (revenues) for the same fiscal period.
2. A good budget provides information for policy making, public scrutiny, and accountability.

CASE

A Lesson in Political Muscle

A Philadelphia university that failed to work with a state lawmaker advocating for home-schooled students has itself been given a lesson in the Pennsylvania House of Representatives.

    State Rep. Joseph A. Petrarca, a Democrat, believed the admissions policies of the University of the Arts placed an unfair burden on the home-schooled child of a family in his western Pennsylvania district. He and the family objected that the private university's standards for determining whether a home-schooled student had completed a high-school-level education were stricter than the state's. Mr. Petrarca says he had repeatedly tried to reach university administrators to discuss his concerns. Last week, out of frustration, he persuaded the House to vote 106 to 97 to deny the university its annual state-aid appropriation—about $1.2 million. Officials of the university "found my phone number all of a sudden," he says. After the institution's interim president, William Mea, agreed to meet with Mr. Petrarca to discuss his concerns, the House took the matter up again and voted 156–46 to give the university the money. Mr. Mea said that he was not aware of Mr. Petrarca's calls and that the House vote to cut off his institution's funds took him by surprise. He said the university went out of its way to recruit home-schooled students.

Reprinted with permission. Schmidt, 2007, p. A16. *The Chronicle of Higher Education.*

Thinking It Over

    1. What does this case say to you about accountability and responsiveness in the use of public resources?

    2. What definition of budgeting applies to this case?

    3. In your opinion, was Representative Petrarca justified in using his power of the purse to hold a *private* university accountable? Why?

    4. How does this case illustrate the difference between stewardship and serving a voter or constituent in one district?

3. A good budget serves legal and political purposes by (a) meeting legal obligations and requirements; (b) aiding decision making by being timely and addressing what is important in budgetary politics (listed in table 1.2); and (c) being understandable and comprehensive, leaving out nothing that matters in decision making (termed **materiality**).

4. A good budget preserves leaders' credibility and public confidence by presenting comparable, consistent, accurate, reliable, valid data, analyses and explanations.

5. A good budget is persuasive and speaks to target audiences, including decision makers; taxpayers, voters, citizens, service users; employees; the investment community; other organizations and professional associations; and oversight agencies including auditors, grantors, and donors.

Materiality—a matter is "material" if there is a substantial likelihood that a reasonable person would consider it important.

A good budget gives us a financial handle on public action and inaction. It tells us what we agree is important and what our public priorities are. It should also tell us what we are not doing or not doing well enough, and what we are not funding (see chapter 9). Recent experiences with the construction and upkeep of the levees in New Orleans, a bridge in Minneapolis, and poorly financed health care and pensions nationwide dramatize the importance of a *good* budget.

THUMBNAIL

Public budgeting is different from personal or business budgeting. It is supposed to be. Public budgeting is making choices about scarce resources for the fiscal period *through the political process.* Budgeting focuses on political purposes; calls for accountability, transparency, responsiveness, and stewardship centering on sustainability; and relies on public participation and public scrutiny. Although these values and mechanisms are important in business environments (especially for corporations regulated by the Securities and Exchange Commission), the degree of public participation, scrutiny, and accountability is much, much greater in public budgeting. Political authority is broken into bits and pieces among many institutions and many players participate in an open process. The political choices are written into law, making them harder to change, but also harder to fudge.

WEB SITE RESOURCES

- Cutbacks and Priorities
- Fiscal Year
- Further Resources
- Internet Resources
- The Paradox of Efficiency
- President Barack Obama, video, "Welcome to Recovery.gov"

REVIEW QUESTIONS

1. What accepted limits on competition over the budget are said to "take the fun out of money?"
2. What did Einstein mean when he said, "Not everything that can be counted counts, and not everything that counts can be counted?" What does this mean when applied to the budget?
3. How are citizens able to learn enough about the budget process to hold public officials accountable for their decisions?
4. Why is transparency in the budget process important for a democracy?
5. Why might an *efficient* budget not necessarily be a *good* budget?

2

⌒∞⌒

We the People: Power and Participation

This chapter answers four questions:

- Do We Vote Our Budget Choices?
- Are Citizens Self-Interested Rational Actors?
- Is Lobbying Legitimate in Budgetary Politics?
- Does Public Opinion Influence Budgetary Politics?

> What did Bob Marley, the Jamaican reggae musician and activist, say about power and participation in "Get Up, Stand Up"?

> Democracy is the theory that the common people know what they want and deserve to get it good and hard.
> H. L. MENCKEN (1880–1956)

Most Americans believe that a democracy depends on the consent of the people for effective, legitimate government. After all, the Declaration of Independence declares that governments derive "their just powers from the consent of the governed." The citizens' voluntary cooperation that flows from their consent contrasts dramatically with the force relied upon by authoritarian governments. In turn, consent relies upon open, accountable, and responsive government.

In this chapter we examine how citizens influence budgeting and for what purposes. Citizens participate in budgeting through (1) public meetings, (2) advisory committees, (3) surveys, (4) focus groups, (5) lobbying, and (6) voting. They may organize like-minded citizens into associations for grassroots political action. Associations may link with other groups in coalitions to amplify their voice in decision making. By encouraging participation, many public leaders hope to increase trust and legitimacy, educate voters and taxpayers, marshal support for budget proposals, and get input and feedback for decision making about the budget. Both leaders and participants anticipate changing

25

how much is spent, on what, and how it is financed. This, after all, is the point of participation.

What is the citizen's role in budgeting? Participation means a lot more than saying okay. Is public participation meaningful? We look at how citizens voice their spending and tax choices through voting, interest groups, lobbying, and opinion polls when deep social divides (or **cleavages**) translate into different interests. Is the public so polarized and are the budget debates so bitter that consent and therefore democracy are threatened? How responsive is government to these different and opposing interests? How should political leaders interpret shifting and conflicting public opinion?

Here we see how budgeting in a democracy affects and is affected by electoral participation and partisanship, advocacy, and lobbying. In sum, this chapter is about how citizens bring power and preferences into play in budgetary politics.

DO WE VOTE OUR BUDGET CHOICES?

In a republic or representative democracy, public participation in decision making is most often filtered through elected representatives. Rather than making decisions directly, citizens elect public leaders to make decisions. Candidates for national, almost all state, and some—but certainly not all—local offices are endorsed by political parties. Endorsed candidates run in more-or-less partisan campaigns that associate them with a party and its positions on many public policies, including budget issues. (Many local elections are nonpartisan, particularly in cities with appointed chief executive officers, usually given the title of **city manager**.) The public expects candidates in partisan elections to support the party's position, and the public may use the party label as a shortcut to efficiently sidestep close study of each candidate's stand.

Unfortunately, this idealized version of citizen participation has serious practical problems.

- The first and most important problem is the low rate of voter turnout. When voter turnout is low, how do people learn about their rights as citizens, their responsibilities to the community, and their relationships to government? Far more people experience political relationships and responsibilities through budgeting than participate in electoral politics (see chapter 7). Low voter turnout means citizens in the United States and other countries learn about their rights and duties through the tax system. (People also learn about politics through popular music; for the link among democracy,

---

Cleavage—a sociological or socio-economic category or division that cuts society into broad parts (such as gender, race, and class) with which interests are associated that may affect voting and support for budgetary issues.

City Manager or County Manager—an official appointed and employed by an elected governing body to manage the local government's operations and services on a day-to-day basis.

corruption, and responsiveness, listen to "El Costo de la Vida," by Juan Luis Guerra, the popular Dominican merengue artist.)

- A second problem is that party labels are imperfect guides to specific decisions about particular issues. The fact is that each voter casts a single vote, but an election is usually about a bundle of issues. This further reduces the usefulness of party labels for predicting candidates' stands on particular issues once they are elected.
- A third problem is about leadership and the public's power. How closely do officeholders listen to the citizens' voices? How much power do citizens believe they have?

Voting Bundles, Not Budgets

Although some voting is specifically on budget matters (such as voting on the budget at a New England town meeting), electoral politics usually swirls around the many issues at stake in a general election. It is often difficult for citizens to pinpoint exactly where a candidate stands on spending, taxes, and debt. The difficulty compounds when many issues are at stake.

Even a specific campaign promise may be fudged when the candidate takes office and learns that trade-offs and compromises are needed to put together legislative support to get something done. A well-known example of this behavior is when soon-to-be-president George H. W. Bush, in his acceptance speech at the 1988 Republican National Convention, pronounced: "Read my lips: no new taxes." In a famous political turnabout in 1990, he signed the bill that raised income-tax rates for high-income earners in order to offset a growing deficit. (An ironic twist is that he delivered the address at the New Orleans' Superdome, now a symbol of governmental failure in disaster relief.)

General elections often involve many issues, each with a different priority in the candidates' and public's minds. Citizens respond by using any one of six decision rules to cast their vote, each with important consequences for budgeting:

1. *Calculus.* Voters may weigh and compare candidates' positions and vote for the one who overall most closely represents their own views. Even an increase in Independent voters (meaning not affiliated with Democrats or Republicans) does not necessarily mean more voters do this kind of calculation. It demands a lot of time and information, plus some faith that the candidates actually will follow through on their campaign promises.

2. *Trump.* A single-issue voter may agree with a candidate on a top priority and shrug off disagreements over other issues. Other times, a single-minded focus on budget impacts substitutes for a meaningful discussion of public policy as a way of effectively closing the door on a policy option labeled a "budget buster." In local politics, property taxes, public schools, or economic development may trump other concerns. To voice their preference by voting, citizens more passionate about an issue may turn out in higher numbers than those who are less passionate (see box 2.1).

BOX 2.1

James Madison, The Federalist #10, 1787

Among the numerous advantages promised by a well constructed Union, none deserves to be more accurately developed than its tendency to break and control the violence of faction....Complaints are everywhere heard from our most considerate and virtuous citizens, equally the friends of public and private faith, and of public and personal liberty, that our governments are too unstable, that the public good is disregarded in the conflicts of rival parties, and that measures are too often decided, not according to the rules of justice and the rights of the minor party, but by the superior force of an interested and overbearing majority. However anxiously we may wish that these complaints had no foundation, the evidence, of known facts will not permit us to deny that they are in some degree true.

By a faction, I understand a number of citizens, whether amounting to a majority or a minority of the whole, who are united and actuated by some common impulse of passion, or of interest, adversed to the rights of other citizens, or to the permanent and aggregate interests of the community.

Under the pen name "Publius," Alexander Hamilton, James Madison, and John Jay wrote eight-five essays in 1787–1788 advocating ratification of the new constitution.

---

3. *Trade-off.* Voters may decide that certain issues are more important than others at a particular time and cast their votes accordingly. All policy proposals have budget consequences, of course, but sometimes voters are willing to trade their budget preferences for what they see as more pressing policy concerns. This level of priority is often associated with national security or economic issues. Sometimes voters seem willing to make trade-offs in favor of their social concerns, such as abortion or same-sex marriage. The Pew Center tells us that in 2007 a majority of Americans favored helping "more needy people even if it means going deeper into debt." By 2009, however, the large debt incurred during the Great Recession of 2007–2009 may have led more citizens to worry about federal debt levels. Appeals to the political center try to convince voters to make trade-offs that favor one or another political party; wedge issues divide the voters into different camps so that voters see certain trade-offs as unacceptable.

4. *No Show.* Some citizens stay away from the voting booth. They may be overwhelmed by the number of or the complexity of the issues, or by the biting tone of the campaign. Frustrated citizens may see the issues as so distant from their concerns that they do not vote. Apathetic citizens, unconnected to the political system, do not care deeply enough to vote. Low voter turnout works to the advantage of more extreme voters.

5–6. *Voting party affiliation and core beliefs.* These approaches are so important to understanding budgetary politics that they deserve a closer look.

Voting Political Parties

Party affiliation is changing: a map of the states colored red, blue, and swing (meaning no stable party majority) looks very different today than it did several decades ago. Today Democrats and Republicans are about equal in number. Voters increasingly classify themselves as independent and these now are about one-quarter of all adults. The analysis relies on public opinion polls because citizens have to declare a party affiliation when registering in only about twenty states (and this information is publicly available).

The picture changes if we look at voters who report that they are "leaning independent" rather than those who report that they are registered as Independents. Now we see that the largest single percentage of the American public considers itself open-minded in elections and policy disputes. Almost two-fifths of the people report that they are independent, apolitical, or leaning independent. This is about what it was in the 1970s, but higher than the 1950s–1960s. Data from the American National Election Studies shows that Independents (open to persuasion) outnumber those who identify themselves as strongly partisan (firmly decided), and both groups each represent about 30–40 percent of the adult public.

The important moderating influence of independent and independent-leaning voters on elections and policy may be overlooked when we focus on citizens who are strongly committed to a political party and have already made up their minds. About one-third of U.S. citizens declare that they are strongly partisan, or committed to a particular political party. This proportion has risen since the 1970s, but the strong partisanship reported in the 2000s is no greater than what it was in the 1950s and early 1960s.

A candidate's stand on budget issues cannot always be predicted accurately from campaign promises or party labels. Even so, the public, candidates, commentators, and the media often associate budget positions with different political parties. Conservative Republicans are generally thought of as fond of cutting taxes and services while liberal Democrats are presumed to prefer increasing both. These stereotypes do not necessarily predict a candidate's stand on a particular issue.

The same can be said of the voters. Political parties appeal to a broad public, and different constituencies may have different policy preferences; after all, these differences are what make representation important in the first place. Also, these stereotypes unrealistically simplify and narrow the range of practical solutions to the real problems of public policy. Actually, a candidate's principles may give way to an officeholder's pragmatism in the face of, for example, threats to national security, a natural disaster, or changing economic times.

From a partisan viewpoint, budgetary politics is full of surprises. President Clinton campaigned for president in 1991 on a promise to "end welfare as we know it," but turned his attention first to health reform and the deficit. As the majority party in the 104th Congress (1995–1996, the first Republican-controlled session of Congress since 1952), Republicans introduced their first welfare-reform proposal as part of the 1996 Budget Reconciliation Act. Democratic President Clinton twice vetoed their versions of welfare reform before compromising with the Republican Congress to transform welfare from a right to be claimed by all those eligible into a program offering temporary benefits that is described by its name, The Personal Responsibility and Work Opportunity Reconciliation Act of 1996. His signature on this cost him dearly on the left side of his **political base** (meaning the enthusiastic and reliable political supporters who are counted on to vote). Despite the Democrats' supposed "tax-and-spend" approach to budgetary politics, in 1998 President Clinton oversaw the first surplus reported for the federal budget since 1969.

In another surprising turn of events, and although Republicans are said to prefer limited government and fiscal discipline, Republican President George W. Bush and a Republican Congress in the early 2000s expanded the number of government employees and regulations; increased total federal spending, and spending directed toward congressional constituencies (called **earmarks**). Military operations and the massive and unprecedented economic intervention in 2008 increased the deficit and debt to levels surpassed only during the two world wars of the twentieth century. Federal bailout and loan packages amounted to direct public investment in the private sector and drew bitter complaints from some conservative corners. Many conservative leaders, such as Alan Greenspan, chairman of the Federal Reserve for eighteen years, criticized what they saw as an "out-of-control" federal government—even with Republicans controlling both the White House and Congress. Late in November 2008, Senator John McCain (R-AZ), the defeated Republican presidential nominee, said that one lesson from the election is that that Republicans lost their fiscal discipline.

Public support for assistance to the needy fell in the first Clinton Administration, but re-emerged as a public priority in the first Bush Administration, as figure 2.1 shows. This is not a surprise, because we know that the public's ideological frame of mind and partisan choices cycle between liberal and conservative, and the public's mood in national politics runs counter to the government's policies. (The next chapter explains how this "political thermostat" affects public views of government spending.)

Party orthodoxy and stereotypes about budgetary viewpoints are not always useful for predicting politicians' votes on a single budget issue. Congress and some state legislatures are closely divided into two opposing camps. A split along party lines is often referred to as polarization. The split makes partisan compromise necessary for legislative business, but also potentially more uncertain because even a single vote can change budget decisions.

Political Base—the enthusiastic and reliable political supporters who are counted on to vote.

Earmark—directives put into appropriations or committee reports by individual legislators that tell executive units to spend program money in particular geographic locations, on particular companies, for particular projects, or that grant tax breaks to particular companies or individuals; sometimes labeled as wasteful or corrupt.

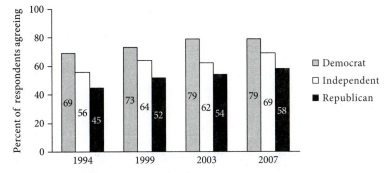

Figure 2.1. Partisan Views on Government Helping the Needy

"These attitudes have undergone a major change since 1994, when the Republicans won control of Congress. In particular, 54% say the government should help more needy people, even if it adds to the nation's debt, up from just 41% in 1994. All party groups are now more supportive of government aid to the poor, though Republicans remain much less supportive than Democrats or independents if it means adding to the deficit."

SOURCE: Pew Research Center, 1994–2007. Retrieved from iPOLL Databank, The Roper Center for Public Opinion Research, University of Connecticut.

Consider how a budget battle waged by one person tipped the U.S. Senate from Republican to Democratic control in 2001. Senator James M. Jeffords from Vermont threatened to bolt the Republican Party unless special education got billions in more funding and the president's proposed tax cuts were scaled back to pay the bill. Had the president and Republican leadership in the Senate caved in, they could have been held hostage to every similar threat. They did not, Jeffords switched his party affiliation, and the Democrats took control of the Senate for the first time since 1994. Another tax cut provides a second example of how a single vote matters. In 2003, the tax cut favored by the Bush Administration passed by one vote. When the Senate vote tied, Vice President Dick Cheney exercised his constitutional duty and cast the tie-breaking vote.

Voting Core Political Beliefs

Although elections are about public policies, candidates' character, spending, and taxes, elections are also about deeply held beliefs and core values. Then-presidential-nominee George H. W. Bush said in his acceptance speech to the Republican National Convention in 1988, "The truth is...this election is about the beliefs we share, the values that we honor, and the principles we hold dear....An election [is] about ideas and values...about philosophy." In fact, feelings and convictions are critical to the way people vote and to political strategies for effectively influencing public opinion. The public's feelings and central political beliefs influence budgetary politics.

Core political beliefs are distributed unequally across the political landscape. The American public tends to see itself as conservative or moderate rather than liberal. Self-proclaimed conservatives continue to outnumber liberals (by two-to-one

Table 2.1. Decade Average of Self-Reported Political Philosophy

Average response to the question, "How would you describe your own political philosophy—conservative, moderate, or liberal?"

	CONSERVATIVE	MODERATE	LIBERAL
1970s	32%	40%	18%
1980s	36%	40%	18%
1990s	38%	41%	18%
2000s (to 2005)	35%	40%	18%

SOURCE: Reprinted by permission. Harris Poll, 2005, table 4.

in table 2.1, but by less according to some other sources). Many voters identify themselves as moderates.

The general pattern of basic political attitudes (called philosophy in table 2.1) has not changed a great deal over the past decades. This leads us to question the widespread view that a *new and more intense* polarization of the American electorate affects all politics today, including budgetary politics. It is neither new nor more intense *for the general public* than in the past. Except among the more strongly partisan and less moderate voters, party identification coupled with central beliefs may mean different things, at different times, and for different issues.

What is different is partisan electoral strategy. For example, instead of appealing to voters at the political center (called the **median-voter** strategy), the Republican Party adopted the strategy of appealing to the party's more conservative base. Republican strategists calculated the loss of conservative votes *versus* the gain of moderate votes if it shifted toward the center; they went with the numbers, and built electoral dominance around turning out the conservative vote. The 1994 election campaign was energized by conservative opposition to the passage, on straight party lines, of the 1993 tax increase. This issue helped sweep conservative Republicans into the majority in the House of Representatives (104th Congress).

Coupled with outstanding organization, fundraising, and tactics designed to turn out their voters on election day, the electoral success of the Republican shift to the right directly affected the political dynamics of budgeting in Washington, D.C. and in many states. Many victors had signed on to a policy agenda (the *Contract with America*) that backed (1) a reduced role for government, (2) increased accountability, and (3) measures to make both tax increases and deficits difficult. The immediate result in Washington was a flurry of initiatives in budgetary politics in 1995 (see the Web site resource, Chronology).

Median Voter—a theory holding that contested decisions turn on the views of the voter in the middle (such that the vote becomes 51/49 instead of 50/50); a theory of electoral politics that explains the tendency of political parties to appeal to as many voters as possible by taking positions at the center of the issue(s).

Toward the end of 1995, a budget standoff developed between the Democratic president and the Republican majority in the House. Federal agencies closed down as federal employees were furloughed. The "aggressive chicken-game strategy" (Shaviro 2007, 134) showed that budgeting in a government divided along party lines goes smoothly only when both sides prefer bipartisan compromise and political horse trading to a high-stake, winner-take-all conflict. Some observers see signs that this hardnosed behavior has spread to the most exclusive of all clubs, the Senate. "With the Senate populated by a record number of former House members, the rules of the Old Boys' Club are giving way to the partisan trench warfare and party-line votes that prevail in the House. States once represented by common-ground dealmakers...are now electing ideological stalwarts" (Weisman 2007, A04). When compromise is rejected—by either party or by both—as an acceptable route to at least some policy goals, victory outweighs governing.

What Does Governing Mean?

Many of today's political leaders of different partisan stripes appear more strident and polarized than many of their constituents. Many voters (including moderates and Independents) are less ideological than the political elites, and many voters are frustrated by the partisan conflict that gets in the way of solving the problems voters face in their daily lives. This difference between the public's perspective and politicians' idea of political leadership contributes to frustration with government and the low level of satisfaction with the way things are going in the country.

Frustration and satisfaction, gauged by Gallup's monthly poll, are seen as predictors of near-future elections. Low levels of public satisfaction fueled Barack Obama's 2008 presidential campaign. Soon after his election, President-elect Obama expressed this dissatisfaction and gave his take on governing: "I think what the American people want more than anything is just commonsense, smart government. They don't want ideology, they don't want bickering, sniping, they want action and effectiveness. When it comes to the budget, people don't want to continue argument about big government or small government, they want smart government and effective government" (Kranish, 2008). History will no doubt judge this president by this standard, as it does all presidents.

Legislative institutions are responsible in part for the ideological and partisan divide between leaders and the public. Committee chairmanships have long been earned through seniority rather than ideology or stands on political issues. Constituents in safe districts, where incumbents are contested weakly and unsuccessfully, send their members back again and again to climb the ladder of seniority. The result is that the more conservative and more liberal members from safe districts climb high. Term limits on the number of terms members may serve break this link in some states, but at the cost of lost knowledge of the process and issues. Members become more dependent on legislative staff and their lack of name recognition deals the executive a stronger hand.

The different perspectives of leaders and voters, the public's frustration, and the low level of satisfaction damage a democracy (see box 2.1, above). These three factors chip away at the public's trust and are demoralizing. They also contradict the claim that elected representatives are responsive to citizens' concerns.

Can Citizens Speak to Political Leaders?

After they take their oaths of office, can elected leaders hear what the public has to say? We now know that voting and party labels are imprecise guides to what the public wants. In fact, the public is many publics, divided and subdivided by political party, income, education, age, race and ethnic group, sexuality, geography, tax burdens and program benefits, and core political beliefs. How can leaders figure out the many and mixed messages on budget issues?

Politicians may see their job as serving as either trustee or delegate, or as some combination.

Trustees make decisions primarily using their own judgment and conscience, much like what we think of when we use the term *statesmanship*. They may appeal sincerely to principal, but it need not be a democratic principal. Some elitist leaders may try to hide their arrogant contempt for the public by claiming stewardship, as if saying, "I know best," or "You would agree with me if you had all the information that I have," (see box 2.2).

Delegates, on the other hand, make decisions that they believe reflect the will of their constituents; they act more like an agent than a statesman. Self-serving politicians may act as agents, but for **special interests** promoting their self-interest instead of their constituencies' interests. Still other delegate-type leaders may ignore the broader public good and exclusively serve the voters in their own districts.

Leaders may switch from one role to the other as the issues and the strength of public feelings change. Incumbents may change from delegate to trustee as they spend more time in office, become experts in certain policy arenas, and enjoy a comfortable margin of support from the voters. Frequent elections encourage elected officials to act as delegates, while longer terms (such as the six years in the U.S. Senate) are intended to promote the trustee outlook.

Whether trustee or delegate, savvy political leaders pay attention to other players and decision makers, not just their own consciences or constituents. For example, David R. Obey (D-Wis.) is a very powerful player in budgetary politics because of his position as the chairman of the House Appropriations Committee in the 110th Congress that began in 2007. About striking a deal with the administration he said, "I don't have the luxury of creating policy in my image.... I push

---

Trustee—a role orientation of elected officials that places priority on their use of judgment and conscience in making decisions.

Delegate—a role orientation of elected officials that places priority on voting the will of the people; in contrast to Trustee role.

Special Interest—an individual or organization supporting a position or program that may fail to benefit the general public or benefits a few far more than the public at large and the costs of which may outweigh the general benefit.

BOX 2.2

Delegate or Trustee?

How leaders see themselves—as delegate or trustee—affects the politics of budgeting and also the arguments leaders use to justify their stands on budgetary issues. The recent history of the State Children's Health Insurance Program (SCHIP) is one example. It began as a deal struck in President Clinton's second term to exchange a cut in the capital gains tax rate for a new entitlement program. SCHIP provides government-sponsored health insurance coverage for children whose families make too much to qualify for Medicaid but for whom paying for private insurance is a financial burden. SCHIP is financed jointly by the federal and state governments and administered by the states. Within broad federal guidelines, each state chooses its program design, eligibility groups, benefit packages, payment levels, and procedures. The 1997 SCHIP legislation granted states a capped amount of funds on a matching basis for federal fiscal years 1998–2007.

Polls in 2007 showed that a clear majority of Americans supported the bill to renew and extend SCHIP, as did many from both parties in Congress, most U.S. governors, business and health insurance interests, many religious organizations including the Roman Catholic Church, advocates for children and health including the American Medical Association, and the AARP. (The AARP, formerly known as the American Association of Retired Persons, boasts about 35 million members nationwide.)

President George W. Bush used his veto power for the fourth time in his presidency when he vetoed the bill in October 2007 to reauthorize (renew) and expand SCHIP. The House could not override the veto. The 2007 bill was to have been financed by a $0.61 increase in the federal tax on cigarettes. President Bush objected to the bill on several grounds, including fiscal responsibility; he saw it as too expensive and an expansion of an entitlement. His press secretary said that the president wished to avoid "additional government-run health care, socialized-type medicine." Reassuring congressional opponents of this popular bill, a White House spokesperson said, "Good policy is good politics, and if members stand on principle, they'll be just fine" (Weisman and Lee, 2007, p. A01).

In February 2009, President Obama signed legislation extending SCHIP to an additional 4 million children and authorizing an additional $32.8 billion through September 2013 financed by a $0.62 increase in the federal tax on cigarettes (to $1.01 a pack). He said, "In a decent society, there are certain obligations that are not subject to tradeoffs or negotiations, and health care for our children is one of those obligations" (Phillips 2009).

Both presidents explained that they were acting as trustees. Both called upon principle to support their position. They made different decisions.

---

forcefully for what I believe. But if I sense there's a different balance point, that's where I have to go" (Williamson 2007, p. A19). As a result, the voters may not get what they thought they were voting for from either a trustee or a delegate.

The public seems to want leaders to both listen and lead on budgetary matters. The public offers little consistent direction about the type of leadership it wants and expects. Electoral politics communicates mixed and vague messages.

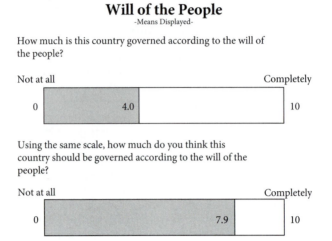

Figure 2.2. **Americans Believe that They Should Participate in Governing**

"Americans are not satisfied with the extent that the will of the people does govern. Asked, 'How much is this country governed according to the will of the people?' and asked to answer on a scale with 0 meaning 'not at all' and 10 meaning 'completely,' the mean response is 4.0. Asked how much the country should be governed according to the will of the people, the mean response is 7.9. 'Eighty-three percent of respondents say that the will of the people should have more influence that it does.'"

Reproduced by permission. World Public Opinion, 2008.

Americans believe that they *should* participate in policymaking and that they have much to contribute (see figure 2.2).

The public's assessment of its influence on government and the government's responsiveness to its wishes reflects the muddles in American politics about what leadership should be like and what influence the public should have on decision making. Many Americans do not believe that they effectively influence government. They believe that they "don't have any say" or "don't think that public officials care much" what they think. By contrast, data from the American National Election Survey in figure 1.4 show that a majority (about three-fifths in 2004) sees government as responsive; government pays attention "to what people think when it decides what to do" and that "having elections makes the government pay attention to what the people think."

Transparency and Meaningful Participation

Voting in general elections is an important way the public participates in budgetary politics, but it is a challenge to interpret the messages voters are sending. Political systems around the globe encourage accountability and transparency to spell out the message more clearly. Budget decisions and the processes that produce them need to be open, understandable, and documented in readable records so that the public can participate and the public and media can examine them.

So that decision making about budget issues is open to public view and participation, governments hold, and often televise, public hearings about budget proposals, post budget documents and videos on the Internet, provide briefing materials to the media, and invite public input. The city of Portland, Oregon publishes user-friendly explanations of the budget and financial documents on its Web site to support its community budget process. The New York City Independent Budget Office publishes understandable citizen's guides for the operating and capital budgets. Many other state and local governments do the same (see the Web site resource, Citizen's Guide to Budgeting in Alexandria, Virginia). The Association of Government Accountants promotes the publication by governments of brief, understandable "citizen-centric" reports about the government's financial condition and performance. The U.S. Government Accountability Office publishes a citizens' guide to the federal government's financial report.

Open government is protected by **freedom of information** laws that define the ways the public and media can gain access to public documents. The federal Freedom of Information Act (FOIA) was signed into law in 1966 and many states followed with their own versions. **Sunshine** laws also promote openness by requiring that most government business be conducted in public sessions. Most states have adopted sunshine or open-hearing laws.

Delegate-type elected officials usually value responsiveness to the public and even trustee-type leaders are held accountable for their decisions. If they are not responsive, they will not hold office for long. Even if there are problems with voting, the mainstay of accountability in a representative democracy is the next election, when incumbents answer for their decisions and hopeful challengers offer new promises.

Despite all these efforts, the public believes that transparency fails to meet their needs. The Association of Government Accountants' 2008 national survey found that 90 percent of American adults believe they are entitled to transparent financial information from government and 57 percent give the strongest possible response in favor of a government obligation to explain how government raises and spends public resources.

Voting Directly on Budget Choices

In many state and local governments, citizens can exercise their democratic rights by voting directly on the budget and other specific legislation. One option is the

---

Freedom of Information Laws (FOI)—a legally defined process for individuals and organizations (especially the press) to gain access to public records.

Sunshine Laws—or open meetings laws, to require meetings to be conducted in public session so decision-makers are accountable to the public.

Referendum—proposal placed on the ballot by petition to repeal or revise an existing law.

Initiative—proposal for a new law that is placed on the ballot by collecting a certain number of citizens' signatures on a petition.

referendum, a proposal placed on the ballot by petition to repeal an existing law. An **initiative** is legislation or a constitutional amendment that starts with a citizen group getting enough signatures on a petition to get a proposal on the ballot. According to the Initiative and Referendum Institute, voters approved about two-fifths of the more than 2,300 statewide initiatives that have appeared before voters in twenty-three states from 1904 (when Oregon introduced the initiative) through 2008. Voters in twenty-three states considered initiatives and referendums about tax issues in November 2008 (see the case concluding chapter 7). Other budget questions on the ballot may start in the legislature. Some governments are required to put proposals for borrowing or tax increases on the ballot for citizen permission. All states except Delaware require citizen approval of constitutional amendments.

These "**tools of direct democracy**" play an important role in budgetary politics. They permit citizens to express their views on a focused issue in a way that voting for candidates cannot. They allow citizens to force governmental responsiveness, bypass elected officials, voice dissatisfaction, and control specific policy.

There are other, less direct ways by which the public can directly express its views and try to influence the budget. The National League of Cities (reprinted by permission) provides an example of citizen-based budgeting in Davenport, Iowa.

> [This]…allows citizens to affect the budget and the city to educate residents about financial challenges. The process has five steps: evaluation, education and feedback, budget development, budget implementation and monitoring and reporting. During the evaluation stage, the city takes a survey of citizens and uses focus groups to measure the quality of existing services. Then a series of forums, called Community Connectors, are held to present the survey results, explain any financial challenges facing the city and further discuss the issues with residents. Departments use the information gathered from these events to balance out pay and work.

As is so often the case with political mechanisms, these tools are double-edged. Direct participation in budgetary decision making heightens the democratic process by offering citizens and taxpayers a chance to make choices that affect their quality of life and pocketbooks. On the other hand, direct democracy raises the specter of the tyranny of the majority under which the concerns of the minority are swept aside. The more direct the democracy, the more open it is to manipulation through selective phrasing and half-truths. The vote is usually for "yes" or "no" only, so there is no opportunity to compromise or to refine the proposal. As the case at the end of this chapter suggests, voters may respond to an appealing idea without examining its broad impacts or full costs. We may wind up with simple-minded approaches that make complex problems worse.

Tools of Direct Democracy—refers to Initiative, Recall and Referendum; may also include town meetings.

ARE CITIZENS SELF-INTERESTED RATIONAL ACTORS?

People are led by their emotions when they vote. This view is very different from the way many political analysts explain voters' behavior. After examining voters' incomes, education, age, race, gender, party affiliation, ideology, and more, analysts sum up the information as the notion of self-interest. They then expect rational actors to act on this interest, defined as economic self-interest.

The reality is that economic self-interest is not always the voters' main focus; political choice, as choices in other spheres of life, is not a rational calculus. Factors such as life experiences and perceptions of risk come into play during decision making. The way a problem is presented affects people's decisions, much the same way as phrasing in a public opinion poll affects people's responses. When Thomas Franks posed the question, *What's the Matter with Kansas?* (the title of his book), he was trying to understand why lower-middle class voters voted for a party advocating views contrary to their economic self-interest. He explains this apparent contradiction by pointing to a socially conservative political agenda that is linked to potent symbols, draws on emotional ties, and trumps economics. Findings from the World Values Survey indicate that, while material concerns matter to people, they define their well-being by what they think is important in their lives, rather than solely by their economic interests.

The emotional basis of decision making also explains the failure of so many efforts to reform budgeting over the past century (many of these efforts are entries in the Web site resource, Chronology of Federal Budgeting). Reformers have tried to make budgetary decision making more rational by reducing the role of emotion and turning instead to analytic techniques.

Emotional Language of Budgetary Politics

Words and images are powerful political tools because they trigger emotional responses. The images and language in budgetary politics—tax cuts, fiscal discipline, security, and fairness, for example—have emotional content and political consequences. Advocates frame issues as competing value systems rather than as programs or policies competing for resources.

In today's heated budget battles, emotional language manipulates the voting and taxpaying public. Labels may substitute for coherent budgetary policy or help market a political agenda. The tax levied on a deceased's estate morphed into the "death tax" not too many years ago. Promised cost savings in programs are advertised as spending cuts. This language reduces the chances for citizens to weigh in on the issues and details of specific programs.

Do we make rational choices with an eye to getting the most value (maximizing utility) from public resources? Self-interest and reason certainly play a part, but so do other considerations. Research in cognitive psychology, economics, and other disciplines confirms that there is something going on other than a straightforward calculus of costs, benefits, probabilities, and risks. Ideology, emotion, selectivity, and biases powerfully affect decisions. Also add popular fallacies, widespread but false beliefs, and ingrained personal biases to the list of barriers to rational decision making in budgetary politics. We just can't blame all illogic, absurdity, and failure on special interests and lobbying.

How Political Ideology Affects Budgeting

Ideology is a systematic set of beliefs and values that shape our understanding of the world. These beliefs and values are the basis for political preferences. Ideology has always influenced the politics of budgeting and continues to play a forceful part. An example is the impact of the approach called **Starve the Beast** (STB). It developed among conservative Republicans in response to the failure to check mounting federal spending since the early 1980s. The theory behind STB is straightforward: make future spending less affordable in order to reduce the role of the federal government in American society. STB consists of three steps.

Step 1. If federal revenues are cut but federal spending is not, then we end up with higher budget deficits.

Step 2. Public opposition to high deficits financed through borrowing or debt should force Congress to cut spending on domestic programs and on entitlements such as Social Security, Medicare, and Medicaid.

Step 3. The result should be that tax cuts force spending cuts and changes in social policy. We should end up with a smaller role for the federal government. Also, because the federal government funds, at least in part, many big-ticket programs with the states, STB should force changes in social policy at the state level as well.

The federal tax cuts in 2001 and 2003 can be viewed as part of this ideologically driven agenda. The approach went awry when the Republican Congress increased domestic spending and the federal government's domestic role. Additionally, the public has not yet risen up against high deficits and a ballooning national debt. In sum, deficits and debt are not as important (or politically *salient*) to the voters as their tax bill is.

Although many observers of the federal political scene were aware of the STB approach, it itself was not on the radar screen for most taxpayers and voters. It was not a part of the public discussion about the extension of Medicare to cover prescription drugs, which made Medicare even more shaky financially at existing tax rates. (Medicare served more than 43 million people and paid out more than $400 billion in benefits in 2006.) This is not to say that the public would not approve; a majority very well might. The point is that accountability and transparency in a democracy require candor or openness about motives (see box 2.3).

Ideology—a systematic set of beliefs and values that shape our understanding of the world. These beliefs and values are the basis for political preferences.

Starve the Beast—a political approach to check government spending by reducing revenues and increasing debt in order to squeeze discretionary spending.

BOX 2.3

Fiscal Transparency Defined

1. For a look at fiscal transparency in the breach, see Groucho Marx in the scene of the cabinet meeting in the 1933 film, "Duck Soup." (This film made the American Film Institute's list of the 100 funniest American films.)

2. "Fiscal transparency is defined...as openness toward the public at large about government structure and functions, fiscal policy intentions, public sector accounts, and projections. It involves ready access to reliable, comprehensive, timely, understandable, and internationally comparable information on government activities—whether undertaken inside or outside the government sector—so that the electorate and financial markets can accurately assess the government's financial position and the true costs and benefits of government activities, including their present and future economic and social implications" (Kopits and Craig 1998, 1, reprinted by permission).

3. "Broadly defined, government transparency is the overall degree to which citizens, the media, and financial markets can observe the government's strategies, its actions, and the resulting outcomes."(Alt, Lassen, and Rose 2006, 30).

Although those favoring STB did not reduce federal domestic spending or the role of the federal government, underfunding certainly did not increase the federal government's capacity to cope with increasingly complex administrative challenges and deliver certain services as well as monitor performance of certain programs. The cost of both increasing capacity and its falling short are high. The discreditable performance of the Federal Emergency Management Agency (FEMA) in the wake of Hurricane Katrina is a case in point.

Another example of a shortfall in governing capacity is contract oversight and compliance. Almost every public organization is engaged in contracts for various services. Unfortunately, the media and legislative audit agencies do not have to dig too deeply to uncover a problem in the complex ways bureaucracies get in trouble spending public money through contracts. This issue is spotlighted by the Department of Defense because it spent more than two-thirds of the total dollar value of federal contracts in 2000–2007. The House Armed Services Committee in 2007 confronted reports of contracting and procurement (purchasing products and services) scandals in Iraq. Although this is a war zone, where needs are urgent and paperwork is secondary, the usual suspects in the contracting scandals included corruption and understaffing.

Domestic federal programs are increasingly performed by contractors, and many federal agencies rely on them to perform core functions. Effectively managing more than $400 billion worth of federal contracts represents an increasing workload, but the number of contract and procurement employees remained at little more than 100,000 during the buildup in contracting in 2001–2005.

The nonpartisan congressional audit office has identified managing federal contracts as a high-risk area since 1992 (GAO, 2007). In truth, the United States has had more than two centuries of problems with government contracts: "Procurement fraud has been with us since the beginning of the republic. The very first congressional investigation, a 1792 inquiry into an Indian victory over troops serving under Major General Arthur St. Clair, was an eighteenth-century version of a defense procurement scandal. Blame for the disaster was placed on the War Department, particularly the quartermaster and supply contractors, who were accused of mismanagement, neglect and delay" (Lewis and Gilman, 2005, pp. 245–246).

IS LOBBYING LEGITIMATE IN BUDGETARY POLITICS?

Citizens may raise their voices to be heard. Trying to influence decisions, citizens organize grassroots campaigns, they visit capitols and executive offices, write to policymakers and the media, and hold press conferences. Activists distribute leaflets, prepare mass mailings and media kits, and work telephone banks. These activities are protected under the First Amendment. These activities also are called lobbying.

Many of us associate lobbying with hired guns paid by special interests and high-powered organizations to wine, dine, entice, and coax legislators. We imagine lobbyists helping to fill campaign war chests and promising votes from mass memberships, or support from influential elites. Campaign contributions to candidates routinely are given with an eye on the prize: access and influence. For example, Congress passed and the president signed an extraordinary "bailout" of the financial industry using $700 billion of public funds in early October 2008. As one account sees it: "Here's pressure: The financial, real estate, and insurance industries—those people who brought us the economic meltdown (and who stand to benefit from the bailout)—so far this year have contributed $339.6 million to party politics, supporting both Republicans' and Democrats' campaigns" (Teichner, 2008). The word *lobbying* triggers suspicion, images of smoke-filled rooms, lush golf courses, and high-profile scandals. Yet, most lobbying is not glamorous and is not corrupt.

How and Why We Lobby

Lobbying is defined by its purpose and method: it is the direct promotion of a particular viewpoint in order to influence what government does. The advocate may be an individual, group, or coalition of groups. Advocacy runs the gamut from a citizen's complaint to a city council person about needing more community policing, to national associations with a paid, professional staff of lobbyists, researchers, and media specialists.

Lobbying—the direct promotion of a particular viewpoint in order to influence what government does (spends, taxes, regulates).

The many players reflect the power of budgeting and the size of the purse. **Public interest** and nonprofit organizations, and professional associations lobby to influence public policy, executive regulations, and legislation at all levels of government. Corporations, business and trade associations, colleges, churches, charities, domestic and foreign governments, coalitions of nonprofit social service agencies and health providers, retirees, farmers, professional associations (for doctors or lawyers, for example), employee unions, taxpayers groups, environmentalists, real estate developers, governors and mayors, and many, many others actively try to exert influence on the budget process. Many legislators become lobbyists after they leave the legislature for the private or nonprofit world.

Here is a case in point. Student lobbyists from the nonpartisan U.S. Public Interest Research Groups (PIRG) weighed in at news conferences, press briefings, and committee hearings about the overhaul of the national loan program for college students. The College Cost Reduction and Access Act of 2007 increased Pell Grants, allowed loan forgiveness for many public service careers (including the military service), and provided other benefits.

Another example is the intense lobbying that swirled around the federal interventions (economic stimulus and financial bailouts) in 2008. Congress passed and the president signed an extraordinary "bailout" of the financial industry using $700 billion of public funds early in October 2008. In late September, more than fifty powerful business and trade associations (including the National Association of Manufacturers, the American Banking Association, and the National Association of Realtors) banded together to urge Congress to approve this "Wall Street" bailout package in order "to prevent a meltdown" of the country's credit markets. Testifying effectively before Congress and, therefore, the nation in late 2008, automakers pleaded for and received billions in financial assistance. Public higher education leaders promoted a "Higher Education Investment Act" in partnership with the federal and state governments as part of a short-term economic stimulus and long-term economic strategy.

Lobbying is more than persuading legislators through direct communication. Lobbyists also identify and secure government contracts for their clients; help draft legislation, rules, and regulations; prepare and submit written reports to agency officials; meet with legislators and their aides; contribute to campaigns; and use the grassroots lobbying techniques described above. Promoting a viewpoint requires research on public policy; analyzing and tracking legislation; monitoring proposed regulations; building and working with coalitions; and attending and testifying at legislative and agency hearings (see the Web site resource, Advocacy Politics). Knowing that credibility is a political asset, witnesses also know that it is illegal to lie ("misrepresent knowingly") about facts when testifying at legislative hearings.

Public Interest Group—a collection of like-minded persons organized together for political action that the group claims benefits the general public.

Some—but not all—lobbying promotes a special interest. A **special interest** speaks for a position or program that (1) fails to benefit the general public or (2) benefits a few far more than the public and whose costs outweigh the general benefit. Public interest organizations, professional associations, think tanks, and mass public-advocacy organizations are counterweights in the competitive system of influencing decision makers. Many participants and players believe that lobbying is a legitimate and necessary part of the democratic political process. Lobbying, in this view, gives voice to different opinions and brings different information to bear on government policy.

Lobbying is widespread in the executive and legislative branches at all levels of government. Almost 40,000 registered, paid lobbyists work state governments on behalf of about 50,000 business firms and organizations. Already a $1 billion-a-year industry, lobbying state government is a growth industry, according to the Center for Public Integrity (CPI 2005). For example, the Wisconsin Government Accountability Board reports that more than $62 million and 477,000 hours were spent on lobbying in the 2007–2008 legislative session (Wisconsin 2009). In many states, lobbying is controlled by campaign finance laws and lobbyist registration and disclosure laws. Some cities, such as Albuquerque, also require lobbyists to register.

Many government agencies have legislative liaisons who are in effect lobbyists, although not formally. The liaisons have the advantage of not having to register while often having access to the floor of the legislature during debate. Senior officials and agency heads are often called as witnesses in budget hearings. (For limits imposed by the president's budget office on agency advocacy in federal budgeting, see Web site resource, Rules of the Game in Washington.) Agency heads, such as local police chiefs, are advised by their experienced colleagues and professional associations to promote their departments' interests in the budget process. A local public safety director in Georgia explains:

> To succeed as the leader of a police organization, the chief must be able to maneuver successfully in the political environment.... Those leaders who are able to work within the political system are more successful at gaining support and resources for their agencies.... [D]eveloping relationships with the finance department is probably one of the most important tasks for a police chief. Explaining the department's unique challenges and involving staff from the finance department to develop proposed solutions increases the police department's support for funding requests to meet these needs (Orrick, n.d., pp. 1, 9–10, reprinted by permission).

State and local governments and nonprofit agencies providing educational or mental health services, for example, may help organize the people they serve as a way of supporting more services (translation: more staff, more programs, and a higher agency budget). Government agencies with a broad base of supporters in many electoral districts may even work with advocacy organizations to achieve their shared budget goals.

Special Interest—an individual or organization supporting a position or program that may fail to benefit the general public or benefits a few far more than the public at large and the costs of which may outweigh the general benefit.

Issue Networks

The cooperation among executive branch agencies, those they serve, and legislative spending committees is called the **iron triangle** because of the strength of the mutual support among them. Because of increased communication technologies, more specialized issue arenas, and more sophisticated lobbying techniques, mutual support has evolved over the past few decades into more fluid, temporary coalitions, or **issue networks**. One such network is a coalition of business interests whose support helped President George W. Bush move a tax cut (the Economic Growth and Tax Relief Reconciliation Act) through Congress in 2001. Financing this network's lobbying activities was no problem because its 1,000 members include many national business associations representing 1.8 million businesses; after all, as the lobby's architect points out, "Major tax bills are the World Series of lobbying" (Birnbaum, 2007, p. A17). Supporting an increase in the Social Security Administration's budget, another issue network of forty organizations, including AARP, Easter Seals, and labor unions, organized letter-writing to members of the House appropriation subcommittee that oversees the agency's funding (see the Web site resource, Advocacy Politics).

Lobbying pervades government and is legitimate within certain boundaries. The boundaries are established by laws and regulations that take aim at unacceptable behavior such as bribery. The way of life at state capitols has changed as far as lobbying and lobbyists are concerned. States are regulating lobbyists more and limiting or banning gifts to legislators. Some rules, such as requiring the disclosure of campaign contributions, are designed to protect the public against bias in decision making and conflicts of interest.

There are no rules that level the playing field. Different individuals, groups, and coalitions enjoy different amounts and types of resources that make for effective participation. These resources include money, yes. But political participation also turns on information; access to decision makers; and political, organizational, and communication skills.

DOES PUBLIC OPINION INFLUENCE BUDGETARY POLITICS?

A responsive government means that public opinion affects decisions about public policy, and changes in opinions fuel changes in public policy and spending in certain policy arenas. Citizens can and do make their opinions known through public opinion polls. Decision makers study polls at every level of government and members of the media are certain to include them in their news coverage. Political actors use polls to support their positions and try to shape public opinion as well.

Iron Triangle—cooperation among executive branch agency, those who receive the services, and legislative spending committees; considered a formidable team for higher spending.

Issue Network—fluid, temporary coalition around an issue.

For these reasons, polls may be seen as tools of democracy and as important sources of information for political leaders and the public.

Public leaders know that public opinion changes in response to changing circumstances. Media exposure, the availability of new information, the calming effect of the passage of time, and other factors affect the public's judgments. Perhaps a new crisis pushes an earlier concern off the radar screen. This is reassuring because it means that many in "the public" are flexible, not dogmatic, and have the capacity to learn. Because public opinion can and does change, "snapshot" surveys taken only once are less useful than when the questions are repeated over time and trends are identified.

Politicians face multiple issues at the same time. Some of these are framed as budget issues and some are not. Public response to a budget question outside of the larger political context may not give useful guidance to public leaders. (For some problems with polls, see Web site resource, Opinion Polls in a Democracy.)

In most polls, respondents can only answer questions using the answers provided, and so do not help set the policy agenda. Other polls are open-ended, such as the Gallup question, "What do you think is the most important problem facing this country today?" Budget concerns—such as taxes and the deficit—often make the list and are on the public's radar screen, but the public typically expresses more concern about war, terrorism, the economy, and other issues.

Do Leaders Listen?

Acting as the delegates, some political leaders let polls shape their decisions; their policy positions follow shifts in public sentiment. Opinion polls can help trustee-type leaders stand firm against special interests that are trying to claim broad public support. Polls may limit decision makers' ability to make unpopular choices or encourage them to ignore minority viewpoints. Some political leaders cherry pick supportive statistics in a self-serving way; others genuinely consider the public's views as a resource in decision making.

Policy makers in Washington generally may have a low opinion of the public's understanding and knowledge of public policy and low confidence in public opinion polls. Although the great majority of political leaders and media specialists claim to understand public opinion on important issues, only about one-half of the public agrees with them (Brodie et al., 2001, p. 13).

The American public does not see itself as incompetent or beside the point. In 2008, 94 percent of Americans expressed the belief that leaders should be influenced by opinion polls and that the public should have more influence with decision makers (see figure 2.3). Long preferring public officials who listen to majority opinion on public policy issues, Americans repeatedly tell decision makers that they favor the delegate model. The public believes that elected officials also should consider their own sense of what is right and choose policies that mesh their values with the majority's view.

The public's dissatisfaction with unresponsive government reduces the public's trust in government. When Gallup asked Americans to identify the "most

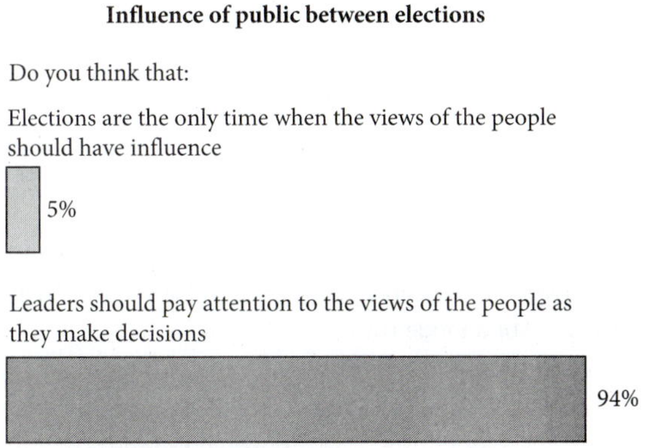

Influence of public between elections

Do you think that:

Elections are the only time when the views of the people should have influence

5%

Leaders should pay attention to the views of the people as they make decisions

94%

Figure 2.3. The Public's View of Public Opinion
Reproduced by permission. World Public Opinion, 2008.

important problem facing the country" in 2007, the way government was working—or not working—ranked among the top issues. In 2008, World Public Opinion conducted a national survey of the United States that found the American public's dissatisfaction is traced to its perception that it should have more influence over decisions and that elected officials act in their own self-interest by favoring special interests and party agenda over the public interest. The public's attitude may bring to mind traditional American populism: people want the political system to stand up for them and live up to its ideals.

Interpreting Public Opinion

Interpreting public opinion is anything but easy. Polls may communicate contradictory, shifting, vague, and confusing messages (see box 2.4 and the Web site resource, Opinion Polls in a Democracy). Opinion polls can also target public feedback about spending, taxes, and services. Some governments and nonprofit agencies ask citizens directly about budget and service priorities, but most do not. Some surveys are designed to gather public opinion about government performance. This subjective data may be supplemented by information about the actual quantity and quality of performance. Citizen satisfaction surveys may influence where local governments and agencies put resources.

THUMBNAIL

Participation is important because citizen's consent and voluntary cooperation relies upon open, accountable, and responsive government. The point of participation is to influence decisions on how much is spent and on what, and how it is financed. More people experience political relationships and responsibilities by paying taxes than by voting.

Voting has a limited impact on budgetary politics. A candidate's stand on budget issues cannot always be predicted accurately from campaign promises or party

=============================== **BOX 2.4** ===============================

The Federal Budget: People's Chief Concerns in 2006

- More than half of Americans say that reducing the budget deficit should be a top priority for Congress in 2007, but other issues rank higher
- Half of Americans say the federal budget deficit is a "very serious" problem
- Health care costs and jobs going overseas rank higher as economic concerns than the federal budget deficit
- Americans say about half of every tax dollar is wasted by the federal government
- Seven in ten voters say only "some" or "not much" of their tax money goes to government programs they personally support
- Two-thirds of Americans say wealth should be more evenly distributed but are divided on whether the government should redistribute wealth
- Survey responses on the size of government vary depending on how the question is worded
- Half of Americans say federal income taxes are too high, but six in ten say the income tax they pay is fair
- The number of Americans who say federal income taxes are "too high" has declined since the 1990s
- A plurality of Americans say the local property tax is the "least fair," and that number has increased since 1994
- Large majorities say corporations and upper-income Americans pay "too little" in taxes
- Americans are divided on whether the IRS is too tough when it comes to enforcing the nation's tax laws
- Americans are divided on whether it's becoming more difficult for people to cheat on their taxes and many say they don't know
- Most Americans say they would be more likely to vote for a candidate who would reduce the federal budget deficit by canceling tax cuts rather than cutting spending on social programs

Reprinted by permission. Public Agenda, 2007.

labels. The public's ideological frame of mind and partisan choices cycle between liberal and conservative, and the public's mood in national politics runs counter to the government's policies.

Voting and party labels point unclearly to what the public wants. The public is many publics. Voting in general elections is an important way the public participates in budgetary politics, but it is a challenge to interpret the messages voters send. Electoral politics communicates mixed and vague messages.

The public's feelings and central political beliefs influence budgetary politics. Many voters are less ideological than the political elites, and many voters are frustrated by partisan conflict. Economic self-interest is not always a voter's main focus, and political choice is not necessarily a rational calculus. Advocates of a particular policy often frame it as competing value systems rather than as programs or policies competing for resources. Ideology also influences the politics of budgeting.

Many Americans do not believe that they effectively influence government. The public believes that the current level of transparency fails to meet their needs. The *tools of direct democracy*, including the referendum and initiative, play important roles in budgetary politics; they permit citizens to express their views in a focused way.

CASE

Advocacy Strategy, Advocacy Ethics

Why does a certain program or service deserve legislative support? When the program or service can draw on external support from, for example, the general public or powerful organized groups, then budget advocacy is often about communication and persuasion, or marketing. By way of example, the poster shown in figure 2.4 suggests that while firefighters' equipment may be costly, the real cost is best measured not in dollars, but in the value of life.

This argument in effect changes the subject from dollars to something highly valued and against which it is difficult to argue. The strategy links the program or service with something that is so valuable and important that many make the case that it cannot or should not be reduced to dollars and cents. The usual calculus does not apply; rather, the strategy implies that any amount of money is justified. The life of a firefighter and the life of a child are obvious examples, but subtler ones include winning the war, supporting troops in the field or, in the past, putting a man on the moon. Economic development with its promise of jobs often is treated the same way in local politics. Similar arguments have been made about military, medical, and police services, as well as education.

Politicians and professional budgeters cannot deal well with arguments for unlimited value because available resources are always limited and choices must be made. Because budgeting *must* translate value into dollars and a budget simply cannot handle nonmonetary value, the strategy may backfire. Some decision makers may even resent one special interest claiming that it is above the competition…and therefore trying to box in the decision makers. They may object to the view that one special interest's claim is exceptional; after all, the disabled or veterans can and do pack the visitors' gallery. Decision makers also are all-too-familiar with strategies based on intimidation: Give us the money or we close down, give us the money or we will die, give us the money or we will support your opponent. Decision makers may find these types of advocacy strategies too simple to accept and object to making choices in terms of who yells loudest and has money for advertising and public relations campaigns. Nonetheless, organized interest

Figure 2.4. Advocacy Strategy

Courtesy of www.FireFighterCloseCalls.com, the National Fallen Firefighters Foundation, and the Canadian Fallen Firefighters Foundation.

groups contribute to democracy by representing many people's interests, promoting political participation, and adding information to policy debates.

Thinking It Over

1. Is it true that life is so highly valued that only nonmonetary terms apply?

   Standard evaluation techniques assign a monetary value to life. In assessing road construction, "the monetary value of fatalities . . . is what the economist means by 'the value of life'. . . . Governments cannot avoid the trading of lives for money, but they may establish the terms under which that trade takes place. The trade is unavoidable because governments take responsibility for activities—health, transport, environmental protection, civil order, and especially national defense—where lives can be saved at a price" (Usher 1985, pp. 168, 185). In civil lawsuits, when measuring the value of a lost life, lawyers often declare that a price tag is a poor gauge, but that is all there is. Experts are often asked in court to place a financial value on the loss of a limb or bodily function, and they do!

2. Are these advocacy strategies unethical or illegitimate? Or is it inevitable that organized special interests will use these strategies in a democratic system that allows freedom of speech (which translates into no limits on spending to get out the message)?

Valued participation in a democracy relies on organized groups, which we call special interest or public interest groups (depending on the view of their goals). Organizations must be effective if they are to survive, and so their advocacy strategies are geared to effective participation in budget competition. Democracy is loud, messy, and often unfair. See the Web site video, "Arnoldbucks," and the Web site resource, Advocacy Politics in Budgeting.

3. Is there a moral core to budgeting?

Claims on resources pit ethical values, social goals, and future possibilities against one other. Is it a public leader's duty in the budget process to forge a new or deeper understanding by creatively redesigning the questions and options? The *Federalist Papers* no. 57 reads, "The aim of every political constitution is, or ought to be, first to obtain for rulers men [sic] who possess most wisdom to discern, and most virtue to pursue, the common good of the society."

In this spirit, do we turn to elected leaders and top professionals in the hope that they will think broadly, include the voiceless in their calculus, reach out to stakeholders, and remember the public interest and future generations? If there is little direct incentive to do these things in a system of democratic elections, must we rely on the integrity and thoughtfulness of our leaders? In his message to Congress on April 27, 1961, President John F. Kennedy said: "The ultimate answer to ethical problems in government is honest people in a good ethical environment. No web of statute or regulation, however intricately conceived, can hope to deal with the myriad possible challenges to a man's [sic] integrity or his devotion to the public interest."

WEB SITE RESOURCES

- Advocacy Politics in Budgeting
- "Arnoldbucks" video
- California Dreamin': Tools of Direct Democracy
- Chronology of Federal Budgeting, 1789–2008
- Citizen's Guide to Budgeting in Alexandria, Virginia
- Further Resources
- Internet Resources, Lobbying and Lobbyist Roster; Professional Associations; Public Interest, Professional, and Advocacy Organizations; and Financial Condition and Performance Measurement
- Opinion Polls in a Democracy
- Rules of the Game in Washington: Confidentiality, Testimony, and Communications

REVIEW QUESTIONS

1. Why is looking at a candidate's party affiliation not a good way to predict the candidate's stand on a specific budgetary issue?
2. How might a candidate following a delegate model of leadership approach a budgetary problem differently from one who follows the trustee model?
3. How does emotion play a role in the budgeting process? Would budgetary politics produce better decisions if participants focused more on costs and benefits and left emotion out? Why?
4. In what ways have efforts to increase the accountability of government officials to the electorate made the job of lobbyists easier? More difficult?
5. Despite the numerous rules designed to make the lobbying process ethical, "there are no rules that level the playing field."
   a. What types of groups or organizations are the most effective lobbyists and why?
   b. Does the fact that the lobbying process is inherently unequal necessarily make it unethical as well?
   c. Is it appropriate for a department head and other appointed public leaders to encourage their clients and issue networks to lobby for more funding for the department?

3

⚛

Fairness and Trust in
Budgetary Politics

This chapter answers five questions:

- What's Fair?
- Are Taxes Fair?
- Is Spending Fair?
- Are Citizens Satisfied with Performance?
- Does Citizen Trust or Distrust Matter?

> What does Pink Floyd tell us about money and about fairness
> in "Money"?

> Injustice is relatively easy to bear; what stings is justice.
>
> H. L. MENCKEN

The clashes in budgetary politics are often over the big political questions and deep divisions in modern society. We know that public support for government spending on individual programs changes with how the issue is presented (the so-called framing effect). Issues may be framed in ways that either increase or decrease the political impact of partisanship and deep divisions in society on public support. For example, although majorities of people in numerous surveys support increasing spending on many government programs, welfare (framed as cash assistance to the poor) is an exception; this is a program a majority usually would like to cut. Some scholars argue that this is because welfare has become a racial symbol. Political leaders, pundits, right-wing talk-radio hosts, and left-wing talking heads use cleavages for political mobilization—to stir up popular support or opposition to public policies and programs.

Race and ethnic identity, gender, income and class, age, sexual orientation, geography or region, ideology, and religion can foster *cleavage* issues. Cleavages may affect elections that, in turn, affect spending priorities. (The battle for the White House in 2008 made it obvious that generational, gender, and racial identities affect voting.)

Cleavage issues are very often fought out in the political arena in which budgeting is the core decision-making process. The stakes are high because public budgeting pinpoints who and what pays for and benefits from the use of public resources. We also often see in budgeting contests over **wedge** issues that are exploited to divide the public for political advantage; these contests also promise big prizes.

We use two cross-cutting questions about fairness and trust to examine the big political issues.

1. What do citizens see as fair in budgeting and what are their attitudes about who gets and who pays?
2. How satisfied are Americans with the performance of public institutions, and how does the decline in the public's trust of these institutions affect public budgeting?

Through budgeting we try to answer these questions. After all, the endpoint in each round of budgetary politics is to produce a budget—the most important statement of public policies and the core values underlying them. By exploring citizens' understanding of fairness on the one hand and satisfaction and trust on the other, we see the politics of budgeting in action in a democracy.

The economic stimulation and recovery packages of 2008 and 2009 illustrate the link between fairness and trust in American politics. In September 2008, the Bush Administration sent to Congress an extraordinary $700 billion plan for a financial bailout of financial institutions. Much of the public's negative reaction to the proposal hinged on what many saw as excessive pay and bonuses for corporate executives in the financial industry. The outcry delayed but did not prevent passage of the 2008 Emergency Economic Stabilization Act. Over the next few months, the public responded with outrage to tales of excessive corporate spending on executive bonuses, luxurious retreats and offices, and corporate jets. Shortly after taking office, President Obama signaled his responsiveness to public indignation by issuing rules to limit executive compensation. In February 2009, Congress took the limits a step further when it passed the $787 billion recovery package. But the compensation restrictions in the American Recovery and Reinvestment Act did not apply to the 359 banks that had already taken government aid, a.k.a. taxpayers' money, and so there followed a predictable political firestorm over bonuses handed out by American International Group, Inc. (AIG) in March 2009.

WHAT'S FAIR?

The authors disagree with Winston Churchill who noted, "All the great things are simple, and many can be expressed in a single word: freedom; justice; honor; duty; mercy; hope." Whole books have been written about the idea of fairness because it is complex and important. Despite Churchill's summary judgment, no single or

---

Wedge—a divisive issue such as abortion that often is associated with ideology and social values and that may be used to promote electoral support for one side and erode support for the opposing position and candidate, with consequences for budgetary politics.

simple definition captures all of its many meanings. On the other hand, we must not be too specific if we are to keep this idea politically meaningful. Sometimes we use the word *fair* to mean justice and to suggest impartiality rather than self-interest or personal bias. Alternatively, fairness may call to mind using set procedures and following the rules. Other times, the focus may switch to equality, but even this widely used meaning causes some confusion. One standard of fairness in public finance is to treat everyone the same (horizontal equity); another standard calls for treating people differently in different circumstances (vertical equity). Some of us think of a level playing field or equal opportunity. Believing that a fair *outcome* is what counts, others have in mind that the price, tax, benefit, service, or share seems reasonable and expected, or is what they believe they or others deserve. Little wonder, then, that people hold different beliefs about what is and is not fair and interpret political decisions and proposals differently.

Some or all of these meanings are used in American politics. Actually, the ambiguity is politically useful because the use of this one word can promise whatever the listener wants to hear. One thing we all probably understand is that the cry, "It's not fair!" is a call to combat that expresses a sense of betrayal. This is why fairness and trust are examined together in this chapter. Another link between the two ideas is that sometimes a sense of unfairness builds into a package of grievance, blame, and distrust labeled "the politics of resentment." Sometimes this package is used as a marketing device or a political scam.

ARE TAXES FAIR?

Policy makers usually claim that tax fairness is a core principle in their revenue decisions. (Chapter 7 discusses tax fairness and equity further.) The politically savvy have long believed that some sort of tax fairness affects the public's acceptance of taxes, and this acceptance is crucial to political success. Expressing this political imperative, King Louis XIV's finance chief observed, "The art of taxation consists in so plucking the goose as to get the most feathers with the least hissing." It is widely believed that taxes that the public sees as *fair* cause less hissing.

Many experts and ordinary citizens believe that tax fairness is a moral necessity rather than simply a political need. In his highly influential *Wealth of Nations*, published in 1776, Adam Smith advocated that people should pay taxes in relation to their ability to pay and that a tax system should aim to level out inequality by sparing the poor and taxing the rich. The famous American humorist, Will Rogers, implied that Americans have a moral view of taxes when he observed, "People want *just* taxes more than they want *lower* taxes. They want to know that every man [sic] is paying his proportionate share according to his wealth."

This moral aspect invests debates over taxes with intense feelings that are easily tapped for political advantage. There is much contradictory evidence on citizen opinions about taxes but, if public opinion were not so important, there would be far fewer polls on taxes. Some things are certain: emotions draw on moral sentiments, can run high, and do overcome hardheaded calculus and financial self-interest.

The Public's Perspective

The tax attitudes expressed in opinion polls are treated as basic constraints on leaders' leeway in making policy decisions. After all, public acceptability is important in a democracy. In the end, public acceptance defines what is politically practical.

Nationally, the belief that state income taxes are somewhat or not at all fair is common, and even more people believe that local property taxes are somewhat or not at all fair. The current debates over the federal **estate tax, alternative minimum tax,** and tax cuts provide plenty of convincing evidence that many citizens view the federal tax system as unfair (see Web site resource, Fairness and the Federal Income Tax). Many complain especially about its complexity when they judge the federal income tax harshly. The fact that perceptions vary with party affiliation, age, and income suggest that perceptions about tax fairness have significant political implications. The Tax Foundation's annual surveys on American attitudes on taxes show that the issues of tax complexity, fairness, and burden are top concerns.

Notions of Tax Fairness

Tax fairness comes in four different flavors:

1. Everyone pays something.
2. Taxes paid in line with services and benefits received.
3. Willingness to pay or political acceptability.
4. Ability to pay (tax burden or effective tax rate).

These ideas about fairness lead to different public policies and different payers. Because the definition of what is fair is loaded with political content and conflict, the proposal in figure 7.4 seems so far-fetched. Here, the devil is in the details.

Americans seem to like the idea that everyone should contribute something. Surveys by the Tax Foundation in 2006 and in 2007 posed the question, "Last year 43.4 million Americans—that's one-third of all taxpayers—paid no federal income tax after deductions and credits. Thinking about your own tax burden, do you think this is fair, or do you feel everyone should be required to pay some minimum amount of tax to help fund government?" More than three-fifths responded that everyone should pay something.

A second version of tax fairness relates the amount paid in taxes to benefits received from public services. It may come as some surprise that this popular and seemingly hardheaded approach is not really easy to use in policy making. Do taxpayers calculate the costs and benefits over their lifetime or as a market-like transaction for a particular service at a particular moment? Do taxpayers think

---

Estate Tax—a tax on the monetary value of the remaining assets after a person's death.

Alternative Minimum Tax (AMT)—a parallel federal income tax structure originally enacted in 1982 that allows fewer exemptions and deductions and with fewer rates than the standard income tax; designed to catch higher-income individuals with little income taxed through the normal tax structure.

about the value received from an educated electorate, combating epidemics, or political stability? Do taxpayers honestly state their true preferences or do they try to hitch a free ride?

A third interpretation of tax fairness centers on taxpayers' **willingness to pay**, meaning their acceptance of (or resistance to) taxes. In contrast, a crude version says that the more I pay—the higher the price to me—then the less fair I judge the tax. Although some taxpayers may deny that they lean toward this cost-shifting, me-first attitude, it does appear to be widespread.

The fourth approach to tax fairness looks at **ability to pay** rather than willingness to pay. Advocated by both Adam Smith and Will Rogers, this approach is concerned with **tax burden** (or **effective tax rate**). Tax burden measures taxpayers' ability to pay by dividing their income by their tax payments. (Note that tax burden is proportional to income, not wealth, and definitions of income vary.) With the basic idea that a fair *share* of income should go to taxes, this approach looks at the percent of income paid in taxes, not the number of dollars paid.

Tax Burden

On average, the national tax burden rose from almost 6 percent of income in 1900 to almost 31 percent in 2008. The Tax Foundation informs us that the average American worked 22 days to pay taxes in 1900 but today works 133 days. But who is average?

Economists divide the public into five equal groups, from low- to high-income earners. Middle income means the 20 percent of households whose income is in the middle or can mean the 60 percent that includes everyone except the lowest 20 percent and highest 20 percent. The *median* household income in the United States in 2006 was over $48,000, and the middle 20 percent earned from about $38,000 to $60,000. About one-half of the families in the lowest 20 percent have incomes below the government's poverty line. Usually 60–80 percent of Americans label themselves as middle class (Prante, 2007).

Whether we agree with the many respondents to opinion polls who say that the same flat percentage should be paid by everyone, or we believe that higher-income earners should pay a higher percentage of their incomes in taxes, odds are that not many of us believe that it really is fair for lower-income taxpayers to pay a larger share of their income in taxes than taxpayers with higher incomes. (Taxes that burden lower income taxpayers more than higher income taxpayers are labeled "regressive.")

Willingness to Pay—an acceptance of taxation.

Ability-to-Pay Principle—the idea that a person's tax burden should be based on the person's capacity to pay the taxes, with capacity usually measured as taxes paid as a percentage of the taxpayer's income.

Tax Burden—total tax payments divided by total income; taxes expressed as percent of income.

Effective Tax Rate—the amount of tax paid expressed as a percentage of income.

Yet, most state and local taxes take a greater share of income from middle- and low-income earners than from high-income earners.

Disliked taxes are not necessarily "the third rail" and politically fatal if they are linked to citizen's positive assessment of the spending side of the budget, or performance. The public trumpets its dislike of the local **property tax** in opinion polls, but this judgment does not translate into a negative attitude about local government. The public sees the property tax as the "worst" or *least fair* tax. Next come, in order, the federal income tax, state sales tax, and state income tax. Yet, overall, the public sees local government as relatively cost-effective, giving taxpayers the most for their money; the federal and state governments are runners-up. "Probably the most significant long-term trend is the decline in the public's support of the federal government and corresponding increase in support of state and especially local governments. Beginning with almost equal levels of support in the early 1970s, a gap of 22 percentage points in 2006 separated the public's views of which governments (federal or state-local) give them [sic] the most for their money" (Cole and Kincaid, 2006).

Taxes and Income Inequality

Taxes are front and center in any public debate about budgets. The average federal tax burden fell from 1979 to today. This period spans the tax cuts of the Reagan (1980s) and Bush administrations (2000s). A median family's federal tax burden is at its lowest level in almost one-half century (Piketty, 2007 and Shapiro, 2002).

Despite the drop in the federal tax burden, anti-tax sentiment persists. Three widespread beliefs shape anti-tax sentiment:

1. Taxes are too high.
2. The tax burden is unfair.
3. Government performance is unsatisfactory, so the return from taxes is unfair.

The Libertarian Party takes the argument a step further and says that taxes are unfair by their very nature because government threatens liberty, self-reliance, and the free-market economy. Arguing on the grounds of economic efficiency and fairness not necessarily related to ability to pay, many tax-cut advocates argue that a lower federal tax burden is good public policy to (1) stimulate the economy, (2) maintain income mobility and reward hard workers and private-sector innovators, and (3) encourage savings and investment. As the case at the end of this chapter shows, many activists promote reducing the state and local tax burdens, or at least halting the growth of taxes.

The irony is that American public opinion supports more public spending when taxes are relatively low. More people always favor spending increases over cuts. It appears that a perfectly responsive government would find itself cutting

---

Property Tax—a tax levied on real and/or personal property according to the assessed valuation and the tax rate.

taxes, only to face a more demanding public that favors spending. (This calls to mind Anthony Downs' classic article, "Why the government budget is too small in a democracy.")

Another perspective looks at the effect of tax policies on the distribution of income. Many recent and proposed changes in the U.S. tax system add to the already widening income gap by making after-tax incomes less equal at the very same time as income inequalities are growing. Some political activists and experts see adding to income inequality as bad public policy and offer five reasons.

1. A widening income gap threatens political stability.
2. Large income differences are fundamentally undemocratic; the majority of Americans believe that income differences are too large.
3. A widening income gap is an economic drag on an economy that depends on mass consumption.
4. Income inequalities discourage economic growth and encourage corruption.
5. Taxes that *add* to income inequality are unfair.

Consider some of the political implications of a widening income distribution.

[The] widening gulf between the rich on the one hand and the poor and middle class on the other hand can reduce social cohesion, trust in government and other institutions, and participation in the democratic process. Growing income inequality also has widened discrepancies in political influence—a particular problem given political candidates' heavy dependence on private contributions. This may have contributed to the increase in the number of Americans who feel that their elected officials do not care much about the views of ordinary citizens (Bernstein, McNichol, and Nicholas, 2008, p. 19).

The view that a *fair* political system is the basis for economic growth and political stability is widely shared. In 2005 when still Chairman of the Federal Reserve, Alan Greenspan warned that the large and fast-growing income gap between the rich and the non-rich might threaten the stability of the political-economic system. The next year, in his first major speech as Treasury Secretary, Henry Paulson identified growing income inequality as a leading challenge for the United States. (Paulson would become one of the architects of the government's intervention strategy to deal with the 2008 financial crisis and freezing credit markets.) A wide and increasing gap between the rich and the poor can threaten the political consensus that is needed to tackle the many challenges facing the nation.

The distribution of income affects the demand for publicly financed services in a community. Income distribution also affects taxpayers' ability and willingness to pay. In turn, these affect a state's ability to finance public services or fiscal capacity.

The most widely used measure of income inequality is the **Gini Index** (or coefficient). A higher Gini means there is more inequality in the distribution of

---

Gini Index or Coefficient—a measure of income inequity.

income; a lower means there is less; a value of 0 means complete equality and a value of 100 represents "perfect" *in*equality. U.S. Census data tells us that the Gini Index has risen over the past four decades. In fact, income inequality in the United States has increased to what it was before the Great Depression.

The income distribution in the United States is different from the income distribution in many countries with which we often compare ourselves. The United Nations' Human Development Indicators ranks 177 countries. With a Gini Coefficient above 40, the United States has greater income inequality than Canada, Australia, Great Britain, or Japan, for example. The United States has less income inequality than Russia or Mexico. When a Harris Poll asked adults in China, Great Britain, France, Germany, Italy, Japan, Spain, and the United States in 2008 about the gap between the rich and the poor, a large majority in each country responded that the gap is too wide.

The income gap surfaced as a political issue in the financial crisis of 2008. In late September, public resentment and mistrust stalled government intervention. Widespread public opposition is credited with the defeat in the House of Representatives of the first version of a $700 billion bailout bill for the financial industry. More than one trillion dollars in value in the stock market was wiped out in one day, September 29, 2008. Subsequent legislation included restrictions on pay and bonuses for corporate chieftains, investment bankers, and financial moguls on Wall Street.

Fiscal Federalism and Tax Fairness

The federal structure of U.S. government affects overall tax fairness. The extremes of Mississippi, with the lowest average federal tax burden, and Connecticut, with the highest, together show how a low or high average personal income turns into a low or high average federal tax bill. With the statewide average personal income almost 30 percent higher than the national average, Connecticut ranks highest among all the states. Its total personal income is more than double that of Mississippi, at 77 percent of the national average. As a result, Connecticut taxpayers have a relatively high average federal income tax bill, while taxpayers in Mississippi have a relatively low average bill.

The difference in tax burdens among the states brings us to four important points.

1. We have a federal system of shared authority and separate (as well as shared) policy arenas and government programs and services. State and local services, such as education and public safety, are financed largely through taxes at the state and local levels of government, even in the poorer states. As a result, the total tax burden includes federal, state, and local taxes.

2. State and local income and property taxes are allowed as itemized deductions on the federal income tax, called the **federal offset**. The higher-income

---

Federal Offset—state and local income and property taxes are allowed as itemized deductions on the federal income tax.

earners who itemize their deductions on their federal taxable income in effect export part of their state and local tax burden to the rest of the country. This so-called federal **tax expenditure** and the exclusion of interest on state and local bonds from federal taxation are estimated to cost the federal budget about $85 billion each year (see chapter 7).

3. Fiscal federalism means that federal, state, and local governments interact by either reinforcing or undermining the policy objectives and fiscal capacity of the other governments.

4. The types of revenue used and their structure affect tax fairness at all levels of government. These policy choices are made through political processes at the federal, state, and local levels of government.

IS SPENDING FAIR?

The question of fair spending asks, "Who gets, how much, who decides, and why?" Yet, the public's views on spending often express broad political assessments rather than judgments about policies or particular programs. In 2005, a World Public Opinion poll asked the U.S. public, "How would regular people divide up the budget if given the chance?" The pattern of responses showed support for cutting defense spending and support for increasing social spending. That the public would alter the Bush Administration's budget in significant ways was a forewarning of the November 2006 election that changed the majority in both houses of Congress and in public offices around the country.

Spending attitudes serve as a "political thermostat" (Wlezien, 1995) that helps curb the effect of electoral victory on public spending for *specific* programs.

> We know that public opinion on government spending generally runs counter to the views of current policy (and the current party control of the White House)....We see this in particular with respect to preferences on government spending, where a government policy that increases spending on a certain program usually reduces the percentage of people who support spending "more" on that program (and vice-versa for spending less) (Ellis and Stimson, 2007, p. 30).

Americans' attitudes toward public spending *in general* are ideological and partisan. Most Americans oppose super-sizing public spending as a matter of general principle. National surveys since 1992 have asked Americans whether they would favor "smaller government with fewer services" or "larger government with more services," 50 percent or more always opt for smaller is better as a matter of principle (see figure 3.1). Spending attitudes are related to party affiliation, with a majority of Republicans and Independents but only a minority of Democrats favoring smaller government in late 2007. The general principle does not translate into particular policy preferences. There is little public support for cutting most domestic programs and strong support for increasing spending on education, health, and more.

Tax Expenditures—revenue foregone by government or reductions in income tax liabilities from special tax provisions or regulations that provide tax benefits to particular taxpayers.

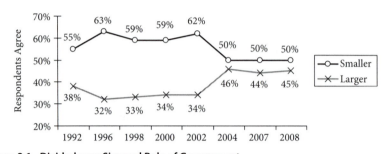

Figure 3.1. Divided over Size and Role of Government

SOURCE: ABC News and The Washington Post, 1985–2006. Retrieved from iPOLL Databank, The Roper Center for Public Opinion Research, University of Connecticut.

Where we live, how old we are, our racial or ethnic identity, education, income, partisan affiliation, and ideology influence attitudes about fair spending. Spending preferences signal more than financial self-interest; they mirror the problems people encounter around them on a daily basis. Support for spending by government is generally greater among African Americans and women and declines as education, income, and age increase. With priorities different from those of city residents, suburbanites are less concerned about programs they think of as urban programs.

Spending preferences also mirror deep divisions in American society. Public support for spending on education, roads, sewers, garbage collection, and programs for the disadvantaged in U.S. metropolitan areas falls as racial and ethnic diversity increases. Areas with less diverse populations tend to have more income redistribution and public spending. Racial, ethnic, language, and religious differences are a big part of the reason spending on income-transfer programs, such as unemployment insurance, food stamps, welfare, health care, and pensions, is lower in the United States than in European countries.

The fact that the United States is becoming more diverse surely will affect the amount spent and on which services in the future. For example, the population of Hispanic and Latino origin is projected to almost double as a percentage of the total U.S. population by 2050, to almost one-quarter of the population. The traditional response to diversity suggests that public support for public spending will decrease in the future, unless other factors exert a counter influence.

America's increasingly diverse future leads us to expect more varied service demands, plus different expectations about the proper role of government and individuals' relationships with government and the community. Are members of a new immigrant group accustomed to turning to government or to their own network for assistance? What is the attitude toward tax compliance and participation in politics and civic life? In *Bowling Alone*, Robert Putnam directs our attention to the idea of **social capital**, the organizational networks, norms, and social trust that aid working together for common benefit. He argues that a rich stock of social capital increases community members' preference for shared public benefits.

Higher social connectedness translates into support for higher levels of public spending. Relative need does not. Higher levels of income inequality are not associated with more government spending in the United States and many other countries.

The Politics of Redistribution

Public enthusiasm for spending is affected strongly by the type of spending, that is, whether the program is **distributive** or **redistributive**. The costs and benefits of distributive policies and programs such as Social Security, Medicare, environmental protection, and national security are delivered widely. In redistributive programs, costs are shared widely but benefits are targeted to narrow segments of the public. So-called safety-net programs such as Medicaid, food stamps, and poverty programs are redistributive.

The values and behavior of empathy and altruism are common among Americans and most (90 percent) agree that people should be willing to help those less fortunate. Empathy, meaning being understanding of and sensitive to others, is higher among those supporting increased redistributive spending. Why, then, do the public and political leaders so weakly support spending on poverty programs and foreign aid and so often target them for cuts? Why is racial and ethnic diversity so important to public spending?

Part of the answer lies in Americans' fondness for a relatively limited role for the federal government, at least in the abstract. That Americans dislike taxes also needs to be taken into account. Although two-thirds of responses to a Gallup poll in 2007 favored a more even distribution of wealth, they split over whether the government should redistribute wealth "by heavy taxes on the rich" (Newport, 2007).

Another part of the answer lies in the disconnect between what people say and what people do, the difference between what is politically correct and what is politically probable or practical. Another part of the answer lies in political images and self-images. The American approach to redistribution is colored by the often-stated belief that the poor, especially of other racial and ethnic groups (see box 3.1), are lazy and personally at fault. This view is different from the view in many other societies that the poor are unfortunate victims.

A myth of self-reliance underlies Americans' tendency to think about poverty in individualistic moral terms such as merit, hard work, and initiative. This idea

---

Social Capital—organizational networks, norms, and social trust that aid working together for common benefit.

Distributive Policy—government programs where both costs and benefits are distributed widely.

Redistributive Policy—costs are distributed widely and benefits are concentrated on narrow segments of the population; examples include Medicaid, food stamps, and poverty programs.

BOX 3.1

Who Is Poor in the United States?

- Different sources and different federal and state programs define income differently. See http://www.census.gov/hhes/www/income/compare1.html, http://www.census.gov/hhes/www/poverty/poverty.html, and http://aspe.hhs.gov/poverty/index.shtml for different income definitions.

- The U.S. Census Bureau uses money income before taxes to define poverty. This definition includes earnings, unemployment compensation, workers' compensation, Social Security, Supplemental Security Income, public assistance, veterans' payments, pensions, pension or retirement income, interest and dividends, educational aid, alimony, child support, and other various sources, but does not include capital gains or noncash benefits such as public housing, Medicaid, and food stamps.

- People whose poverty status cannot be determined include students living in college dormitories.

- As of 2006, 12.3 percent of the population or 36 million were living in poverty. Non-Hispanic Whites account for 44 percent of the American poor and 66 percent of the total population.

RACIAL/ETHNIC GROUP	POVERTY RATE
Non-Hispanic Whites	8%
Blacks	24%
Asians	10%
Hispanics	21%

SOURCE: U.S. Census Bureau, 2007, Table 1, p. 5.

---

was captured by Barry Goldwater when he kicked off his presidential campaign in 1964: "I ask that you join with me in proving that every American can stand on his own, make up his own mind, chart his own future, keep and control his own family, asking for help and getting help only when truly overwhelming problems, beyond his control, beset him." Forty years later, country singer Keith Urban captured it again in his song, "Stuck in the Middle."

Asked in 2000 whether "most people who want to get ahead can make it if they're willing to work hard, [or] hard work and determination are no guarantee of success for most people," respondents opted three-to-one for work doing the trick. Asked a year later, "Would you say you are doing well financially primarily because of your own efforts and abilities, because of good luck, or because of things other people have done for you," 86 percent chose own efforts and abilities (Money, 2003, p. 48). The belief in self-reliance and hard work supports the idea of the *American dream* of class mobility and personal success. It is labeled a myth because, *overall*, the single best predictor of individual wealth is the country in which you are born coupled with the wealth or class of your parents.

Now take a look at many voters' and taxpayers' rejection of the last fifty years of civil rights and welfare-related redistributive programs. This working class or middle-class *politics of resentment* reshaped American politics by overturning the class and racial alliances of Franklin D. Roosevelt's **New Deal**. Many political scientists have written about the resentment that builds on what some Americans see as threats to their (real or imagined) privileges and identity. In contrast to politics based on economic interests, such as benefits and services (like old-fashioned populism), we see here status-based politics about who we are and would like to be. Status politics raises issues about identity (such as immigrants and racial minorities), prestige, respect for one's values, and reassurance. Status politics fires up conflicts over non-economic values and expresses grievances and resentments as moral issues. The resentment builds on five factors.

1. Some people are voicing their dissatisfaction with governments' performance and this attitude is their protest vote.
2. Some people are alienated, intolerant, and lack social trust.
3. Some are unhappy with the way the political system works, distrust political institutions, and doubt their own political effectiveness.
4. Some people respond to fear with resentment.
5. Some people's resentment is an expression of racism.

Resentment affects opinions about the fairness of redistributive programs and the public's willingness to support public spending. Redistributive politics redefined fair from helping those in need with cash assistance to helping those in need who deserve it because they are working and supposedly on their way to self-sufficiency. The "end of welfare as we know it" slogan in favor of the Temporary Assistance for Needy Families (TANF) program in 1996 illustrates the shift to assisting the working poor; each year the program accounts for about $17 billion of the federal budget. In a country in which almost nine out of ten residents are native born, resentment over spending public resources appears in states whose voters and taxpayers feel especially burdened by illegal immigrants (or aliens). Arizona, Colorado, Hawaii, and Rhode Island passed laws in 2006 excluding illegal immigrants from some government programs. Other state legislatures also are considering refusing government benefits to residents with an unlawful status. The politics of resentment has had other political fall-outs as well (see Web site resource, The Politics of Redistribution and Resentment).

Generational Politics

The United States is not only getting more diverse, it also is getting older. Fairness among different age groups now and fairness across current and future generations

---

New Deal—the name given to the programs advanced by President Franklin D. Roosevelt during the Great Depression.

BOX 3.2

Giving a Heads Up on Demography and Spending

"A recent study argued that, without an overhaul of entitlement programs (which largely favor older persons) or tax-revenue reform, the ever-expanding Social Security, Medicare, and Medicaid budgets will tighten the squeeze on other domestic spending (including programs for children, welfare, education, the environment, community development, housing, energy, and justice—programs that reach the majority of *all* Americans.) But, others argue that there are potentially catastrophic outcomes associated with the redistribution of federal resources among age categories. For instance, the safety nets for the most vulnerable may be interrupted. Costs might be transferred to the states, with limited capacity to absorb the additional expenditures. Individuals may be unable to assume the additional responsibilities asked of them.

"There is no generally accepted rule in welfare economics for how an age group's interests ought to be represented in public decision-making....[W]e are continually faced with two questions. First, do we care about our collective future—the commonwealth—or only about our individual futures? And, if we have collective concerns, we face an even more difficult decision about what mix of private and public responsibilities will best serve the needs of the generations."

SOURCE: Shrestha, 2006, pp. 24–25.

are political problems that stare out at us from the budget numbers and population projections (see box 3.2). Americans aged 65 or older will increase from 13 percent in 2010 to almost 20 percent of the population by 2030, according to the U.S. Census Bureau.

The public consistently favors health and education programs, and national opinion polls generally show that the public supports increased spending on education in preference to other spending options (see figure 3.2). Numerous statewide surveys show opposition to cutting spending on education, even in the face of looming deficits. At the same time, the public expresses strong opposition to cuts in Social Security and Medicaid, programs at the other end of the generational spread.

Responsiveness to citizen preferences does not come cheap in an open democratic society with a changing demographic profile. Health benefits redistribute resources primarily to the elderly but education redistributes to the young. Competition between these uses of public resources is nothing new. As budgets are squeezed even tighter in the future, we expect intergenerational conflict over redistributive spending to heat up.

Think about the possible effects on public spending of the changing age, income, and occupational structure in our society. Families with two wage earners and single heads-of households demand preschool and after-school programs. These demands face off against the service demands associated with

Figure 3.2. The American Public Supports Spending on Education

longer life spans and retiring baby boomers. The increasing numbers of elderly in good health and self-supporting may retire to new locales or stay in their homes. Either way, their decisions affect both communities and public budgets; their decisions convert into demands for social, emergency, and recreation services and help shape housing demand, local businesses and jobs, and property taxes.

The age groups costing the most in state services are children (schools), young adult males (criminal justice), and seniors (health). There is no easy way to balance these demands in public decision making or to determine how an age group's interests are best represented, unless we can imagine a world without politics. The political balance among these demands is tricky, at best.

Figure 3.3 shows that people in the United Kingdom receive fewer services and benefits just when their tax contributions are highest. The U.S. pattern is the same: spending and taxation for each individual varies with age. If we think in terms of households rather than individuals, then the taxpaying young parents' demands on public spending are pitted against the demands of their aging parents. This lifecycle perspective goes a long way toward explaining anti-tax sentiment among American taxpayers and voters. This anti-tax perspective, however, focuses on immediate paybacks and ignores the broader benefits over one's life span and for the community from public programs.

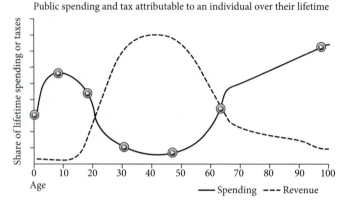

Figure 3.3. **Life Cycle and Government Resources in the United Kingdom**
How does public spending change with age?
Reproduced by permission of the United Kingdom. United Kingdom, Treasury, 2007.

It is also politically difficult to balance fairly among current budget demands and future generations. **Intergenerational equity** is the widely accepted standard of fairness that requires the generation enjoying the benefit to pay for it. Problems of accountability, acceptability, and fairness arise because the beneficiaries being handed the bill did not participate in the original choice (see chapters 5 and 8).

Spending across the States

Should each state get back from the federal government about as much as its taxpayers pay in federal taxes? According to the Tax Foundation, New Jersey receives the least among the states in federal spending per dollar of taxes paid, sixty one cents. New Mexico, at more than two dollars, receives the most. Is this fair? If yes, then why is it fair? If you don't think it is, then what standard of fairness do you think we should use?

For sake of argument, let us say that it would be fair for federal spending to be spread around about equally to each person, meaning that states should receive federal spending in proportion to their population. At less than $6,000 per person and with a small population, Nevada receives the least among the states in federal spending per person. Alaska, also with a relatively small population, comes in highest, at almost $14,000. Is this fair?

A third alternative is to give each state the same amount, for the same reason that each state has two votes in the Senate. Each state is an equal in the federal system of fifty-one sovereign parts; the federal system includes the fifty states and the federal government. Is identical treatment fair?

Intergenerational Equity—fairness across age groups or generations; often thought of as requiring the generation enjoying the benefit to pay for it.

Federal spending passes political tests. Spread around so that every state gets something, some spending aims at getting enough votes in Congress to fund the program. Other federal spending is geared to having the states carry out the policy goals set in Washington. The location of military bases and other federal facilities means federal spending is different in different states. It also means that public opposition to closing or relocating these facilities is widespread and faces resistance among the "losing" states' congressional delegations.

Poverty programs advantage regions such as the South, with a higher proportion of residents in poverty. For Medicaid, an **entitlement** program available to individuals who meet the eligibility standards, eligibility depends on income. This program provides medical care for more than 59 million people. It is financed jointly by the federal government and the states, and there is no cap on total spending. Medicaid costs the federal budget almost $216 billion, or more than two-thirds of all federal spending on aid to state and local governments. Medicaid represents about 22 percent of total state spending and is driving state spending even higher.

Some federal grants to the states are based on a formula that may or may not use measures of need; other funds are available to states, localities, and private businesses and organizations that apply in a competition. The many different federal agencies that provide grants post their grant announcements and application packages on the government-wide system http://www.grants.gov

Grants are financial incentives the federal government uses to get state (and local) governments to carry out federal policies and programs. Homeland security is a federal function that involves thirty-two federal agencies and their budgets. The departments of Homeland Security (DHS), Defense, Health and Human Services, Justice, and Energy are the big players. Since its creation in 2003 as a response to 9/11, DHS alone has administered almost $23 billion in federal grants to states, territories, urban areas, and transportation authorities. For the first few years, widely dispersed grants helped ensure the popularity of the new programs. Public and congressional critics complained that popularity outweighed the needs of high-risk locations, such as big cities and shipping ports. Now assistance is more targeted, although funding still goes to all the states. President Bush's budget for fiscal year (FY) 2009, submitted to Congress in 2008, explained the more targeted assistance:

> To optimize limited resources and minimize the potential social costs to our free
> and open society, we must apply a risk management approach across all homeland
> security efforts in order to identify and assess potential hazards … and prioritize
> and allocate resources among all homeland security partners, both public and
> private, to prevent, protect against, and respond to and recover from incidents.

Entitlements—federal outlays funded by law other than annual appropriations and considered "mandatory" or nondiscretionary until the law is changed; includes programs such as Social Security, Medicare, Medicaid, food stamps, federal civilian and military retirement benefits, veterans' benefits, and unemployment insurance.

Today grant programs in DHS combine the principles of spread and targeting for distributing federal money.

Federal aid to state and local government today finances almost one-quarter of all state and local spending. Because state and local governments depend upon this aid, proposals to cut federal aid meet with a lot of opposition from state and local leaders, public-interest organizations, nonprofit agencies, and members of Congress. Almost one-half trillion federal dollars is at stake, along with policy priorities in a federal system.

Political and Budgetary IOUs

A spending crunch is created by the increasing number of people eligible to receive benefits from redistributive entitlement programs, such as Medicaid, and the more costly federal entitlement programs primarily for seniors, Medicare and Social Security. These programs represent political promises made many years ago. (Both health programs were signed into law in 1965 and Social Security dates from 1935.) A large and increasing share of federal and state resources are devoted to entitlements and other accumulated IOUs such as payments on debt, unfunded pensions, and employees' and retirees' medical benefits.

Public-sector retirement benefits have been favorite targets of political manipulation. Benefit expansion is a relatively painless substitute for salary increases because today's decision makers will not be held accountable for tomorrow's tax bill. Inadequately funding benefit plans is a relatively hidden spending cut that comes with the additional "advantage" of pushing the costs of current programs and services off onto future taxpayers. Although the picture varies a good deal among the states, their accumulated bill in unfunded benefits for retirees approaches a trillion dollars. The federal budget does *not* include the more than $90 billion in post-employment benefits earned by—but not yet due to be paid to—federal employees in fiscal year 2007.

For the federal government alone, the bill in 2004 for all unfunded promises and IOUs stood at about $40 trillion, and the sum keeps growing. Today the bill is on the order of about $60 trillion (see figure 3.4). This long-term perspective adds together the current public debt and the present value of future resources needed to finance current policies. Divide the figure by the population and the result is . . . staggering. Now add in the states' and localities' IOUs plus crumbling infrastructure (see chapter 8) and the figure tops $100 trillion.

Whether you and current and future taxpayers and voters see this spending as fair or not, you can bet that the people who get the benefits see them as what is *rightfully* coming to them. They feel entitled, and many people have planned their futures around these programs. Entitlements are financial and legal obligations that cannot be changed without a change in the law.

To say that changing these entitlements is politically difficult is to understate the political reality. Proposals to change eligibility or reduce benefits are met with howls of betrayal. Facing opposition from constituents, lobbyists,

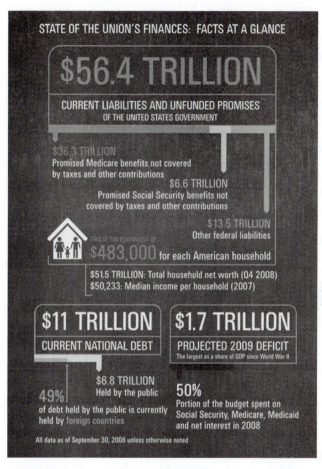

Figure 3.4. Federal IOUs
Reprinted by permission. Peter G. Peterson Foundation, 2009.

organized advocacy associations, and more, the elected officials who cast their vote on the floor of the legislature find it difficult to reduce these programs. They discover that promise-keeping and stability in public policy are at issue, as well as voters' support. Keeping the laws on the books today is a statement of ongoing political and financial commitments. Yet, keeping a promise has a downside: "[I]f not keeping explicit promises is costly, then transparency might lead politicians to keep promises when not doing so might be better" (Alt, Lassen, and Rose, 2006, p. 32).

The United States faces a big problem built out of arithmetic and politics. The costs cannot be met without crowding out other domestic spending or raising taxes beyond what is likely to be politically tolerated or financially practical (see box 3.3). In the crunch, current political leaders see their flexibility and scope for decision making reduced. Citizens and taxpayers face reduced accountability

---

BOX 3.3

Train Wrecks and Blinders

A Republican member of the House Budget Committee said, "It's a train wreck....
The government is making promises to people right now it knows it can't keep,"
(Montgomery, 2008).

"The blinders put on budget policy today threaten the very basic functions of
government as they apply to many programs, particularly those affecting children
and working families....[W]e are not creating a budget that adapts to the needs of
our time, and the reason is simple. Both political parties compete to tell us that we
are entitled to get not give, to receive not contribute, and along the way to confuse
appeals to greed with righteousness" (Steuerle, 2004, reprinted by permission).

---

because current officeholders did not make the decisions that drive current
spending.

> Make no mistake about it. This particular type of fiscal crisis is unique in our
> nation's history. Never before has the law pre-ordained so much of our future
> spending patterns. Never before have dead and retired policymakers so domi-
> nated officials elected today. And never before has so much of policy bypassed
> the traditional set of breaks applied through normal democratic decision-making
> (Steuerle, 2007, reprinted by permission).

ARE CITIZENS SATISFIED WITH
PERFORMANCE?

A budget is a statement of purposes and policies, but whose purposes are these
and are the policies what the public wants? Citizen assessments and preferences
raise the issues of accountability and responsiveness that are central to democratic
governance and turn attention to performance and results. These issues are so
important in a democracy that best budgeting practices include an assessment
element. Many governments and nonprofit agencies routinely keep a watchful eye
on performance and results.

The public gives Washington poor grades on both performance and responsiveness. Figure 1.4 in chapter 1 sketches the public's feelings about responsiveness
through 2004. As for performance, the Pew Research Center found in 2007 that
almost two-thirds of Americans agreed that "when something is run by the government, it is usually inefficient and wasteful." For decades, surveys have asked the
public, "Do you think that people in the government waste a lot of money we pay
in taxes, waste some of it, or don't waste very much of it?" Figure 3.5 shows that for
decades a majority has believed that government wastes "a lot" of money.

What the public expresses about how well or how poorly government uses
public resources is a sign of the times, a political thermometer of public satisfaction.

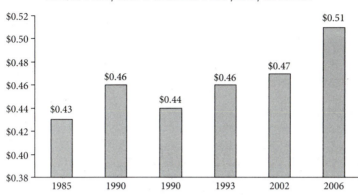

Figure 3.5. Public Evaluations of Federal Government's Efficiency

SOURCE: ABC News and The Washington Post, 1985–2006. Retrieved from the iPOLL Databank, The Roper Center for Public Opinion Research, University of Connecticut.

The public's evaluation of performance and responsiveness is influenced by people's feelings toward the party in office. People whose political party is in office are more likely to express a more favorable evaluation and people whose party is not in office tend to express a more negative view. Sharp upturns in public perceptions about a lot of waste echo shifts in public sentiment that translate into electoral shifts. These attitudes imply that more efficient management of government programs is unlikely to change public attitudes that are general political judgments rather than specific performance assessments.

The public believes tax money is wasted, but prefers spending more on selected programs. The public voices opposition to tax increases, but often opts for more spending over tax cuts. Is the American public foolish or irrational, or can these seemingly contradictory attitudes be explained another way?

The explanation is that attitudes toward spending, taxes, and performance are overall political assessments, expressions of satisfaction, and expressions of trust. Since 1979, every month Gallup has asked Americans if they are satisfied or dissatisfied with the way things are going in this country. In 2007–2008, satisfaction was tracking below the historical average of 43 percent. Frustration with the federal government's performance on domestic matters typified almost one-half of the adult public (Newport, 2008). A majority of Americans rate local and state governments favorably, but a majority expresses an unfavorable opinion of the federal government (see figure 3.6). The decline in the public's favorable attitude toward the federal government and the increase in the public's favorable attitude toward state and local governments since the 1970's show up again when Americans are asked which government gives them the most for their money (Cole and Kincaid, 2006, p. 456).

Political leaders pay attention because they believe that voters link their views about the budget to their evaluation of how good a job their leaders are doing.

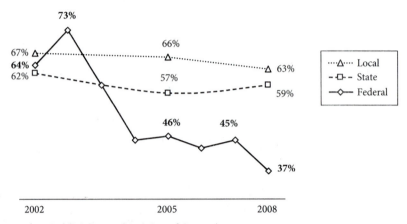

Government Favorability

Figure 3.6. Public's General Opinion of Government

QUESTION: Is your overall opinion of your government...very favorable, mostly favorable, mostly unfavorable or very unfavorable. Responses shown combine "very" and "mostly favorable."

SOURCE: Pew Research Center for the People & the Press, 2002–2008. Retrieved from the iPOLL Databank, The Roper Center for Public Opinion Research, University of Connecticut.

Some surveys suggest a link between the public's awareness of a governor's proposed budget and the public's approval rating. Leaders believe that budget outcomes could then have political costs or advantages for them. In reality, the effect goes the other way: the public's general judgments about satisfaction and performance affect the public's view of specific budget outcomes.

The widespread perception of government waste is less an assessment of performance than an echo of reduced confidence in political leadership and institutions. The readings on the political thermometer of public satisfaction with government performance signal a serious political problem: a crisis of confidence.

DOES CITIZEN TRUST OR DISTRUST MATTER?

General public trust or distrust of government institutions and leaders affects budgetary politics. Public support for spending on domestic programs rises and falls with rising and falling levels of trust in government. Citizen trust affects attitudes and behavior. Trust influences voting and other kinds of political participation, and encourages people to obey the law on matters such as paying taxes. Public opinion about the federal government's performance and waste reflects decreased general confidence in political leaders and institutions. Many polls find that trust varies by racial and ethnic groups, education, and partisan affiliation. General political trust affects public support for both distributive and redistributive programs and may even cancel out ideological differences in public support for spending.

Citizen trust is low by historical standards and a global concern. The United Nations (2007) declared, "Today, building trust in government is a worldwide concern. When people do not see themselves and their interests represented by their

Excerpts from the Association of Government Accountants' 2008 survey of public attitudes reveal two major findings about trust and transparency:

1. There is a large "expectations gap."

   - The public overwhelmingly believes government has the obligation to report and explain how the government generates and spends its money; however, government is not meeting expectations.

   - Across all levels of government, those surveyed held being "open and honest in spending practices" vitally important but felt that governments did extremely poorly in terms of being "responsible to the public for its spending."

2. There is a problem with trust.

   - Poor performance on financial management reporting has created a problem of trust between citizens and their governments with regard to spending practices.

   - American adults believe governments are failing to practice open, honest, and responsible spending while doing a poor job of providing understandable and timely financial management information.

   - These gaps between expectations and performance…are extraordinary and demonstrate how far off performance is from citizens' expectations.

---

political leaders and their government, trust is compromised and the general public interest is undermined." A 2008 survey in nineteen nations with 59 percent of the world's population found that people in most of the countries have low trust in government. "Trust in government appears to be highly related to how much people perceive the government as being responsive to the will of the people" (PIPA, 2008). Publics in all western democracies share this attitude. The American public is no exception.

Budgetary politics and practices in the United States reflect the decline of trust in government and also contribute to it. Accountability, transparency, perceived efficiency, and trust are interrelated. Americans point to government waste and inefficiency as a leading reason for distrust. The public also blames government for failures in accountability and transparency (see box 3.4).

Americans are willing to consider tough choices only if ways are found to increase their confidence that their leaders will spend public resources responsibly. A study of public attitudes about the fiscal challenges Americans face—the IOUs described earlier in this chapter—concludes, "The main obstacle to building public support for difficult choices on our nation's finances and future is not public opposition to tax increases or to program cuts, nor is it public lack of interest; the main obstacle is a deeply felt and pervasive mistrust of government" (Rosell, Furth, and Gantwerk, 2006). A nonpartisan project on federal fiscal challenges argues, "But people will only be willing to make…hard [budget] choices if they trust their leaders to act responsibly, so that their sacrifices are not wasted" (Facing Up to the Nation's Finances, n.d.).

THUMBNAIL

The big political issues of fairness and citizen satisfaction and trust play out in the politics of budgeting. Although people have different beliefs about what is and is not fair, policy makers usually claim that tax fairness is a core principle. Public acceptance ultimately defines what is politically practical. In general, public attitudes toward spending, taxes, and performance are overall political assessments.

Nationally, the total—including federal, state, and local taxes—average tax burden stands at almost one-third of income. The average federal tax burden has fallen over the last three decades. Many citizens view the federal tax system as unfair and excessively complex. People see the local property tax as the "worst" or *least fair* tax, but believe that they get the most for their tax dollar from local government.

The federal structure of government in the United States affects the impact of tax policies and spending patterns. Fiscal federalism means that federal, state, and local governments affect the policy objectives and fiscal capacity of the other governments through policy choices made through separate political processes at the federal, state, and local levels of government. Because state and local governments depend upon federal aid, proposals to cut federal aid meet with a lot of opposition.

Americans' attitudes toward public spending *in general* are ideological and partisan. They are divided over whether government should be large or small and the quantity of services it should deliver. The general principle does not translate into particular policy preferences. More people always favor spending increases over program and service cuts. Spending preferences mirror deep divisions or cleavages in American society and the increasing diversity of the U.S. population will affect public spending in the future. Noneconomic or status-based politics (in contrast to politics based on economic interests) has reshaped American politics by overturning traditional class and racial alliances. Public enthusiasm for spending is affected strongly by whether the program is distributive or redistributive.

A large and increasing share of federal and state resources are devoted to accumulated legal obligations. These affect accountability: many of these obligations were made years ago, but keeping them in place is a current policy decision. The costs cannot be financed in the near future without significant changes to other public programs and/or taxation.

Citizen assessments and preferences raise the issues of accountability and responsiveness that are central to democratic governance. Public attitudes toward spending and taxes in general are a political thermometer, a gauge of overall political satisfaction. The same is true of the public's views about government performance, and the widespread perception of government waste is less an assessment of performance than a sign of reduced confidence in political leadership and institutions. Budgetary politics and practices in the United States reflect this decline of general public trust and also contribute to it.

CASE

What Do *You* Think?

Two proposals for state budgeting have dedicated advocates and vocal opponents. The first is a state constitutional amendment the "Taxpayer Bill of Rights," or TABOR. It restricts the growth of revenues or spending to the annual change in population plus inflation, and requires that voters approve going over the limits. (Notice how the use of this formula means that the current budget structures future budgets and how cuts made during an economic downturn have a long-term impact.) The second proposal is to oppose all tax increases under all circumstances. (See also the case in chapter 7.)

What is TABOR?

TABOR is a state tax and expenditure limit that includes the following elements: it is a constitutional amendment; it restricts revenue or expenditure growth to the sum of inflation plus population change; and it requires voter approval to override the revenue or spending limits. In Colorado, where the so-called 'Taxpayer Bill of Rights' or TABOR was adopted in 1992, public services have deteriorated significantly. For example, between 1992 and 2001, Colorado declined from 35th to 49th in the nation in K–12 spending as a share of personal income. Colorado now ranks 48th in higher education funding as a share of personal income—down from 35th in 1992. Between 1991 and 2004—a period in which the percentage of children who are uninsured declined nationally—the proportion of low-income children who lack health insurance in Colorado doubled. Colorado now ranks last in the nation on this measure. In addition, between 1992 and 2002, Colorado declined from 23rd to 48th in the nation in access to prenatal care, a sign of funding shortages in local health clinics.

Allowing revenue or expenditures to grow with population and inflation may sound reasonable, but it falls far short of being able to fund the ongoing cost of government. In an era in which health care costs are growing far faster than inflation and populations are aging, limiting the rate of spending growth to inflation plus population growth forces annual reductions in the level of government services.

TABOR shrinks the scope of what government can accomplish and creates conditions that each year pit programs and services against each other for survival. And once such limits are embedded in a state constitution, they usually cannot be removed or modified. They undermine existing services for children, youth, and families and make any new initiatives virtually impossible to undertake.

In Colorado, the only state with a TABOR, voters decided in November 2005 to suspend their TABOR amendment for five years so that the state could begin restoring cuts in public services and avoid making even more drastic cuts. Yet organizations dedicated to shrinking government —such as Grover Norquist's Americans for

Tax Reform, Americans for Limited Government, the CATO Institute, and Americans for Prosperity Foundation, among others—are still pushing for the adoption of TABORs in other states. In 2005, TABOR proposals were introduced in about half of the states; none passed. In 2006, TABOR legislation and ballot initiatives were pushed aggressively in at least a dozen states. In five of these states, signatures were turned in for initiatives, but the initiatives were thrown out by the courts. In three states, TABOR initiatives did make the ballot, but were soundly defeated.

Reprinted by permission. Center on Budget and Policy Priorities, n.d.

Thinking It Over

1. What do you think of these two ideas? When forming your opinion, what are three important questions to ask, and why are they important?
2. In 2008, Colorado voters defeated Amendment 59 that would have weakened TABOR. The Colorado Commission on Taxation commissioned a poll in 2001 in which a majority of respondents approved of the TABOR Amendment and a larger majority approved the provisions requiring that voters approve tax increases and setting limits on taxes and spending. Link this chapter with chapter 2 to answer these questions: Does public opinion influence your thinking? Should it?
3. What are the implications of these proposals for accountability, responsiveness, fairness, and public trust?
4. In what ways do these proposals illustrate the politics of budgeting?

Exploring the Case Further

1. AmericansforTaxReform,http://www.atr.org/state/projects/govtransparency map.html
2. CATO Institute, http://www.cato.org/fiscal/index.html
3. Center on Budget and Policy Priorities, http://www.cbpp.org and video
4. http://www.cbpp.org/taborvideo.htm
5. Tax Foundation, http://www.taxfoundation.org

The Taxpayer Protection Pledge

The pledge was started in 1986 as the first project of Americans for Tax Reform (see figure 3.7).

I, _____, pledge to the taxpayers of the _____ district of the State of _____ and to all the people of this state, that I will oppose and vote against any and all efforts to increase taxes.

Signed _____   Date _____

Witness _____   Witness _____

Figure 3.7. The Taxpayer Protection Pledge
Reprinted by permission. Americans for Tax Reform.

WEB SITE RESOURCES

- Fairness and the Federal Income Tax
- Further Resources
- Health Care Basics and the Budget
- Internet Resources
- The Politics of Redistribution and Resentment
- Resources on Different Approaches to Fairness and Participatory Budgeting in Developing Democracies

REVIEW QUESTIONS

1. What are some reasons that Americans typically prefer less government spending than Europeans on redistributive income-transfer programs, such as food stamps and welfare?
2. Why do you think many middle-class and working-class Americans may be unwilling to support a tax structure that is targeted primarily at the wealthy?
3. Why is the age of a community's population important to consider when making budgetary decisions?
4. How do entitlement programs make creating a fair budget difficult?
5. Why would more efficient management of government programs be unlikely to change the popular notion that the government wastes a lot of taxpayer money?

4

⟨∞⟩

Process Matters

This chapter answers six questions:

- How Is the Budget "Game" Played?
- How Did We Get Here?
- What Is Executive Budgeting?
- How Does Executive Budgeting Work?
- Why Take a Political Perspective?
- How Does the Federal Entitlement Process Work?

> These things do not happen by chance. There is much less luck
> in public affairs than some suppose.
>
> CALVIN COOLIDGE (1872–1933)

How decisions are made affect *what* decisions are made. Process matters, institutions matter, and so do rules in their various forms, including laws, procedures, and guidelines. These all influence political decisions and public policy. A major study of modern democracies finds that forms of government (presidential *versus* parliamentary) and rules about elections (majority *versus* proportional) affect total government spending, welfare spending, and the size of budget deficits (Persson, Torsten & Tabellini, 2005, pp. 270–274). The Organisation for Economic Co-Operation and Development (OECD) keeps a database on budget practices and procedures of several dozen countries and the National Association of State Budget Officers (NASBO) and National Conference of State Legislatures (NCSL) do the same for the American states. For a sense of how process matters, think of how decisions are made in legislative committees, when members' votes are needed to pass a proposal. When decision making is decentralized among different players who are equally important to the outcome but who disagree, the typical way to make a decision is either to split the difference or to take turns.

Public priorities and policies written into a budget often emerge from finding the middle ground and compromising rather than a straightforward reckoning of what is efficient and effective. Many other considerations come into play, including accountability, transparency, responsiveness, law, fairness, existing policy commitments, and public participation.

Many political players and institutions get in on the action. Informal influences, interactions, and relationships, along with custom and habit, influence decisions and affect results. Negotiation, bargaining, accommodation, horse-trading, and collaboration are needed to cut a deal and get something done, and these interactions *usually* govern decision making. By way of example, look at two powerful actors on the national political stage: the chairperson of the House Ways and Means Committee who has jurisdiction over revenue and big entitlement programs, and the chairperson of the House Appropriations Committee. As powerful as these representatives are, they still share power with other players. The House Ways and Means Committee chairman observed that "you can only demonstrate power when you have the votes. That means consensus, and that means the sharing of whatever political power… [there] is" (Cohen, 2007). The chairman of the House Appropriations Committee pointed out, "If you want to be trusted around here and you want to be somebody people can work with, you have to make d*** sure the other guy always gets something.… Everyone has to have a stake in it" (Williamson, 2007, p. A19).

The complex, dynamic public sector uses formal rules and legal authority to make big-ticket decisions. The effect of separation of powers, federalism, and vigorous public and private sectors on the American political world is that authority is fragmented; power is dispersed among branches of government as well as different governments and organizations. The result is that no single person or institution makes an important budget decision alone.

The neat frameworks of formal procedures, timetables, documents, and deadlines trace the decision-making process as if it were played out in a series of defined steps. (In fact, much of this chapter is organized according to the broad steps in the budget cycle.) But beware! Policy proposals often inch along at what may first appear to be a straight line, only to be sidetracked or sideswiped by events or new information that transform the political landscape, erupting into shifts in political support. Decisions get nudged, snagged, bumped, and buffeted by competing influences and pounding pressures that come in from many sides and many sources. The case at the end of this chapter shows that deals may underlie a budget decision; compromises are struck and bargains made. But **feedback loops** and overlapping moves can magnify small changes, causing deals to unravel. The budget process in a democracy is open to many influences, many pressures, and many players.

Feedback Loop—the method by which policies are subject to revision based on the influence and effect of prior decisions; using information about implementation and performance to adjust processes and routines.

The process is more like a three-dimensional interactive video than a two-dimensional sequence of steps. But we must sacrifice shadings, tones, and looping interactions to get the big budget picture in our sights. In political decision making, the reality of formal and informal influences is usually more complex and often more dramatic than a diagram can capture.

This chapter focuses on the process for adopting the **operating budget**, which provides goods and services to be consumed during the fiscal period for which the budget is adopted. (Chapter 8 examines the capital budget, which finances long-lived projects such as bridges and buildings.) All public-sector organizations use an operating budget, of which the greatest part is usually the **general fund**. The general fund includes all resources not required by law to be accounted for in another fund—an independent **self-balancing set of accounts** established by law and open to all allowable purposes (all other funds are restricted to specific purposes). The general fund usually includes most of an organization's current expenditures and revenues. The general fund almost always is required by law and professional practice to be balanced. When people talk about *the* budget and a balanced budget, they usually are talking about the general fund.

HOW IS THE BUDGET "GAME" PLAYED?

Some elements of decision-making processes are formal, embedded in written rules and sometimes in laws, charters, or constitutions. Other elements are informal, the products of habit, custom, preference, or on-the-fly adjustments to circumstances, such as political advantage (see box 4.1). While the formal elements are easier to identify and trace, both the formal and informal elements are important to budgeting.

Governmental budget processes are different from budgeting in other organizations for the five reasons listed in figure 4.1. One difference is that a government's budget process results in a law. For a government budget to become a law, it must be passed by the legislative body and signed by the chief elected official. Only by law (called an **appropriation**) may resources be used. The general rules of how a bill becomes a law apply, but budget rules often have some special features. These

---

Operating Budget—finances goods and services consumed in the fiscal period.

General Fund—an accounting fund to account for all financial resources that the organization can legally engage in, except those legally required to be accounted for in a more specialized fund; usually accounts for most government programs, thereby making it the most visible and competitive avenue for funding a program.

Self-balancing Set of Accounts—the accounting equation, assets = liabilities + equity; alternatively stated as assets − liabilities = equity.

Appropriation—law passed by the legislature and signed by the chief executive that permits the obligation for and spending of government resources.

BOX 4.1

Presidential Stamp on the Budget Process

The Bush administration established a budget review board to set spending priorities and arbitrate budget disputes between cabinet members and OMB. Because Vice President Dick Cheney chaired the budget review board, he had "direct and indirect power over the federal budget—and over those who must live within it." The OMB director in 2001–2003 said that he never saw a cabinet secretary make a direct appeal about the budget to the president (Becker and Gellman, 2007, p. A01). In effect, the vice president had veto power over public policy.

The budget process in the Obama Administration also suits the president's style and political agenda. President-elect Barack Obama pledged, "We will go through our federal budget—page by page, line by line—eliminating those programs we don't need, and insisting that those we do operate in a sensible cost-effective way....That is what the OMB will do in my administration—it will not only help design a budget and manage its implementation, it will also help make sure that our government—your government—is more efficient and more effective at serving the American people" (OMB, 2008).

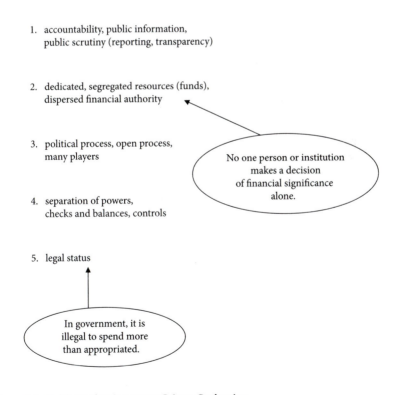

1. accountability, public information, public scrutiny (reporting, transparency)

2. dedicated, segregated resources (funds), dispersed financial authority

3. political process, open process, many players

   No one person or institution makes a decision of financial significance alone.

4. separation of powers, checks and balances, controls

5. legal status

   In government, it is illegal to spend more than appropriated.

Figure 4.1. Public Budgeting *versus* Private Budgeting

may include distinctive approval paths involving budget committees, requirements for public hearings, or other features aimed at ensuring accountability and transparency because budget decisions involve taxes and governments' coercive powers.

The timing of budget legislation is important to the legislative process. The budget often is passed toward the end of a legislative session because the promises and deals it includes give legislative leaders a way to enforce party discipline or put together a voting bloc, as the case at the end of this chapter illustrates. Second, if a new budget is not passed on time and before the start of the new fiscal year, all but legally required government payments and essential services grind to a halt.

Formal procedures, institutional arrangements, and the structure of budgets vary meaningfully across states and local governments. For an example, look at Nebraska, where nonpartisan elections fill the seats in a unicameral (or one-house) legislature. The federal budget process is different from state and local budgeting in ten fundamental ways. This chapter especially highlights the first two differences. Other chapters examine other major differences.

1. Executive/legislative powers (these also vary from state to state and among localities).
2. Procedures and practices, such as fiscal year, **line-item veto**, budgeting by **budget authority** *versus* appropriations, legislature's receiving agency requests, requirements for balance, **accounting** practices, **fund structure**, and arrangements for handling emergencies (such as **contingency funds** and supplemental appropriations).
3. Openness, visibility, and public awareness, perceptions, and opinions.
4. Citizen participation and public perceptions of budgets' significance (saliency) and usefulness of participation (efficacy).
5. Capital budgeting.
6. Revenue sources, structure, and **intergovernmental transfers.**
7. Major spending categories, impact of labor costs, and impact of entitlements.

Line-item Veto—the chief elected official's authority to pick out specific items in the budget and veto them without vetoing the whole appropriation bill.

Budget Authority (BA)—provided in law to federal agencies to enter into legal obligations resulting in current or future government outlays.

Accounting System—the total set of records and procedures that are used to record, classify, and report information on the financial status and operations of the organization.

Fund Structure—the financial system of all the accounting funds in the organization.

Contingency—a budgetary resource set aside for emergencies or spending not anticipated or known at the time the budget is adopted.

Intergovernmental Transfer—payments made by one government and distributed to another government, usually through some predetermined formula.

8. Drivers of budget growth and change.
9. Scope of government, size, and impact on economy.
10. Functional responsibilities such as **monetary policy**, national security, and education.

HOW DID WE GET HERE?

The historical development of governmental budgeting in the United States affects the way budgeting is done today. Federal budgeting after the American Revolution began with four annual appropriation acts: for the Treasury Department, for the War Department, for civilian employees, and for all else (see box 4.2). Except in wartime, Congress dominated federal budgeting throughout the nineteenth century and until after World War I. Government agencies prepared their estimates, submitted them to the Treasury Department, and Treasury turned them over to Congress. The president did not take part, and there was no integrated budget for the government as a whole. Congress' main concerns were raising enough revenue and whether spending was legal, rather than the purpose and effective use of resources.

Many central features of federal budgeting today were put in place in the nineteenth century. The House established the Ways and Means Committee as a standing committee in 1802 and the Senate followed suit with its Committee on Finance in 1816. A two-step process of legally allowing the activity (authorization) and then permitting spending on it (appropriation) began in the House of Representatives in 1837 and in the Senate in 1850. The House created its Appropriations Committee after the Civil War. As the century drew to a close, standard accounting practices were adopted with the passage of the Dockery Act in 1894. Each new institution or procedure usually was grafted onto the existing process. (For more on the current federal budget process, see Appendix A and the Web site resource, How to Read Highlights of the Federal Budget.)

As society grew larger and complex, so did government and the broader public sector, including **NGOs** (or nongovernmental organizations) providing social, health, and educational services. The nineteenth century was a time of change and turmoil. The frontier pushed westward; immigration fed urban growth and squalor; railroads changed transportation; industrialization and labor unrest transfigured the workaday world; electrification transformed life's rhythms in the cities; and the reaction to partisan corruption and party bosses changed politics and budgeting.

Governments' role expanded in response to this transformation—and so did public expectations. Many state and local governments responded to the rising clamor of political demands by launching public-safety, health, transportation, and education services. Washington began expanding the reach of federal regulation

---

Monetary Policy—actions by the Federal Reserve, done as the central bank to influence the availability and cost of money and credit.

NGO (nongovernmental organization)—term used around the world to refer to organizations that are neither public (governmental) nor private business.

============================= **BOX 4.2** =============================

The First Federal Appropriations Act

Annual appropriation acts in 1791–1794 amounted to a few lump-sum appropriations, with one appropriation covering Treasury warrants, another the civil list, a third the Department of War, and a fourth other expenditures. Appropriating $639,000, Congress passed the first general appropriation act on September 29, 1789:

> Be it enacted by the Senate and House of Representatives of the United States of America in Congress assembled, [t]hat there be appropriated for the service of the present year, to be paid out of the monies which arise, either from the requisitions heretofore made upon the several states, or from the duties on impost and tonnage, the following sums, *viz.* A sum not exceeding two hundred and sixteen thousand dollars for defraying the expenses of the civil list, under the late and present government; a sum not exceeding one hundred and thirty-seven thousand dollars for defraying the expenses of the department of war; a sum not exceeding one hundred and ninety thousand dollars for discharging the warrants issued by the late board of treasury, and remaining unsatisfied; and a sum not exceeding ninety-six thousand dollars for paying the pensions to invalids.

Go to the House and Senate Appropriations Committees (http://thomas.loc.gov/links) and compare current budget documents to the 1789 appropriation act. Compare it also to the 2001 emergency appropriation in figure 4.4. How has the budget and budget process changed? See also the Web site resource, How to Read Highlights of the Federal Budget.

---

by establishing the first regulatory commission in 1887 for surface interstate commerce. New tasks followed from a new definition of the public good in a society undergoing rapid change.

The nineteenth-century system of **legislative budgeting** was caving in under these new demands at all levels of government. No one had an overall picture of what executive agencies were doing, at what cost, for what purposes, and who was in charge. Many legislatures could not handle the work burden.

WHAT IS EXECUTIVE BUDGETING?

Governments began to shift to **executive budgeting**, in which a single, comprehensive budget plan was put together by the executive and given to the legislature

---

Legislative Budgeting—a budget process that gives more power to the legislative branch than the executive branch; a budget process in which the units of the executive branch submit their budget requests directly to the legislature and not to the chief executive.

Executive Budgeting—a budget process in which the executive formulates and submits the budget to the legislature and then implements the adopted budget.

for review and appropriation. Beginning in New York City, and then adopted by municipal governments run by professional city managers, executive budgeting aimed for better planning, accountability, and control of public resources. Early in the twentieth century, state and local governments took the lead in adopting executive budgeting. Change came more slowly in Washington, where Congress closely guarded its constitutional powers.

The move to executive budgeting was part of the ongoing tug-of-war between the executive and legislative branches that explains much of budgetary politics over the past century. This move also signaled developing administrative capacity that depended on newly established government agencies and bureaus with expert staffs and on technology for communication and transportation. (Alexander Graham Bell introduced Americans to the telephone only in 1876, and three years later Thomas Edison gave us the electric light bulb.)

Executive budgeting also crowned efficiency as a central value in public budgeting. But efficiency for what purpose? In 1912, President Taft's Commission on Economy and Efficiency defined the purpose of executive budgeting as stewardship.

The federal government adopted executive budgeting in 1921, with the passage of the Budget and Accounting Act. This act also created the Bureau of the Budget to act as the executive's budget staff. (It would become part of the new Executive Office of the President in 1939 and renamed the Office of Management and Budget, or OMB, in 1970.) To counterbalance the shift in budgetary power from Congress to the White House, the 1921 act established a new staff office in Congress, the General Accounting Office (renamed the Government Accountability Office in 2004). This law shifted auditing—examining the use of public funds and making sure that financial transactions are in order—from the Treasury Department in the executive branch to Congress (see box 4.3).

BOX 4.3

What Does the U.S. Treasury Department Do?

Go to http://www.ustreas.gov

- Pays Social Security, veterans' benefits, and income tax refunds to more than one-third the population.
- Collects federal revenues and enforces federal tax laws through the Internal Revenue Service.
- Manages the national debt, federal finances, pays bills, and manages a daily cash flow larger than the budget of many countries.
- Produces U.S. postage stamps, currency and coins, and investigates and prosecutes tax evaders and counterfeiters.
- Analyzes tax policy and makes the official estimate of federal receipts for use in the president's budget.

HOW DOES EXECUTIVE BUDGETING WORK?

The federal government, most states, and most large, complex local governments follow an executive budget cycle. In this cycle, the chief executive's budget staff drafts a budget to propose to the legislature. All executive budgeting goes through these four broad stages:

1. executive formulation and submission,
2. legislative review and appropriation,
3. executive implementation, and
4. audit and evaluation.

(The Web site resource, Portland's Budget Process, traces these stages in a big city.)

The federal cycle is summarized neatly this way:

> Federal budgeting is a cyclical activity that begins with the formulation of the President's annual budget and concludes with the audit and review of expenditures. The process spreads over a multi-year period. The main stages are formulation of the President's budget, congressional budget actions, implementation of the budget, and audit and review.... While the basic steps continue from year to year, particular procedures often vary in accord with the style of the President, the economic and political considerations under which the budget is prepared and implemented, and other factors (Keith and Schick, 2004, pp. 9–10).

(Appendix A traces federal budget formulation and the federal appropriations process.)

The federal and local governments and nonprofit agencies usually adopt a budget for one year. So do most states, but twenty states adopt a budget for a two-year period. (The Web site resource, Fiscal Year, provides more information about the fiscal year.)

Executive Formulation and Submission

Stage One starts with the **budget call** from the chief executive, when forms and general guidelines are sent to the departments and agencies. The chief executive's policy agenda and view of the economy often set the overall framework. The budget call ordinarily sets the limits for agency requests by announcing spending guidelines and the executive's priorities. The instructions ordinarily point to permitted increases or required proposals for cuts. For example, a local government's budget call may look like this:

> The guidelines require a *status quo* budget and call for departments to submit a base budget that reflects these principles:
>
> - No new full-time positions or funding of vacant unfunded positions;
> - No additional hours above current levels for temporary or overtime labor;

Budget Call—in an executive budget process, the chief executive's set of policies and guidelines sent to the spending units for them to follow in drafting their budget requests.

- A 3 percent inflationary increase for items other than salaries, wages, and benefits;
- Capital outlay requests justified from a productivity standpoint.

[Anything above these guidelines requires special forms and justification.]

These instructions treat what is already in the budget differently from proposals for change that are given special scrutiny.

Bouncing Off the Base

Decision making often starts by bouncing off where decision makers see themselves now, or the *base*. The base is (1) the budget adopted last year, (2) the most recent estimates of operations in the current year, or (3) the current cost of continuing existing programs (current services) and revenues under current law. (Some governments include inflation when calculating the base.) Changes to the base are examined with special care. This is an analytic perspective; a way of looking at the world in two broad categories of what is going on now and proposals for change. This political perspective on decision making is, in effect, a learning device or a lens through which decision makers focus on information and issues. It is *not* a set of fixed decision-making rules or relationships.

Bouncing off the base is built right into many of the key budget documents. This is important because the way information is presented and questions are framed influence the decisions made. Four signs point to this perspective, including

1. historical spending arrayed in columns alongside the current requests;
2. using the last appropriation or **current services** as a point of departure for decision making;
3. an emphasis on change, as in many budget messages and narratives that highlight new priorities and initiatives;
4. special detail on and scrutiny of proposed changes.

Conventional formats display figures from prior years right alongside figures for the current cycle. Many budget documents highlight change, expressed in percentages and/or dollars. The executive's budget message and summary narratives and schedules usually lay out proposed changes in detail. Instruction forms sent to the agencies at the beginning of budget preparation commonly require more elaborate justification of proposed changes than of ongoing operations.

Using the base as the starting point for making budget choices is a useful shortcut. It is efficient because so much of the budget is tied up in existing legal obligations (such as contracts, debt payments, and employees' and retirees' accumulated benefits); requirements of intergovernmental aid or **mandates**; and

---

Current Services—budget amount for continuing existing programs, allowing for changes in inflation and law.

Mandate—a binding obligation by law or contract accepted by one organization in order to receive certain benefits or funds from another organization; can be a mandate on use and/or procedures involving the funds.

routine essential services. This approach reserves some power over budget decisions for the legislature at a time when executive power over the public purse is increasing in many governments.

A single decision-making round is driven far less by current agendas and political demands than by spending commitments and revenue choices made in the past. These are in place before the budget call kicks off the new round. They are legally binding, at least until the law is changed, and include obligations such as (1) labor and other contracts, (2) unpaid bills, (3) payments of interest and principal on debt, and (4) court orders dealing with, for example, prisons, education, and mental health services.

To simplify the political task of making choices, decision making about spending in the upcoming budget routinely starts with the prior fiscal year as the point of departure. This approach splits spending into two parts: (1) changes, which usually are the stuff of current political discord and examined closely, and (2) past bargains and compromises that for the most part usually are left in place. As a result, the scope of the budget battle is narrowed.

The National Association of State Budget Officers (NASBO, n.d., p. 100, reprinted by permission) describes the base as

> essentially the next fiscal year's cost of implementing this fiscal year's...decisions....The decisions typically reflect long practice and custom, and may at times seem "automatic." In fact, they are not. They are spending decisions. They represent an agreement on what kind of information is to be considered in subsequent decision making and how micro budgeting decisions are to be simplified.

Starting with the base has its costs. Under ordinary circumstances (1) much of the base goes largely unexamined, (2) obligations made in the past tie up much of the budget, (3) new competitors for the always scarce resources are relatively disadvantaged, and (4) responsiveness to current demands suffers. An observer of state budgeting noticed "the tendency for public agencies to continue what they have been doing in the past without much reexamination" (Morgan, 2002, pp. 40–41). The U.S. Comptroller General, head of Congress' Government Accountability Office (GAO), observed similar results in federal budgeting (see Web site resource, Bouncing Off the Base in Government Budgeting).

Sometimes an approach to decision making that divides the budget broadly into base and change is termed **incrementalism**. This book's authors purposively avoid this term because classical incrementalism represents a whole literature (most notably Wildavsky, 1964) that comes complete with its stubborn fans and unyielding critics. The decision-making rules, relationships, and predicted outcomes of classical incrementalism, such as marginal change, are irrelevant to the perspective described here. The size of the change is also irrelevant to this perspective.

Incrementalism—the budget theory holding that small changes from prior decisions are to be expected due to the limits of time, resources, and ability to evaluate all options; helps describe political/organizational decision-making as influenced by the most recent past.

Practical and pressured, budgeters look out at their budget world from where they are now. Bouncing off the base is their usual platform for beginning many—*but by no means all*—budget decisions in many governments and non-profit agencies (see Web site resource, Bouncing Off the Base in Government Budgeting). About one-half of the states rely on this budget approach, and so do most local governments, school districts, and nonprofit organizations. "Most states use a budget method that is incremental—previous appropriations are increased or decreased by small increments. Due to ongoing funding require-ments, a large portion of the previous year's budget is assumed to be committed. And with an emphasis on accounting and control, the focus is on what money buys (inputs) rather than on the service that is provided (outcomes)" (NCSL, 2008). In Texas, which uses a performance-based approach to state budgeting, the legislature still uses the prior fiscal year as the jumping-off place for decision making (Texas, 2007).

Washington, D.C. and many states and localities saw heroic efforts to shift to different approaches to budgetary decision making; the point of **zero-based budgeting** was to break away from the base (see Web site resource, Budget Formats). Yet, decision making about the budget usually still bounces off the base. The budget world typically is divided into (1) the base or current services and (2) change.

Bouncing off the base is a *political* perspective on budgeting that emphasizes *change* in the long- and short-term. Decision makers start with where they are now, focus on what they can do, and make choices about changes from there. With each budget round, players in the process respond to new demands for new ser-vices and adjust existing services to changing circumstances. The decision-making process draws on many different formal and informal rules (including laws and procedures), routines, and relationships, advocacy for different and opposing interests, leadership and personalities, skills at building coalitions and consensus, policy leanings, executive-legislative deals, and more.

To say that the base is the starting point for putting together the next budget is not at all to say that the base remains static or never changes. On the contrary, the base is reshaped by changes in, for example, the number of people eligible to receive benefits, such as when a growing or changing student population swells preschool enrollments or special education. Changes in the cost of providing particular ser-vices, such as health care, influence the base. Changing fuel prices show up in the costs of gassing up police cruisers and school buses. Cuts in state aid or declining housing values alter revenue estimates. New political demands along with court orders, natural disasters, and other environmental developments also affect the base (see the Web site resource, How Budgets Interact with Economic Conditions.) A change in political consensus can lead to revisiting and even sharply reducing or eliminating a program that no longer enjoys majority legislative vote support.

Zero-Based Budgeting—a budget format approach that places an emphasis on re-justifying each program anew each year.

Budget Requests

The agencies then begin drawing up their budget requests within the general boundaries set out in the budget call. Larger agencies may have a budget office staffed by professional budgeters to prepare estimates and analyses. The chief executive's budget staff may prepare the budget requests for smaller agencies.

Legislative Call. At about the same time as the budget call, the chief executive asks the agencies to send in their proposals for the upcoming legislative session. These proposed changes in law may be added to the legislative agenda that the chief executive sends to the legislature. These agency proposals are a source of many of the good ideas competing for resources.

Appeals and Issue Networks. Spending estimates are political strategies as well as estimates of needed resources. After all, there is no universal, meaningful gauge of how much is the "right" amount…deciding this is the point of budgetary politics.

To influence the budgetary decision makers, politically appointed agency heads appeal to reason—the program is effective, efficient and maybe is low cost. They also appeal to emotion—the program is popular with the public, embraces important political symbols, or is traditional. (A sample request is included in the Web site resource, Tracking an Agency's Budget Request.)

The most persuasive evidence that money is well spent and taxpayers are getting value for their money is public and elected leaders' support. Budget requests often are designed to appeal to this political support. Sometimes the audience and service beneficiaries are inside the government; for example, the personnel office wants another analyst. Then the budget request must rely on workload data and technical arguments. If the agency has an outside constituency to support it, then the argument may appeal to external political support. Program advocates, program beneficiaries, and lobbyists make up this constituency, sometimes labeled special interest groups. Programs that have broad support and are seen as serving the public interest can draw on symbols, support, and arguments that are quite different from more narrowly targeted services. There are different audiences that must hear and respond to an appeal. If a program appeals directly to the public, then political leaders are more likely to support it; if it is efficient or cost effective, then the budget office may think it is a good idea.

An appeal is made to both reason and emotion in many cases and combines technical and political arguments. The fine-tuning depends upon the service and how it is financed, the audience, the clientele, the chief executive's policy agenda, and legislative support. The balance may shift over time as, for example, when a new program wins the chief executive's support or widespread public backing.

The appropriations committee in the legislature, the constituency, and savvy agency budgeters must work together in a supportive, ongoing relationship if a budget proposal is to successfully make its way through the highly competitive political process. Cooperation and mutual support dominate relationships in this so-called *iron triangle*, formed by the appropriations committee, the constituency, and the agency. They all share an interest in seeing that their program is adequately funded and depend on one other to make it happen. Their mutual dependency is a source of political power for all three. Although this cozy relationship weakens executive leadership over policy and control over the bureaucracy, remember that the chief executive appoints the agency head to implement his or her policy preferences. Usually the agency head serves at the pleasure of the chief executive, and it is the chief executive's budget recommendation that goes to the legislature and frames the discussion.

Budgetary politics today is fluid and dynamic, and constituencies tend to band together temporarily around a particular issue. They then regroup around different issues. As a result, today the iron triangle is better described as an *issue network*.

Budget Strategies. Budget requests ordinarily draw on one or more of five standard strategies. These five are real-world observations but not necessarily recommendations. One strategy is a classic rule of thumb: if you don't ask, you don't get. More assertive budgeters tend to end up with more resources for their agency over time, but risk their professional reputation and the trust of their audience and constituency if their requests seem excessive. Credibility is an asset in the politics of budgeting.

Aaron Wildavsky identified three general budget strategies in his 1964 classic book. The first is to defend the base, to circle the wagons as it were, in order to protect the agency's resource base against cuts. Mindful that the pressure of scarcity is always part of the budget process, and with the objective of protecting the program or agency against the threat of having requests cut, budgeters may try to tie an item or issue to existing law to get it in the base.

The second general strategy is to expand the base by building bit-by-bit on what is already in place. Most aggressive and risky, the third general strategy is to increase the base by simply asking for more, as Oliver does in Charles Dickens' *Oliver Twist*. This strategy is easiest politically when it comes in response to an emergency or crisis such as posed by natural disasters and national security; then the obvious, immediate need short-circuits the usually intense review of new budget proposals.

Although defending the base probably is the most common—and surely the easiest—strategy, the base is **not** sacred. The base is a reference point, a point of departure for decision making in a single budget cycle; it is *not* a fixed, unchanging decree carved in stone for all time. This strategy is no guarantee of budgetary success.

A review of spending from prior years may be thorough, methodical, and program by program. Or external events, such as the loss of a grant or an extreme price change, may foster reconsideration. Scrutiny may be driven by chance, such as when a public employee retires or takes a new job and the position is frozen (no one is permitted to be hired) or allocated elsewhere by the central budget office.

Today, after repeated episodes of budget cuts and streamlining techniques, such as retirement incentives and contracting with private companies to provide services, probably no base, no agency, and no service has escaped untouched. Some programs and even some agencies have been "zeroed out" (or eliminated). New revenue sources arise and established ones fade. Some items are hard to change and others easier, but even laws can be and are changed. When we broaden the time horizon beyond a single budget round, we see significant shifts in spending and revenue patterns as well as in programs and services.

The last strategy is padding the budget, but certainly it is not recommended for reasons of ethics, democracy, and professionalism. Padding occurs when budget estimates are fudged and distortions are hidden in order to build in some insurance against anticipated cuts made by the chief executive or legislature. Picture this scenario: spending totals must fall within revenue estimates, a tax increase is out of the question, and a budgeter expects the city council or state legislature to trim the agency's request. To defend the base, the budgeter exaggerates the demand for services, cost increases, or another factor.

To the extent that agency heads are protecting programs from anticipated budget cuts that translate into devastating service cuts, they may see themselves as trying to protect the public interest. They may be trying to create and defend enough slack to operate comfortably and to provide managerial flexibility and adaptability so that, when the unexpected happens, a crisis does not erupt. Some agency heads and professional budgeters may see themselves operating in a game-playing environment, where some seem to get away with it, others are tempted to try it, and the central budget office contributes an incentive by making **across-the-board** cuts (equal percentage to all agencies), which are not targeted and made without regard to efficiency, costs, or needs.

The problem is that the strategy of padding sacrifices accuracy, accountability, credibility, and honesty on the altar of budget success. Accountability and honesty are sacrificed because padding, in effect, means agency heads are faking their resource needs to the chief executive who appointed and relies on them; this behavior does not breed trust. By fudging or fabricating and then attempting to hide the misrepresentations, budgeters put the brakes on transparency and accountability. Padding undercuts the legislature's legal authority to allocate public funds. By padding their budget, a small group of unelected public servants decides that their particular agency or service defines the public interest. Padding amounts to putting organizational loyalty above law, professionalism, and democratic values.

Padding occurs far less frequently than commonly believed and should *not* be thought of as routine behavior. Because spending estimates are political strategies, agency heads and their budget staff usually prefer to guard carefully their political

---

Across-the-board—Applied equally to all participants, such as cutting all agencies' funding by an equal percentage.

asset, credibility. They know that padding is easily visible, usually does not pay off, and invites cuts to their requests.

> The development of the budget and decision making process requires the involvement of many parties working in a cooperative way to build consensus, while recognizing and not compromising their respective roles. The executive budget analyst must be capable of playing different roles at different times with different groups, while maintaining integrity and credibility. The same data that convinced the executive analyst must also be provided to legislators and the legislative staff, with all the arguments and supporting information. Timely, accurate, and complete information from the agencies is critical to the success of an analyst (NASBO, n.d., reprinted by permission).

Padding is contrary to professional standards advocated by, for example, the National Association of State Budget Officers and the Government Finance Officers Association. Professional budgeters usually build in a margin of safety and provide some flexibility and adaptability for the jurisdiction. Conservative forecast revenues aim at making sure that there is enough money coming in to cover the payroll and pay bills. Half of the states require that expenditures come in under the official revenue forecast for the budget period; in these twenty-six states, the revenue forecast "binds the budget" (NCSL, 2008). Expenditures, on the other hand, are often estimated more expansively, because the amount fixed in the budget (the appropriation) is the resource ceiling. If these estimates are within a reasonable range of possibilities, open rather than hidden from the governing body and the public, and publicly discussed by elected officials in open sessions, then this behavior is very different from padding.

When budget officers in a central budget office provide estimates without disclosing fully the assumptions, range of estimates, and risks, then we have a version of padding, and the same objections apply. Elected officials should be given the opportunity to decide how much risk they are willing to bear (and bear it they will in the next election). Another version of padding is budgeting as if every position will be filled yearlong, despite the likelihood of turnover and vacancies, and not publicly revealing this built-in slack before the legislature adopts the budget.

Some budget officers may try these things for self-protection and others to ensure that the year ends happily, with a surplus (see Web site resource, Information is Power). These behaviors work to dampen political demands on public resources by exaggerating scarcity. They lead to over taxing, lost opportunities, and shift decision making from elected officials to staff offices.

In a democracy, the budget game has widely accepted rules and is supposed to be fair, accountable, and transparent. These values require making realistic revenue estimates that are neither stingy nor generous and then appropriating less than promised. The *reliability* of the estimates and projections—rosy scenario or wishful thinking? smoke and mirrors? politically useful tall tale?—are as important to understand as the numbers themselves. As the first Secretary of the U.S. Treasury Department, Alexander Hamilton, said, "In political arithmetic, two and two does not always equal four."

Significance of Stage One

The action really starts when a chief executive puts forward his or her policy agenda in a series of recommendations to the legislature. By establishing the agenda, the chief executive usually frames the discussion and dominates subsequent legislative action (see figure 4.2). A chief executive's policy agenda ordinarily amounts to only a small proportion of the total budget. The scope of change in any single budget round may be a small percentage of the entire budget, but a small percentage change represents many dollars and the impact of small decisions mount over time.

What are the broad political consequences of not revisiting all budget choices every year? As is so often the case in politics, the answer includes positives and negatives. First, citizens, taxpayers, budgeters, and those receiving services probably would not want the entire budget revised, because they prefer some stability and predictability in public policy and public services.

The fate of the federal program for abstinence education is an example of the importance of stability in budgeting. The program was part of the welfare reform laws of 1996 but lived on through many short-term extensions after 2002. Despite about $50 million available in federal money, state participation dropped to only one-half of the states by the fall of 2008. A headline of *The Oklahoman*

Figure 4.2. The Chief Executive Today Frames the Budget Debate, But These Great Presidents Did Not. Why Not?

Ranger Ed Menard, National Park Service, October 22, 2007.

proclaimed, "States abstain from program." A staff member of Idaho's Department of Health and Welfare explained, "The funding stream became inconsistent. We didn't know from one quarter to the next whether we'd be getting the rest of the money" (Associated Press, 2008, p. A8). Of course, stability is anticipated only in the short term because repeated budget rounds allow for rapid change in small steps compounded over the years.

Second, a narrower perspective helps decision makers meet timetables and deadlines to put a budget in place before the beginning of a new fiscal year. Third, keeping past commitments in place keeps competition in bounds and reduces conflict in the political system. The fourth consequence is a serious negative in a democratic system: if most of a budget is built up from past decisions and commitments, then accountability and responsiveness are reduced today and in the future. New ideas are disadvantaged in the competition for resources, emerging problems may be ignored, and evidence-driven rethinking is throttled.

Legislative Review and Appropriation

The drama is in Stage Two, when deals are cut, bargains struck, and so much is made public. Although deals can be made at any stage in the process, this stage is associated with bargaining and negotiating because it takes a legislative majority to pass a budget. Under the media spotlight, legislators swing from standing fast on principles to compromising on dollars. Legislators learn that it is easier politically and personally to trade dollars than programs and principles.

Despite the political drama and media limelight, a legislative session ordinarily has a small impact on budget totals. These totals are driven first and foremost by pre-existing commitments. Yet, a small percentage of a large budget equals many dollars. What is at stake is which current demands get funded.

Review of the Executive Budget Request

In some governments, individual agencies submit their budget requests directly to the legislature as well as to the chief executive. Most state legislatures receive agencies' budget requests (NCSL, 2008). Receiving the agency's request increases the legislature's budget powers because its review starts with two numbers representing different assessments of program priorities and service needs. This is all about executive-legislative balance, the power of persuasion, framing the discussion, and setting the agenda (see figure 4.3). A related mechanism, freedom of information laws, requires that all public records be available to the public and may require that agency requests and even worksheets be made public (see the case at the end of chapter 10).

In other governments, including the federal government and eight states, the legislature receives only the executive's proposal. This strengthens the chief executive's hand because a single proposal dominates the discussion. Federal agencies have been barred from bringing their requests directly to the legislature since the beginning of executive budgeting in 1921. OMB's regulations require that agency requests be kept confidential (see Web site resource, Rules of the Game

Report For: Main Operating Appropriations Bill   Version: As Introduced

Appropriation Amounts—Comparison of Request to Executive   General Revenue Fund

Totals by Agency	2004:	Estimated 2005:	Request FY 2006:	Exec. FY 2006:	$ Change Req. to Exec.*	% Change Req. to Exec.**	Request FY 2007:	Exec. FY 2007:	$ Change Req. to Exec.*	% Change Req. to Exec.**
ADJ Adjacent General	$ 10,007,501	$ 10,049,795	$ 10,043,735	$ 10,043,735	$ 0	0.00%	$10,043,735	$ 10,043,735	$ 0	0.00%
DAS Administrative Services Department of	$ 128,820,255	$ 143,114,219	$ 182,850,103	$ 180,847,507	[$ 1,802,508]	-1.11%	$ 162,650,103	$ 161,381,940	[$1,258,163]	-0.79%
AAM African American Commission on	$ 271,504	$ 252,000	$ 282,000	$ 282,000	$ 0	0.00%	$ 282,000	$ 282,000	$ 0	0.00%
JCR Joint Committee on Agency Rule Review	$ 308,102	$ 370,750	$ 379,780	$ 379,700	$ 0	0.00%	$ 387,334	$ 387,334	$ 0	0.00%
AGE Aging, Department of,	$ 110,213,571	$ 132,150,500	$ 142,173,213	$ 151,682,653	$ 9,509,440	0.50%	$153,585,277	$ 150,585,711	$ 8,000,434	3.01%
AGR Agriculture, Department of	$ 19,553,400	$ 20,058,904	$ 20,053,905	$17,430,289	$ 2,828,818	-13.10%	$ 20,058,906	$ 17,080,073	[$ 2,987,832]	-14.50%
AIR Air Quality Development Authority	$ 7,700,559	$ 9,748,914	$ 7,580,822	$ 7,890,914	$ 70,002	0.09%	$ 7,630,518	$ 9,554,814	$ 2,015,008	26.78%

Figure 4.3. Ohio's Legislature Reviews the Governor's Proposed Budget

Reprinted by permission. Excerpt from State of Ohio, Legislative Service Commission, 2005. Calculations and amounts are as shown in the original.

* Dollar difference between department's request and executive's recommendation.

** Percentage difference between department's request and executive's recommendation.

in Washington). Of course, internal documents often are leaked and experienced
agency budgeters know how to "arrange" a legislative request for their agency's
budget information. Based on their credibility, they have established solid working relationships with legislative staff. There are limits to this behavior because
disregarding executive-branch confidentiality this way also risks their credibility
(and perhaps even their jobs).

Limits on Legislative Powers

Congress and almost all state legislatures have few or no limits on their budget
powers and may increase or decrease the executive's recommendations for spending and revenues. Yet some legislatures are prohibited by constitution or statute
from increasing spending and are limited to cutting the executive's proposed
budget. Others may not change revenue estimates based on existing law and may
increase revenues only by raising taxes or other revenues. Restrictions written into
the state constitution or city charter are more difficult to change than statutory
limits. Also, state laws and regulations, including limits on legislative powers, are
important limits on budget powers at the local level, as chapter 5 explains.

It turns out that legislatures are not freewheeling, do-as-you-please decision-
making forums. Limitations on operating budgets date to the 1930s. They were
and are a popular response to perceived extravagance or waste or to the political success of special interest groups opposing taxes. Tax-and-expenditure limitations (TELs) of various types currently operate in most states. One example is
California's Proposition 13, adopted by referendum in 1978 and described as a
"political earthquake" (Moore, 1998). Figure in the need for a "supermajority" to
adopt a budget, and you can understand the budget turmoil in California (see the
Web site resource, California Dreamin').

Line-Item Appropriations and Veto Power

This stage of the process is designed to produce a budget for spending (appropriation) and revenue. When signed by the executive, the budget becomes law.
An appropriations bill may be written in broad categories of spending or in the
narrow detail called line items (see Web site resource, Budget Formats). A **line-
item appropriation** is the legislature's most important control over executive
operations in the third stage, implementation. As a source of legislative power, the
line-item appropriation has remained a characteristic feature of federal budgeting
for two centuries and is common (but not universal) among the states and local
governments.

In forty-three states and many local governments, the chief executive has
the authority to veto specific portions of the spending bill. Florida's governor, for
example, has the constitutional authority to "veto any specific appropriation in
a general appropriation bill." The president and other executives without line-
item veto authority may veto or sign only the entire appropriations bill. Many

---

Line Item—the smallest expenditure detail in a budget.

presidents, including Reagan, Bush, Clinton, and G.W. Bush advocated giving the chief executive authority to veto portions of appropriations bills as a tool to reduce spending. Gallup Polls dating to 1945 show public support for giving the president line-item veto authority. The Line Item Veto Act was passed in 1996 by a Republican Congress and signed by a Democratic president. The U.S. Supreme Court declared it unconstitutional two years later because it violated Article I, Section 7, Clause 2 of the U.S. Constitution that specifies that laws are passed and vetoed as a whole.

Budget Blackout

Some features of the formal process in the stage of legislative appropriation push decision makers toward compromise and stimulate consensus building. Deadlines at the end of the fiscal year and at the end of the legislative session work to force all budget players to come to terms with legislative arithmetic: it takes a majority (or supermajority) to pass a budget. State legislative leaders have been known just to unplug the clock in the chamber to extend the time to reach a budget compromise and adopt a budget.

The National Conference of State Legislatures (2008, reprinted by permission) describes the state situation: "Generally, far more cooperation exists between the legislative and executive branches than is typical for Congress and the president. . . . Late budgets and vetoes are most likely when a state is experiencing serious fiscal difficulties. Otherwise, executive and legislative negotiations are intended to resolve budget disagreements and avoid vetoes and late budgets."

One historical example of the power of formal deadlines is the budget stand-off between the Democratic president and Republican Congress in November 1995. When the fiscal year started without spending laws in place, federal agencies closed. About 800,000 "nonessential" employees found themselves temporarily furloughed. Under President Ronald Reagan in the 1980s, the federal government shut down under similar circumstances.

All public agencies and programs do not necessarily face a drop-dead deadline when timetables are missed. First, legal obligations, such as payments on debt, are met. Second, critical services may continue under governments' constitutional obligations to provide for the public health and safety. Third, lawmakers may agree to extend spending authority temporarily, until agreement on a new budget can be reached. The federal version is a **continuing resolution** that usually provides for spending at the same rate as the year before.

Similar mechanisms operate at the state and local level. For example, Connecticut uses two-week extensions of spending authority as mini-budgets when the regular budget fails to pass before the start of the new fiscal year. In 1991,

---

Continuing Resolution—interim appropriations bill providing authority for federal agencies to continue operating at specified level until a specified date or until regular appropriations are passed; sometimes used to fund some or all government operations for the year; must have presidential signature.

when the fiscal year began without a budget in place, for the first time in over a century, Connecticut saw special sessions, agency closings, employee furloughs, and mini-budgets. This impasse was so politically draining that, when the governor vetoed the initial budget in 2002, the approaching new fiscal year pushed agreement.

Implementation and Audit

The implementation and **audit** stages of the budget process are less about politics and policy than about the mechanics of managing public resources, but they operate in a political context and have policy consequences. Budget implementation is primarily the executive's job, although the legislature and judiciary control their own budgets to protect their independence.

Allotments and Rescissions

The budget office makes funds available to agencies on a schedule called **allotment** in state and local budgeting and **apportionment** at the federal level. The schedule usually calls for equal quarterly installments. The schedule helps prevent agencies from spending more than was appropriated. When resources are especially tight, a small percentage of the appropriation may not be allotted but held back as a kind of insurance against running in the red. (Red ink flags a negative number, or deficit.) The central budget or finance office monitors revenues and expenditures as the budget is implemented during the course of the fiscal year.

In most states, the governor has some authority to reduce spending during the budget year below the amount appropriated. The president also has some power to reduce appropriations without going back to Congress for approval but only for limited and technical reasons. A reduction (or **rescission**) is not permitted because the president disapproves of a program that is part of a bill already signed into law. President Richard M. Nixon's refusal to spend certain appropriated funds was one factor contributing to the adoption by Congress of budget reform in 1974. A rescission under the sole authority of the executive is in effect a line-item veto, which the Supreme Court declared unconstitutional in 1998 because the president must sign a bill in its entirety rather than pick and choose among its pieces.

Audit—a review of the financial and/or performance operations of a program, agency, department, spending unit or the entire organization.

Allotment—a schedule at the state and local levels by which the budget office makes funds available to agencies (for example, quarterly).

Apportionment—a schedule at the federal level by which the budget office makes funds available to agencies (for example, quarterly).

Rescission—reduction, often by chief executive, of spending authority during budget implementation below the amount appropriated.

Supplemental Appropriations

During the implementation stage, legislatures may respond to unanticipated events and emergencies, such as natural disasters, by adopting supplemental appropriations for the current fiscal year. Supplementals, as such legislation is called, permit flexible and timely responses, but at the cost of sidestepping the regular funding process with its deliberation, competition, and trade-offs. In Washington, supplementals labeled "emergency supplementals" are fast-tracked and so become magnets for unrelated, nonemergency funding. This bundling is a legislative strategy primarily aimed at evading a presidential veto. Some funding in emergency supplementals goes to programs that were squeezed out during the regular appropriation process or are habitually under-funded to escape the caps on federal spending. In the summer of 2008, a supplemental appropriation bill for military operations included funding to expand college benefits for veterans.

Over 1,000 pages long, the $787 billion economic recovery package (American Recovery and Reinvestment Act) was passed as an "emergency supplemental" and signed into law in February 2009. It is different in one large respect from the emergency supplementals that funded the military operations in the Bush Administration because the recovery package is on-budget (see the Web site resource, How to Read the Highlights of the Federal Budget).

> Even if the funds were emergency designated, including them in the regular budget and appropriations process provides greater transparency. When full funding information is not included in the regular budget and appropriations process, it understates the true cost of government to policymakers at the time decisions are made and steps can still be taken to control funding, which is even more important in a time of constrained resources (GAO, 2008, p. 17).

War and the Federal Budget Process

Historically, when war strains political institutions, Congress has responded by changing the budget process. The Civil War led to the creation of appropriations committees in both the House and Senate. The aftermath of World War I saw the adoption of an executive budget process and new institutions, the GAO and OMB.

According to federal law, a declaration of war triggers the suspension of certain rules in the congressional budget process (see the Web site resource, How War Affects the Formal Federal Budget Process). However, the rules were not suspended for the Persian Gulf War or the armed hostilities in Iraq and Afghanistan because no declaration of war was ever made. "Congress and the [p]resident met the additional spending needs associated with these hostilities largely by using procedures that allow such spending to be declared 'emergency requirements,' thus freeing it from budget enforcement constraints" (Keith, 2004, p. 1).

Under spending rules in force through the end of 2002, the declaration of something as "an emergency" cancelled spending caps and the requirement to find a way to offset or pay for the expenditures. The purpose of this rule is speed and flexibility. This is the way Congress enacted in just four days the $40 billion appropriation in response to the terrorist attacks on September 11, 2001 (see figure 4.4).

PUBLIC LAW 107–38—SEPT. 18, 2001

Public Law 107–38
107th Congress

An Act

Sept. 18, 2001

[H.R. 2888]

Making emergency supplemental appropriations for fiscal year 2001 for additional disaster assistance, for anti-terrorism initiatives, and for assistance in the recoveryfrom the tragedy that occurred on September 11, 2001, and for other purposes.

2001 Emergency
Supplemental
Appropriations Act
for Recovery from and
Response toTerrorist
Attacks on the United
States.

Be it enacted by the Senate and House of Representatives ofthe United States of America in Congress assembled, That the following sums are appropriated, out of any money in the Treasury not otherwise appropriated, to provide emergency supplemental appropriations for fiscal year 2001, namely:

EXECUTIVE OFFICE OF THE PRESIDENT AND FUNDS APPROPRIATED TO THE PRESIDENT

EMERGENCY RESPONSE FUND
(INCLUDING TRANSFERS OF FUNDS)

For emergency expenses to respond to the terrorist attacks on the United States that occurred on September 11, 2001, to provide assistance to the victims of the attacks, and to deal with other consequences of the attacks, $40,000,000,000, to remain available until expended, including for the costs of: (1) providing Federal, State, and local preparedness for mitigating and responding to the attacks; (2) providing support to counter, investigate, or prosecute domestic or international terrorism; (3) providing increased transportation security; (4) repairing public facilities and transportation systems damaged by the attacks; and (5) supporting national security: *Provided,* That these funds may be transferred to any authorized Federal Government activity to meet the purposes ofthis Act: *Provided further,* That the Congress designates the entire amount as an emergency requirement pursuant to section 251(b)(2)(A) of the Balanced Budget and Emergency Deficit Control Act of 1985: *Provided further,* That $40,000,000,000 shall be available only to the extent that an official budget request, that includes designation of the $40,000,000,000 as an emergency requirement as defined in the Balanced Budget and Emergency Deficit Control Act of 1985, is transmitted by the President to the Congress: *Provided further,* That the President shall consult with the chairmen and ranking minority members of the Committees on Appropriations prior to the transfer of these funds: *Provided further,* That of the $40,000,000,000 made available herein, $10,000,000,000 shall not be available for transfer to any Department or Agency until 15 days after the Director of the Office of Management and Budget has submitted to the House and Senate Committees on Appropriations a proposed allocation and plan for use of the funds for that

Figure 4.4. (*Continued*)

Department or Agency; $20,000,000,000 may be obligated only when enacted in a subsequent emergency appropriations bill, in response to the terrorist acts on September 11, 2001: *Provided further*, That the President shall transmit an amended budget request proposing an allocation of funds: *Provided further*, That not less than one-half of the $40,000,000,000 shall be for disaster recovery activities and assistance related to the terrorist acts in New York, Virginia, and Pennsylvania on September 11, 2001, as authorized by law: *Provided further*, That the Director of the Office of Management and Budget shall provide quarterly reports to the Committees on Appropriations on the use of these funds, beginning not later than January 2, 2002: *Provided further*, That the President shall submit to the Congress as soon as practicable detailed requests to meet any further funding requirements for the purposes specified in this Act.

Reports.

GENERAL PROVISIONS

SEC. 101. Funds appropriated by this Act, or made available by the transfer of funds in this Act, for intelligence activities are deemed to be specifically authorized by the Congress for purposes of section 504 of the National Security Act of 1947 (50 U.S.C. 414).

SEC. 102. Funds appropriated by this Act, or made available by the transfer of funds in this Act, may be obligated and expended notwithstanding section 10 of Public Law 91–672, section 313 of the Foreign Relations Authorization Act, fiscal years 1994 and 1995, and section 15 of the State Department Basic Authorities Act of 1956.

This Act may be cited as the "2001 Emergency Supplemental Appropriations Act for Recovery from and Response to Terrorist Attacks on the United States".

Approved September 18, 2001.

LEGISLATIVEHISTORY—H.R. 2888 (S. 1426):
CONGRESSIONAL RECORD, Vol. 147 (2001):
    Sept. 14, considered and passed House and Senate.

○

Figure 4.4. Federal Appropriation in Response to September 11, 2001
SOURCE: Library of Congress, 2001.

Introduced on September 14 and passed without amendment in the Senate by a 96–0 vote, the appropriation became Public Law 107–38 on September 18, 2001.

Although the spending rules had lapsed, the practice of passing emergency supplemental legislation continued. This is how the military operations in Iraq and Afghanistan were funded. The emergency supplemental legislation for the military operations also was off-budget until 2009, so the spending did not show up in the federal totals. Funding military operations through off-budget emergency supplementals raises problems of accountability, transparency, and oversight through the routine appropriations process.

If a government wants to wage a war it cannot or will not pay for now, then it borrows and pays later. Rather than raise taxes and cut other spending, the United States did just that when it added the war costs to its deficit financing amount. America's (and other countries') history shows that financing war by debt is a common practice. Past political leaders borrowed to pay for the American Revolution and for World War II (see box 4.4). One big difference is that now only about one-half of the publicly held debt is in American hands (see chapter 5).

After the Books Are Closed

The audit stage occurs after the end of the fiscal year, when the books are closed. An audit of records and transactions is a critical step in financial reporting and fundamental to accountability. The audit is the single most important control over executive implementation exercised after transactions are made.

An independent auditor certifies that the financial records for the year are a good representation of what actually happened to the public's money. When the books are closed on the fiscal year, management prepares financial statements. Auditors test (or sample) transactions to see if they correctly trace back to the financial statements.

A key political issue is that auditors are independent so that their results have credibility. One way to ensure their independence of the executive is to have them report to the legislature. The Government Accountability Office (GAO), the federal government's auditing office, reports to Congress. Many other governments and nonprofit agencies hire outside financial auditors whose professional code of conduct requires them to avoid any conflict of interest that might color their judgment.

Auditing is a concept that covers **financial audits** as well as performance audits. The aim of most audits is to ensure that financial transactions are reported accurately. Some audits, called program audits, check to see whether the goals of the program are being achieved; these audits are politically sensitive. Performance audits look for places where efficiency or effectiveness could be improved or

---

Financial Audit—a review of the organization's accounting system, usually by an independent accounting firm, to attest that the organization's financial statements present fairly the financial results for the fiscal year; it is not designed to catch fraud, waste and abuse.

====== BOX 4.4 ======

Borrowing to Pay for War

The first Secretary of the Treasury under the new Constitution was Alexander Hamilton. He faced what was then thought of as a large debt from the Revolutionary War.

> Hamilton's first official act was to submit a report to Congress in which he laid the foundation for the nation's financial health. To the surprise of many legislators, he insisted upon federal assumption and dollar-for-dollar repayment of the country's war debt of $75 million in order to revitalize the public credit: "[T]he debt of the United States...was the price of liberty. The faith of America has been repeatedly pledged for it, and with solemnities that give peculiar force to the obligation."

SOURCE: Department of the Treasury, Office of the Curator.

Much of the war cost of World War II was financed by borrowing from the public through the sale of so-called war bonds. By the end of the war, almost $61 billion had been raised through sales campaigns appealing to patriotic sentiment, as the poster below shows.

See Web site video, Uncle Sam Speaks, video clips promoting savings bonds.

Figure Box 4.5. Borrowing to Pay for War
"We Can...We Will...We Must"
SOURCE: Reprinted by permission. Smithsonian Institution. Design by Carl Paulson, 1941.

where there is evidence of waste or abuse. These reports can be politically sensitive, too.

At the federal level, the Government Accountability Office still does financial audits but shifted its primary role in recent years to performance auditing and searching for waste and abuse. This newer role has this nonpartisan, professional agency more active in policy disputes, especially when the Congress and the president are from opposite parties and congressional members seek to investigate what they see as the misdeeds or programmatic excesses of the executive branch.

The routine audits of state and local governments are aimed at checking that the financial reports fairly represent financial results. These financial audits ordinarily do not catch waste, fraud, and mismanagement. In addition to reporting on their own revenues and expenditures, these governments have to report to the federal government on any federal money they receive. The audits at the state and local levels are public information about the financial condition of the government and whether the budget is in fact balanced.

While cities routinely do financial audits, only a handful have performance auditing offices. Performance audits, as opposed to financial audits, are often controversial. They can be used to embarrass political opponents or used by reformers to demand change. Because of this high profile, maintaining the independence of the performance auditors is an ongoing battle.

State and local governments, as recipients of federal grants, must comply with federal rules and regulations. The federal Single Audit Act was passed in 1984 to streamline the intergovernmental financial system by establishing uniform requirements for comprehensive, **single audit** of federal grant recipients. State and local government auditors must follow federally mandated auditing standards, often called the *Yellow Book*. The GAO issues these audit standards. Today, professional practice established by the American Institute of Certified Public Accountants requires that CPAs follow the *Yellow Book* when doing all audits of state and local governments.

Even the federal auditing arm gets audited! For example, in 2005 the GAO reported, "Once again we have received a clean audit opinion on our financial statements, and ... [in] this report we have included the external auditor's report stating that we presented our financial statements fairly.... The auditors also reported no instances of noncompliance with applicable laws and regulations" (GAO, 2005).

The most common type of audit verifies that transactions are properly reported and controlled. Audited financial results provide critical feedback about actual operations and financial management. They are included in the **Comprehensive Annual Financial Report** (CAFR), required of state and local governments

---

Single Audit—the federal government allows recipients of its financial aid to provide it with one locally-generated audit (a single audit) of all federal dollars.

Yellow Book—the compilation of generally accepted auditing guidelines for state and local governments receiving any federal funds; published by the U.S. Government Accountability Office (GAO) in a book with a yellow cover.

Comprehensive Annual Financial Report (CAFR)—annual financial report prepared by state and local governments that adhere to generally accepted accounting principles (or GAAP).

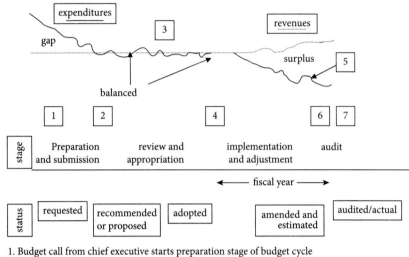

1. Budget call from chief executive starts preparation stage of budget cycle
2. Executive proposes relatively small changes to existing base
3. Legislature makes relatively small changes to executive proposal
4. Fiscal year begins
5. Surge in 4th quarter spending before annual spending authority lapses
6. Fiscal year ends and annual spending authority lapses
7. Books are closed within a few weeks, audited, and CAFR issued

Figure 4.6. Schematic Executive Budget Process: Stages, Status, Gap, and Balance

Reprinted by permission. Lewis, Carol W., 2003. Budgeting in the Public Sector. In Jack Rabin, Robert F. Munzenrider and Sherrie M. Bartell (eds.). Principles and Practices of Public Administration. New York: Marcel Dekker.

by **generally accepted accounting principles**, or GAAP. The Governmental Accounting Standards Board (GASB) issues guidelines governing the CAFR. The mission of this nongovernmental, independent nonprofit organization is "to establish and improve standards of state and local governmental accounting and financial reporting that will result in useful information for users of financial reports and guide and educate the public, including issuers, auditors, and users of those financial reports" (GASB, n.d.).

Summary of the Executive Process

Figure 4.6 pictures a prototypical executive budget process, from the budget call through the end of the fiscal year and audit. As the process moves through the four stages, the status of the budget changes. The sequence over the fiscal year is (1) agency request; (2) chief executive's recommended or proposed budget;

Generally Accepted Accounting Principles (GAAP)—A uniform standard for financial accounting and recording, encompassing the conventions, rules, and procedures that define broadly-accepted accounting principles; allows ease of comparison of financial results over time and across similar organizations; GAAP for state and local governments established by the Governmental Accounting Standards Board; GAAP for private business and nonprofit organizations established by the Financial Accounting Standards Board; GAAP for the U.S. Government set by the Federal Accounting Standards Board.

BOX 4.5

The Perfect Exam

Three ways in which federal budgeting is different from state budgeting are

    a) the federal government has no capital budget but many states do,

    b) the president does not have the line-item veto but most governors do,

    c) the president does not have to submit a balanced budget but governors in forty-four states do, and Congress does not have to adopt a balanced budget but forty-one states legislatures do,

    d) all of the above.

---

(3) adopted budget; (4) amended, revised, and estimated; and (5) audited, or actual. Notice how balance, the foremost fiscal goal of budgeting, involves adjusting the relationship between revenues and expenditures throughout the first three stages. Although the executive budget process produces similar general contours in budget processes, there are significant variations among governments (see box 4.5).

WHY TAKE A POLITICAL PERSPECTIVE?

A political perspective on decision making defines a *good* budget, policy, or program by its political success: the fact that it musters the support that translates into a legislative majority and executive signature. ("Good" does not necessarily mean it agrees with any particular citizen's personal preferences, because government services are not a cafeteria line to pick only those services a citizen wants.) In any given budget cycle and under routine circumstances, decision makers tend to concentrate on proposed changes—increases or decreases expressed in dollars or percentages—in spending and revenue. Most budget messages and media reports highlight proposed changes. The decision making aims at answering the question, "What's new?"

A political perspective emphasizes today's wins and losses in the competition for resources. Under time pressure to reach agreement and pass a budget, the players' attention is directed to what can be done in the current budget round for the next fiscal year. Here the question is, "What now?" The practical players are concerned first and foremost with those things they can do something about, that are within their scope of decision making and action. For hardheaded realists interested in solving problems and providing services, the question becomes, "What can be done?" (see table 4.1).

In most public organizations, decision making about the budget also draws on specific roles, accepted decision rules, and shared expectations. All players anticipate sharing in the action—increases or decreases—and returning again to compete for resources in future budget cycles. Individual and institutional participants

Table 4.1. Political Decision Making in Budgeting

FOCUS	QUESTION
• Change	What's new?
• Action/Discretion	What can be done?
• Current round/fiscal year	What now?

in the budget process fall into two broad camps: program **advocate** or promoter, and resource **guardian**, reviewer, or naysayer. It is important to understand the different roles in budgetary decision making because decisions emerge from negotiations and accommodations among many, many players, including the chief executive, agency bureaucrats, professional budgeters, legislators, lobbyists, advocacy and public interest groups, employee associations, taxpayer groups, the media, and others. This factor affects the dynamics on the executive side and the state budget director's job. "The job requires an accountant's eye and a politician's ear. The numbers have to work, but so do the politics. Doing one or the other is child's play" (Pazniokas, 2009, p. A9.) "On the legislative side, the budget approval process at the local level is much like herding cats. Cats are independent, and often change their focus or priorities. They will work together when it is in their best interests. In some cases, their success may rest in the hands of others" (Braga, 2007).

Credibility and reputation are important because long-term relationships and strategies develop as players come back to the table in each budget round.

> The process of budgeting requires the collaboration and interaction of a variety of entities and individuals.... The budget is the final product of the political interaction among all of these players and reflects the priorities that emerge after consideration of all the interests expressed by various entities (NASBO, n.d., reprinted by permission).

The long-term relationship fosters compromise. "'To get something done or to get what you want or most of what you want, you've got to compromise,' said Nicholas E. Calio, who served as Bush's first legislative affairs director" (quoted in Eggen and Kane, 2008).

Of course, sometimes the expected roles, rules, and norms of behavior may break down. Crises, extreme partisanship, personality conflicts, and actors better described as autocratic barons than responsive players may at one time or another dethrone the traditional and derail the process. Today, routine budget processes are under pressure from many sources, including

1. built-in and deepening strains between demands and financial resources;
2. new tools for transparency and accountability, including e-government;

Advocate—a promoter of a particular program who pushes for funding for that program.

Guardian—the budget role characterized by protecting public resources by saying "no" to spending advocates and opposing spending increases.

3. new demands, including counter-terrorism and emergency preparedness;
4. the weight of cumbersome rules and procedures accumulated over many decades that are opaque instead of transparent and limit citizens' understanding and access;
5. the build-up of financial commitments that reduce responsiveness and accountability.

HOW DOES THE FEDERAL ENTITLEMENT PROCESS WORK?

The federal process is set apart by many factors. Different from state and local governments, for example, it does not use a **capital budget**. The president does not have the authority to veto individual lines in a budget he signs. The federal government is not on the receiving end of rules and regulations slapped on as a condition of receiving aid (mandates).

In fact, Congress does not even pass a budget as it is known in other public organizations. Congress adopts a **budget resolution** with totals for spending, revenues, the deficit or surplus, and the debt limit. This budget resolution is the framework within which are made the budget decisions, including the appropriations bills that usually are twelve in number. Also different is the fact that Congress does not vote directly on spending levels in appropriations. Instead, Congress approves budget authority that allows agencies to acquire financial obligations that will lead to spending. Not all of the new budget authority passed for any given fiscal year will be spent or obligated that year (see Web site resource, How to Read Highlights of the Federal Budget).

Another important difference is that only about one-third of federal spending goes through the annual appropriations process. Spending controlled through annual appropriations is called **discretionary spending** and treated differently from the other type, **mandatory spending**. These terms refer to the legislative process governing the spending, not the program's importance.

Capital Budget—plan for financing long-lived projects such as bridges and buildings; the first year of the capital improvement program with a detailed source of financing for each of the specified capital projects for implementation during the upcoming fiscal year.

Budget Resolution—congressional agreement that is not a law (and does not require the president's signature) that sets revenue, spending, and other budget targets; developed by House and Senate Budget Committees and then conference report produces a concurrent budget resolution.

Discretionary Spending—outlays on programs funded by annual appropriations under the jurisdiction of the House and Senate Appropriations Committees; represents about one-third of most federal spending, including most defense spending and, for example, education and housing programs.

Mandatory Spending—federal budget concept meaning spending is controlled by federal laws other than appropriations acts; includes spending for entitlement programs and interest on the national debt.

Mandatory spending is budget authority and outlays provided in authorizing legislation rather than in appropriations acts. Some entitlement programs get their budget authority in the form of a permanent appropriation in the legislation authorizing the program. Interest on the public debt is classified as mandatory spending. Mandatory spending also includes spending on entitlement programs, such as Social Security and Medicare, that provide benefits to people who meet the eligibility criteria set out in law. The government cannot control total spending on these programs because (1) the federal government is legally obligated to pay eligible recipients the amounts to which the law entitles them, and (2) there is no dollar cap on the total spending the government is obligated to pay for these programs. To make matters worse, government pays for but does not provide or manage Medicaid services. The result is that no one decides how much is too much; no one is accountable for budget impacts. Entitlement programs and net interest payments consume about two-thirds of the budget. Current projections indicate that this proportion is likely to increase in coming years.

There are only two ways that entitlement programs can be changed. First, entitlements can be changed by the authorizing committees, among which the Ways and Means Committee figures prominently. This committee handles mandatory spending on Social Security programs, Supplemental Security Income, Temporary Assistance for Needy Families (TANF), unemployment compensation programs, and Medicare, but does not have jurisdiction over food stamps, Medicaid, or the State Children's Health Insurance program referred to as SCHIP. Ways and Means also has jurisdiction over trade and revenue bills. Because Article I, Section 7 of the Constitution requires that revenue bills start in the House and because of the weight of mandatory spending on federal spending, this committee and its chairman are very powerful in the national political system. A permanent committee since 1802, it reaches today into almost all, if not all, homes. Social Security alone covers more than 150 million workers and pays benefits to almost 50 million people.

Because bills to reauthorize entitlement programs may come up only every four or five years and revenue legislation is irregular, Congress may turn down the second avenue: reconciliation. The House Committee on Rules defines **reconciliation** as a "procedure for changing existing revenue and spending laws to bring total federal revenues and spending within the limits established in a budget resolution." The budget resolution sets overall spending and revenue goals, including goals for mandatory and discretionary spending. In reconciliation instructions, the budget resolution may direct authorizing committees to propose changes in the laws governing the entitlement program. For example, the congressional budget resolution for FY 2008 instructed two committees to take this action for FY 2008.

Reconciliation—an important political tool, instructions to congressional authorizing committees to change existing spending and revenue laws by a set date so that the targets set in the budget resolution can be met.

An important political tool, the reconciliation process was designed to help reduce the deficit. In 1990, reconciliation was used to cut entitlement spending. It was used three times during the Clinton presidency, once to push through welfare reform. Spending cuts took the reconciliation route in 2006 and the Republican Congress used it in 2001 and 2003 to pass the tax cuts advocated by President George W. Bush. An important political tool operating under congressional rules different from the regular appropriations process, reconciliation amounts to a budget short-cut: it is not subject to a filibuster and needs only a simple majority to pass.

PAYGO (for pay-as-you-go) is another rule affecting entitlements. It requires that any proposal to expand entitlements or other mandatory spending must be paid for by either increased revenues or by cuts in other mandatory programs. Introduced into federal budgeting in 1990, it was intended to make it easier to balance the budget by requiring that changes in mandatory spending not increase the deficit (to be "deficit neutral"). Although the law requiring the offset lapsed in 2002, the House and Senate have incorporated this rule into their own rules. The addition in 2003 of the prescription drug benefit to Medicare shows that the rule does not stop all growth in entitlements. It does make expansion more difficult politically because the specific trade-off must be identified or the rule waived. Following the PAYGO rule helps to ensure that the federal government has the resources to respond to public demands over the long-term. "PAYGO rules—and, most importantly, adherence to them—ensure that when the public asks the government to respond, it can" (OMB Watch, 2007).

THE ART OF THE BUDGET PROCESS

In 1919, before he became president, Calvin Coolidge remarked, "Politics is not an end, but a means. It is not a product, but a process. It is the art of government." The same is true of budgeting.

So many voices are raised by so many players: the many governments, non-profit organizations, contractors managing and providing services, committees and advisory groups, lobbyists, and more. Add to these the many laws and regu-lations, professional standards, and customs. We see that budgeting in complex public organizations in a federal system of government resembles a Rube Goldberg invention. Rube Goldberg, the twentieth-century cartoonist, was famous for his overly complicated contraptions designed to accomplish a relatively simple task.

Where can citizens look to see how well public organizations work and what taxpayers are getting for their tax dollars? It is difficult to know for sure who is doing what, with whom, for what purpose, and at what cost. Nonprofit organizations and

---

Pay-as-you-go (PAYGO)—current payment of current expenses; rule introduced into federal budgeting by the 1990 Budget Enforcement Act that requires increases in mandatory spend-ing or decreases in revenues be offset (or paid for) so that the change does not increase the deficit (is deficit neutral); used in state and local government to describe a financial policy by which the capital program is financed from current revenue rather than through borrowing.

governments, at all levels and across the country, deliver goods and services through contracts, public-private partnerships, regional networks and co-operative agreements, and intergovernmental arrangements. These form an intricate, dense web of interrelationships and responsibilities. Governments sign contracts with nonprofit agencies for social services. Private firms landscape town squares, haul trash, run prisons and schools, construct roads and bridges, and build weapons systems under contracts with governments. This complexity muddies accountability. Who is responsible for the services and costs and how can citizens hold them accountable?

Here is another the problem: the decision makers in many governments and public organizations are caught in a bind. Budget processes are supposed to be open and transparent—everyone can play and everyone can understand. At the same time, these processes must be carefully controlled to prevent fraud and waste, and we expect decisions to be based on efficiency as defined by technical analysis. Budget processes are supposed to be accountable—we hold the top decision makers responsible. Still, much of the budget is the result of decisions made in the past. Budget processes are supposed to be responsive, but constitutional requirements, existing law, current services, intergovernmental mandates, lobbying limits, and more constrict responsiveness. There is some comedy and much politics in processes designed to accomplish so much.

THUMBNAIL

As a core decision-making process, budgeting injects important stabilizing elements into the political system: the goal of balance in the context of relative scarcity (the gap between available resources and public demands); the need for timely outcomes; allowing if not ensuring that the public's voice and priorities are heard and responded to; maintaining the honesty and integrity of the numbers and credibility of the participants; and other elements.

The decision-making process itself changed from legislative budgeting to executive budgeting early in the last century. It is still evolving, and today is more centralized, top-down, and dominated by the executive and the central budget office in many more governments than it once was. These shifts reflect to some degree the exposure of communities and their budgeting processes to events outside their and their leaders' control. These events include natural and human-caused disasters (for example, September 11, 2001) and economic disruptions from, for example, corporate relocations and the loss of jobs from the local economy.

The results of the process change over time. We see considerable change when we look at budgets from years ago and compare them to public budgets today. Simply put, we are both raising and spending our resources differently from the way we used to. Today, much of the budget is not susceptible to annual decision making, but rather tied up by legal obligations before the start of the current budget round. The challenge this poses for democracy and accountability is that past officials made decisions that bind and limit present officials, and present ones do the same. How can citizens now and in the future have a meaningful say?

CASE

A Package Deal

by Representative Denise W. Merrill (D, 54th District), Connecticut General Assembly
House Chair of the Appropriations Committee in 2008 and House Majority Leader in 2009

The University of Connecticut decided to ask the state legislature to fund a football stadium in 1999. As the representative from the 54th District, home to the state university's main campus, I naturally was expected to be an ally for any proposal that came from my largest constituency base. Also, the proposal was championed by the Speaker of the House, a die-hard University of Connecticut football fan, graduate of the institution, and a man who, not coincidentally, had done me many favors. At the time, I had been in office for only five years and, although I was seen as an authority on higher education policy in the legislature, I relied heavily on the Speaker for any benefits for my district or myself politically.

I was, however, opposed in principle to the building of a football stadium with public dollars. For one thing, I felt that a 1A football program, needing substantial public support for the newly expanded football program, would draw down funding for the university's academic programs. Moreover, the cost of building the stadium, some $90 million, did not seem justified for the six games a year that would be played there. In my eyes, this was a clear case of the interest of my very singular constituent—the University of Connecticut—colliding with the interests of the state taxpayers, who would be asked to subsidize this public-private venture of uncertain return.

Compounding my political distress was the fact that my district constituency—most of whom were directly or indirectly dependent on the university—was divided on the issue. Some saw the stadium as a direct benefit to the university; others saw it as its ultimate intellectual demise. This schizophrenia turned out to be a blessing in disguise for me.

I really didn't want to take sides, but I knew that the speaker and those who were determined that the state would have a 1-A football program would undoubtedly bring the stadium project to a vote. My choices, as a rank-and-file legislator, were limited. I could shut up, support the stadium and the speaker, or do what both my conscience and my good sense told me was the right thing and refuse to commit a large number of taxpayer dollars to a dubious venture.

To the last minute, I had no idea what I was going to do.

But I didn't count on the speaker, who was, among other things, a very clever politician. In order to soothe those who shared my concerns, he packaged the project with a bill to fund a large economic development project in Hartford, the state capital. Both the governor and the legislature saw the project as the salvation of an impoverished and financially distressed city. It would produce a large-scale convention center, along with enhanced housing and retail development, key to redeveloping a blighted urban site and to the developer ready to underwrite the project. The pairing of these two projects ensured the support of the governor (of the opposing party) and mollified those who saw the stadium as nothing more than one more benefit for the university.

My conscience was clear. I voted for the package as part of a larger economic development plan for the state. And while some voters at home grumbled about the expense, most felt the tradeoff was worthwhile. The speaker neatly avoided testing my loyalty, and today the football stadium is seen by all as a reasonably successful venture, filled to the brim with happy football fans every weekend in the fall. I still wonder whether such a commitment of dollars could have been better spent. I'll never know.

Thinking It Over

1. What do you think of the speaker's game plan, in which the budget is a package, a bundle of political obligations and interests, and the art of the possible? (A federal version of bundling is an **omnibus appropriations bill**).
2. Bundling is a sophisticated version of **logrolling**, the exchange of votes by legislators in order to pass the bills that interest each of them. Does the bundling strategy serve the public interest or give us a package everyone can support but programs that otherwise would not be funded?
3. What could Representative Merrill have done differently, had she been House chair of Appropriations in 1998 instead of a rank-and-file member? An attorney first elected to the state legislature in 1993, State Representative Merrill has served for nine terms and was the House chair of the Appropriations Committee for three sessions, 2005–2008. She often runs unopposed. Connecticut's state legislature, the General Assembly, uses joint (House and Senate) committees and subcommittees. In 2008, Merrill was elected by her colleagues to the powerful position of House majority leader. Do you expect her changing role in the legislature to affect her decision making, and how and why?
4. Do you think Representative Merrill voted the way she should have? Does her justification convince you?
5. Why was a divided constituency a political advantage in this case? Note that the 54th District is relatively liberal and that many of Merrill's constituents would support the Hartford project.
6. In what other ways does the process of making decisions about the budget affect the decisions made and outcomes of the budget process?

WEB SITE RESOURCES

- Bouncing off the Base in Government Budgeting
- Budget Formats
- California Dreamin': Tools of Direct Democracy
- Citizen's Guide to Budgeting in Alexandria, Virginia
- Fiscal Year
- Further Resources
- How Budgets Interact with Economic Conditions
- How to Read Highlights of the Federal Budget
- How War Affects the Formal Federal Budget Process
- Information is Power
- Internet Resources
- Portland's Budget Process

Omnibus Appropriation Bill—a bundling of bills at the federal level authorizing spending by various agencies on various projects.

Logrolling—an exchange of votes among legislators to pass legislation that achieves the goal of each legislator in the exchange; agreement (often unspoken) among legislators to support public spending in each other's legislative districts without questioning the need or purpose.

- Rules of the Game in Washington: Confidentiality, Testimony, and Communications
- Tracking an Agency's Budget Request
- Uncle Sam Speaks

REVIEW QUESTIONS

1. In what important ways is the federal budget process different from budgeting in state and local governments?
2. Why is it important that the Government Accountability Office reports to Congress rather than to the president?
3. Why does only one-third of all federal spending go through the annual appropriations process? How does this affect the politics of budgeting?
4. Does budgeting in your state "bounce off the base?" What is your evidence?
5. Look at the budget process. Go to the Web site of a major city (population 100,000 or more), read about its budget process, and look at its most recent operating budget and the transmittal letter from the city manager or mayor.

   City _____

   URL _____

   a. Do electoral politics or other political considerations play a role in formulation of the city's budget? Cite evidence for your answer. (See especially the summary narrative and the transmittal letter.)
   b. Does the city use an executive or legislative budget process? Cite evidence for your answer.
   c. Are there signs of an analytic perspective that starts from the base? Cite evidence for your answer.
   d. Does the proposed budget spotlight change? Cite evidence for your answer.

5

Putting the Puzzle Together

This chapter answers four questions:

- What Rules Guide Putting the Budget Pieces Together?
- What Is a Balanced Budget?
- What Happens When There Is No Budget or the Budget Is Not in Balance?
- Is the Budget Sustainable Over Time?

> [B]alancing the budget is a little like protecting your virtue:
> You just have to learn to say "no."
>
> PRESIDENT RONALD REAGAN,
> SPEECH AT KANSAS STATE UNIVERSITY, 1982

> Annual income twenty pounds, annual expenditure nineteen
> nineteen six, result happiness. Annual income twenty pounds,
> annual expenditure twenty pounds ought and six, result
> misery.
>
> ADVICE FROM MR. MICAWBER TO DAVID COPPERFIELD IN
> CHARLES DICKENS' NINETEENTH-CENTURY ENGLISH NOVEL

Each budget cycle begins with a gap between available resources and all the political demands and public needs to which these resources could be directed; this is what scarcity means. Decision makers adjust revenues and spending to each other; this is what balance means. How do they make these hard choices and put the pieces together? And what happens when balance is just a fleeting concept?

Budget theories tell us a lot about how the different pieces of budgeting should fall into place. Unfortunately, they do not offer a meaningful solution to the puzzle of aligning long-term and short-term goals or individual and community concerns about spending and revenue. The theory of rational choice suggests that the budget reflects the decisions of individuals who make decisions to serve their economic and political self-interest such as advancing their reelection prospects or wanting to manage a larger budget. Bureaucratic or political self-interested behavior is different from illegal actions that directly line their pocketbooks. Rational choice theory also focuses on citizen preferences for a low-cost public sector that provides quality services. As a competing theory, incrementalism suggests that budget policy usually is the accidental result of many small decisions that bounce off the base and tinker with current practice. From an incremental perspective, the result is less a coherent policy than an accumulation of nickel-and-dime band-aids.

Neither theory grapples with the harsh reality of budgetary balance. Public leaders prefer to (1) dodge or defer tough decisions, perhaps by fudging revenue forecasts, and (2) spread the pain by imposing across-the-board cuts. Each theoretical explanation may be a necessary but not sufficient explanation for the lack of budget balance. Neither predicts how a particular public agency moves toward balance.

An important piece of the puzzle is understanding the institutions and rules that drive budgetary choices toward balance. These norms or fiscal-constraint rules may be stated as mandates or just preferences of those in power. Debate rages over the need for more or fewer constraints, as in: Should the focus be on "starving the beast" of government or should government come to the rescue of society? For every taxpayer or group that answers it one way, there is always someone on the other side who loudly argues for the opposite position. Budgeting is a political process that allows different ideas to influence revenue policy and spending choices.

Fiscal constraint rules can come in many different forms. They can be in constitutions or, at the other end, just framed as policy pronouncements by the chief executive. In terms of hard-to-change law, state constitutions often prohibit taxing property used for religious purposes, and the state imposes rules on local governments. President George H. W. Bush announced a "no-new-taxes" policy but then abandoned this rule. President Bill Clinton stated that he was going to balance the budget, and he did, if a certain definition of balanced budget is used. Just because Tennessee may face budget pressures it is highly unlikely that the state's elected politicians will change the state's "no income tax" rule to fill the budget shortfall. Other steps are more likely, such as cutting spending, deferring maintenance, offloading costs to local governments and raising rates on existing taxes and charges for services. The task of setting and following fiscal rules that advance the fiscal goals of the public organization is not easy but the American experience shows that it happens—to some degree—every year in nearly 90,000 units of government. Each one typically has to legally adopt a budget *before* it can spend a penny.

As children we learned that we should treat others as we would want to be treated—the **golden rule**. How does this rule, called **reciprocity**, apply to

---

Fiscal Constraint Rule—a law, policy, practice or procedure that has financial implications.

Reciprocity—principle of mutual exchange or supporting behavior, such as in the *golden rule* that calls for treating others as you would like to be treated.

"Harry, she just said her first words! She said, "Why have you saddled my generation with the huge national debt?"

Figure 5.1. Intergenerational Equity

Reprinted by permission of www.cartoonstock.com

public budgeting? It means that the annual budget should cover all the year's costs. Otherwise, today's generation of taxpayers pushes its costs onto future taxpayers. Both **intergenerational equity** and **fiscal sustainability** focus on the future impact of today's decisions. This point can be made in more direct terms: the generation of this book's authors (both baby boomers) should not expect college-age readers to pick up the bill for the older generation's bevy of unfunded promises. Figure 5.1 fittingly conveys this point.

WHAT RULES GUIDE PUTTING THE BUDGET PIECES TOGETHER?

Governments must follow and obey **fiscal-constraint rules** embedded in constitutions, statutes, ordinances, laws, and expressed through policy statements

---

Intergenerational Equity—fairness across age groups or generations; often thought of as requiring the generation enjoying the benefit to pay for it.

by elected and appointed officials. There are both hard and soft fiscal-constraint rules. Hard rules, such as in a constitution or its amendments, are imposed directly by voters, making them hard to change. Soft rules, by contrast, are enacted by a governing body or imposed by the executive, making them easier to change than having to appeal to the voters.

Fiscal Rules for the Federal Government

The legal basis for a federal income tax is a good example of a **hard fiscal rule**. Article I, Section 9 of the U.S. Constitution says: "No Capitation, or other direct, Tax shall be laid, unless in Proportion to the Census or Enumeration herein before directed to be taken." As stated, Congress had the authority to levy an income tax only in proportion to each state's population. However, President Abraham Lincoln persuaded Congress to disregard this prohibition when Congress enacted the Revenue Act of 1861 to finance the Civil War. That law imposed a two-tiered rate structure: 3 percent on taxable incomes up to $10,000 and 5 percent on higher incomes. Once that revenue was no longer needed, the tax was abolished in 1872. A flat-rate income tax was enacted in 1884 but the U.S. Supreme Court ruled it unconstitutional the next year. In 1913, the negative hard rule ("no") was replaced by the 16th Amendment permitting but not requiring Congress to enact a tax on income: "The Congress shall have power to lay and collect taxes on incomes, from whatever source derived, without apportionment among the several States, and without regard to any census or enumeration." Generally, the U.S. Constitution grants Congress wide latitude in its taxing, spending and borrowing powers. For example, Article I, Section 8 of Constitution gives Congress broad power "to lay and collect Taxes…provide for the common defense and general welfare…(and) borrow money on the credit of the United States."

Congress and the president impose numerous soft rules. Statutes are frequently changed. One president's executive orders can be replaced by those of the next president.

Fiscal Rules for State and Local Governments

State and local governments, in contrast, face a complex web of hard and soft constraints centered on what can be taxed, at what rate, and how much can be collected, as well as limits on debt and on the rate of growth of spending. Table 5.1 frames the issue. For example, Texas is prohibited from imposing a state income tax unless it is approved by state voters, while Oregon must obtain voter approval for a state sales tax. A supermajority legislative vote is required in fifteen states before taxes can be raised. Colorado's **TABOR** places a limit on the amount of

---

Fiscal Sustainability—an ongoing ability to match what a government owes to what it can claim as resources.

Hard Fiscal Constraint Rule—rule imposed by another level of government or rule that cannot be changed by government officials on their own, but rather voters have to ratify any changes or, in the states with initiatives and referendums, the voters can impose hard rules on their own.

TABOR—"Taxpayer Bill of Rights," a statutory limit on government's power to raise tax levels without the specific consent of the voters.

Table 5.1. Examples of Hard and Soft Fiscal Constraint Rules on Taxation, Debt and Budgeting by Level of Government

	BASE LIMIT	TAXATION RATE LIMIT	COLLECTION LIMIT	DEBT	BUDGET
Hard Constraint					
State Example	Texas Constitution prohibits income tax without voters' approval	Constitution in 15 states require supermajority legislative vote to raise taxes	Colorado's TABOR limits revenues to amount collected in prior year, plus allowance for population growth and inflation	Kansas has $1 million limit on general obligation debt	Balanced-budget required; California Constitution requires a 2/3 legislative vote to approve general fund expenditures for all except education; Arizona Constitution limits appropriations to no more than 7.41 percent of total state personal income
Local Example	Louisiana cities are prohibited from enacting a local income tax	Local sales tax rate limited by state statute; city charter earmarks 1/3 of a local tax to 2/3 to general fund	State law requires automatic roll-back of local property tax rate if higher property values would generate higher tax revenue	State law limits total amount of local general obligation debt	State law requires local balanced budget
Soft Constraint					
State Example	Statutes create sales tax exemptions such as no sales tax on purchase of girl scout cookies	Statutes on sales tax rate	Policy to limit collections to amount received in prior year	Maryland's written policy on acceptable ratios of debt to state personal income and debt service to revenues	Policy to balance the budget from governor's submission to legislative adoption and at end of fiscal year, despite constitution's silence on balancing the budget
Local Example	State grants a local option sales tax but local officials have not imposed it yet	Property tax rate can change yearly, based on amount needed to cover the budget, but local officials have written policy that calls for a level tax rate; city officials may increase water utility fees to reflect annual inflation but the written policy is not to do so every year	Written policy to roll back property tax rate instead of collecting more revenue from higher property values	Written policies on acceptable debt ratios	Written policy to budget only 95 percent of most likely revenue estimate

revenues that can be collected; amounts in excess of the calculated ceiling must be returned to citizens. These examples illustrate how different rules can target the **tax base**, the **tax rate**, and/or the amount that can be collected from the tax.

Debt is a claim on future resources, so it makes sense to put limits on the amount of debt that locks in a claim on future taxes and ties up spending on debt repayment instead of on tomorrow's services. As with other fiscal rules, **debt limits** can come in hard or soft varieties. A soft debt limit, imposed by management or a governing body, is subject to change as circumstances change. For example, a soft debt-limit policy could be stated as no more debt per capita than the average of similar-sized jurisdictions in the state, based on the rationale that it is best to stay in the middle of the pack. What if a city used debt to jump-start economic activity in a downtown destination district, as a way to encourage more people to frequent and therefore contribute to the downtown area? Using public debt for **infrastructure** improvements in a downtown district may be considered a wise investment, thereby requiring a revisiting of the prevailing debt limit policy. Soft-debt limits allow that to happen more easily than do hard rules.

Debt limits placed on the books (that is, the state constitution or local charter) by citizens are hard fiscal rules. Kansas, for example, faces a hard debt limit of no more than one million dollars of debt backed by its full taxing power (rather than by more limited resources), unless approved by the voters. But just how hard is hard? Kansas found a way around the limit because it has about $4 billion of debt outstanding backed by dedicated revenue sources or the pledge, but not the legal burden, to appropriate money yearly to pay debt service. Hard budget constraints include requirements to balance the budget (more on this rule later) and limits, such as California's hurdle to obtain a two-thirds vote of its legislature to approve most general fund expenditures. A different type of limit, this one on the budget itself, is illustrated by Arizona's limit on appropriations to no more than a specified percentage of total state personal income.

Municipal and county governments face their own set of hard fiscal constraints. For example, the Louisiana Constitution prohibits local governments from enacting a local income tax, most states limit the sales tax rate that local governments can impose, and many states require local governments to **roll-back**

Tax Base—that which is taxed, such as property, consumption, or income.

Tax Rate—portion of the tax base that is taken in tax.

Debt—a legal obligation to repay borrowed money.

Debt Limit—a rule limiting the amount of debt a borrower can have.

Infrastructure—publicly owned fixed assets such as roads, bridges, curbs and gutters, streets and sidewalks, drainage systems, lighting systems and similar assets that are immovable and of financial value only to the government unit.

Roll-back—the tax rate which would generate the same *ad valorem* tax revenue as was generated the previous year that usually but not always excludes changes in taxable valuation resulting from new construction, annexation or de-annexation.

the local property tax rate to avoid having higher **property values** result in higher collections. Many states require local governments to balance the budget, and many states limit the total amount of debt backed by property tax revenues (often expressed as a specified percentage of the total value of taxable property values).

Hard fiscal rules cannot be changed by government officials on their own. Voters have to ratify those changes or, in the states with initiatives and referendums, voters can impose hard rules on their own. For local governments, hard fiscal rules can be imposed by the state legislature as well as by local **home rule charters**.

In contrast, **soft rules** are guides to practice that are subject to change without appealing directly to citizens or higher levels of government. For example, soft rules can be enacted by the city council governing a city or self-imposed by the city's executive leadership to guide its fiscal behavior. There are also professional standards and best practices that can be followed (see Web site resource, Internet Resources). Because statutes can be amended, revised, or abolished by subsequent legislation, they are termed soft rules. Similarly, governing officials establish fiscal policies and procedures from time to time, and these can be changed or modified at whim. State legislators, for example, can amend statutes to exempt items from the retail sales tax or raise tax rates (if the state's constitution permits it), limit its collections, change written policy on how much debt the state can afford, and/or pass a budget built on low-balled revenue estimates. For their part, local officials may have the latitude to raise the property tax rate and capture the full extent of property value increases, increase utility fees, set target debt levels, and budget less spending than the revenue they actually expect to collect.

Fiscal Rules Are Norms

Keep in mind that both hard and soft rules are normative, specifying what those in power at the time should or should not do. These rules are not necessarily based on hard evidence from scientific research on what works or what should guide practice. Instead, politics determines what rules will guide or dictate practice, and time tells whether future voters and policymakers will obey or implement them or change them. When Congress grew tired of President Nixon's not spending appropriated funds, it imposed limits on what a president could refuse to spend (**impoundments**). At the same time, Congress changed the federal budget process

---

Property Value—the estimated monetary value of property.

Home Rule Charter—a grant of authority by a state government to designated local governments allowing these sub-state jurisdictions to operate with flexibility unless specifically mandated otherwise by state law.

Soft Fiscal Constraint Rule—a rule governing an organization's fiscal affairs that it controls and can change at will.

Impoundment—presidential method to withhold spending authority without legislative approval; Congress prohibited the practice.

to give Congress a comprehensive view of the federal budget in advance of the president's submission and during congressional adoption of the budget appropriations. As budget deficits grew in the 1980s, successive Congresses responded with a series of laws setting out **deficit targets** (a form of soft limit). Political gridlock resulted, leading President George H. W. Bush to rescind his pledge of "no new taxes" in 1990 and Congress to yield to President Clinton's budget (and tax increase) after two government shutdowns in 1995. Aided greatly by a booming economy that kicked revenues up, the result was balanced budgets at the end of the Clinton presidency and the first reduction in federal debt since the 1960s. At the time of the budget surpluses, there was talk and even forecasts that the national debt could be wiped out in the near future, but this goal proved to be far off-target. The only time the United States had no federal debt was under President Andrew Jackson, the founder of the modern Democratic Party and a populist who preferred small government.

Ideology and philosophy are soft constraints. What is the role of government in the society and the economy? Arguably the most important fiscal matter, this question is seldom asked outright during the budgetary process. A budget's funding and makeup reflect a view of the proper role of government. Although the U.S. capitalistic society rewards entrepreneurial risk-taking, Americans tend to support government's assuming more of the risks, from natural disasters to bailouts of financial institutions considered "too big to fail." In 2001, for example, the Republican Administration of President George W. Bush laid aside its small-is-better philosophy regarding government employment when it created tens of thousands of new federal jobs to fulfill the mission of the Transportation Security Administration and its airport-screening function. Then again in 2008, the Bush Administration chucked its preference to reduce market regulations, or what President Reagan termed the **regulatory tax**, when it bailed out financial giants Fannie Mae and Freddie Mac (see box 5.1), Wall Street securities firms, local banks around the country, the insurance giant AIG, and two of the three domestic automobile manufacturers. In November 2008, in his address to the World Financial Summit, President Bush conveyed his dilemma: "Those of you who have followed my career know that I'm a free market person—until you're told that if you don't take decisive measures then it's conceivable that our country could go into a depression greater than the Great Depressions" [sic]. This statement showcases that a president's governing philosophy, itself a soft constraint, is subject to change due to events and circumstances.

Citizens have an almost insatiable appetite for more government-provided services. At the same time, citizens express a preference for low taxes. The government budget has to simultaneously balance citizen needs against fiscal responsibilities—a difficult balancing act.

Deficit Target—a focus of federal budgeting that sets an allowable upper limit to the deficit.

Regulatory Tax—the costs of obeying government requirements and, although not classified as a tax, is the loss of alternative uses of the income.

BOX 5.1

Fannie Mae and Freddie Mac

Congress created Fannie Mae in 1938 and Freddie Mac in 1970 as **government-sponsored enterprises (GSEs)** to buy home mortgages from local lenders, allowing local lenders more money to lend. The GSEs packaged hundreds of individual mortgages into a mortgaged-backed security and sold shares to investors around the world. Once individuals started to lose value in their homes and default on their mortgages, the value of the packaged pool of mortgages decreased. Investors in mortgaged-backed securities fled to higher quality investments. This exodus helped trigger the financial crisis. Still, these two GSEs have, for many decades, allowed millions of homeowners to borrow money for mortgages at competitive rates because local mortgage lenders were able to quickly sell-off these long-term mortgages (some up to thirty years) and turn them into immediate cash for lending to other borrowers.

WHAT IS A BALANCED BUDGET?

In arithmetic terms, a **balanced budget** means raising enough money to meet spending plans. Budget plans, however, can go awry when reality kicks in or, as the eighteenth-century Scottish poet Robert Burns said, the best-laid plans of mice and men often go astray. Budgets are drafted and adopted days, weeks, or months before the start of the fiscal year that the plans cover. Many months may pass between the calculation of spending needs and the start of the fiscal year (see Web site resource, Fiscal Year). Spending assumptions are built on the expected cost of goods and services, which can be wildly off if inflation surges, fuel and other commodity prices skyrocket, labor prices suddenly change, or unexpected events occur that demand extraordinary services.

Revenue estimates on which spending plans are based can be very different from the number of dollars actually collected. In the summer and fall of 2008, consumers reacted to their fear of (if not actual) loss of a family member's job, a lower market value of their home, the decline in retirement savings, and high gasoline prices by quickly changing their consumption patterns. How does such behavior affect government budgets? For governments that rely on retail sales taxes, less consumer purchasing leads to lower sales-tax collections. Also, when workers lose their jobs and do not receive paychecks, governments that levy income taxes do not receive the tax receipts they expected. Businesses and individuals earning income other than by a paycheck cannot just wait until the end of the year to pay

---

Government-Sponsored Enterprise—quasi-independent entities created by the government for a specific purpose and run on a business or commercial basis.

Balanced Budget—a balanced budget arises when the government entity estimates the same amount of money from revenue collection as it is appropriating for expenditures.

taxes; they have to pay estimated taxes, usually quarterly, to ensure they have paid enough to cover the yearly amount due. The flow of tax payments provides critical information to governments on the evolving state of the economy. As tax receipts veer from what the government revenue department expected for that month or quarter, pressure builds to revise the current public budget to reflect lower-than-expected revenue collections.

Revision of the Budget during the Year

Political coalitions that came together to approve the original budget may not agree with the changes necessary to revise the budget within the year. Revision is especially difficult when a supermajority is needed. California, for example, needs a two-thirds vote of the legislature to approve the budget. Early in December 2008, Governor Arnold Schwarzenegger called a news conference to put pressure on the state legislature to pass his budget revisions. He said that California was "heading towards a financial Armageddon" with a current year deficit of almost $15 billion that was growing by $470 every second, $28,000 every minute, $1.7 million every hour, and $40 million every day that the legislature failed to act (see the Web site resource, California Dreamin'). By the time Governor Schwarzenegger and the legislature resolved the budget impasse through tax increases and budget cuts, the state deficit had swelled to $41 billion. As of mid-2009, California's revenues continued to evaporate and the budget hole grew even deeper.

The "Is" of a Balanced Budget

When is a budget considered balanced? Is it balanced when the chief executive submits the budget to the governing body, when the legislative body passes the budget, every day during the fiscal year, or at year's end? In fact, it may be at each of these key points along the budgetary process. Table 5.2 shows all of the states' balanced-budget requirements.

The law may specify that the chief executive submit a balanced budget. But what if the governor, for instance, proposes new taxes that have not yet been passed by the legislature and bases the budget plan on the higher revenue? The legislative body, in such a case, is placed in the untenable position of having to choose whether to adopt the new tax, cut spending back to the old tax level, or pass an unbalanced budget without the new tax. Once announced, the governor's budget plan ordinarily becomes the minimum amount that program advocates expect. Now the political burden shifts from the governor to any legislator willing to pull money from the governor's funding plan. Tampering with the governor's budget and its financing is not for the politically faint of heart. Until the law was changed in the late 1980s, Louisiana governors could submit a balanced budget premised on new taxes; now the spending plans have to be based on current revenue policy. A Louisiana governor can still propose a new tax or a rate increase on an existing tax, but the change in law makes the governor's policy initiative more transparent. The legislature can just adjust the budget based on current taxes and current services, and reject the package of spending proposals tied to the proposed tax.

Table 5.2. Balanced Budget Requirements

STATE	GOVERNOR MUST SUBMIT BALANCED BUDGET	NATURE OF REQUIREMENT	LEGISLATURE MUST PASS BALANCED BUDGET	NATURE OF REQUIREMENT	GOVERNOR MUST SIGN BALANCED BUDGET	NATURE OF REQUIREMENT	MAY CARRY OVER DEFICIT
Alabama	X	C,S	X	S	—	—	—
Alaska	X	S	X	S	X	S	—
Arizona	X	C,S	X	C,S	X	C,S	—
Arkansas	X	S	—	—	X	S	—
California*	X	C	X	C	X	C	X
Colorado*	X	C	X	C	X	C	—
Connecticut	X	S	X	C,S	X	C	—
Delaware	X	C,S	X	C,S	X	C,S	—
Florida	X	C,S	X	C,S	X	C,S	—
Georgia	X	C	X	C	X	C	—
Hawaii*	X	C,S	—	—	X	C,S	—
Idaho*	—	—	X	C	—	S	—
Illinois	X	C	X	C	X	S	—
Indiana*	—	—	—	—	—	—	X
Iowa	X	C,S	X	S	X	S	—
Kansas	X	S	X	C,S	—	—	—
Kentucky	X	S	X	C	X	C,S	—
Louisiana*	X	C,S	X	C,S	X	C,S	X
Maine	X	C,S	X	C	X	C,S	—
Maryland*	X	C	X	C	—	C	—

State							
Massachusetts	X	C,S	X	C,S	X	C,S	—
Michigan	X	C,S	X	C	X	C,S	X
Minnesota*	X	C,S	X	C,S	X	C,S	—
Mississippi	X	S	X	S	—	—	—
Missouri	X	C,S	—	—	X	C	—
Montana	X	S	X	C	—	—	—
Nebraska	X	C	X	S	—	—	—
Nevada	X	S	X	C	—	—	—
New Hampshire	X	S	—	—	—	—	—
New Jersey	X	C	X	C	X	C	—
New Mexico	X	C	X	C	X	C	—
New York	X	C	X	S	X	—	—
North Carolina	X	C,S	X	S	—	—	—
North Dakota	X	C	X	C	X	C	—
Ohio	X	C	X	C	X	C	—
Oklahoma*	X	S	X	C	X	C	—
Oregon	X	C	X	C	X	C	—
Pennsylvania	X	C,S	—	—	X	C,S	—
Rhode Island	X	C	X	C	X	S	—
South Carolina	X	C	X	C	X	C	—
South Dakota	X	C	X	C	X	C	—
Tennessee	X	C	X	C	X	C	—
Texas	—	—	X	C,S	X	C	—
Utah	X	C	X	C,S	X	—	—
Vermont*	—	—	—	—	—	—	X

(Continued)

Table 5.2. *Continued*

STATE	GOVERNOR MUST SUBMIT BALANCED BUDGET	NATURE OF REQUIREMENT	LEGISLATURE MUST PASS BALANCED BUDGET	NATURE OF REQUIREMENT	GOVERNOR MUST SIGN BALANCED BUDGET	NATURE OF REQUIREMENT	MAY CARRY OVER DEFICIT
Virginia*	—	—	—	—	X	C	—
Washington*	X	S	—	—	—	—	X
West Virginia	—	—	X	C	X	C	—
Wisconsin	X	C	X	C	X	C,S	X
Wyoming	X	C	X	C	X	C	—
Total	44		41		37		7

Codes: C = Constitutional   S = Statutory

Notes

CALIFORNIA—MAY carry over deficit from current year to budget year. However, the budget for any year must be balanced when enacted.

COLORADO—IN Colorado, the Governor cannot sign a budget that is not balanced.

HAWAII—A fiscal year may end with expenditures exceeding revenues for that fiscal year, if available carryover balances from prior years are sufficient to offset the deficit and result in a positive net ending balance for the fiscal year.

IDAHO—THE Governor is not required to submit a balanced budget, but it would be politically unwise not to do so. The constitution requires that the legislature pass a balanced budget. The Governor, as the chief budget officer of the state, has always insured that expenditures do not exceed revenues.

INDIANA—STATE may carry over annual deficits, but cannot assume debt (per the Indiana Constitution).

LOUISIANA—AGENCIES cannot knowingly spend into a deficit pos tion. However, should this occur, there are several procedures available to rectify the situation. The Louisiana Revised Statutes Title 39:76 (Elimination of year-end deficits) states, "If a deficit exists in any fund at the end of the fiscal year, that deficit shall be eliminated no later than the end of the next fiscal year." The preamble of the general appropriations bill states, "The state treasurer is hereby authorized and directed to use any available funds on deposit in the state treasury to complete the payment of General Fund appropriations for the Fiscal Year 2066–2007, and to pay a deficit arising there from out of any revenues accruing to the credit of the state General Fund during the Fiscal Year 2007–2008, to the extent such deficits are approved by the legislature." The preamble also reiterates and authorizes the governor pursuant to Article IV, Section 5(G)(2) and Article VII, Section 10(F) of the constitution that "If at any time during Fiscal Year 2007–2008 the official budget status report indicates that appropriations will exceed the official revenue forecast, the governor shall have full power to reduce appropriations in accordance with R.S. 39:75. (Avoidance of budget deficits) The governor shall have the authority within any month of the fiscal year to direct the commissioner of administration to disapprove warrants drawn upon the state treasury for appropriations contained in the Act which are in excess of amounts approved by the governor in accordance with R.S. 39:74. (Avoidance of cash flow deficits) The governor may also, and in addition to the other powers set forth herein, issue executive orders in a combination of any of the foregoing means for the purpose of preventing the occurrence of a deficit."

MARYLAND—The budget bill, when and as passed by both houses, shall be a law immediately without further action by the Governor.

MINNESOTA—The state constitution limits the use of public debt. The limit implicitly requires the state to have a balanced operating budget. M.S. 16A.11 Subd. 2 requires the Governor's budget recommendations to show the balanced relation between the total proposed expenditures and the total anticipated income.

OKLAHOMA—The legislature could pass and the Governor could sign a budget where appropriations exceed cash and estimated revenues, but constitutional and statutory provisions reduce the appropriations so that the budget is balanced.

VERMONT—In practice, a deficit has not been carried over.

VIRGINIA—The balanced budget requirement applies only to budget execution. The Governor is required to insure that actual expenditures do not exceed actual revenues by the end of the appropriation period. The Governor must execute, not sign, a balanced budget.

WASHINGTON—Although the legal requirement for a balanced budget only applies to the Governor, the legislature has always passed a balanced budget using the official General Fund forecast. State law forbids expenditures without supporting revenues. An agency may receive permission to carry over a temporary cash deficit, however longer term deficits would result in an expenditure authority reduction by the Governor, or a legislative budget change to bring the fund back into balance.

SOURCE: Reprinted by permission. National Association of State Budget Officers, 2008. Calculations in original.

=================== **BOX 5.2** ===================

Twenty Years of Late Budgets: What's the Problem?

According to Common Cause of New York:

> [New York State's]...budget process lacks the necessary qualities of transparency and accountability. The way the system currently functions, state agencies' budget requests to the Governor are not public, certain key programs don't appear on the budget at all, and there is no failsafe in case the state leaders are not able to agree on a budget by the start of the fiscal year.
>
> Furthermore, current interpretations of the State Constitution allow the Governor an unusual amount of budgetary power and give the Legislature little recourse to respond. The Governor may insert serious changes to state policy (like complex school funding formulas) into his budget, and legislators cannot amend budget items (or the accompanying policy changes) in any way or pass their own separate appropriations. The only power they have is to strike out budget items or reduce the dollar amount of appropriations, leaving legislators with no choice but to accept the executive budget as-is or refuse to pass it at all, entirely breaking down the process.

Reprinted by permission. Common Cause of New York, 2005.

Does the legislature face the burden of adopting a balanced budget, or can it enact an unbalanced budget? Most state laws require the budget to be balanced when adopted and at year's end. Executive budget powers are illustrated by the State of New York's experience, because New York did not adopt a budget by the start of the new fiscal year for more than twenty years. The reason is that legislative leaders balked at the power of the governor, as explained in box 5.2.

Balancing the budget on one-time money is also a problem. Doing so builds in a future budget hole because, by definition, balancing the budget on one-time money cannot be repeated—it is not sustainable. Windfalls are budget seductions; they may provide immediate pleasure but seldom offer long-term satisfaction. A nonprofit organization may receive a grant or donation to start a particular program or serve a certain clientele, but when the one-time money is gone, the recipients continue to expect services. Although nearly all the states quickly accepted the money made available to them through the American Recovery and Reinvestment Act of 2009, so they could cover their immediate budget holes, this behavior just forestalls the budget day of reckoning if their economies continue to falter. For years, many governments around the country coasted along by assuming that end-dated grant programs (perhaps federal, state, or corporate) would be renewed in the future. Bubbles burst. Basic operating budgets are best built on recurring resources rather than resources that are here today and gone tomorrow. Residents of a community expect continuity of services.

Even if a balanced budget is adopted on time and on routinely available resources, it says little about the reliability of the revenue and spending estimates.

Although nearly every state and many local governments have had to cut spending deeply during the recession that started in December 2007, the all-too-common practice is to overestimate expenditures so that by the end of the fiscal year actual spending falls below the budgeted amounts (see chapter 4). Budget theory suggests that spending plans are set higher than needed. Incrementalism explains this behavior as managers taking steps to guard their unit's proposed spending plans from the expected cut by higher-level budget reviewers. Public choice theory looks at the same behavior as evidence that managers are **budget maximizers**, interested in self-advancement rather than in achieving policy goals.

Overall, spending less than appropriated combined with higher-than-estimated revenues at the end of the fiscal year produce a **surplus** (excess) that feeds into the government's **fund balance**. The surplus and any amounts still remaining from prior years combine to form the fund balance, which is equal to the difference between assets and liabilities. Broadly speaking, fund balance is a key indicator of financial condition (discussed further in chapter 9). The "unassigned" amount of the fund balance not yet set aside for a particular use is available for appropriation in the future (see later discussion of the rainy day fund). Shortsighted political or financial pressures may encourage ethically and professionally troublesome behavior designed to hide the expected surplus both from those who want more spending and those demanding lower taxes. If this is not enough to show the political tension surrounding fund balance policy, add in the expectations of the investors in the jurisdiction's debt that there will be a sufficient cushion of money to safeguard debt repayment against short-term **cash flow** problems. Political discussions increasingly center on the appropriate size of the fund balance.

WHAT HAPPENS WHEN THERE IS NO BUDGET OR THE BUDGET IS NOT IN BALANCE?

In Article I, Section 9, the U.S. Constitution states that "no money shall be drawn from the treasury, but in consequence of appropriations made by law." Implementing this provision, the Anti-Deficiency Act prohibits all officers and employees of the federal government from entering into obligations before Congress approves an appropriation. This means that federal employees cannot work during a lapse in their agency's

---

Budget Maximizers—theory that those in charge of the budget are more interested in self-advancement than they are in achieving policy goals.

Surplus—when revenues are greater than spending in a fiscal period.

Fund Balance—the difference between assets and obligations (liabilities) in a governmental fund; a positive ending fund balance from one fiscal year is available as a resource for the following fiscal year's activities; the ending fund balance for one fiscal year is the same amount as the beginning fund balance for the following fiscal year.

Cash Flow—actual money (cash) coming in and going out of an organization in a fiscal period.

spending power. Does the government shut down if there is no budget approved? President Clinton and the Republican Congress shut down the "nonessential" parts of the government twice in late 1995 because they could not agree on the budget.

How does part of the federal government remain open when there is no budget? Some parts of government operations have a permanent appropriation that is not subject to yearly approval. For example, Social Security beneficiaries will get their monthly checks. Military operations to protect the country will continue, but civilian employees in the Defense Department are considered, for the most part, nonessential and cannot work during a government shutdown. If essential parts of the federal government continue without even the kernel of a budget, then the mere fact that a budget is not passed and signed into law is not going to cripple all operations of the federal government.

When the budget is not in balance, one of two possibilities occurs: **surplus** or **deficit**. If it is a surplus, the surplus amount can be used to offset a cut in taxes, send some or all citizens a share, save for use in the future, or pay off debt. While getting political consensus on what to do with a surplus is not without its own political give-and-take, we turn to the more current and politically troublesome problem of what to do with a deficit budget, especially at the federal level.

Financing the Deficit by Issuing Debt

Revenues ordinarily should cover expenditures, but what happens when spending is more than revenues? Although cutting spending or increasing revenues (or a combination of the two) would appear to be the right answer, for some governments there is another option, however poor a choice it is. For the U.S. government, a deficit occurs when **outlays** exceed revenues and require the government to borrow money.

The U.S. Treasury issues **securities** (obligations to pay in the future) to investors who are willing to lend money to the U.S federal government, instead of lending money to another borrower around the world. Foreign investors are attracted to these Treasury securities because the U.S. government is unlikely to skip out on paying back investors. (An organization's probability of **default** on its obligations is termed **credit risk**, with an independent **credit rating** firm paid by the

---

Surplus—when revenue is greater than spending in a fiscal period.

Deficit—when total spending is greater than total revenues in a fiscal period; the result when spending (and other uses of funds) exceed revenues (and other sources of funds).

Outlays—the outflow of cash paid for assets, goods or services.

Securities—the form of a debt instrument.

Default—a failure to honor an obligation, as in not paying debt service on time.

Credit Risk—the likelihood that an organization will default on its debt.

Credit Rating—an independent assessment of risk, meaning the likelihood that an organization will not repay the debt, including principal and interest, on time.

organization to make that assessment.) Evidence of the impact of low credit risk appeared in the 2008 financial crisis when investors offered cash to the Treasury without accepting anything more than a return of their cash investment when repayment was due; that they did not expect any interest or return on their money is a very unusual event. These investors seemed to follow the sage advice of humorist Will Rogers who said that he was more concerned with the return *of* his principal than the return *on* principal.

Foreign investors are major lenders to the U.S. government; they own about half of all publicly held debt. Figure 5.2 shows the increasing role of foreign investors. There is a risk that foreign investors could, at some point, threaten to disinvest in Treasuries as leverage to change American public policy on an issue that is important to them. This scenario is unlikely as long as Treasury securities are preferred to most other investment options. Also, acting out this behavior could reduce U.S. demand for the country's products and, in this way, lower the investor country's economic growth. Yet, as the credit crisis of 2008 worsened, foreign investors sold large amounts of their holdings in the debt securities of U.S. government-sponsored enterprises, such as Freddie Mac and Fannie Mae. This trend contributed to the need for the federal government to bail out these entities that enjoyed an unwritten but understood guarantee of federal backing. U.S. officials did not want there to be any reason for foreign investors to avoid buying Treasury securities. Both President Bush and President Obama's recovery

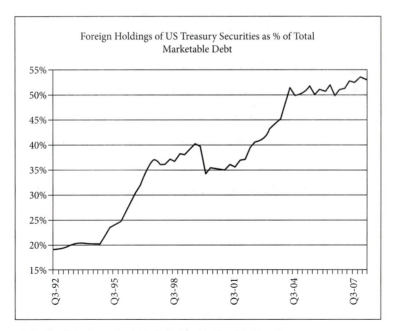

Figure 5.2. The U.S. Government Is Beholden to Foreign Investors
SOURCE: Department of the U.S. Treasury, 2008.

packages, and the resulting large budget deficit, rest on continued demand by foreign investors for Treasury securities.

Borrowing money from the public causes the federal debt to increase, but there is a second way that it increases. This result is due to changes in the **intra-governmental account**. The way this works is that, as the federal government receives Social Security and Medicare payroll taxes (Federal Insurance Contributions Act, or **FICA**), the "surplus" cash received (over and above the payouts for current benefits) is invested in Treasury securities. This way the amount of outstanding federal debt increases even if the budget itself is not running a deficit because the Treasury swaps its securities for the cash.

Total federal debt includes both debt held by the public and intra-governmental debt. As of December 30, 2008, total federal debt outstanding was $10,553,014,664,691.60 (that is trillions!), with 60 percent held by the public and the rest by intra-governmental accounts. Given the bailouts and stimulus package, the national debt is increasing quickly.

The amount of debt held by the public gets the most policy attention because of the obligation to repay public investors. Although the sheer amount outstanding is important to monitor, what is more important from an economic perspective is the ability of the borrower to repay the money. In the case of the United States, this ability to pay is measured by the American wealth base. The common measure used around the world to assess a country's wealth base is its **gross domestic product** (GDP), or the total value of all goods and services produced in the country (see Web site resource, Using the Gross Domestic Product). In fact, countries in the European Union are expected to meet set Debt-to-GDP ratios. For its part, the United Kingdom calls such a ratio as its "sustainable investment rule," with government net debt (including its local governments) to stay below 40 percent of GDP. (Unlike the U.K. where its sub-national governments do not borrow on their own credit but receive money from the central government, American state and local governments do borrow on their own credit so that their debt is not counted in the federal government's totals.)

As figure 5.3 shows, the U. S. federal government's public debt during World War II was a small dollar amount by today's standard, but it represented over 100 percent of the national economy at that time. The debt declined significantly until the Reagan Administration, when tax cuts and budget deficits grew faster than the underlying economy. More recently, publicly held debt as a percent of GDP again declined significantly. The tax increases of the early 1990s reduced the need for debt while the expanding economy made the outstanding debt a smaller percentage of

---

Intra-governmental Account—federal debt held by its own accounts, especially governmental trust funds such as Social Security; debt other than sold to the public investors.

FICA (Federal Insurance Contributions Act)—the legal name designating social security taxes.

Gross Domestic Product (GDP)—a measure of the income generated by the production of goods and services on U.S. soil, including production financed by foreigners.

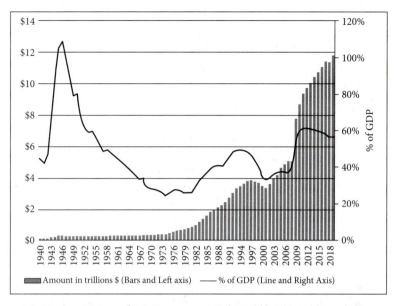

Figure 5.3. Modern History of U.S. Government Debt Held by the Public and as a Percentage of Gross Domestic Product

Publicly-held debt excludes the U.S. Treasury debt instruments issued to serve as the investments of intra-governmental accounts such as Social Security and Medicare. Projections to 2019 are based on current law as of January 2009. In current dollars.

SOURCE: Calculated by authors based on Office of Management and Budget, 2008a and Congressional Budget Office, 2009.

the overall economy. President George W. Bush oversaw a reversal of these trends and a turn to lower taxes and higher deficits. Figure 5.3 reflects projections to 2019 based on current law as of January 2009. It does not fully capture the impact of the economic recession (starting in December 2007) and the large recovery program enacted in February 2009. All of these actions increase the amount of public debt relative to the nation's economic wealth as measured by GDP.

Before 1941, Congress was involved every time the Treasury had to borrow money. Now, Congress sets a lid and allows the Treasury to make decisions on the amount and timing as long as the total debt does not exceed the lid. Table 5.3 traces the history of the federal government's **statutory debt limits**. The first trillion dollars of accumulated debt in the nation's history was reached early in President Reagan's first term and the second trillion was reached in that same term. As of January 1, 2009, the debt limit stood at $11.3 trillion. The February 2009 stimulus package increased the debt limit to $12.1 trillion.

Voting for an increase in the federal debt limit is politically charged (see chapter 6). Typically, the party in control of Congress has to produce the votes for

Statutory Debt Limit—restriction in the law that limits how much debt a government or public organization can owe.

Table 5.3. Federal Debt Limit, Selected Years 1950–2009

AS OF JANUARY 1	LIMIT IN BILLIONS $	% INCREASE
1950	$275	
1960	$295	7.27%
1970	$377	27.80%
1972	$430	14.06%
1980	$879	104.42%
1982	$1,080	22.84%
1990	$3,123	189.19%
1992	$4,145	32.74%
2000	$5,950	43.55%
2001	$5,950	0.00%
2002	$5,950	0.00%
2003	$6,400	7.56%
2004	$7,384	15.38%
2005	$8,184	10.83%
2006	$8,184	0.00%
2007	$8,965	9.54%
2008	$10,615	18.40%
2009	$11,315	6.59%
as of February 2009	$12,104	6.97%

SOURCE: Calculated by authors based on data from the Office of Management and Budget, 2008; the U.S. Department of the Treasury, 2009; and the American Recovery and Reinvestment Act of 2009.

this must-pass legislation, even if the presidency is held by a member of the opposition party. The minority party, in contrast, can be counted on to exploit this opportunity to cast the other party as wasteful spenders. In turn, by stalling until the last moment to increase the debt limit, the majority party may put pressure on opponents by labeling them as the cause of the federal government's almost defaulting on its obligations. This must-pass legislation often is saddled with deficit reduction plans or unrelated legislation to gain the votes needed for passage. Not only has the federal government never defaulted on a debt payment, but many financial experts believe that default would destabilize finances on a global scale. This widely held belief is used as political leverage to obtain the votes to pass an increase in the debt limit.

State and Local Government Debt
American state and local governments do not make a practice of borrowing to cover budget deficits. In fact, most of these governments are prohibited by their state constitutions from borrowing for operating purposes. From time to time, California, Connecticut, and Louisiana have yielded to this temptation and issued multi-year debt to pay current bills; the result is to push the cost onto future taxpayers. When state governments are allowed to end the fiscal year with a deficit, they often have other rules (typically soft ones) that require that the next year's budget cover this deficit. Local governments may face a hard fiscal-constraint rule to end the fiscal year with a balanced budget. This demand puts a premium on closely monitoring the budget during the year in order to have time to make cuts sufficient to achieve

a balanced budget by year's end. Instead of just stepping up to the plate and making the hard choices publicly, some officials disguise the situation by pushing the burden of balancing the budget into the future by cutting back on maintenance of public facilities, such as roads, sewer system, vehicles, and more. Such behavior violates budget transparency, accountability, and equity principles.

Budget Cutbacks

Sometimes the looming gap between revenue collections and spending is so large that cuts in spending are needed. In early 2009, governors and mayors from all across the country welcomed President Barack H. Obama with insistent demands for hundreds of billions of dollars to help offset their expected budget cuts. The argument was that the federal government, with its large tax capacity, responsibilities for monetary and national fiscal policy, and the legal option of using deficits to finance spending, is the perfect "deep pocket." In tune with the American bias for government decentralization and self-reliance, the counter-argument called for local services to be funded by local taxpayers, not by a higher-level handout.

American fiscal federalism reflects differences between the levels of government. State and local governments have a smaller tax base and more fiscal-constraint rules, including more hard and soft rules, than the federal government. Plus they have to follow federal mandates linked to their use of federal money. Fundamentally, local governments are creatures of their state, and so subject to the state's rules. For local governments that rely on property taxes and also must balance their annual budgets, hard lids on tax rates or tax-base growth cut into the governments' ability to respond flexibly to a downturn in property values or state aid. Supporters of such lids would argue that this is exactly what the limits are supposed to do. Then, too, it makes little sense for the federal government to try to stimulate the economy when state and local governments are cutting back on spending. Hard rules get in the way of using the budget to stimulate or dampen down the economy, but the rules also serve to dull the appetite for more government spending and express anti-tax sentiment.

If revenue and/or spending growth are limited to prior-year(s) levels, then revenue shortfalls and deep spending cuts during recessions ratchet down public revenue for years to come. Colorado faced this scenario after the dot.com bust of 2000–2001 and had to lift its hard TABOR-imposed ceiling to allow revenue growth to catch up with population changes and voters' desires.

Recent market changes have whipsawed investment earnings. From July 1 to October 30, 2008, Harvard University's endowment lost 22 percent of its value (or about $8 billion), prompting its president, Drew G. Faust, to institute "a range of capital and operating budget-reduction scenarios" that led to a hiring freeze by its college of arts and sciences (Faust, 2008). Budget reduction is another name for **cutback management**. An organization that operates under a balanced-budget

---

Cutback Management—another term for budget reduction, or reducing the amount of money spent on government functions.

rule and sees a looming deficit has to quickly take steps to get spending back in line with the new revenue expectations. The sooner action is taken the better; if the deficit is discovered late in the fiscal year, the impact of cuts shoehorned into the few remaining days can be large... and painful.

Budget managers must constantly monitor spending against the budget and respond as soon as possible to a looming deficit. (The Web site resource, The Paradox of Efficiency, shows what lax monitoring can do.) Any delay leaves less of the fiscal year in which to respond and magnifies the impact of needed spending cuts. For example, if a yearly budget is built on $100 of planned spending per month (for a total of $1,200 for the year) and a 10 percent cut is needed, cutting out $120 at the beginning of the year would leave $1,080. If the same amount were cut after six months ($600 already spent), then the $120 cut would be out of the unspent $600, and $120 now amounts to a 20 percent cut.

Two common budget-cutting approaches are to cut the same percentage from all programs, termed an across-the-board cut, or to prioritize programs and cut the less important ones first. Prioritization is easier said than done. Most politicians hate to revisit their budget choices and label some programs as less important than others. At the least, it exposes them to political attack by program advocates and opens the door for someone to challenge their reelection. Political concerns often lead to an across-the-board cut that gets decision makers off the hook by imposing the same percentage reduction on efficient programs as well as programs operating less efficiently. This strategy penalizes the well-run programs. A different approach is to use the occasion to target cuts in those areas that are less efficient and/or less effective in their programs. **Right-sizing** is a related term, meaning to determine what is most important and reduce the rest. Politics reminds us that what is "right-sizing" to one is likely to be "wrong-sizing" to another!

Financial pressures typically lead to spending cuts instead of raising revenues for several reasons. First, revenue constraints are hard to overcome quickly, with some requiring direct voter approval or decisions by other levels of government (for example, a state government has to authorize a city's increase in its sales tax rate). Second, elected officials can predict at least initial public resistance to proposals for increases in revenues over which the officials do have some say; the best that officials can hope for is public acceptance, not enthusiasm. Third, the public's expectation that existing services will continue into the future acts to limit slack in the future budget for new programs. Fourth, the public ordinarily and repeatedly expresses a preference for cutting services rather than raising taxes in the abstract, but not when the choices come down to specifics.

Political leadership, vigorous public dialogue, and a well-crafted package of options are what it takes to fund the gap. Despite general preferences, public attitudes toward closing the budget gap are flexible. The public responds to a package of budget proposals differently from a simple proposal to raise taxes. Preferences are

---

Right-Sizing—the term used to describe a variety of policies and practices that seek to reduce the size and scope of an organization or government.

=========================== BOX 5.3 ===========================

Budget Reduction Options

Basic Techniques

Freeze hiring
Freeze promotions
Cut overtime
Use temporary employees
Use volunteers
Freeze or reduce budgeted raises
Reduce or change employee benefits
Reduce work week
Furlough or forced-leave without pay
Encourage early retirement
Downgrade position
Contract-out or privatize services and programs
Do not replace empty positions once someone leaves
Layoffs and Reduction in Force (RIF)
Manipulate pension assumptions
Change work rules
Simplify the work process to work more efficiently with fewer resources

GFOA Fiscal First Aid Techniques

Audit revenue sources
Improve billing and collections procedures
Explore fees for services
Propose taxes with a strong (physical) nexus
Assess organization structure
Conduct a tax lien sale
Restructure debt
Evaluate financial condition & get benchmark data
Inventory programs and ascertain their costs
Audit certain recurring expenditures
Make managers manage
Divest of loss-generating enterprises
Revise purchasing practices
Seek state, federal and/or regional assistance
Pursue inter-organizational cooperation
Identify sources of liquidity
Revisit control system
Develop cash flow reporting
Centralize financial management and human resource activities
Establish a culture of frugality
Recognize opportunities within crisis
Manage perceptions
Be willing to spend money to save money
Network with peer agencies and individuals
Sell assets
Obtain better returns on idle cash

Use short-term debt to pay for vehicles
Outsource
Revisit interfund transfer policies
Close facilities (or reduce hours of operation)

Reprinted by permission. Excerpted from Government Finance Officers Association, 2009.

affected when the budget problem is widely recognized as severe and choices about closing the budget gap include certain types of taxes and certain types of spending.

Belt-tightening shows up in a common tactic: postponing maintenance of buildings and equipment as long as possible. Deferred maintenance is often short-sighted and inefficient; for instance, a leak in a worn roof is not fixed, and the next storm brings interior damages and higher repair costs. Saving maintenance dollars in one year can lead to higher repair bills later. Frankly, there is no constituency for a bridge until it is about to fall down. Clearly, this cost-cutting measure can be used only so long.

Labor costs constitute about 75 percent of the operating budget in local government. Freezing the workforce is the single most common approach to closing a budget gap taken by local government. Other methods are listed in box 5.3.

Local governments that fail to meet the fiscal rules of their states are subject to penalties, which vary by state. An Ohio local government, for example, is considered faltering and added to a formal state "watch" list when it has a year-end deficit equal to one-twelfth of its revenues. Failure to resolve the problem during this "watch" status can lead to direct state oversight and state control of local fiscal affairs.

IS THE BUDGET SUSTAINABLE OVER TIME?

A budget balanced for the current year does not mean that it will be balanced next year. The general rule is that one legislature cannot bind its successors. If this were allowed to happen, there would be little left for a new legislature to do because options for changes in the budget would be lost. There are exceptions, though, when one legislature can bind its successors. If legally enacted, a contractual agreement has to be honored, including the duty to pay long-term debt obligations. Other than for such exceptions, change can occur quickly if the votes are there to do it. A balanced budget in one year may be followed by an unbalanced one. Politicians and voters may decide to follow a different strategy of deep tax cuts and large spending increases in such a way as to produce an unbalanced or out-of-whack budget.

More common is a balanced budget that is not actually balanced because policymakers push spending burdens into the future. One way to satisfy current needs but push up future costs is to add new employees during the year, agree to wage and salary increases but only starting in the next budget year, or increase retirement pay. The City of Vallejo, California filed for federal bankruptcy in 2008 because, years before, city officials signed labor contracts that led to overall compensation levels for public safety officers well above those in surrounding areas and above what the city's limited tax and revenue-raising powers could pay. In effect, the city bargained away its fiscal flexibility. City leaders approached bankruptcy as a way to replace the expensive labor contracts with more fiscally sustainable plans. As you might imagine, the affected public safety officers were not pleased with this and argued that it was not their fault but rather mismanagement by city officials.

In another California example, elected and key appointed officials of the City of San Diego contrived ways to maintain current services by manipulating the amounts paid to city pension accounts. The practical effect was to push the cost burden onto future taxpayers. Although this was poor fiscal management, what got them in real trouble was committing **securities fraud** by borrowing money without revealing the true status of the city's financial condition. As a consequence, they agreed to federal securities regulators' demands for more controls on handling these decisions in the future. The controls meant independent overseers and auditors.

Rainy Day Budgeting

Budgeting involves the trade-off of one budget year against all future ones. A common policy prescription is for each government to have a **rainy day fund**: resources put aside into a particular fund now in case revenue is temporarily reduced in the future. Money is set aside to be used to stabilize the budget over the business cycle (of economic booms and slowdowns) or cover emergencies. This policy decision leads to follow-up questions: How much money should be set aside in this savings account and under what conditions can the money be withdrawn—that is, just what *is* a "rainy day"? Money could be set aside in a separate account or the surplus of revenues over spending could be allowed to accumulate in the fund balance. Savings attracts spenders—who see rain everywhere. State and local government officials often establish policy on when savings can be accessed (what is a "rainy day") and the appropriate amount to save—such as 5 to 10 percent of current year revenues or an amount equal to one month of expenditures. Although personal-finance gurus assert that individuals should have at least six months of savings in order to cover the bills until finding another job, governments have taxing power that translates into more stability in revenue flow providing more security than the average citizen enjoys.

Public Sector Employee Benefits

Historically, public-employee wages and salaries were well below those of comparable jobs in the private sector. To attract and retain employees,

---

Securities Fraud—a violation of law in the selling and/or trading of securities.

Rainy Day Fund—resources put aside into a particular fund now in case revenue is temporarily reduced in the future.

government officials offered generous employee benefits, such as the right to a retirement plan after ten years (known as **vesting**); to retire after twenty years at a high percentage of the employee's highest three-year average salary; and to receive guaranteed (free or low-cost) health care benefits during retirement. However, the only employee-benefit costs that showed up in the annual operating budget were the yearly pension contributions and health care premiums. Supposedly, these contribution levels were set to cover the current value of future benefits based on many assumptions about future costs—the amount of investment income that might offset some of these costs and the future workforce composition, to name just a few of the assumptions embedded in public-employee benefit programs. There was limited information available on the amount of the unfunded **pension liability** and often none on the amount of "**other post-employment benefits**" (**OPEBs**). Only recently have state and local governments had to place a dollar value on these long-term liabilities and report them along with all other claims against assets. These generally accepted accounting principles would make it harder for current officials and taxpayers to shift part of the cost of current public services onto future taxpayers.

Budget Sustainability

Citizens and their governments face a big problem. Federal government budget trends are not sustainable in the long run and were not even before the recession that began in December 2007. As discussed more fully in earlier chapters, there are several key parts of the federal budget that are not reviewed yearly. In fact, they are on autopilot, meaning that certain programs have a **permanent authorization** to exist and the right to an unlimited draw for cash from the U.S. Treasury to pay beneficiaries who meet eligibility standards. The two biggest programs are Social Security and Medicare (see chapter 6 on entitlements). There is a growing mismatch in numbers between retirees drawing public benefits from these programs and workers paying taxes. Add another problem: the federal debt. As the federal debt increases so will interest payments to the investors. Going forward,

---

Vesting—point at which the employee has a permanent legal right to certain employer-provided benefits even if the employee no longer works for the employer.

Pension Liability—a shortfall in pension funds to cover the employer's agreed-upon pension obligation to its current and future retirees; calculated by using assumptions about life expectancy and interest rates (actuarial assumptions).

Other Post-Employment Benefits (OPEB)—benefits other than pensions earned by employees over their years of service that will not be received until after their employment ends; benefits provided to eligible retirees may include health insurance and dental, vision, prescription or life insurance.

Permanent Authority—the legal ability of a federal government program to continue in existence unless the law is changed.

the federal budget cannot sustain this level of financial commitment under its current revenue policy (see figure 6.4).

A **sustainable budget** is one that focuses on balance not just in a single year but for many years into the future. Organizations enjoy **structural balance** when the annual growth rate of revenues is equal to or lower than the growth rate of spending for the same past time-period (such as the last five fiscal years). Although this growth-rate comparison assumes that current tax and spending patterns persist into the future, it does set the stage for difficult questions about the flight path of financial commitments as they play out in the future. The point is to take a multi-year perspective when applying the budget-balance rule.

The concern with sustainability is so strong and widespread that sustainability now ranks among the values important to public budgeting (see table 1.2). There is a movement to make state and local government accounting rules reflect sustainability issues. Federal government accounting rules are also adding fiscal sustainability reporting expectations (see box 5.4). As the federal government assumes a more substantial role, up to *near* nationalization, in extending bailout terms for some investment banking firms, commercial banks, and mortgage intermediaries (such as Fannie Mae and Freddie Mac), these commitments may become part of the federal budget and its **balance sheet**. Transparency demands more complete disclosure of the future impact of current decisions.

THUMBNAIL

There is no free lunch. Everything must be paid for, sooner or later. This chapter describes the rules that guide budget behavior toward the goal of annual balance. Putting the budget pieces together is never easy, as figure 5.4 hints. There are many hard and soft fiscal-constraint rules that govern the process. Hard rules are those placed in constitutions and city charters by the voters and so are hard to impose and change. Soft rules, in contrast, are not set in stone, but much easier to alter when circumstances change or an election changes officeholders or the legislative majority. Defining a balanced budget is not altogether easy. Is it balanced on a windfall, on the assumption that a new tax will be enacted, on fishy assumptions, or just utter disregard for the future impact of current decisions? Facing up to an unbalanced budget is not any easier. Does a public

---

Sustainable Budget—a budget in which current resources cover current benefits and services received by current taxpayers and residents and also any future costs associated with these current benefits and services.

Structural Balance—when the growth rate of revenues is equal to or greater than the growth rate of spending.

Balance Sheet—the basic financial statement that discloses the assets, liabilities, and net assets of a reporting entity as of a specific date, such as year-end; a snapshot of the financial condition.

BOX 5.4

Defining Fiscal Sustainability

STATE AND LOCAL GOVERNMENT

[The following terms are defined by the Governmental Accounting Standards Board, which establishes accounting standards for American state and local governments.]

Economic Condition: Economic condition is a composite of a government's financial position and its ability and willingness to meet its financial obligations and service commitments on an ongoing basis. Economic condition includes three components: financial position, fiscal capacity, and service capacity.

Financial Position: Financial position is the status of a government's assets, liabilities, and net assets, as displayed in the basic financial statements.

Fiscal Capacity: Fiscal capacity is the government's ability and willingness to meet its financial obligations as they come due on an ongoing basis.

Service Capacity: Service capacity is the government's ability and willingness to meet its commitments to provide services on an ongoing basis.

However, the concept of fiscal sustainability relates to economic condition has not been deliberated [as of February 2009].

SOURCE: Reprinted by permission of the Financial Accounting Foundation, 2006.

FEDERAL GOVERNMENT

[The following terms are defined by the Federal Accounting Standards Board, which establishes accounting standards for the U.S. Government (but not for private firms, nonprofit organizations or state and local governments).]

Stewardship Objective: Federal financial reporting should assist report users in assessing the impact on the country of the government's operations and investments for the period and how, as a result, the government's and the nation's financial condition has changed and may change in the future....

Fiscal Sustainability Reporting should provide information to assist readers of the [Consolidated Financial Report]...in assessing whether future budgetary resources of the U.S. Government will likely be sufficient to sustain public services and to meet obligations as they come due, assuming that current policy without change for federal government public services and taxation is continued....

Reprinted by permission of the Federal Accounting Standards Advisory Board, 2008.

---

organization cut spending, raise revenues, or borrow its way out of an immediate problem? Increasingly, the public and its officials are starting to focus on how to make the budget sustainable over the long term. A new budget value, sustainability, focuses on paying for today's liabilities, not pushing them off on a later tax-paying generation. Given that cash is king, there must be money to pay public bills. These imperatives are sure to drive hard decisions about public budgets.

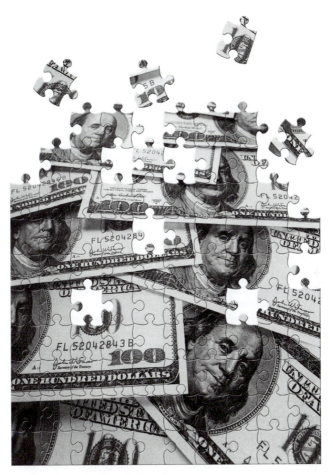

Figure 5.4. Putting the Budget Puzzle Together
Reprinted by permission of Stockxpert.com

CASE

Insulating Politicians by Letting a Commission Do the Heavy Lifting on What to Cut

Politicians and citizens alike disagree about what should be cut from a budget, so it is hard to come to a quick resolution in a political environment. There are mechanisms that have been used by the federal government and several states to insulate politicians from the dirty work when across-the-board cuts no longer work (and they just delay the budget day of reckoning) and the politics is too tough for surgical cuts. The idea is to set up a process outside the normal budgetary process to review programs or departments based on criteria other than "I will not vote to cut your favored program, if you will not vote against mine." Two mechanisms of particular interest are closure commissions and sunset legislation.

Inside the Washington beltway, delegating the heavy lifting to a commission is a time-honored dodge. The federal government started the concept of a closure commission with the Base Realignment and Closure Commission (BRAC, found at www.brac.gov). It was first created by law in 1988 and re-created most recently in 2005. Congress embraced this process for deciding which military bases in the United States to close. The goal was to create a process to ensure that decisions about closing bases would be made on need and cost justifications rather than on political grounds. Congressman Dick Armey (R-TX) called attention to this problem in 1988: "The fact is, unfortunate as it is, that historically base closings have been used as a point of leverage by administrations, Republican and Democratic administrations, as political leverage over and above Members of Congress to encourage them to vote in a manner that the administration would like" (Lockwood and Siehl, 2004, p. 2). The other problem the new process sought to avoid was the slow process of law making in Congress. Under normal committee review and typical House and Senate rules, legislative amendments could allow powerful lawmakers or coalitions to influence the decision on which military bases to close or keep open. Under the BRAC law, an independent commission appointed by the president, with the advice and consent of the Senate, considers the facts obtained from the military and other interested parties, including from public hearings, and then makes recommendations on which military bases to close or reorganize. Both the president and the Congress have to make quick decisions on whether to proceed with the recommendations. Congress faces an up-or-down vote on the commission's recommendations without amendment. These votes are politically damaging when home-state bases or favored activities are on the closure list, so the process is not totally immune from presidential and congressional influence. For the most part, however, the BRAC process has worked to pare down the number of military bases in the United States and realign them to meet the military's missions.

President George W. Bush proposed a similar model for the rest of the budget. Under that concept, an independent commission would review existing programs and departments against their results (a "results commission") and recommend restructuring and consolidation of programs. The proposal would commit the president and Congress to a fast-track, no-amendment vote.

States look at the success of the BRAC model in crafting their own solutions for politically difficult budget issues. For example, the State of Kansas created a commission to decide which state mental health hospitals to close and, based upon its 1996 recommendations, the legislature accepted the commission's identification of particular hospitals to close. This success bred other applications. The independent-commission model has been proposed in Kansas to (1) ease the vote on difficult issues, including a reduction in the number of local governments (even school districts) in Kansas; and (2) review the entire state budget and come up with recommendations for budget cuts. In 2009, Kansas Governor Kathleen Sebelius resurrected the closure commission model to revisit the remaining social service facilities, an announcement made just before she was announced and later confirmed as President Obama's Secretary of Health and Human Services.

New York State liked the BRAC model, too. In 2005, Governor George E. Pataki and the state legislature formed the Commission on Health Care Facilities in the 21st Century to reconfigure the state's health care system with particular attention to state hospitals and county-owned nursing homes. The commission's recommendations in November 2006 had to be treated as a whole by the legislature

(Perez-Pena, 2006). A similar approach for paring back the number of prisons was proposed by the succeeding governor (Confessore, 2007).

A different mechanism is a sunset commission, used by some states, but not the federal government. This mechanism automatically ends the life of an agency after a fixed number of years. An independent commission reviews the agency before the end of its fixed term. The agency terminates automatically unless a vote is taken to extend its life. An example is the Texas Sunset Advisory Commission, which was created in 1977. According to its Web site (www.sunset.state.tx.us), this commission "questions the need for each agency, looks for potential duplication of other public services or programs, and considers new and innovative changes to improve each agency's operations and activities."

Thinking It Over

1. What are the political advantages of these types of mechanisms to frame solutions to hard budget choices?
2. Would you support a BRAC- or sunset-type independent commission to help deal with the federal budget deficit?
3. Is it a good idea in a democracy to use automatic mechanisms so that elected representatives can dodge the vote and the heat?

WEB SITE RESOURCES

- California Dreamin': Tools of Direct Democracy
- Chronology of Federal Budgeting
- Fiscal Year
- Further Resources
- Internet Resources
- The Paradox of Efficiency
- Using the Gross Domestic Product to Measure the Role and Size of Government

REVIEW QUESTIONS

1. What is the difference between a hard and a soft fiscal rule? How does each affect the politics of the budgetary process?
2. What does it mean that the budget is balanced?
   a. Why might a budget that was balanced when it was originally adopted by the legislature actually end up generating a budget surplus at the end of the year?
   b. What can be wrong with balancing the budget on a "whistle and a prayer," if the goal is to pass a budget so spending can start and a shutdown avoided?
   c. If a significant tax cut is assumed to foster strong economic growth a few years out, is it acceptable for public officials to vote for a deficit budget this year? Why or why not?
   d. Look at the most recently adopted budget for your state's capital city. Is the budget balanced? How do you know? Use the budget message and other

sources as needed to identify one hard and one soft rule that guides decision making about the budget.

3. Do you consider debt a (negative) four-letter word? Why worry about a high debt-to-GDP ratio? What are the parallels to an individual's financial situation?

4. Why do public leaders typically adopt a strategy of cutting spending when faced with a budget shortfall?

5. Why is it politically and financially important to make spending and revenue decisions so that a balanced budget is sustainable in the long run?

6

⚜

Spending Public Resources

This chapter answers six questions:

- How Much Are We Spending?
- Why Is Some Federal Spending Kept Secret?
- What Is the Cost of the "War on Terror"?
- What Does Counterterrorism Cost?
- What Are We Getting for the Money?
- Why Do Budgets Grow?

> That most delicious of all privileges—spending other people's money.
>
> JOHN RANDOLPH (1773–1833, MEMBER OF CONGRESS)

> A billion here, a billion there, and pretty soon you're talking about real money.
>
> ATTRIBUTED (PROBABLY FALSELY) TO
> ILLINOIS SENATOR EVERETT DIRKSEN (1896–1969)

How much should we spend, and on what, and for whom should we spend it? With government alone weighing in at about one-third the U.S. economy, these questions have concrete, important consequences on Main Street, Wall Street, and Pennsylvania Avenue. Our key political processes provide the answers to these core political questions.

How public resources are spent tells us *what* and *how much* citizens, taxpayers, and public leaders think public organizations should do. V.O. Key, Jr. posed *the* question about public spending in 1940: "On what basis shall it be decided to allocate X dollars to activity A instead of activity B?" Some may like answers that use ideas such as efficiency, marginal utility, opportunity costs, or performance measures. But, at the end of his essay, Key told us that spending choices reflect political philosophy. His answer was correct then and is still right. Spending choices are political judgments that help define our society and political life. They also help shape our future (see the Web site resource, How Public Spending Helps Define Us and Our Future: The Story of Hurricane Katrina).

Public spending serves four main purposes: (1) to finance operations, (2) to assign public resources to different uses, (3) to implement **fiscal policy**, and (4) to redistribute resources. First, public expenditures pay for public programs and services, and for the equipment and personnel involved in these operations. Second, public resources are divided among different uses (or functions, such as defense, education, health, and others). The pattern of the division is a statement in dollars of public priorities. In speeches, press releases, and budget messages, political leaders explain their spending proposals in terms of their political agenda. Because spending choices have political content, both leaders and the public pay close attention.

The third purpose of public spending is to help form fiscal policy, associated with the economist John Maynard Keynes (and his *The General Theory of Employment, Interest and Money*, first published in 1936). Basically, Keynesian theory is taken to mean that the government's revenues and expenditures, including its surplus and deficit positions, can influence the overall economy. High employment is the top goal because when people have jobs they demand goods and services, and so jobs are created to make these products and provide these services. Instead of flexing their taxing and spending power to influence the economy, national leaders since World War II for the most part emphasized instead the need to reduce the influence of government on private economic activity. The focus was on lowering taxes, reducing the role of government, and encouraging investment. Federal deficit reduction became the mantra until September 11, 2001, when the political and, therefore, the budget scenario changed. Deficits climbed as a direct result of the nation's reaction to the terrorist attacks coupled with the Bush Administration's tax cuts. When signs appeared of a slowdown in the economy and unemployment started rising, Washington returned to fiscal policy by issuing **tax rebates** in the winter of 2008. As the deepening global recession took hold, leaders in China, France, Italy, Britain, Spain, and the United States turned to **fiscal stimulus** packages in 2008 and 2009. This strategy uses massive public spending programs to upgrade and build bridges, roads, power plants, pipelines, and more in order to jump-start the economy by creating jobs and pouring public resources into the economy. Using spending rather than tax cuts and/or rebates, and using government programs rather than private business to quicken the economy does not enjoy universal approval among economists and is opposed by some conservative analysts and decision makers (see figure 6.1).

Tax Rebate—a refund of a portion of the amount of taxes paid.

Stimulus—an effort by the government to spur certain economic activity.

Fiscal Policy—a government's policies on revenues, spending, and debt anagement as these relate to government services, programs and capital investment; using government's revenues and expenditures, including its surplus and deficit positions, to influence the overall economy.

The fourth purpose of spending is to *re*distribute resources among segments of the population, geographic regions, and economic activities. In the Great Depression, U.S. Senator Huey Long from Louisiana captured a lot of national attention with his call to adjust wealth and income by what he termed "share the wealth." Although well short of his extreme position, governments do use tax and spend power to influence who gets what. Some spending policies benefit a particular group of people while costs are spread more broadly. A prime example

Figure 6.1A. Tax-Based Approaches to Fiscal Policy

President Reagan addresses the nation from the oval office on tax reduction legislation, July 27, 1981.

Reprinted by permission. Ronald Reagan Presidential Foundation and Library.

Figure 6.1B. Tax-Based Approaches to Fiscal Policy

Using "Tax Rebates" to Stimulate the Economy in 2008.

AP Photo/Susan Walsh.

Figure 6.1C. Tax-Based Approaches to Fiscal Policy
Opposition to President Obama's stimulus package in January 2009.
Reprinted by permission of The Cato Institute.

is **pork barrel** projects that benefit a single community or industry. Programs such as Medicaid redistribute resources from high-income earners to the poor and Social Security from taxpayers of working age to retirees. Governments in the United States and other countries spend an enormous amount of money each year to help their residents improve their human capital, from pre-kindergarten

Pork Barrel Politics—politics surrounding spending designed to support incumbents' reelection by letting them direct spending such as capital projects or grants to their districts, usually through the tacit agreement among legislators to support public spending in each others' districts.

programs to doctoral programs at research universities. This is redistribution in action: helping individuals earn higher income in the long run by spending tax money today.

Redistribution also is embedded in tax policy. Who pays? That question alone implies that some do and some do not. Although too much redistribution can skew self-interest, there is no known dividing line between too little and too much. The payoffs of public budgeting add up politically to who and what gives and gets.

What shapes spending and what drives it? Spending and program decisions are affected by what is going on within the programs; these are micro-factors, such as the perceived quality of services delivered and the way each unit of service is actually produced and its cost. Developments in the socio-economic and political environment also affect spending; these macro-factors include demographic change, economic conditions, public preferences, natural disasters, war, and level of economic development (see box 6.1). Some macro-factors, such as the 2008 global recession, may shock the system and affect spending at every level of government and throughout the economy.

Decision making about spending begins with a political eye on likely revenues. Bouncing off each other, spending and revenue decisions are made at the same time, and each affects the other as the budget's balance is adjusted. As a matter of fact, every budget cycle begins with the same problem: how do we fund the gap between available revenues and all the political demands and public needs to which resources could be directed? If spending is shaped first and foremost by the pressure of scarcity, what causes public budgets to grow?

HOW MUCH ARE WE SPENDING?

Total government current spending was almost $4.5 trillion early in the twenty-first century, or more than $15,000 for every person living in the United States. This is about one-third of the gross domestic product (GDP), a measure of the size of the economy. On the eve of the New Deal, states and local governments were spending more than twice what the federal government was spending. Within less than eighty years, the relative weights had reversed and the federal government was spending 60 percent of all government spending (see table 6.1). Federal spending rose from less than 3 percent of the GDP in 1929 to more than 20 percent of the GDP in fiscal 2006. The sweep of the historical pattern is plain, and more recent data that show federal stimulus and recovery spending and state and local spending cuts would just amplify the trend.

Measuring Spending
There are a lot of zeroes in a trillion dollars, twelve to be exact. What does all this money mean? (See box 6.2.) A simple count of the dollars does not tell us what even Goldilocks knew: is this too big, too little, or just about right? Is a program change affordable? Are the totals responsible or excessive? What do decision makers such as legislators, analysts, and taxpayers think about?

===== **BOX 6.1** =====

A Comparative Look at Government Spending

On the average, spending by the central government in developed countries accounts for less of the country's GDP than does spending in developing countries (see table box 6.1). This pattern reflects a stronger private sector. Characterized by a higher GDP, developed countries on the average spend a higher percentage of their GDP on "modern state functions" such as health and social services than do developing countries. The patterns for defense and education shown in the table box 6.1 deserve some thought.

Table Box 6.1. Central Government Expenditure by Function, 1990–2002

	COMPLETE SAMPLE	DEVELOPED	TRANSITION	DEVELOPING
Traditional State Functions	5.3	3.9	3.8	6.1
G. administration and public order	2.9	2.1	1.9	3.4
Defense	2.4	1.8	1.9	2.7
Modern State Functions	17.8	25.0	22.1	14.5
Education	3.6	2.9	2.5	4.1
Health	2.5	3.8	3.1	2.0
Other social services	7.4	14.9	12.4	3.9
Economic Services	4.3	3.5	4.1	4.5
Interest Payments	3.0	3.4	2.4	3.0
Other Expenditure	2.1	2.6	3.0	1.7
Number of Countries	111	21	19	71

NOTE: Percent of GDP, domestic prices, simple averages.

_____

Reprinted by permission. United Nations Online Network in Public Administration and Finance, n.d., Table 4.b.

Usually decision makers consider first the impact of spending on taxes and other own-source revenues, and then think about spending in relation to (1) internal dynamics, such as **percent change** and **growth rate**; (2) external developments, including changing prices, economic growth, socio-economic change;

_____

Percent Change—change in a data series from the initial value expressed as a fraction of 100; calculated as [(newer number minus older number)/older number) times 100] to convert to a percent.

Growth Rate—a constant percentage rate at which a data series would grow or contract on a yearly basis to reach its current value (formally known as the compound annual growth rate).

Table 6.2. U.S. Government Spending, Fiscal 1929 and Fiscal 2006*

	FY 1929				FY 2006				1929–2006
	BILLIONS $	% GDP	PER CAPITA	% OF TOTAL	BILLIONS $	% GDP	PER CAPITA	% OF TOTAL	COMPOUND ANNUAL GROWTH RATE
State & Local	$5.6	5.4%	$45	68%	$1,784.4	13.5%	$6,016	40%	7.8%
Federal	$2.6	2.5%	$21	32%	$2,692.2	20.3%	$9,076	60%	9.5%
Population (in 1,000s)	1930 123,203				2005 296,639				

* The figures here are estimates only. Sources round to different figures (trillions, millions, thousands) and calculations here introduce further rounding errors; the 2006 data are estimates; and the population figures are for calendar years 1930 and 2005.

SOURCE: Calculated from Bureau of Economic Analysis, 2006 and the Census Bureau, 2006.

BOX 6.2

What Does the Money Mean?

What did Tom Cruise have to say about money in the 1996 film, *Jerry Maguire*?

"All sorts of things have been used as money at different times in different places.…*Amber, beads, cowries, drums, eggs, feathers, gongs, hoes, ivory, jade, kettles, leather, mats, nails, oxen, pigs, quartz, rice, salt, thimbles…vodka, wampum, yarns, and zappozats (decorated axes)*" (Davies, 2002, p. 27).

Figure Box 6.2. 20 Shillings, First Government-Issued Paper Money, Issued by the Massachusetts Bay Colony in 1690

SOURCE: National Numismatic Collection, Smithsonian Institution.

and (3) political factors, such as citizen preferences. The different questions decision makers and citizens ask prompt different ways of thinking about spending that highlight different political goals and interests.

To understand spending, we give the simple number of dollars meaning by comparing the number to other things, such as the size of the economy, population, and total spending. These comparisons give different views of what the dollars mean. Because no single measure tells the whole story or answers all the questions, current best practice among professional budgeters is to use several different budgetary measures. For example, OMB's historical tables on the federal budget show major areas of government spending—such as defense, human resources, and interest on the debt since 1940—in millions of dollars, as a percentage of total outlays, and as a percentage of GDP.

Think of examining spending as looking at a slide under a microscope. Each cut into the subject and each level of magnification gives us a different view of reality. One general category of information is whether spending is looked at through the lens of internal dynamics or external developments—what is happening beyond or external to the service. Another general category is how a particular factor affects spending. Some changes, such as changing prices, affect spending directly; other effects may be indirect, but even roundabout influences may be costly.

The impact of different factors on a budget depends on the level of government and the type of service under the microscope.

Internal Dynamics: Percent Change and Rate of Growth

It is common practice to compare spending today with spending in the past by showing dollar change, percent change, or growth rate. We make this comparison when we say, for example, the increase in general-fund spending by the states is estimated at 1 percent for FY 2009, compared to more than 5 percent in FY 2008, and that the last two budget rounds kept state spending increases below the historical average of 6.7 percent over more than three decades (NGA and NASBO, 2008, pp. vii, 3). This example uses the states' own history as the standard for comparison. The change may be expressed in dollars in a budget or as percent change in an explanation. Either way, the effect is to draw attention to the increase or decrease.

External Developments

Budgeting and governments' financial performance do not take place in a bubble protected from the outside world. On the contrary, budgeting is deeply affected by external circumstances. Natural disasters, such as Hurricane Katrina, are one example, and war is another. Other developments affecting budgeting include changing prices, economic change, social change, and political change.

Changing Prices. Decision makers consider changes in the dollar's value over time because prices of programs and services change. The dollars spent today (**current** or **nominal dollars**) are worth what the dollars actually can buy (**real** or **constant dollars**). It is important to think about changes in the purchasing power of the dollar when comparing spending over time.

In February 2008, President George W. Bush submitted his $3.1 trillion budget proposal for FY 2009 to Congress. In 1901, the federal budget stood at $525 million (OMB, 2007, p. 21). To understand what these figures mean, we turn to **price indexes** such as the **Consumer Price Index** (CPI) to determine the impact of changing prices (see the Web site resource, Using the CPI). Converting current dollars into a constant dollar value compensates for the effects of **inflation** and allows meaningful comparisons between periods.

Inflation or the threat of inflation has been and remains a central concern with heavy political content. A historical example is that inflation is "credited" with helping to bring down the Weimar Republic and usher in Nazi Germany. Along with economic stability and employment, inflation concerns underlay monetary policy, meaning what the Federal Reserve does as the central bank to influence the availability and cost of money and credit. In 1913, Congress delegated its power of coinage and the money supply to the Board of Governors of the Federal Reserve Bank through the Federal Reserve Act. The Federal Reserve System is responsible for establishing and implementing monetary policy. In inflationary periods, the purchasing power of the dollar declines, the purchasing power of fixed revenues declines, and prices of goods and services rise. When, as in 2008, the availability of **credit** evaporated for even good borrowers, the Federal Reserve stepped in to prevent severe financial problems, thereby forestalling the collapse of prices caused by no one buying anything (a **depression**). No economic actor, public or private, can plan for the future, if he or she are whipsawed by inflation or deflation, and the inability to borrow money at reasonable rates. As a result, monetary policy is very important to budgeting.

Economic Change. Changing macroeconomic conditions affect budgeting (as shown in the Web site video on the effects of the economic downturn on Boston's budget).

Current Dollars—a count of the number of dollars without paying attention to how much they are worth or their purchasing power.

Real Dollars—when monetary values are adjusted for changes in the value or purchasing power of the dollar.

Price Index—a statistical manner of tracking prices over time to determine the impact of inflation.

Consumer Price Index (CPI)—a statistical description of price levels provided by the U.S. Department of Labor; the index is used as a measure of the increase in the cost of living.

Inflation—decreasing purchasing power of the dollar; the overall general upward price movement of goods and services in an economy.

Credit—money lent with expectation of being paid back (with interest) in the future.

Depression—an economic event with severe reductions in employment, personal income and gross domestic product that resets the economy at a lower level for an extended period.

Some affect the budget directly; changing interest rates affect investment income and the cost of borrowing. Other changes in macroeconomic conditions affect budgets indirectly; for example, rising unemployment affects revenues by affecting the ability of residents to pay their property taxes. Both direct and indirect impacts are different at different levels of government and for different programs and revenue sources.

When the economy softens and people lose or cannot find jobs, demand rises for publicly financed social services. The costs of certain programs go up, as more people are eligible and more apply for benefits; unemployment compensation and income-related or means-based entitlements such as Medicaid are examples. The cruel reality is that, at the same time, revenue declines from taxes sensitive to economic conditions such as the income tax, payroll tax, and sales tax. Rising unemployment and falling personal income may mean that people have a hard time paying their property taxes and mortgage payments, with the result that foreclosures increase and the collection rate for property taxes falls (see box 6.3).

The opposite effects are expected during periods of economic expansion. When employment increases, revenue rises from income tax, payroll tax, and sales tax. By pushing up revenues without a change in tax rates, a strong economy generates politically-free revenue increases. In inflationary periods, the purchasing power of the dollar declines, but rising wages boost tax revenues. On the other hand, the costs of labor, goods, and equipment increase, and therefore the cost of providing public programs increases. As inflation pushes higher the program benefits adjusted for the **cost of living (COLAs)**, the costs of programs such as Social Security increase. The increase of 5.8 percent in Social Security benefits in 2009, the largest increase in almost three decades, meant approximately $100 more a month for the average retired couple.

Economic conditions affect initial revenue projections and expenditure estimates, and changing conditions contribute to departures from the adopted budget. Because economic conditions affect a government's financial performance as well as residents' economic well-being, an economic report often accompanies or supplements budget analyses. According to the National Association of State Budget Officers, thirty-eight states include economic analysis in the budget. Kansas law, for example, requires an annual economic and demographic report to accompany the governor's yearly budget submission. At the federal level, the annual *Economic Report of the President*, written by the chairman of the Council of Economic Advisors, is transmitted to Congress no later than ten days after the president's budget is submitted. The Congressional Budget Act of 1974 requires the Congressional Budget Office, a nonpartisan professional office in Congress, to submit reports about fiscal policy to the Committees on the Budget.

The broadest indicator of economic output is the gross domestic product (GDP), the most widely used indicator of a country's economic well-being. Its change over time reflects the pace of economic growth. Thinking about spending

---

Cost of Living Adjustment (COLA)—an adjustment in pay or benefit levels to cover the impact of inflation.

BOX 6.3

How Do Falling Housing Prices Affect Local Budgeting?

After almost doubling since 2000, home prices peaked in mid-2006, and then started to decline. From the peak of the housing market in 2006 through the end of 2008, home values declined by $6.1 trillion. About 12 million or nearly one out of every six homeowners had negative equity (meaning that their mortgages were higher than the house was worth) by the close of 2008*, the year that the Concise Oxford English Dictionary added *subprime* and *credit crunch* to its dictionary.

Homeowners with mortgages more than the value of their house could no longer use home-equity loans to bail them out of mounting credit card debt, and many faced the prospect of paying their mortgage and property taxes late or not at all. If they can neither make their payments nor refinance the loan, then they face the prospect of foreclosure.** Real estate foreclosures in the United States rose 75 percent in 2007, to an average rate of more than 1 percent of all households. By the end of 2008, 2.8 percent of all U.S. mortgages were in foreclosure, with Florida, California, and Nevada taking the lead (Heffley and Lenon, 2009, p. 9).

Foreclosures affect local budgeting in several ways (see figure box 6.3):

- The collection of local property taxes may be delayed while properties are tied up in foreclosure. Some properties may be abandoned and owed taxes accumulate. Although the taxes will be paid sometime in the future, the revenue is not available to support current programs and services. The result is that spending and services must be cut or taxes on other properties must be increased.

- Housing values fall in areas with many foreclosed properties. The result is a lower tax base to support the local government. Property taxes provide more than 70 percent of local governments' revenue.

- Falling housing values reduce people's net worth and sense of financial well-being, which may affect charitable donations. The result is reduced revenues for local charities and nonprofit agencies.

- With a reduced tax base, governments may reduce subsidies to or service contracts with local nonprofit agencies. This puts further pressure on local charities and nonprofit agencies.

- Personal financial pressures may increase the demand for local services such as school medical and nutrition programs, shelters, food pantries, and soup kitchens.

* Double this number owns the home free and clear, without a mortgage.

** The Economic Report of the President defines foreclosure as a "legal process in which a lender seeks recovery of collateral from a borrower (in the case of home mortgages, the home itself is the collateral), with several possible outcomes, including that the borrower sells the property or the lender repossesses the home. Foreclosure laws are based on the statutes of each [s]tate" (Council of Economic Advisors, 2008, p. 54).

- Foreclosures put pressure on rental housing in the area; increased rents may push out lower-income residents, effectively exporting pressures to other communities.

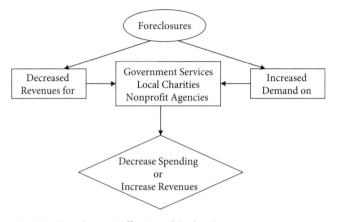

Figure Box 6.3. Foreclosures Affect Local Budgeting.

See the Web site video, City of Boston, Ways & Means Committee, on the effect of the economic downturn on the FY09 City of Boston budget.

in proportion to economic activity suggests the relative priority in society for a particular use of governmental resources (see Web site resource, Using the Gross Domestic Product).

Looking at the relative priority of a particular use of resources suggests that it is possible to imagine other uses. These other uses with their other benefits are called **opportunity costs** (see Web site resource, Analyzing the Costs of Public Programs). This is what Benjamin Franklin was talking about when he wrote in 1783, "What vast additions to the conveniences and comforts of living might mankind have acquired, if the money spent in wars had been employed in works of public utility."

Comparing spending to the GDP considers the alternative uses of all resources, but decision makers can allocate only the resources available to them. Public budgeting concerns public resources only. This point is illustrated by spending on national defense, which was somewhat more than 4 percent of the GDP in 2008, but did not include spending on security in the private sector, which some estimate was more than double the public budgets of all law enforcement agencies in

Opportunity cost—what must be given up in order to have something else.

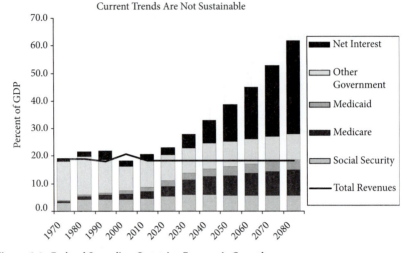

Figure 6.4. Federal Spending Outstrips Economic Growth
Government Accountability Office, 2009, p. 7.

the United States. An opposite illustration is spending on health care that includes all spending, both public and private. According to the Department of Health and Human Services, spending on health totaled $2.2 trillion in 2007, or one-sixth of the U.S. national economy.

Spending priorities that are either different from policymakers' preferences, or possibilities that are unrealistic in political or financial terms represent a call to action. The projected growth of entitlements is a case in point; it is widely understood in Washington that the current path is unsustainable and threatens the country's long-term prosperity and strength (see figure 6.4).

It also is useful to compare state and local spending to the size of the economy. Average state spending is somewhat volatile because it is affected by changing economic conditions. Average state spending measured as a percent of the GDP initially increased in the twenty-first century, but then declined to below its average in the 1990s.

Social Change. Between 2000 and 2005, the U.S. population grew by more than 15 million, or almost four times what the entire population was in 1790. Little wonder, then, that government is spending more money. Spending per person (or per capita) helps decision makers get a handle on spending relative to the residential population (see table 6.1).

Measuring spending relative to the population is common, but may be misleading and so misdirect decision makers. Spending is related to legal residents counted in the census, but they are not necessarily the only or main service recipients or the only taxpayers. What about commercial and industrial taxpayers, commuters, and tourists needing services? In many cities, such as vacation resorts and metropolitan centers, the population count does not match service demand and does not address ability to pay or tax effort.

A Slice of the Pie

Where public resources go is often expressed as a pie divided into slices of the total budget devoted to activities or programs. **Budget share** directs our attention to the activity's relative priority *within the public organization*. For example, state and local spending now is more than $2.5 trillion. Primary and secondary education and higher education account for more than one-third and public welfare represents almost one-fifth of all state and local spending. Federal spending has changed a good deal over the last forty years as well (see figure 6.5).

Changes in budget share show shifts in public or governmental priorities. As useful and widespread as it is, this perspective says nothing at all about the size or growth of the budget or economy. It ignores efficiency, effectiveness, and changes in demand and need.

Cost Structure Makes a Difference

The building blocks of spending for one program are not necessarily the same as they are for another. The costs of different activities are likely to be quite different, and precisely where the dollar goes is driven by each program's **cost structure**. Some programs are affected by changes in prices; the price of gasoline for police vehicles and heating oil for homeless shelters fluctuates in a sometimes-volatile market. Road-building costs reflect commodity prices for concrete and asphalt (tied to oil prices) as well as labor costs. The Defense Department, for its part, spends an additional $130 million when the price of fuel goes up by $1 (Barr, 2008, p. D01).

Workforce and Payroll

A service is termed labor-intensive when most of the spending goes to pay workers' salaries, wages, and employee benefits. Knowing whether a service is labor-intensive is important because the relationship between labor costs and the amount and quality of services is inescapable: significant cuts in labor-intensive services mean layoffs and vice versa: **layoffs** translate into service cuts.

More than half of all state and local spending is on education and public safety. Here are the teachers, firefighters, police, and corrections officers. Employing more than one-tenth of the national civilian workforce, state and local governments employ two-thirds of all government employees and are responsible for almost three-fifths of the total government payroll. State and local government

---

Budget Share—a calculated percent of the total budget, often represented as a budget pie.

Cost Structure—a focus on compiling, processing and using cost information; covers both pricing of services and charging for their provision; addresses the planning and implementing of a costing system and the management decisions.

Layoff—a mandatory temporary separation from a job.

State and Local Spending, FY 2006

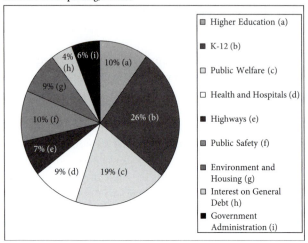

Figure 6.5A. A Slice of the Pie

NOTE: Spending is as percentage of direct expenditures. Capital outlays are excluded. Public safety includes police, fire, corrections, and protective inspection and regulation. Environment and housing includes natural resources, parks and recreation, housing and community development, sewerage, and solid waste management.

SOURCE: Compiled from U.S. Census Bureau, 2008, Table 1.

CHANGING COMPOSITION OF SPENDING

Federal spending is divided into five major components: net interest, Social Security, Medicare and Medicaid, national defense, and everything else.

COMPOSITION OF FEDERAL SPENDING (% OF TOTAL SPENDING)

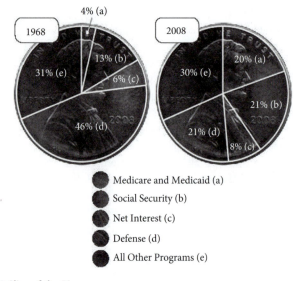

Figure 6.5B. A Slice of the Pie

Reprinted by permission. Peter G. Peterson Foundation, 2009.

employment has increased by more than 2.5 million since 1990. The public's clamor for labor-intensive services, such as education and public safety, translates over the long haul into governments' growing labor force.

Total civilian government employment is more than 22 million, as figure 6.6 shows. The federal government employs about 2 percent of the national civilian workforce of 137 million, compared to the states at 3.4 percent. As an employer, local government is almost twice the size of the federal and state governments combined.

Another key factor in the public sector workforce is that wages and occupational mix differ from the private sector (see Web site resource, You Can Pay Me Now or Let Them Pay Me Later). While two-thirds of public sector jobs are professional and administrative (such as teachers, police officers, social workers, and public health officers), these types of positions represent only about half of the private sector. In general, the public sector overpays low-skilled workers but underpays high-skilled ones.

Of course there are wide variations among the states and local governments in their pay and employee benefit packages. Whatever they do pay is usually public information. Because labor costs are typically the single largest part of local spending, effective local budget management in local government translates into effective workforce management.

Employee Benefits and Unpaid Bills

Labor costs affect more than the current payroll. It is more common for state and local governments to provide more generous benefits to employees than the private sector. The cost of employee benefits in state and local governments averages over $12 per hour, or almost one-third of the total cost of labor, according to the Bureau of Labor Statistics. Benefits include insurance; paid leave, such as vacations, holidays, sick leave, personal leave, military leave, and funeral leave; retirement and Social Security; Medicare, unemployment insurance, workers' compensation, and more. The single most costly benefit is health insurance.

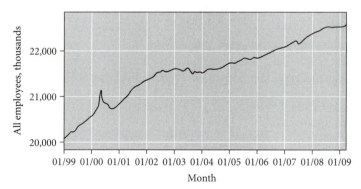

Figure 6.6. Total Government Employment, 1999–2009
U.S. Bureau of Labor Statistics, 2009.

What we are *not* spending is also related in part to labor costs. Unfunded **liabilities** amount to future bills for costs acquired but not yet paid. These obligations can build up over time to massive sums and promise future trouble. The trouble did not wait for San Diego. In 2003, a scandal over city employees' pensions triggered lawsuits, criminal indictments, and the mayor's resignation (see chapter 5). The trouble is now a time bomb, and the ticking can be heard across the country. State and local governments owe current and future retirees about $400 billion more than is in their pension funds and are about $1.5 trillion short of their commitments to retirees' health care. The median level of funding for state employees and teachers' retirement is only 83 percent of the sound or **actuarial** level, according to the National Association of State Retirement Administrators' Public Fund Survey for FY 2007.

WHY IS SOME FEDERAL SPENDING KEPT SECRET?

Transparency and accountability in a democracy mean that the budget should be public and openly debated. This openness is tempered by the need to preserve and protect the country, which may require keeping secret sensitive matters of national security. Keeping this information from one's enemies means for all practical purposes keeping it hidden from nearly every citizen as well.

The budget for sensitive national security spending traditionally is secret. In his confidential message to Congress in 1803, President Thomas Jefferson asked for an appropriation of $2,500 for the Lewis and Clark expedition (see figure 6.7). The existence, cost, and pace of development of the Manhattan Project's atom bomb during World War II were secret; President Roosevelt forbade a Senate committee investigating the war's costs to question the high spending or to learn what the project was about (Cooke, p. 350). Like the atom bomb, some development and purchasing of weapons and certain intelligence activities are secret today. This secret spending is called the **black budget**; it is blacked out because it is classified information.

Details on classified weapons and research projects are not made public, so their costs are unknown, and even the totals for intelligence spending is secret. Intelligence spending usually has been secret since the late 1940s, the early years of the Cold War. Members of the two congressional intelligence committees (established in the 1970s) can see the figures in the classified documents that go along with authorization bills, but the rules of the House and Senate prohibit members from revealing classified information. The U.S. intelligence community involves numerous agencies (for example, the Central Intelligence Agency and the Defense

---

Liability—amounts owed.

Actuarial—the present value of future cash flows, as in today's value of the future payments of a pension obligation.

Black Budget—spending on national security that is kept a secret because the information is classified.

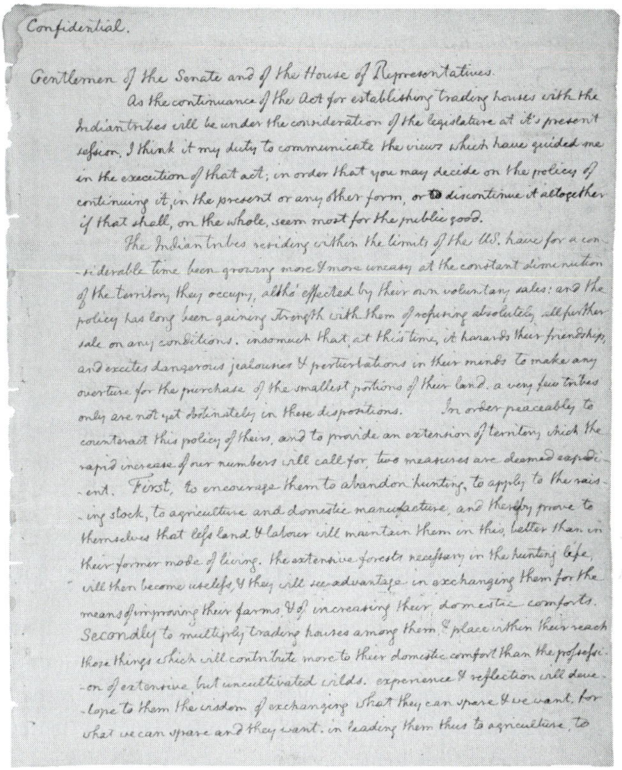

Confidential.

Gentlemen of the Senate and of the House of Representatives.

As the continuance of the Act for establishing trading houses with the Indian tribes will be under the consideration of the legislature at it's present session, I think it my duty to communicate the views which have guided me in the execution of that act; in order that you may decide on the policy of continuing it, in the present or any other form, or discontinue it altogether if that shall, on the whole, seem most for the public good.

The Indian tribes residing within the limits of the US. have for a considerable time been growing more & more uneasy at the constant diminution of the territory they occupy, altho' effected by their own voluntary sales: and the policy has long been gaining strength with them of refusing absolutely all further sale on any conditions. insomuch that, at this time, it hazards their friendship, and excites dangerous jealousies & perturbations in their minds to make any overture for the purchase of the smallest portions of their land. a very few tribes only are not yet obstinately in these dispositions. In order peaceably to counteract this policy of theirs, and to provide an extension of territory which the rapid increase of our numbers will call for, two measures are deemed expedient. First, to encourage them to abandon hunting, to apply to the raising stock, to agriculture and domestic manufacture, and thereby prove to themselves that less land & labour will maintain them in this, better than in their former mode of living. the extensive forests necessary in the hunting life, will then become useless, & they will see advantage in exchanging them for the means of improving their farms, & of increasing their domestic comforts. Secondly to multiply trading houses among them, & place within their reach those things which will contribute more to their domestic comfort than the possession of extensive, but uncultivated wilds. experience & reflection will develope to them the wisdom of exchanging what they can spare & we want, for what we can spare and they want. in leading them thus to agriculture, to

Figure 6.7. A Tradition of Secrecy

First page of confidential letter from President Thomas Jefferson to Congress, 1803.

SOURCE: National Archives and Records Administration (NARA).

Intelligence Agency) whose programs and staff are largely—but not necessarily wholly—tucked within the Defense Department's large budget.

The secrecy meant to protect the country also means that it is difficult to piece the whole picture together to get some sense of the size of the black budget. An intelligence official revealed that the total amount spent on intelligence in 2005 was \$44 billion. This figure was last made public in 1998, when spending on intelligence totaled almost \$27 billion (Shane, 2005). Simple arithmetic tells us that spending on intelligence increased more than 60 percent in seven years. One estimate puts the black budget for weapons purchasing, research, and development at \$34 billion in FY 2009 (Kosiak, 2008). Including war-related funding in the 2008 supplemental appropriations pushes the figure higher.

The arguments for and against secrecy swirl around five central issues (Best and Bazan, 2007). These are

1. the constitutional requirement for public reports on spending,
2. the value of open political discussion,

3. the risk of revealing potentially harmful information to opponents,
4. the risk of revealing details when aggregate figures are discussed,
5. the loss of executive and congressional scrutiny when information is classified.

The fifth concern on the list hints that secrecy protects the bureaucracy from public criticism as well as the country from its adversaries. So, add the issue of bureaucratic insulation to the list of concerns. Another issue is the temptation to use the black budget to hide spending that is not directly related to national security, such as an earmark for a representative's home district.

When the environment is seen as threatening, the balance among an open society, government transparency, and national security readily tilts toward secrecy. Yet, the relationship between secrecy in budgeting and national security is not clear-cut. The 9/11 Commission recommended in 2004 that the funding totals for national intelligence and its component agencies be made public as a way to *strengthen* national security.

WHAT IS THE COST OF THE "WAR ON TERROR"?

The question, "How much?" is asked about all policies and services throughout the public sector and under all administrations. Asking this question does not imply an answer to another question, whether the money is well spent or wasted. The answer to this second question is a political judgment, but the judgment cannot be informed without knowing the costs.

The Congressional Budget Office (CBO) answered the question about the cost of the "war on terror" before the Budget Committee of the House of Representatives in July 2007. From September 2001 through June 2007, funding for military operations and other defense activities in Iraq, Afghanistan, and other countries totaled $533 billion. Funding for diplomatic activities, economic support and war-related foreign aid, reconstruction, training and equipping indigenous forces, and U.S. veterans' benefits and services raises the war-related total to more than $602 billion, with the hostilities in Iraq accounting for more than 70 percent. Specifically war-related appropriations averaged about $93 billion a year in 2003 through 2005, rose to $120 billion in 2006 and then to $170 billion in 2007. In 2008, more than $12 billion per month supported operations in Iraq.

Regular and **emergency supplemental appropriations** have since added hundreds of billions of dollars to the total reported by CBO. A 2008 congressional report estimated the total cost of the Defense Department's military operations in the war on terror from 9/11 through the appropriations of June 30, 2008. The estimate excluded the costs of interest on war-related debt, reconstruction assistance, diplomatic security, veterans' benefits, and other activities by other agencies and

---

Emergency Supplemental Appropriation—an addition to the regularly adopted budget that is passed in response to or under rules applicable to unusual and unanticipated circumstances.

BOX 6.4

One Economist's View of the Costs of War

Economists think about cost as a part of the broader discussion of choice. People choose to spend their money in one way rather than another because the chosen way produces better benefits than the way not chosen. We forego certain opportunities in favor of others in order to obtain benefits that are better than others. This approach to costs means that not all costs are created equal.

It is particularly important to use the economic concept of cost rather than the accounting concept when evaluating the spending for a war....It also makes sense to evaluate ongoing defense or war fighting costs in terms of the benefits of security. Clearly, if the costs approximate the benefits, then such a dreadful thing as war has an economic justification. If not, then citizens will vote to end the conflict.

Reprinted by permission of the Heritage Foundation. Beach, William W., 2008.

---

is in terms of budget authority, not outlays. The cost in 2008 in current dollars exceeded $800 billion, or somewhat more than 1 percent of the nation's economy. World War II, by comparison, weighed in at almost 36 percent of the GDP. When long-term and indirect or associated costs, such as interest on the debt and veterans' education and health benefits are added, the costs of the "war on terror" reach into the trillions of dollars (Stiglitz and Bilmes, 2008).

To be fair to the men and women in the middle of these military operations, we remember the human costs and that not all the costs of war show up in the budget. Even the costs that are or will be in the budget are subject to different ideas about costs...and different views on war (see box 6.4).

WHAT DOES COUNTERTERRORISM COST?

Claiming almost 3,000 lives and costing about $85 billion, the attack on September 11, 2001 was the most deadly and costly international terrorist attack in U.S. history. This type of attack is classified as a low-probability, high-consequence event. This means that it happens rarely but, when it does, the costs are moderate-to-high in terms of deaths, casualties, infrastructure, short-term economic impact, confidence in the government's ability to protect its citizens, and government credibility at home and abroad.

Given that the human toll is far lower than automobile accidents, HIV, or malaria, some citizens, taxpayers, and political leaders think it is wise to ask how much the United States is spending on security and whether this is the way we should be using resources. Any politically useful answer must take into account the dreadful prospect of another type of low-probability, high-consequence event: a catastrophic attack with a chemical, biological, radiological, or nuclear weapon of mass destruction.

One consequence of 9/11 was that the United States redirected some public (and private) resources toward security. Likely critical targets such as water and power plants and communication and transport facilities are "hardened" to minimize the possibility and effects of an attack. Military installations and government buildings also are hardened. Security measures for computer systems and data storage translate into protecting financial systems, bank and land records, marriage and birth records, and much more. Disaster assessments and emergency response plans are drawn up, extended, and updated, while specialized emergency response teams are equipped and trained. All these and many more efforts are costly. Is this is the best way to spend public resources?

It is difficult to compute the overall cost of counterterrorism policy and programs.

> Most countries do not reveal how much is spent on some components of counterterrorism or homeland security, since it may be in a country's strategic interest to keep this information secret. This is particularly true of the intelligence budget. Even when this information is available, there is still the problem as to what counts and what does not count as counterterrorism actions. That is, does the US-led invasion of Afghanistan against the Taliban and al-Qaida count? Most researchers classify this war as a proactive response to a terrorist threat.... Moreover, homeland security involves many activities including control of immigration, inspection of imports, hardening of targets, gathering of intelligence, guarding of borders, security at airports, and other activities (Sandler, Arce, and Enders, 2008, pp. 29, 34, quoted by permission).

Not all security spending targets terrorism. Only a portion of DHS spending is aimed at countering terrorism. Homeland security includes programs aimed at natural and both natural and human disasters such as a hurricane, flood, wildfire, or an accidental spill of hazardous chemicals. Also, not all acts of violence are necessarily terrorism. For example, in its 2008 budget request, the Department of Homeland Security (DHS) requested an increase of $35.6 million for the protection of candidates and nominees during 2008 presidential campaign. In 2004, DHS related 66 percent of its total budget directly to terrorism-related activities.

The DHS budget does not tell the whole story, however. Thirty-two federal agencies, all states, and many local governments are involved in security activities. For example, the National Counterterrorism Center (http://www.nctc.gov) was created in 2004 and is staffed by the Central Intelligence Agency (CIA) and departments of Justice, State, Defense, Homeland Security, Energy, Treasury, Agriculture, Transportation, Health and Human Services, and others.

The estimated *increase* in federal and private sector spending on homeland security in the United States was almost $44 billion in 2005, or about 0.5 percent of the GDP. Spending by state and local governments is excluded from this estimate. A broader method, counting federal spending on homeland security, the wars in Afghanistan and Iraq, other related federal spending (such as some foreign aid), state and local spending on homeland security, and private sector spending

($10 billion), puts total U.S. spending at $92 billion, or still less than 1 percent of GDP each year since 9/11 (Sandler, Arce, and Enders, 2008).

> Government officials realize that a single terrorist incident—like 9/11—could result in [large losses]...If such losses are not weighted by the appropriately small likelihood, then overspending on security follows. People often over-respond to very low probability catastrophic events when compared with more certain events with small losses....But more deadly and damaging attacks in the future may eventually justify the high cost of defensive and proactive expenditures. Surely, this fear drives U.S. expenditure on homeland security and its global war on terrorism (Sandler, Arce, and Enders, 2008, pp. 43, 53, quoted by permission).

WHAT ARE WE GETTING FOR THE MONEY?

What do public resources accomplish when the budget is implemented? Are the policies put into action, and are the purposes met? Are resources wasted, or are operations efficient and effective? These questions highlight performance, accountability, and results. Best practices in budgeting call for performance measurement and evaluation (see Web site resource, Internet Resources, on best practices and on financial condition and performance measurement).

More than one-half of states' budgets and many local governments include performance, productivity, and/or effectiveness measures in the budget documents of some or most agencies (see figure 6.8). These measures may play a role in decisions about new or revised programs, or when service alternatives such as **contracting out** or **privatizing** are being considered. Measuring the performance of federal agencies has been on the agenda for almost a century, but recent steps have focused more attention on federal agency performance and measurement.

Public agencies must be especially careful to measure performance in a meaningful way. Decision makers, the media, and the public should be cautious when interpreting the results. Some measures base the evaluation on citizen assessments, which certainly are important. The problem is focus. Asking the public to evaluate performance in the abstract is a different matter from asking for an evaluation of specific services and actual experiences with public agencies. Abstract or general questions ask for citizen's political assessments and preferences. Chapter 3 argues that the people's general judgments about political satisfaction affect their view of specific budget outcomes. For these reasons, gauging performance should draw on different measures, including clearly targeted objective measures of output, efficiency, and effectiveness. Narrowly focused, objective measures help overcome the political thermometer effect, discussed in chapter 3.

Contracting out—an agreement by one government with a non-governmental unit or another government to carry out a function or provide a service that would otherwise be done by the contracting government.

Privatization—transferring the production and delivery of a service and/or operation and administration of a function formerly performed by government to a private entity.

Performance measures help determine the quality and cost efficiency of government services. They identify the results achieved and the benefits delivered to citizens and indicate how well government resources are being used. In addition to improving accountability to the public, performance measurement data can guide public officials in making resource allocation decisions and can aid organizational managers in program evaluations.

The following chart explains how performance measures work:

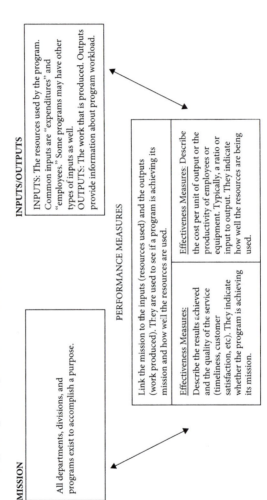

MISSION

All departments, divisions, and programs exist to accomplish a purpose.

INPUTS/OUTPUTS

INPUTS: The resources used by the program. Common inputs are "expenditures" and "employees." Some programs may have other types of inputs as well.
OUTPUTS: The work that is produced. Outputs provide information about program workload.

PERFORMANCE MEASURES

Link the mission to the inputs (resources used) and the outputs (work produced). They are used to see if a program is achieving its mission and how well the resources are used.

Effectiveness Measures: Describe the results achieved and the quality of the service (timeliness, customer satisfaction, etc). They indicate whether the program is achieving its mission.

Effectiveness Measures: Describe the cost per unit of output or the productivity of employees or equipment. Typically, a ratio or input to output. They indicate how well the resources are being used.

Although performance measures can indicate areas that may need attention, they will not identify the reason a program is performing that way or how it can be improved. In addition, data comparisons between units of government can be misleading since each jurisdiction will have unique methods of service delivery and data collection.

Figure 6.8A. Best Practices in Budgeting Include Performance Measurement

Performance Indicators for Raleigh, NC, Fiscal Year 2005–2006.

Reprinted by permission. Raleigh, City of, North Carolina.

Department: Community Services

   Division: Parks and Recreation Target Range

   Section: Parks and Recreation Target Range

Goal Statement:

To operate a safe, supervised, and non-threatening target range that encompasses all aspects of the shooting sports for recreational shooters, law enforcement and military.

Performance Measure	2009 Quarter 1	Prior Year Quarter 1	2009 Year to Date	2009 Annual Projection
Cost per user (in dollars)	4.98	7.00	4.98	9.88
Customer satisfaction rating	3.82	4.75	3.82	4.00
Gross revenue collected	314,388	275,807	314,388	1,036,980
Number of uses	33,203	31,237	33,203	105,000

Figure 6.8B. Best Practices in Budgeting Include Performance Measurement

Reprinted by permission. Broward County, Florida, 2009.

Measuring performance is aimed at increasing efficiency or reducing total costs, or both. It also is about effectiveness and outcomes. Using public resources wisely and saving money obviously are good ideas. Unfortunately, no tool is up to solving the political challenges that stare out from the budget numbers. No assessment technique will let the political process evade them.

Consider this scenario. National opinion polls usually show that the public supports increased spending on education in preference to other spending options. Numerous statewide surveys show opposition to cutting spending on education, even in the face of looming deficits. The public also expresses strong opposition to cuts in Social Security and Medicare, programs at the other end of the generational spread. The costs of both public elementary and secondary education and Medicaid are increasing, and each already is about a fifth or more of state spending.

The battle over public spending is about to heat up. States grapple with spending pressures from court orders (on prisons and education funding, for example), public employees' and retirees' pension and health care, Medicaid costs, and more. Almost one-half of all federal spending, excluding defense and interest on the debt, goes to the elderly. The impacts of trade-offs, compromises, and sacrifices among economic and age groups are potentially politically explosive.

WHY DO BUDGETS GROW?

Public attitudes toward federal spending increases and spending cuts are dynamic; not rooted in simple self-interest or carved in ideological stone. In fact, public support for spending increases in 2008 was at its highest level since the 1980s (when pollsters began asking) and support for spending cuts stood at a relatively low level. Sometimes the public appears less concerned about deficits or taxes than about programs or services. Sometimes, too, the American public seems to agree with the playwright George Bernard Shaw who observed, more than a century ago, that "the balance sheet of a city's welfare cannot be stated in figures. Counters of a much more spiritual kind are needed, and some imagination and conscience to add them up, as well" (Shaw, 1904, p. 169). Shaw was speaking specifically of cities, but in a way that could easily be extended to the rest of the public sector.

If we start with scarcity and throw in the general dislike of tax increases, then why does spending by the public sector increase over the years? Here are ten reasons for the growth of public spending.

1. Electoral politics. In competitive elections, candidates make many promises and try to keep at least some of them. Yet, many politicians promise not to raise taxes, and still budgets grow. As the number of people proposing spending from a common revenue pool increases, so does public spending.

2. Automatic pilot. Revenues from sales and income taxes rise as economic activity increases, and so tax increases may not be needed. Some politicians promise not to touch entitlements, such as Social Security or Medicare, but

the increasing number of people eligible for existing benefits drives up the costs of these entitlements even when the line is held on benefits.

3. Advocacy politics. New needs arise as society becomes more complex, educated, and politically savvy; technology adds to our capacity to organize around special issues and to organizations' ability to voice political demands. Advocates on behalf of existing, expanded, and new programs emerge among the public, the bureaucracy, the business and nonprofit communities, and elected political leaders.

4. Structure of government. Intergovernmental mandates (a symptom of federalism) push up costs for other governments, and the courts (separation of powers) may mandate spending on, for example, prisons or special education.

5. Decision-making process. How decisions are made in a responsive democratic political system affects budget outcomes. Although some features of the decision-making process dampen new demands on public resources, some demands do make it into the budget. An existing program has developed its beneficiaries and advocates in the public, the bureaucracy, and the legislature.

6. Purchasing power of the dollar. Inflation pushes prices up in many programs, especially programs that are indexed, or linked to the CPI. These programs include Social Security, some other entitlements, and many public pension plans.

7. Productivity, unionization, and professionalization. In some states and localities, unionization has influenced the variety and cost of salaries, wage, and employee **fringe benefits**; in some areas, low wages, poor benefits, and low morale have affected the workforce's productivity; professional standards for service and training push up some services' costs.

8. Accountability shortfalls. Corruption and outmoded or inadequate accountability systems push up costs; sometimes the problem lies with relatively uncontrolled service providers under poorly managed contracts with government.

9. Emergency and Military Spending. As society becomes more interdependent and more fragile, emergency preparedness and emergency management become more important and affect spending. War also drives up costs during the hostilities and beyond, for post-service benefits, survivor benefits, advances in weaponry, and re-arming and re-equipping the military.

10. Changing possibilities. Technology may be efficient, but it also is expensive and pushes up public spending. The human imagination drives spending

---

Employee (Fringe) Benefits—contributions made or obligations for the benefit of employees beyond the employee's salary or wage; the organization's share of the costs of employee medical insurance, pension coverage, federal Social Security and Medicare programs, and payment for timed not worked (sick leave and annual leave).

up by thinking up new ideas and devising new inventions, which in turn lead to new political demands on public resources. (In 2008, the last budget of the Bush Administration ushered in the e-budget—the first budget submitted electronically to Congress.)

THUMBNAIL

Public expenditures serve four main purposes: financing operations and services, allocation, fiscal policy, and redistribution. Spending is shaped by internal factors specific to an activity, such as cost structure. Spending is affected by environmental factors, including economic change, demographic change, and public opinion.

Spending is measured in total dollars and relative to revenue. Percentage change and growth rate, and other commonly used measures reflect internal dynamics. Changing prices, economic change as measured most broadly by the GDP, social change, and political factors focus on external dynamics. Spending is commonly measured on a per capita basis. When government and community agencies are responsive and responsible, a diverse population translates into varied demands on public resources. Issues of intergenerational equity are among the more pressing budget challenges. Demographic change coupled with past promises (entitlements and accumulated financial obligations) reduce current political leaders' flexibility and accountability in the budget process.

The proportion of the total budget devoted to an activity or program shows spending priorities in a public organization. Changing proportions show shifts in spending priorities. The specific cost structure of a program also affects spending. The labor-intensive services of education and public safety absorb more than one-half of all state and local spending. Workforce-related unfunded liabilities amount to hundreds of billions of dollars.

The public voices spending preferences for education and entitlements for the elderly. The public often chooses more spending over tax cuts. Electoral politics, advocacy politics, governmental structure, the decision-making process, inflation, and other factors contribute to spending growth.

CASE

A Difficult Dilemma

National Conference of State Legislatures, Denver, Nov., 2006, pp.18–19. Reprinted by permission.

(See the Web site for the video version.)

"A state senator in the Midwest faces a tough choice. He believes it is wrong to vote for unfunded [public employee] pension benefits and has never done so. His Senate president, a man who has done a lot for him, including appoint him chair of the Appropriations Committee, asks for his vote on an expansion of an unfunded pension benefit bill. Should he go along with something he doesn't believe in?

"The senator's leader, to whom he feels indebted, has asked him for a favor that goes against his beliefs. Put yourselves in the senator's shoes and think about his values that are in conflict: his loyalty to his leader versus his opposition to unfunded pension benefits."

Thinking It Over

1. Why could someone believe it is *wrong* as a matter of principle to vote for extending public employee pension benefits without paying for them? What principles and ethical obligations are involved here?
2. Is this a true ethical dilemma? Why not just go along? After all, being a team player is critical in politics.
3. Should the senator's understanding of his duties be affected by his being the chair of the Appropriations Committee? Whom should the senator serve? Would you consider public employees as stakeholders here?
4. Is loyalty a virtue in politics? Loyalty to whom? What is the difference between loyalty and a **quid pro quo** (exchange of favors)?
5. Legislative leadership often postpones the budget until late in the session. This gives leadership a tool—carrot and stick—to use to enforce discipline on other votes. Is this ethical? What is *logrolling* and is it ethical?

Put yourself in the senator's shoes.

1. What are your options?
2. How do you vote on the bill for unfunded pension benefits?

Ethical Leadership

"The senator explains his choice. He told his leader he would vote for the bill, but he also would introduce a budget amendment to fully fund the pension benefit. In the end, the president found someone else who would support the bill without the money, so...[the senator's] vote wasn't needed. The senator did not choose between the two most obvious options: to carry the amendment or not. He chose a 'third way.' A third way may be a compromise between the two options, or it may be an unforeseen and creative course of action [that calls for using 'moral imagination']. The challenge in choosing a third way is to arrive at the decision in an ethical manner, not by manipulating the decision. He did not vote for an unfunded pension bill and respected his Senate leadership at the same time."

Thinking It Over

1. Was this resolution politically savvy, financially sound, and ethical? Is the senator **right** in considering all three concerns?
2. Knowing this situation that speaks to the senator's ethical standards, would you vote to reelect the senator?

Quid Pro Quo—"This-for-that," receiving something in return for giving something, an exchange of benefits or favors, "I'll do this for you if you do that for me."

WEB SITE RESOURCES

- Analyzing the Costs of Public Programs
- City of Boston, video, Ways and Means Committee, Effect of the Economic Downturn on the FY09 City of Boston Budget
- A Difficult Dilemma, video, parts I and II
- Further Resources
- How Budgets Interact with Economic Conditions
- How War Affects the Formal Federal Budget Process
- Internet Resources
- Public Spending Helps Define Us and Our Future: The Story of Hurricane Katrina
- Using the Consumer Price Index
- Using the Gross Domestic Product to Measure the Role and Size of Government
- You Can Pay Me Now or Let Them Pay Me Later

REVIEW QUESTIONS

1. Why is monetary policy important to budgeting? Why is fiscal policy important to budgeting?
2. Why is it important to consider macroeconomic factors when making budgetary decisions? How does a weakening economy affect budgeting at each level of government and in nonprofit agencies? How does economic growth affect budgeting at each level of government and in nonprofit agencies?
3. What considerations should be taken into account when cutting spending for a labor-intensive service?
4. How does spending on national security and intelligence programs affect transparency and accountability? What trade-offs are involved?
5. Why is saving money by making sure that government funds are spent more wisely and more efficiently *not* enough to prevent having to make difficult political choices about future revenue and spending decisions?

7

꧁∞꧂

A Taxing Subject: Raising Public Resources

This chapter answers six questions:

- Why Do We Pay for Public Services?
- Who Makes Revenue Policy?
- What Types of Revenue Does the Public Sector Use?
- How Do Taxes Work?
- What Are the Five Principles of Taxation and How Are They Applied?
- Can Governments Raise Revenue without Having Taxes?

> Taxes are what we pay for civilized society.
> JUSTICE OLIVER WENDELL HOLMES, JR.

> Don't tax you; don't tax me; tax that fellow behind the tree.
> SENATOR RUSSELL B. LONG, JR. (D-LA), CHAIRMAN OF THE
> COMMITTEE ON FINANCE.

You may feel you are the "fellow behind the tree" because you pay general taxes to support government and charges and fees for particular public services. The average American household pays twenty-nine different types of taxes (see table 7.1). Some activities require that you pay the amount directly, as when you pay sales tax on a purchased item or a user charge for sewerage service. Other activities carry a hidden or indirect tax or fee, such as the one buried among the details on the telephone bill to fund the local 911 system, or the charge imposed by a city for the local electric utility to use public rights-of-way along the streets to string power lines on the poles.

Governments, including most school districts, have the authority to **tax**, that is, to use legal authority for the compulsory confiscation of resources. This authority is both ancient and worldwide. Before the Aswan Dam was built, the silt left

---

Tax—the compulsory confiscation of resources through the use of legal authority.

181

Table 7.1. Types and Amounts of Taxes Paid to Federal, State, and Local Governments, 2004

TAXES PAID TO THE FEDERAL GOVERNMENT IN 2004	
FEDERAL TAXES	AVERAGE AMOUNT PER U.S. HOUSEHOLD
Payroll Taxes (Social Security & Medicare)	$7,069
Individual Income Taxes	$7,062
Corporate Income Taxes	$2,155
Estate and Gift Taxes	$217
Gasoline Excise Taxes	$213
Customs Duties, Etc.	$205
Air Transport Excise Taxes	$107
Telephone and Other Excise Taxes	$92
Diesel Fuel Excise Taxes	$81
Alcoholic Beverages Excise Taxes	$74
Tobacco Excise Taxes	$63
Total Federal Taxes	$17,338

Reprinted by permission of The Tax Foundation. Chamberlain, Prante and Hodge, 2007.

TAXES PAID TO STATE AND LOCAL GOVERNMENTS IN 2004	
STATE AND LOCAL TAXES	AVERAGE AMOUNT PER U.S. HOUSEHOLD
Property Taxes	$2,906
General Sales and Gross Receipts Taxes	$2,240
Individual Income Taxes	$1,984
Other Business Taxes	$425
Corporate Income Taxes	$380
Gasoline Sales Taxes	$298
Other Selective Sales Taxes	$258
Public Utilities Taxes	$190
Insurance Receipts Taxes	$129
Personal Motor Vehicle Licenses	$120
Tobacco Excise Taxes	$108
Business Motor Vehicle Licenses	$67
Severance Taxes	$61
Special Assessments Taxes	$57
Personal Property Taxes	$50
Estate and Gift Taxes	$50
Alcoholic Beverages Excise Taxes	$41
Other Personal Taxes	$36
Total State and Local Taxes	$9,400

Reprinted by permission of The Tax Foundation. Chamberlain, Prante and Hodge, 2007.

behind by the flooding Nile fertilized the fields and meant a good harvest. Rather than directly measuring agricultural production as the basis upon which to tax, the ancient Egyptians used the Nilometre (cubit measurements chiseled into, for example, pillars or steps along the riverbank) to measure the height of the river and calculated taxes from the reading. The ideas of a flat tax and a tax based on ability-to-pay are at least as old as ancient Athens, and scholars argue over tax principles contained in the Bible. The Beatles sang about taxes on everything and everywhere in their 1966 song, "The Taxman."

The obligatory and unavoidable nature of taxes also has long been known and long resented. Legend has it that Lady Godiva rode naked on horseback through eleventh-century Coventry, England in a famous tax protest. Her repeated urgings that her husband, Leofric, cut the taxes he imposed on the people seem to have gotten on his nerves. He said that he would lower taxes when she rode naked through the town at midday. Ever obedient, she did as she was told. The respectful townsfolk did not look except, of course, for "Peeping Tom." Benjamin Franklin wrote, "In this world nothing can be said to be certain, except death and taxes." In the 1936 novel *Gone with the Wind* a character exclaims, "Death, taxes, and childbirth! There's never any convenient time for any of them."

It is difficult today for the average American citizen to keep track of all the payments made, much less to know which government and public leaders to hold accountable for the wise stewardship of all the public funds collected. For example, the federal government taxes **earned income**, state governments impose a tax on gasoline, and local governments charge for water and sewer services. Surveys suggest that citizens often are unable to distinguish accurately among governments, their services, and their taxes. Think of the publicly provided service you used most recently. Is the city, county, state, or federal government responsible for this service? Or was it provided by a nonprofit agency, and how is it funded?

Raising revenue is politically linked with public spending. Much like the classic definition of pornography offered by Supreme Court Justice Potter Stewart (who could not define it but knew it when he saw it), citizens believe they know inefficient government when they see it. For example, seeing four trucks and eight workers apparently lounging around a backhoe digging a hole in the street is sure to cause citizens' complaints. This is a classic view of wasteful spending (even if it is not). Public services include essential items, such as national defense and public safety. Public services also include other services that some citizens might think are less essential (or even frivolous), such as adult-recreation programs and advice on how to live a *good* life (for example, don't smoke, eat healthy, drink responsibly, and abstain from premarital sex). Each public entity needs an accountability system in place that guards against wasteful spending or else the willingness of citizens to pay for public services evaporates. (Will Rogers, an American humorist, whose wit often targeted government, expressed a contrarian view: "Be thankful we're not getting all the government we're paying for.")

Many arguments about revenue policy, revenue decisions, and citizen preferences about taxes rest on the theory of rational choice and its focus on the power of economic incentives. Self-interest is a powerful motivator for individuals, whether

---

Earned Income—includes all the income that is subject to taxation and the wages one gets as either employee or as self-employed.

the decision is about a personal matter or made by public leaders on behalf of the community. This theory also is helpful in understanding why public officials, acting together with others in a cooperative endeavor, choose particular revenue policies.

Because the revenue system is complex and many taxes and charges are hidden, it is beyond the capacity of most (almost all?) citizens to understand. This troubles many observers of budgeting in practice. How much thought do people actually give to taxes when they make decisions about their personal lives or political choices? People do get riled up over taxes but, even so, taxes have never reached the top of the list of the yearly averages of Gallup's "most important problem" since polling on this question began in 1935. Despite media hype and intense advocacy politics over revenue policy and tax increases, the public shows a "lack of urgency" about taxes (Bowman, 2009, p. 105).

Still, the behavior of individuals and firms are influenced by tax policy to some degree. High taxes can discourage workers from working overtime or businesses from making investments in new facilities and machinery. Communities compete for jobs, quality of life, economic development, and more; this competition suggests that the theory of rational choice adds to our understanding of revenue policy.

Knowing the likely impact of their decisions, elected officials—with an eye on the next election—anticipate likely reactions to their revenue choices. Yet, decision makers typically prefer making small and politically acceptable changes in existing revenue policy instead of grand changes. Big changes upset the existing apple cart of who pays and how much and are bound to bring out vocal opponents who feel damaged or even betrayed. Small steps compounded over repeated budget cycles lead to significant shifts that may or may not add up to desirable public policy.

Public officials must get public consent to taxation in a democratic society in which people want services from the public sector but are not always willing to pay for them. What people are willing to pay for drives many policy decisions on public services. A political perspective highlights how revenue decisions are made, by whom, and with what technical and political inputs.

WHY DO WE PAY FOR PUBLIC SERVICES?

Do you like taxes? Few do. Yet, we put up with them. A dislike of taxes that is expressed politically is called **tax resistance**. It can get ugly. Europeans were familiar with tales of savage tax protests from the Middle Ages through the eighteenth century. Colonists in Boston objected to being taxed by the British Parliament and responded with the Boston Tea Party, which helped set the stage for the American Revolution. The violent response in western Pennsylvania to the new federal government's very first internal tax led to the Whiskey Rebellion of 1794, when President Washington responded by calling out the militia. The case at the

---

Tax Resistance—a dislike of taxes that is expressed politically.

end of this chapter is a more recent example of tax resistance (see also the case in chapter 3) and modern "tea party"-type labels are used to promote vocal complaints against government activity.

Even so, people often express a willingness to pay more, if the payment is directly linked to a particular service they support, such as education. We live together in communities that provide some much-needed services. We need to prevent the spread of disease, see to it that one person or business does not poison the water we use, and safeguard our physical safety from speeding cars, criminals, terrorists, or foreign armies. The community's members must pay for these services somehow. Taxes are literally the price we pay for civilized society.

Most of us do not like to pay taxes and would rather have someone else foot the bill. Pulling this off legally—by using rules in the tax code that allow tax breaks—is **tax avoidance**. **Tax evasion**, on the other hand, is the use of illegal methods to escape paying. American history is rich with well-known examples of tax evaders. The famous mobster, Al Capone, departed Chicago in 1932 to serve time in Alcatraz prison for federal tax evasion. In 1973, Spiro T. Agnew pleaded no contest to charges of tax evasion and resigned as vice president of the United States. Singer Willie Nelson faced a $32 million bill from the IRS in 1991; he released "The IRS Tapes" to help cover his tab. Tax problems dogged several nominees to top posts early in the Obama Administration.

Willingness to Pay

The core political question budgetary politics must answer is, "What are people willing to pay?" What are they willing to pay for a new sports arena, a program to fix highways and streets, to subsidize the zoo, or any other of the many programs and services the public asks elected officials to fund? In a representative democracy, the basic answer comes from our delegation of responsibility to elected officials, who are free to make these decisions tempered by their having to stand for reelection later. Sometimes, the decision has to be submitted directly to voters in a referendum (see chapter 2), with the question framed something like this: "Should the City of Sunshine build a downtown arena to be paid for by the receipts collected from a one-quarter percent retail sales tax for three years?"

Officials often look to public opinion polls to gauge voters' willingness to pay. National opinion surveys capture the strong views of citizens on taxes. Respondents typically point the finger at the local property tax when responding to the question, "Which do you think is the worst tax—that is, the least fair?" Why? It could be because

---

Tax Avoidance—the use of legal methods including deductions, credits and allowances, to decrease the amount of taxes owed or tax liability.

Tax Evasion—the use of illegal methods to escape paying the amount of taxes legally owed or tax liability.

the retail **sales tax** is buried in the fine print of the sales ticket, and the income tax bite is less obvious in a paycheck showing after-tax, take-home earnings. By contrast, the property tax is up front and visible as a large payment made by homeowners either directly to the government or through monthly payments with the mortgage.

Property tax limits are common in the states. Expressing their opinion of the property tax, the public continues to approve limits. State lawmakers can climb on the soapbox and support limits because it is not the state, but the local treasury that suffers revenue loss. Limits on general revenue and spending are less common than limits on property taxes.

Revenue Systems Serve Different Functions

Whether the payers like it or not, public organizations must raise revenue. All sources of funding bundled together form a revenue system. Although not everyone agrees on the appropriateness of each one, public revenue systems can serve six functions:

1. to finance public organizations and services;
2. to reward and penalize certain economic and social behaviors (for example, speeding and parking tickets; tax advantages for education and retirement savings, childcare, and home mortgages; "sin" taxes on alcohol and tobacco; and incentives for investment);
3. to redistribute resources through privileged treatment or tax breaks (exemptions, deductions, or credits) among individuals, activities, economic and other groups, and geographic regions;
4. to affect demand by charging for particular services (such as parking meters, tolls, entrance fees to parks and swimming pools);
5. to implement fiscal policy, with higher taxes (and/or lower public spending), to cool off an overheated economy and lower taxes (and/or higher public spending), to stimulate a lagging economy;
6. to engage everyone (in one way or another) in paying for the privileges and responsibilities enjoyed as being part of the community.

Many governments use a hybrid revenue system that serves at least some of these purposes.

Taxes and other revenues are necessary to finance the provision of goods and services that citizens demand from their government. Revenue policies, however, must be fair and clear to all who have the obligation to pay, and avoid unnecessarily hampering private economic decisions on which economic growth depends. Public officials use tax policy to reward or punish certain behaviors, such as providing a tax advantage for savings and discouraging tobacco use by placing a high tax on tobacco products. Tax policy is also an instrument used to reallocate assets among individuals, economic groups, and regions. Taxing the rich at a higher tax

---

Sales Tax—a tax levied on the market price of designated items purchased; the companion tax is the "use tax."

rate than lower-income taxpayers is termed a progressive tax but its effect is a form of redistribution. Therefore, taxation is a complicated policy issue with significant political implications. Fundamentally, government tax policy requires trade-offs because there is no perfect tax or perfect revenue system.

Revenue and Civic Engagement

Voting generally is seen as the most important form of political participation in a democracy. More people in the United States participate in community life by paying taxes than voting in national elections or engaging in any other specifically political activity. Even Donald Duck does his patriotic duty by paying his federal income tax in Walt Disney's 1943 film, *The Spirit of '43*. Paying into the public coffers is a lesson on public duties and a vehicle for participation in civic life for voters, as well as people who are ineligible, unregistered, or unwilling to vote. According to table 7.2, in the 2004 national election, 122 million ballots were cast but about 184 million people filed individual income tax returns. Less than 56 percent of the adult population voted in 2004, compared to the 84 percent of the adult population who filed individual income tax returns. These statistics only deal with the federal income tax. To get a better sense of the political reach of civic engagement through taxation, we should add legal residents, illegal aliens, and even children under eighteen who must pay sales taxes on their purchases. Because so many more people pay taxes than vote, paying for government and other public organizations is actually the main form of civic engagement.

Civic engagement through taxation teaches at least two political lessons. The first is that financing the public life of a community is costly. Supporting government is a big factor in the average family budget that spent more on taxes in 2008 than on food, clothing, and housing combined. The average household paid more than $17,000 in taxes to the federal government in 2004 and more than $9,000 to state and local governments, according to the Tax Foundation. Taxes claimed almost 31 percent of income in 2008, compared to 6 percent of income in 1900.

Another lesson is that the community is complex and so Americans face a long list of different taxes and charges imposed by different governments (as shown in

Table 7.2. Taxation and Voting: Civic Engagement

YEAR	ESTIMATED POPULATION, 18 AND OVER	FEDERAL INCOME TAX FILERS* (MILLIONS)	FILERS AS % OF POPULATION 18 AND OVER	VOTES IN NATIONAL ELECTION (MILLIONS)	VOTES AS % ESTIMATED POPULATION OVER 18
2004	219,973,000	184	84%	122	56%
2000	209,130,000	180	86%	106	50%
1996	199,169,000	169	85%	96	48%

* Estimated Income Tax Filers based on married filing jointly equal to two persons and all other filing status equal to one person. Data currently not available for 2008 filers.

SOURCES: U.S. Census Bureau, 2004, 2008, and 2009; and IRS, 1996, 2000, and 2004.

table 7.1). Citizens look to many different government and public agencies to provide a battery of services, programs, and facilities; they all require money. As a
result, the average American household bears the burden of complexity as well as
the burden of taxes.

Strategies for Public Support

The problem with tax resistance is that many people want government services,
sometimes even the same people who do not want to pay taxes. The political problem is how to fund these services if people are reluctant to pay for them. How can
government get the kind of consent that is necessary in a democracy?

Officials are careful to cultivate public support for taxation. A number of
standard strategies have developed over the years to limit taxes and to earn public
support. Some were devised by public officials and others initiated by citizens or
interest groups. These strategies help explain some of the major characteristics of
and trends in taxation in the United States.

1. *Taxing everyone a little bit* makes taxes both seem bearable and fair ("the least
   hissing" noted in chapter 3), but it results in a lot of different taxes, charges,
   and fees. Politicians pick and choose the sources of revenue that they believe
   are most acceptable to their constituents from among those that the law
   allows. To avoid burdening any one group excessively, politicians tend to use
   a variety of taxes, even if some only produce a limited amount of revenue.
   This nickel-and-dime approach may not be as efficient as fewer taxes that
   collect more money, but it makes taxes less visible, despite their frequency,
   and more politically acceptable (meaning less hissing). When people pay a
   little bit here and a little bit there, they often do not even know that they are
   paying a tax, let alone know how much they are paying. The sales tax shows
   why political leaders prefer hidden taxes and little tax bites. Few people have
   any idea how much sales tax they pay in a year, because ordinarily they do
   not add up the tax on purchases made throughout the year.
2. When politicians seek support from a distrustful public for a tax increase,
   they often *dedicate* the revenue to some popular program or clearly needed
   project. Because money is fungible (a dollar can substitute for another dollar), the resources once going to the newly financed popular program can
   be shifted to other uses. Where distrust is high, elected officials promise
   to spend the new money on education, health care, or bridge repair after a
   major well-publicized bridge collapse. Citizens are less likely to say "no" to
   worthwhile projects that they favor.
3. A third approach is to be selective about the specific type of revenue and
   keep an eye on its political acceptability. Taxes can be made more acceptable to the public if decision makers rely as much as possible on taxes the
   people prefer, while reducing, freezing, or reforming taxes that people dislike. Public acceptability depends on a tax's visibility, affordability, predictability, and how familiar people are with it. No politician wins a citizens'

award for tax innovation. People prefer taxes and fees they can predict and plan for as opposed to taxes that change from year to year. People generally prefer voluntary fees (based on usage) to compulsory taxes and prefer taxes, such as the sales tax, that take repeated, small, and less visible bites to property taxes, which hit in large, noticeable amounts, usually twice a year. It is hardly surprising, then, that property taxes regularly lose out in public opinion polls.

4. People are more likely to accept taxation willingly if the *tax burden is light*. Where taxes are concerned, political leaders assume that there is an equal sign between affordability and acceptability; keeping taxes from climbing too high is a tactic for keeping taxes acceptable. Affordability is accomplished in two different ways. One is to keep the tax burden down across-the-board, and the other is to maintain relatively high taxes but create a system of exemptions from the burdens those rates impose. *Light* is a relative measure and may depend as much on what people are used to as on the actual tax burden, or the proportion of income taken by taxes.

Torn between those who demand additional or better quality services and those who want to pay less in taxes, politicians may freeze taxes in place. They may promise never to raise taxes or not raise taxes for a set number of years. (The case at the end of chapter 3 shows a typical pledge.) As public officials try to meet the seemingly ever-growing demand for public services, they hunt for revenue sources that will provide the needed revenue, while keeping tax resistance as low as they can. Typically, decision makers prefer a lot of revenue sources with smaller yields and to dedicate the revenue to particular spending purposes, especially when voters must approve a tax increase at the ballot box.

WHO MAKES REVENUE POLICY?

The authority to make tax policy and write tax legislation is a key source of political power. Two historical examples illustrate this long-known truth. The first is the Magna Carta, a critical document in the development of democracy and a foundation stone of the British and U.S. legal systems. This Great Charter was granted originally by King John in 1215 at Runnymede. Under threat of civil war, he struck a bargain with his barons to limit his taxing powers. About six centuries later, the U.S. Supreme Court exempted the federal government from state taxes. In the 1819 decision of *McCulloch v. Maryland*, Chief Justice John Marshall famously pronounced that "the power to tax involves the power to destroy." The states "have no power, by taxation or otherwise, to retard, impede, burden or in any manner control the operations of the constitutional laws enacted by Congress."

Today, the executive branch generally sets the revenue agenda by framing the issues and then controlling tax administration. Presidents have a large staff of tax experts, employed by the Department of Treasury, who can examine every conceivable angle of current or proposed tax law. The Treasury's Office of Tax Analysis

(OTA) analyzes the effects of alternative tax programs and makes the official estimates of federal receipts used in the president's budget submission to Congress.

The U.S. Constitution assigns the power to tax to Congress, with the House given the legislative role of originating tax legislation. Both the House and the Senate have assigned responsibility to specialized committees, the House Ways and Means Committee and the Senate Committee on Finance. The majority party in each house dominates the committee by (1) appointing a chairman who controls the agenda and (2) appointing a majority of party members to the committee, which usually assures that the party's position will get a majority vote. When the majority party changes in either house, so does control of the tax committees. These two committees are especially powerful because they have jurisdiction over entitlements as well as tax legislation (see chapter 4). The tax committees are lobbied intensely because the issues they deal with affect so many people in the pocketbook. A book on the intense lobbying for tax reform in 1986 was given the apt title *Showdown at Gucci Gulch* for all the well-dressed lobbyists crowding into the rooms and hallways of congressional power (Birnbaum and Murray, 1987).

Political Pressure on Technical Experts

The complexity of tax law issues led Congress to create the Joint Tax Committee (JTC) in 1926. This committee is joint because it serves both the House and Senate. The JTC is solely devoted to taxation, and is staffed by tax professionals—economists and lawyers—with the nonpartisan technical expertise to advise lawmakers. This nonpartisan status does not insulate the JTC from politically charged issues or from political pressure. The Joint Tax Committee (JTC) is under pressure to take into account the effects of taxation on economic behavior. If taxes are cut by 10 percent, will tax revenue fall by 10 percent? What if the economic stimulus of a tax cut encouraged more taxable economic behavior, resulting in more not less revenue, offsetting the effect of the lower tax rate?

This apparently magical equation (lower taxes rates = more revenue) enjoys more political support, especially among those who want to cut taxes, than called for by social science. Although there are probably some behavioral effects, and tax reductions actually do stimulate economic activity, no one knows the precise size of the effect (see box 7.1). Making revenue estimates based on this equation is called **dynamic scoring**, where dynamic means taking into account how people respond to a tax change, and scoring means estimating the financial effects of a proposed change in law according to set of definitions and rules. Given the JTC's powerful position in the tax legislation process, advocates of tax cuts continue to press the JTC to incorporate dynamic scoring estimates of tax changes more fully and more frequently into their revenue estimates. Even the technical aspects of taxation can become political.

Dynamic Scoring—where dynamic means taking into account how people respond to a tax change, and scoring means estimating the financial effects of a proposed change in law according to set definitions and rules.

BOX 7.1

The Magic of Dynamic Scoring

In 2004, former Federal Reserve Chairman Alan Greenspan asserted, "It is very rare and very few economists believe that you can cut taxes and you will get the same amount of revenue," while Ben Bernanke, the current chairman, testified before Congress in 2006, "I don't think that, as a general rule, that tax cuts pay for themselves" (Conrad, 2006).

An earlier statement on this matter comes from Arthur Okun, the chairman of the Council of Economic Advisors under President Lyndon B. Johnson. "Now, we argued, and I think the facts proved ultimately that there was a good deal of merit in this, that if you did the right thing in terms of either more government spending or a tax reduction of major proportions, that you'd invigorate the economy enough so that incomes would be much higher and therefore you'd get higher revenues as a result of those higher incomes, enough to offset this, that at least the large deficit that would be incurred would be a transitory phenomenon. There were some rhetorical statements made about how you could balance the budget by stimulus and so forth. I'm not sure one could ever demonstrate that indeed you collected more than you gave away, but at least you got a very major offset to this" (Okun, 1969).

Revenue Power Outside the Beltway

Revenue power does not stop at the Beltway, the major and usually congested highway that rings Washington. In state government, the governors most often set the tax agenda. The chief executive has access to the tax department (typically labeled the "revenue department") and the central budget office, while legislators usually labor under an information disadvantage because they do not have similarly staffed offices that can examine the details of tax legislation. Thirty-eight states have legislative fiscal offices, but twelve have no specialized staff for analyzing revenue issues. The states' legislative fiscal offices generally are small and the staffs have a variety of responsibilities in addition to analyzing tax proposals. For example, New Jersey's Legislative Budget and Finance Office is described officially "as the chief fiscal officer for the Legislature and the Legislative Services Commission" with these responsibilities: "collects and presents fiscal information for the Legislature and its budget committees, reviews requests for appropriations, and determines approval for and the transfer of funds among State accounts...and staffs the Joint Budget Oversight Committee." At the local government level, the council or board often has no budget staff of its own, and may depend on the executive budget office for information and analysis.

Outside government, nonprofit advocacy groups may work at building public resentment against taxation or lobby elected officials to curtail taxes. Advocacy groups may also play a role in initiating anti-tax referenda. There are few advocacy groups routinely pushing for more taxation overall, although some groups ask for tax increases on specific activities of which they disapprove (such as smoking or drinking) or tax increases dedicated to programs that they support (such as public schools). As counterpoints to the anti-tax advocacy groups, liberal and union-supported groups conduct their own analyses of important tax issues in an attempt to level the playing field of information.

Political Pressure on Decision Makers

Given our complex economy, it stands to reason that any tax on a particular part of any economic activity is sure to be complex. Competing interests seek advantage at different stages throughout the process, from the initial formulation of tax legislation to the application of tax law to particular events. Lawmakers, at all levels of government, are whipsawed by competing testimony: one side submits data touting the benefits of a tax cut while another group is armed with statistics showing the opposite. Put yourself in these lawmakers' shoes: Who and what should you believe, as you put your elected career on the line with one vote?

A simplifying route, taken by some, is to sidestep the responsibility and sign the "taxpayer protection pledge" shown in the case at the end of chapter 3. Another evasive tactic for a "hot" issue—and decisions about taxes always fall in this category—is to submit the issue directly to the voters through advisory balloting (in order to get a sense of voters' views when a direct vote by citizens is not required by law) or to read carefully public opinion polls. This evasive tactic is built right into the political process in many state and local governments where a binding referendum is required by law.

WHAT TYPES OF REVENUE DOES THE PUBLIC SECTOR USE?

Public organizations use at least nine different sources of revenue, including

1. taxes, including property taxes, income taxes, payroll taxes, sales and use taxes, and excise taxes;
2. service charges and user fees;
3. licenses, franchises, leases, and rents;
4. gaming and lotteries;
5. investment earnings;
6. sale of assets;
7. fines (speeding and parking tickets!);
8. intergovernmental payments (grants-in-aid, reimbursements, and revenue sharing);
9. bequests and gifts.

Nonprofit agencies also draw on government subsidies, payments for contracted services, and donations from charities, foundations, and individual donors.

Although not strictly a revenue source, organizations borrow money to fund the purchase and construction of fixed assets. While the act of borrowing generates cash just like a revenue source, debt has to be repaid, with interest, from a future revenue flow. Even when the borrowed money is to refill an emptied treasury, it has to be repaid. For these reasons, borrowing is not revenue but an advance of future revenue.

Of the different revenue sources, taxes are compulsory payments. Many of the other revenue sources are based on lifestyle and use of publicly provided services (see table 7.1). **Service charges and user fees** are paid in exchange for a specific good or service provided by government and other public entities. You may pay charges and fees daily when riding on a city bus, monthly when paying for public water or sewer service to your home or apartment, each semester when paying a student fee (if you attend a public college), or on those occasions when you renew a driver's license or buy a hunting permit. Parking tickets and speeding fines are levied when you violate the law so, although it is compulsory to pay, the choice to speed is yours. Included in this category are payments by utility companies to string wires and poles along the public right-of-way and by businesses that want logging or drilling permits. Users have to pay directly for many recreation services and for water, sewer, electricity, and other services provided by government-owned enterprises.

Considered voluntary, charges and fees are most appropriate when (1) the benefit can be measured in units that can be counted and priced; (2) the actual recipient can be identified with some certainty; (3) costs are known, so that they can be recovered through the fee, with or without a subsidy from general tax revenues; and (4) equity concerns are not a major consideration. Sometimes the equity issue is handled by charging for a service on a sliding scale that relates the fee to a person's income.

Now that all but two states (Hawaii and Utah) engage in some form of state-sponsored **gaming** activities (from lotteries to casinos and racetracks), part of what people pay to play goes into state treasuries. Publicly sponsored gambling initially was justified in some states as a means of financing public education, and the history of lotteries illustrates the role of political acceptability in selecting revenue sources. **Dedicated revenue** is committed by law to a particular program or purpose. The division of resources into different pots reduces overall budgetary flexibility but is a favored mechanism for (1) justifying new or increased revenue, and/or (2) protecting a pet program.

Service Charge and User Fees—a means of paying for something based on services received or paying to use something, such as a public golf course.

Gaming—use of lotteries, casinos, racetracks, etc., which bring in revenues that are sometimes used for specific purposes, such as education.

Dedicated Revenue—revenue committed by law to a particular program or purpose, meaning that the money cannot legally be spent for other purposes.

The Property Tax

Local governments rely extensively on the property tax. The amount of property taxes owed is based on the estimated fair-market value of the property as appraised for tax purposes and the tax rate, not on the owner's ability to pay. The **appraised value** of a property is often adjusted by a legally mandated **assessment ratio** (say 10 percent for residential property) to set its **assessed value** or taxable value. In turn, the property's taxable value is multiplied by the tax rate to calculate the tax bill. A property that does not change during the year can still have its estimated fair market value adjusted by the government's tax appraiser to reflect sales of similar properties. This means that homeowners, for example, can see their property's taxable value increase without any physical improvements made to the property—just by living there for another year. This fact stokes anti-property tax sentiment.

When assessed values go up quickly in a hot real estate market, local governments could reduce the tax rate so that tax bills would not jump too quickly. When local government officials estimate anticipated revenues, they think about the taxable value of each property added up across all taxable properties. This total amount is the tax base for the property tax. Multiplying the tax base by the tax rate tells local officials how much they can expect in property tax revenue. When property values rise and tax rates remain unchanged, local officials get a politically-free tax increase. But this works only for a while. Big jumps in property taxes are blamed for increasing tax resistance and statewide tax revolts that lead to statewide tax limits, such as California's Proposition 13 in 1978.

One way of assuring that property taxes do not jump quickly from year to year beyond the ability and/or willingness of the public to pay is to require voters to approve an increase in the tax rate. Increases in the property tax rates in school districts in Illinois must first be approved by voters. Some states limit how much the tax yield (or number of dollars collected) can grow in any given year, regardless of whether it is the value of property or the tax rate that pushes the yield higher.

Sometimes the jump is in the wrong direction, at least from the perspective of raising revenue. Falling property values (see box 6.3) mean that in order to raise the same revenue as last year, the tax rate must be increased. Local politicians do not enjoy increasing the tax rate any more than the voters and taxpayers do. The alternative is to cut services, which people also dislike.

Appraised Value—an estimate of the market value of property established through market sales, comparable sales or other methods; set after notification, hearing and appeals, and certification process.

Assessment Ratio—a legal classification that gives some types of property (especially residential) a favorable treatment compared to other (often business) property.

Assessed Value—taxable value of property that may be equal to or less than market or appraised value; reduction often the result of a classification ratio or factor (or legally allowable percent of the market value); used to determine the basis for the tax liability of property owners.

Many states have imposed rules that limit property taxes that local governments can raise and many states offer reduced taxes to make the burden more bearable for some groups of taxpayers. The first is a general rule that applies across-the-board to all properties of a particular classification (such as residential, commercial, and agricultural use), regardless of the property owners' incomes. The second type of rule links the payment more closely with the ability to pay. **Circuit-breakers** reduce the property tax burden on poor, disabled, or elderly households by offering a tax reduction or refund based on the proportion of income that goes to property taxes. If this proportion is considered too high, then the property owner is eligible for the tax reduction. Most of the eighteen states with circuit-breaker programs offer them to homeowners and renters, who frequently pay for property taxes through their rent.

The Income Tax

It was not until 1913, when the 16th Amendment to the U.S. Constitution was approved, that the federal government could legally levy an **income tax** (although Wisconsin had imposed one in 1911). Today, the income tax is the primary tax source for the federal government and most states. The basic structure entails four steps: total sources of income; subtract allowable deductions and exemptions to determine taxable income; apply the appropriate tax rate to determine the amount of tax; then subtract allowable credits to determine the tax due. This four-step process is a simplistic view of what can be very complicated. Taxpayers have to determine if the income received is taxable (certain sources are not taxable), if they are eligible for particular deductions, exemptions and credits, and what tax rate to apply.

The Sales and Use Tax

Taxing consumption appeals to many people who want to avoid taxing income (via an income tax) or wealth (through the property tax). To these advocates, the fundamental appeal of a sales tax is that everyone pays the same tax rate. Those who oppose this form of taxation say that is just the point: a consumption tax does not take into account the taxpayer's ability to pay the tax. The impact of a consumption or sales tax is regressive, meaning that those with a lower income pay a higher share of their income in sales taxes than do those with a higher income. The regressive impact of a broad-based sales tax can be reduced by exempting sales taxes on basic needs, such as milk or bread. Starting with Mississippi, the first state to adopt a retail sales tax, states and local governments across the country now use the retail sales tax. It works this way: the customer pays the tax on a purchase to the retailer who then has to send these tax dollars to the taxing authority. Unlike the property tax, where

---

Circuit-breaker—reduction of the property tax burden on poor, disabled, or elderly households by offering a tax reduction or refund based on the proportion of income that goes to property taxes.

Income Tax—a tax on specific elements of income.

there can be disputes on the market value assigned to a property, the value of the good or service subject to a sales tax is clearly stated at the time of purchase.

Revenue Diversity

American state and local governments use different revenue mixes because they face different fiscal constraints. A state constitution may prohibit the imposition of an income tax, as does Texas. State statutes may limit the rate of sales tax that a local government may impose. Finding the right mix of revenue sources requires a balancing act among what is legally allowed, what citizens are willing to support, and how much money is needed to cover the cost of government.

Each revenue system usually relies on more than one source of revenue. States often dictate the sources available to local governments, and some states regulate the collection procedures and rate of increase. When a state permits but does not require the use of a particular revenue source, the source is said to be a **local option**. Because of the variety among and within the states, analysts calculating tax burden often consider the state and local taxes as a single system so that the combined impact is taken into account. The impact is important; some analysts argue that, in a basic way, individuals and firms express their opinion of the mix or revenue system by voting with their feet and either staying or leaving a state.

A budget built on one revenue source is risky because a disruption in revenue flow can have severe budget consequences. Changing economic conditions, such as seen in the recession and financial crisis starting in December 2007, are a case in point. A tax system that is responsive to changing economic conditions relies upon different revenue sources, with some sources aimed at automatic and politically painless growth and other sources at stability and predictability. In addition, revenue diversity tempers the use by local governments of the widely disliked property tax.

Although most municipalities rely on property taxes for a significant share of revenues, they also impose service charges for utility operations, receive state financial aid, and collect police fines and zoning fees. Many also use a local-option retail sales tax. Cities in Ohio and Pennsylvania (along with St. Louis and Kansas City, Missouri, and Birmingham, Alabama, among others) have access to a local income tax. Although Oregon does not have a general sales tax, it does impose selective sales or excise taxes. Alaska does not have a statewide general sales tax, but does allow a local sales tax. The result is that each state is a little different from the others in what is taxed and which level of government imposes the tax. As Supreme Court Justice Louis Brandeis wrote in 1932, "It is one of the happy incidents of the federal system that a single courageous state may, if its citizens choose, serve as a laboratory; and try novel social and economic experiments without risk to the rest of the country." Elected officials are only too happy to let another one (or another state) go first in proposing a new tax.

Local Option Tax—the grant of authority by a state that allows local citizens to vote for a new local tax.

Table 7.3. The Reliance of State and Local Government Tax Systems on Property, Sales, and Personal Income Taxes, 2005–2006

	PROPERTY TAX	GENERAL AND SELECTIVE SALES TAX	INDIVIDUAL INCOME TAX	OTHER TAXES
RELATIVELY BALANCED*				
California	23%	32%	31%	14%
Colorado	31%	36%	25%	9%
Connecticut	38%	25%	29%	8%
District of Columbia	27%	28%	27%	19%
Georgia	29%	39%	26%	6%
Idaho	28%	33%	27%	12%
Illinois	38%	34%	17%	12%
Indiana	37%	33%	28%	8%
Iowa	33%	33%	24%	10%
Kansas	31%	37%	23%	9%
Maine	38%	29%	24%	10%
Maryland	23%	24%	38%	15%
Massachusetts	35%	20%	34%	11%
Minnesota	24%	33%	31%	13%
Missouri	27%	39%	26%	8%
Nebraska	33%	32%	22%	13%
New York	29%	26%	31%	14%
North Carolina	23%	34%	32%	11%
Ohio	29%	30%	32%	9%
Pennsylvania	29%	29%	25%	17%
Rhode Island	40%	30%	22%	8%
South Carolina	32%	36%	22%	10%
Utah	23%	40%	28%	10%
Virginia	31%	27%	30%	12%
Wisconsin	36%	28%	26%	9%
AVERAGE BALANCED*				
Kentucky	18%	37%	29%	16%
Michigan	38%	33%	19%	11%
Montana	35%	17%	25%	22%
New Jersey	43%	22%	22%	12%
Oklahoma	16%	38%	24%	22%
Vermont	42%	29%	20%	9%
West Virginia	18%	38%	22%	22%
HEAVY RELIANCE* ON SALES TAX				
Alabama	15%	48%	23%	14%
Arizona	28%	47%	16%	9%
Arkansas	15%	53%	23%	9%
Florida	35%	48%	0%	17%
Hawaii	16%	51%	25%	8%
Louisiana	16%	56%	16%	13%
Mississippi	25%	49%	15%	11%
Nevada	26%	59%	0%	15%

(Continued)

Table 7.3. *Continued*

	PROPERTY TAX	GENERAL AND SELECTIVE SALES TAX	INDIVIDUAL INCOME TAX	OTHER TAXES
HEAVY RELIANCE* ON SALES TAX				
New Mexico	14%	46%	16%	24%
South Dakota	34%	54%	0%	12%
Tennessee	24%	59%	1%	16%
Texas	43%	45%	0%	12%
Washington	27%	61%	0%	11%
HEAVY RELIANCE* ON PROPERTY TAX				
New Hampshire	62%	16%	2%	21%
ALL OTHERS				
Alaska	26%	12%	0%	62%
Delaware	15%	12%	30%	43%
North Dakota	27%	35%	12%	26%
Oregon	30%	9%	45%	17%
Wyoming	31%	30%	0%	38%

* Definitions

Relatively Balanced means that no tax contributes less than 20 percent or more than 40 of state and local tax revenues.

Average Balanced means that no tax contributes less than 15 percent or more than 45 percent of state and local tax revenues.

Heavy Reliance means that one tax source contributes over 45 percent of state and local tax revenues.

SOURCE: Calculated from U.S. Census Bureau, 2005–2006).

A measure of revenue diversity for state and local governments combined is known as the **three-legged stool**, meaning that income, property and sales taxes should each constitute about one-third of overall tax revenues. Table 7.3 shows how total state-local tax revenue systems meet a generous definition of revenue diversification. One-half of the states have a relatively balanced combined state and local tax system, with none of the three basic tax sources accounting for more than 40 percent or less than 20 percent of total tax collections in the state. This is up from just twenty states a dozen years earlier. Seven states have an average balanced state and local tax system. Other states prefer to place a heavier reliance on one tax source and not at all or only sparingly use another tax. Texas, for example, does not have a personal income tax.

Three-legged Stool—the principle stating that income, property, and sales taxes should each constitute about one-third of total state and local tax revenues.

HOW DO TAXES WORK?

What will be taxed and at what rate? Fundamentally, revenue policy involves policy decisions regarding the (1) base, (2) rate, and (3) yield. The tax base is that which is taxed, such as property, consumption (typically termed a retail sales tax), or income. The tax rate is the percentage of the base that will be taken in tax. The tax yield is the amount resulting from applying the rate to the base. A 10 percent rate applied to a $10,000 base will yield $1,000 in taxes, assuming that all of the tax liability (or dollar amount owed by a taxpayer) is collected. If you know two of the three factors, you can determine the third:

$10,000 x .10 = $1,000
$10,000 = $1,000 / .10
$1,000 / $10,000 = .10

All taxes, then, can be expressed by this formula: rate x base = yield.

The broader the base, the lower the rate required to achieve a desired yield. A broad definition of each of these three major taxes could include the following tax base options:

- Property tax: land (both improved and unimproved); built structures (such as a house, swimming pool, manufacturing plant, and paved parking lot for an office building); inventory (for example, vehicles in an auto dealer's parking lot or furniture in your home); machinery and equipment; and personal motorized vehicles (automobiles as well as off-the-road all-terrain vehicles).
- Consumption tax: tangible goods (a computer purchased over the Internet); intangible goods (downloaded songs over the Internet); commodities (should we tax Girl Scout cookies or the items sold at a garage sale?); and services (legal services, beautician services).
- Income tax: cash wages and salaries; gross sales (or net, with costs deducted); deferred income; interest and dividends; and gains from investments.

Expenditure plans in most of the public sector depend upon revenue policy. (Not so with the federal government, which has the printing press and no requirement to balance the budget.) The public budgetary process identifies the amount of money needed to pay employees, purchase goods and other services, and make capital improvements.

If the entire budget is financed by only one tax source, then the desired annual spending could be divided by an estimate of the tax base for that same annual period to produce the tax rate that would have to be imposed in order to generate the needed amount of money. For example, if the city budget of $1,000,000 is financed by one tax with a taxable base of $10,000,000, then the tax rate would be 10 percent. A modification of the formula would subtract from the $1 million budget that which can be financed by other revenue sources (such as charges for services, fines, and even other taxes). So, for instance, if the city could offset one-half of the $1 million budget with those other sources, then the formula would be $500,000 divided by the $10 million tax base to yield a tax rate of 5 percent.

The Sticky Problems of Tax Administration

What is actually taxed? Determining the tax base is not always easy. Under payroll withholding, the amount of earned income is reported by the employer, and the amount withheld from the worker's paycheck by the employer is paid to the taxing authority. The worker's end-of-year income tax reporting to government is simple if this job is the only source of income. Things get more complex if this person also earns income not as an employee but as a sole proprietor running a business. Business expenses can be subtracted from business income, requiring detailed bookkeeping. Just as a taxpayer has to track all the income that is taxable, the taxing authority has to use audit procedures to ensure that all taxable income is subject to the appropriate tax.

Tax base considerations also arise with the retail sales tax and property tax. The retail sales tax is collected by the retailer from the customer, and then paid to the taxing authority. Most retailers have electronic cash registers that automatically assign the tax to any customer's bill. What about determining the yearly taxable value assigned to a home that has not changed ownership in decades and that has not had any significant improvements in that period? Is the fair market value the same as the original cost? Has the house depreciated in value as it has aged, as does a computer? What if the neighborhood has experienced turnover in home ownership with house prices escalating (or declining), which reflect the changing economic character of the community? These questions are hotly debated.

States generally impose rules that require frequent appraisal of every real property parcel as the way to estimate its fair market value. Property owners receive notice of these estimated values and are given an opportunity to challenge (or appeal) the appraisal. Taxpayers face a real hurdle when trying to argue convincingly that changes in their neighbors' property values do not affect theirs. Although taxpayers want a low taxable value to minimize their taxes, they want a high sales price to maximize their wealth.

Placing a value on a piece of property is subjective, especially if there is no recent arms-length sale (meaning between two separate parties with equal information). Otherwise, the property value of an apartment complex, an office building, a restaurant, an electricity-generating plant, or even a railroad can be appraised according to its income-earning capability. Associate Justice David J. Brewer stated the principle in an 1897 U.S. Supreme Court case: "Now it is a cardinal rule which should never be forgotten that whatever property is worth for the purposes of income and sale it is also worth for purposes of taxation." So, how much income can the pizza restaurant near campus generate? Do you think we will all agree on this figure? Tax appraisers develop estimates based on the type of restaurant, its particular location, seating capacity, building characteristics, and broad industry trends. These may or may not be close to the actual income generated from this particular restaurant. One thing is plain: determining fair market value for tax purposes is sure to light a fire of passions fueled by dollar signs.

As these base valuations suggest, tax administration has to deal with many sticky problems. Probably your state has a retail sales tax because only Delaware, Montana, New Hampshire, and Oregon do not have a state or local sales tax. How does that sales tax system distinguish between music or software purchased in a retail store versus items downloaded from an Internet site? Regardless of how it is acquired, you owe the tax, even if the "store" does not collect it from you. Your obligation is to pay the equivalent "sales" tax in the form of a **use tax**. Usually people only have to submit yearly the use tax due on all their mail order or Internet-based purchases. To make it easy to comply, many states place a line-item on the state income tax forms for taxpayers to estimate the amount of use tax owed. Actually, few citizens know they have this obligation to voluntarily pay the use tax, although ignorance of the law is no excuse.

Put yourself in the role of the state revenue commissioner who is given a mandate from the state legislature to collect more money by going after tax deadbeats, who owe but do not pay their taxes. How would you estimate the number and monetary value of music downloads in the state as well as identify the individuals who received these taxable items? Assuming you could do all this, how would you set up a system to actually collect the tax? These dilemmas hint at the problems involved in administering a tax in our rapidly changing economy.

Rules that Limit Tax Uses and Tax Increases

Some mechanisms that are applauded as oh-so democratic make it difficult to raise the revenues needed to cover the community's appetite for services. Remember, this appetite also is expressed through the democratic political process. Some of these mechanisms are designed to block revenue increases and drown out service demands.

Citizens and their elected representatives place limits on the use of taxes and often on their increase (called tax-and-expenditure limitations or TELs). Some limits are tighter than others. For the retail sales tax, states typically define a common tax base (some states tax groceries while others exempt these purchases from the sales tax) that applies to all their local governments and then limit the rate that a local government can impose. Voters, who are not necessarily or only taxpayers, mind you, may have to approve all changes in property tax rates. Limits on the tax base can take shape as restrictions on the amount that a residential value may be increased in any single year. Also, the maximum amount of property tax collections may be tied to changes in inflation and population. As a case in point, Colorado's Taxpayer Bill of Rights (discussed in the case in chapter 3) has attracted national attention, but attempts to copy it elsewhere have failed.

States vary in the limits they impose on local governments' authority to tax. Figure 7.1 shows that some states permit cities and towns to use a sales tax, income

---

Use Tax—the obligation to pay the equivalent retail sales tax even if the item is not purchased locally but is purchased out-of-state, in a garage sale, or even over the Internet.

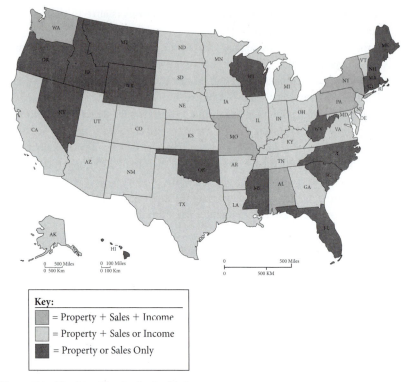

Figure 7.1. Municipal Tax Authority by State

Reprinted by permission of National League of Cities. Hoene and Pagano, 2008.

tax, and a property tax, or some combination. Many New England states permit their cities and towns to use only a local property tax. In contrast, local governments in Oklahoma focus on the sales tax. The most common tax-and-expenditure limits or TELs on local government restrict property taxes. Less common are limits on general revenue and spending. Cities and towns in the great majority of states operate under a TEL (see figure 7.2).

Another rule designed to make it difficult to increase revenues is to require a supermajority vote of each house of the state legislature to approve a tax increase. According to the National Conference of State Legislators, five states (Delaware, Florida, Kentucky, Mississippi, and Oregon) require a supermajority of three-fifths; eight states (Arizona, California, Colorado, Louisiana, Missouri, Nevada, South Dakota, and Washington) require a two-thirds vote; and three states (Arkansas, Michigan and Oklahoma) demand approval by three-quarters of their legislators.

Nominal Versus Effective Tax Rate

The face or **nominal tax rate** is the tax rate written into law (the statutory rate). By contrast, the effective tax rate is the number of dollars actually paid in taxes

---

Nominal Tax Rate—the stated legal tax rate.

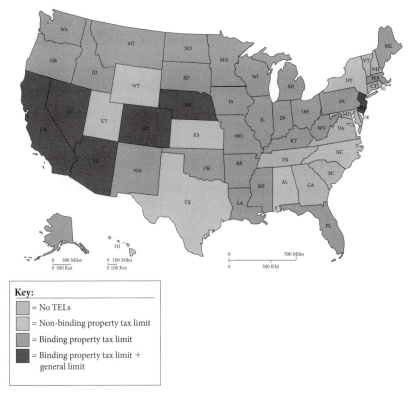

Figure 7.2. Tax and Expenditure Limits on Municipalities

Reprinted by permission of National League of Cities. Hoene and Pagano, 2008.

expressed as a percentage of a given tax base (total income or spending). The difference is who pays on paper and who ends up with a lighter wallet.

If the tax paid is expressed as a percentage of the taxpayer's income, then we are talking about the tax burden. The burden of a tax is determined by its economic effect, not the statutory rate. A retail sales tax rate of 5 percent on a shirt is the same whether it is purchased by a billionaire or a college student who struggles along in poverty, but the financial impact on these two taxpayers is different. In this simple example, the tax burden is the tax paid on the shirt divided by the purchaser's income level.

Debates over taxes get downright confusing when people on different sides of a political issue use different measures, talk about different ideas and, as a result, talk right past each other. One position argues correctly that the retail sales tax is fair because it treats everyone equally by applying the same tax rate to the same economic choice (**horizontal equity**). On the other side is the competing and also

---

Horizontal Equity—a standard of tax fairness that states that taxpayers with the same income should pay the same amount in taxes; a concept of fairness that calls for treating everyone equally by applying the same tax rate to the same economic choice.

correct understanding that the tax is unfair because the economic impact is different (**vertical equity**).

WHAT ARE THE FIVE PRINCIPLES OF TAXATION AND HOW ARE THEY APPLIED?

Given the variety of possibilities for tax design and the serious implications of each decision, tax legislation aims at balancing fundamental principles. The five principles of a sound revenue system sometimes compete with each other and sometimes reinforce each other. A sound revenue system should (Kansas, 1998)

1. foster strong economic growth, job creation, and a rising standard of living for everyone;
2. minimize distortions of private economic behavior by households and business (an efficient tax);
3. yield revenues as low as possible to finance justified levels of expenditures over time;
4. be structured to be simple, understandable, predictable and efficient;
5. have a tax burden that is equitable in impact.

With an eye on these principles and the revenue system's performance, policymakers may have to re-evaluate the system from time to time in order to take into account changing economic, political, and social conditions. (For example, after 2,600 years, China's agricultural tax was abolished as of 2006; the tax had been based on the amount of cultivated land and family size but had become a disincentive to grain production.) Although this framework is a useful approach to assessing tax policy, the ultimate assessment in a democracy is the election.

Applying Tax Principle #1: How Does Tax Policy Affect Economic Growth?

An important tax principle is to foster strong economic growth, job creation, and a rising standard of living. Four criteria are used to measure success. First, tax policy should foster an economic development strategy that benefits both households and businesses. In the United States, the preferred approach to sustainable economic growth is through business investment and private sector job creation instead of through government. Assessing tax policy by its impact on business is a time-honored, potent policy argument. Opponents who label a tax proposal as a jobs-killer can get the upper hand in the public debate. Just as important is the impact of tax policy on households. Voters deserve to know how tax policy impacts their standard of living, including access to jobs and wealth creation. Therefore, tax policy needs to focus both on households and businesses.

Vertical Equity—a standard of tax fairness that calls for treating differently people in different circumstances; a tax is fair if its economic impact is related to income; the principle underlying the idea of tax burden.

Second, a broad tax base is better than a narrow one, because the same tax rate yields more revenue and a narrow base can victimize or benefit certain individuals or groups. Any tax exemption or tax preference should be made known and explained in terms of the competing principles. Labeled loopholes, hidden or narrowly targeted tax favors are viewed suspiciously in an era of low trust of public institutions and public leaders. Are these legal loopholes created by lawmakers to encourage desirable economic behavior or to reward campaign contributors or the politically powerful?

Because taxpayers can gain the same economic benefit from not paying a tax as from getting a direct payment from the government, tax policy invites intense political pressures and fierce jockeying for favored treatment. It is important, then, to know what the favors are worth to the winners and what the favors cost. Tax expenditures are an estimate of the revenue lost to government from each tax incentive, exemption, or loophole. Notice that it is an estimate of a taxing activity that has *not* occurred, and so the estimate is open to intense debate. Not everyone agrees that the lack of tax on an item or activity is properly seen as a "loss" to government, because government can rightfully claim only things that are taxed; trying to claim untaxed (exempted) items as a revenue loss is problematic. This objection is met by thinking of tax expenditures as the value of reductions in tax liability from special tax provisions or regulations that provide tax benefits to particular taxpayers. This means that tax expenditures are valued as benefits received rather than as lost revenue. According to the Tax Foundation, "These policies use the tax code to implement social and economic policy instead of traditional government spending. Lawmakers have come to prefer tax expenditures and credits in recent years because they are less transparent to taxpayers, face less budgetary scrutiny, and allow lawmakers to funnel taxpayer dollars from one group to another without facing criticism that they are big-spending politicians" (Chamberlain, Prante and Hodge, 2007).

Adding up estimates of the exceptions to the general tax code helps decision makers and the public grasp the actual dollar value of tax privileges. This exercise improves transparency by throwing open a window on the policy goals and impacts of tax choices. The federal government and many states compile all the various legal loopholes and their dollar values into a formal report on tax expenditures.

Advocates of fundamental tax reform target many of the current tax expenditures for extinction, but the recipients of those tax advantages will surely fight to maintain their tax favors. In 1786, political economist Vilfredo Pareto observed the fundamental point: "A hundred men from each of whom is exacted one franc will not react to defend their own with as much energy as one man moved by the desire to get hold of those one hundred francs."

Who would reforms affect? Just about everyone. Lists of federal tax expenditures show preferred tax treatment for education savings plans, state tuition programs, and employee retirement plans; the deduction of interest on home mortgages and student loans; untaxed benefits such as from Medicare, employer contributions for medical care and health insurance, and unemployment benefits; and tax credits related to children, the elderly, the disabled, and poor.

A third criterion for the economic growth principle is that tax policy should focus on the long run and not overact to short-run, immediate concerns for any particular firm or market conditions. Lawmakers face a constant and unyielding call for tax incentives or exemptions from individuals and businesses that seek help in tough times, but are not likely to support loss of their tax breaks when times are good. Beneficiaries of a proposed tax incentive often trumpet the net economic benefits that the change would bring, and lawmakers can serve the broader public interest only by demanding hard data about the costs (government taxes not paid by the employer) and benefits (likely new jobs and the taxes paid by those workers).

To compete for economic development advantages, state and local government officials frequently offer an assortment of tax and other incentives to attract a large new business to locate in the area. Incentives might include an outright exemption from a tax or the freezing of tax payments at a low amount for a number of years. Public officials must weigh the benefits from having more jobs in the community and the income, sales and property taxes generated against the absence of tax payments from the business.

Government services, as well as taxes, should be competitive with other states. This fourth criterion for a tax policy that encourages economic growth recognizes that taxes and other revenue sources are supposed to produce revenue to support public services. Therefore, it makes sense to compare both revenues and services to those of surrounding or competitive governments.

Applying Tax Principle #2: What is Efficient Taxation?

By their very nature, taxes interfere with private economic decisions made by households and businesses and divert resources to government. Many policy-makers argue that taxes should be as economically neutral as possible in order to promote the individual choice and limited government upon which capitalism is built. Both the structure and level of individual taxes or the whole revenue system can be designed to keep distortions as small as possible.

Some taxes, however, are specifically designed to interfere with personal behavior. For example, governments impose so-called **sin taxes** to influence tax-payers' choices and discourage certain taxed activities. Cigarettes, alcoholic beverages, and gambling, for example, are taxed separately at high levels, perhaps with part of the tax proceeds dedicated for sin-reduction activities such as gambling addiction recovery programs. The federal government tried to discourage the purchase of luxury products such as personal airplanes, high-priced boats, and expensive automobiles through a now-expired luxury tax. Exceptions to the rule of tax neutrality usually are advocated on the grounds of good policy, but the fact is that sin and luxury taxes are easier to impose than other taxes and therefore are easy targets for tax increases.

Sin Tax—a tax levied on the purchase of goods and services that are considered bad for the health or character such as taxes on alcohol, cigarettes, and gambling.

Table 7.4. 2009 Tax Rate Schedule

MARGINAL TAX RATE IF YOUR FILING STATUS IS SINGLE		
TAXABLE INCOME		
OVER	BUT NOT OVER	MARGINAL RATE
$0	$8,350	10%
$8,350	$33,950	15%
$33,950	$82,250	25%
$82,250	$171,550	28%
$171,550	$372,950	33%
$372,950	and over	35%

MARGINAL TAX RATE IF YOUR FILING STATUS IS MARRIED FILING JOINTLY		
TAXABLE INCOME		
OVER	BUT NOT OVER	MARGINAL RATE
$0	$16,700	10%
$16,700	$67,900	15%
$67,900	$137,050	25%
$137,050	$208,850	28%
$208,850	$372,950	33%
$372,950	and over	35%

SOURCE: IRS, 2009b.

To confirm that tax design meets this neutrality goal, it is best to track the effective tax rates on representative households and businesses. Would you work extra hours if you knew that a higher share of that pay would go to taxes than before? This can happen with a graduated income tax where the tax rate changes at specified income levels. The **marginal tax rate** is the tax on the next dollar of income and it is at that point where economic decisions about work, consumption, and investment can be affected by tax policy. Table 7.4 shows the federal individual income tax rates for 2009. If your filing status is single and you earned $33,949 in taxable income for the year, the next dollar of income would be taxed at 15 percent (15 cents out of the dollar) but that second dollar of income (resulting in a total of $33,951 of taxable income) would be taxed at 25 percent (or 25 cents out of the dollar). That is a 67 percent increase in taxation on the second dollar of income compared to the first. Would that higher tax lessen your enthusiasm for working the extra time to earn the second dollar?

Tax policy debates often focus on the need for low marginal tax rates. Otherwise, a business might avoid hiring new employees or investing in a new

---

Marginal Tax Rate—the tax on the next dollar of income and the point at which economic decisions about work, consumption, and investment can be affected by tax policy.

facility because of the higher taxes on the next increment of income. These disincentives violate the tax principle of efficiency because the business decision would be made on the basis of tax policy instead of the underlying economics of business hiring or investment.

Applying Tax Principle #3: How can Tax Policy be Economical?

Governmental organizations depend on money to run their operations. Unlike business firms that must sell an item to earn income, citizens empower their governments to raise funds from taxation. Wise stewardship and electoral success both demand that taxes be as low as possible to finance politically justified levels of public spending over time.

Forecasting Revenue

Annual budgets depend upon an estimate of revenues to be collected during the year to cover the approved spending plan for the fiscal period. Think about the timing problem caused by the fact that revenue plans or forecasts are developed before the start of the fiscal year and have to last through it. The forecast (unless changed) somehow has to hold for eighteen months or so, during which great and small events will affect spending and investment behavior that in turn will affect revenue collections.

Forecasting revenues (or expenditures for that matter) is both art and science. Studies indicate that individuals with years of experience with a particular revenue system can use their expert judgment to get a fairly close estimate. (There is a "Mack truck" problem—the expert could be hit by a Mack truck one day and the critical expertise is lost.) A host of sophisticated techniques are available, yet they invariably produce competing estimates. It comes down to human judgment on which estimate to use. Many states turn to a consensus revenue-estimating process in which a small group of experts, usually from legislative, executive, and academic settings, come together at set times during the year to compare and discuss estimates based on different assumptions and techniques. They produce one estimate that reflects the best that the group can offer to policymakers.

Studies of actual practice reveal an uncomfortable tendency of decision makers to underestimate revenues but overestimate spending. Public officials adopting this approach stand a chance to end with the year in the black, with a positive balance. Such behavior may be politically preferred. However, this does not make it right or best practice, just politically useful. A former Texas revenue estimator calls for pessimistic revenue forecasts because the "state's leadership can forgive an estimator who underestimates a little. But they don't like those who underestimate a lot or, worse still, overestimate" (Hamilton, 2007).

Forecast—an estimate of the amount (of revenues, spending, or services) expected over a specified period.

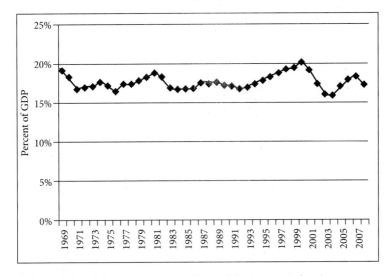

Figure 7.3. The Price of Government Is the Share of the Economy that Supports Government

NOTE: Taxes include individual income, corporate income, social insurance, excise, and estate and gift taxes. Taxes average 17.7 percent of GDP from 1969 to 2008.

SOURCE: Calculated by authors from data from Congressional Budget Office, 2009.

Price of Government

What level of revenue is needed to support government? The **price of government** is the share of the economy that supports government (see Web site resource, Using the Gross Domestic Product to Measure the Role and Size of Government). In figure 7.3, federal receipts for forty years average less than 18 percent of the nation's gross domestic product. The up-tick in revenues during the economic prosperity and higher tax rates passed in President Clinton's term were offset by tax cuts enacted under President George W. Bush.

As a starting point for building a budget, state and local governments can track similar impacts on the economy. Minnesota tracks state and local revenue as a percentage of the state's personal income, a common definition of the tax base of a state. The price of government in Minnesota is about 16 percent in FY 2008, meaning that sixteen cents of every dollar of personal income is paid to the state, local governments, and public school districts. This measure serves "as a financial index for the cost of public services in Minnesota." As another example, the City of Dallas, Texas defines its price of government as the percentage of locally collected city revenue (including all taxes, fees, and charges) as a percent of gross personal income. Indicators such as these help policymakers track the share of the economy taken by government to pay for public services.

Price of Government—an estimate of the cost of government to the economy; often measured as total taxes or revenues as a share of the economy, defined nationally as gross domestic product, and for a state or city often as aggregate personal income.

An economical tax system has to consider five additional factors: responsiveness to the economy, purchasing power, base and rate changes, choice, and budget reserves. Each factor is examined in the following sections.

Tax Elasticity

How sensitive or responsive is the revenue tax system to changes in the economy? **Tax elasticity**, as this is called, is measured by changes in revenues compared to changes in the underlying economy. If revenues change 1 percent from one year to the next, and the economy changes by the same percentage, then elasticity is 1/1 or 1. This shows that revenues move with the economy. If, however, revenues change by 1 percent, but the economy changes by 0.5 percent for the same period, then elasticity would be 1/0.5 or 2.0. This shows that revenues are growing twice as fast as the economy and that that government is taking a bigger share of the economy. Elasticity greater than 1 means that the tax or tax system is sensitive to changes in the economy (elastic); less than 1 shows that it is not sensitive (inelastic tax). If revenues do not change with the economy, then revenues may not keep up with the demand for government services, which tend to increase with economic change. The property tax is not as elastic a revenue source as is the retail sales tax or the personal income tax.

Elastic taxes automatically produce more revenue in a growing economy without political leaders having to raise taxes. In effect, the increase is *politically* free. This is not the case with inelastic taxes, such as the property tax, unless the property tax base itself is growing through construction and rising property values. In many communities today, the property tax base is shrinking and public leaders face the high political costs of slashing spending, raising property tax rates, or both.

Revenue Yield Over Time

Assessing a tax or tax system over time involves shifting the focus from cash received to the impact of inflation and changes in the tax rate and base. This focus may not be persuasive in the political arena, where decision makers and taxpayers are likely to be swayed more by the dollars received than by careful analysis.

When making comparisons over time, changes in purchasing power matters (see chapter 6 and Web site resource, Using the Consumer Price Index). It is possible to raise more revenue than, let us say, a decade ago, but not enough more to make up for inflation. When this happens, more revenue actually translates into less purchasing power. Less purchasing power is not an automatic license for political leaders to raise taxes or charges and fees. Taxpayers may not be persuaded by an inflation argument when they see a higher tax bill.

The flip side is that inflation affects the value of tax exemptions, credits, and, ultimately, tax liability. For example, the IRS says, "By law, the dollar

---

Tax Elasticity—how readily the amount generated by a tax is affected by changes in economic conditions or demand.

amounts for a variety of tax provisions must be revised each year to keep pace with inflation." As a result, more than three dozen tax benefits, affecting virtually every taxpayer, are being adjusted" (IRS, 2009a). Experience with the federal alternative minimum tax shows that failing to link some tax provisions to inflation may have unintended consequences by capturing more income groups in the tax net than expected and thereby stimulating political opposition to a taxing scheme originally designed to reach only higher-income groups enjoying particular tax-advantages (see Web site resource, Fairness and the Federal Income Tax).

Revenues are nudged and tweaked more often than they are overhauled. Trying to keep their head low and head-off a political backlash, political leaders prefer to build on what already is in place rather than raise the visibility and political costs of revenue changes. As a result, most of the frequent revenue changes actually involve minor tinkering with the rate and the base.

Tracking revenues over time can be tricky. Revenue levels can reflect changes in the tax rate instead of the tax base itself. For example, to raise the sales tax rate from $.03 cents per dollar to $.0325 cents might be expected to increase revenue, unless the higher rate discourages consumer spending, as dynamic scoring suggests. The rate itself may not change, but new exemptions can blow a hole in the amount collected compared to the past. For these reasons, the data should be adjusted to reflect changes in tax rates and exemptions before making policy decisions based on revenue trends.

Other Concerns

Because public revenues are raised to cover public spending, it is only logical to keep an eye on the *use* of scarce resources. Resources and spending are two related sides of budgeting. This calls for cost-effective services with built-in incentives to economize. The incentives should work at different levels in the political system and in governmental and nonprofit public organizations. Incentives preserve the choice that is central to both a federal political system and market economy. Choice in a federal system means that state tax policy should not tie the hands of local public leaders and prevent them from meeting local obligations and local demands.

Lastly, to avoid frequent or short-term tax and spending changes that can disrupt economic behavior, adequate budget reserves should be used so that budgets can be balanced. A large **budget reserve** (typically measured as a percentage of yearly revenues or expenditures) can indicate over-taxation. Here the government is taxing to save instead of taxing to spend for useful services. Political opponents can argue the opposite, too: the lack of reserves to deal with an uncertain economy shows mismanagement by the political leaders, both past and current.

Budget Reserve—an amount above yearly expenditures that is collected but not planned to be used in the current fiscal period.

Applying Tax Principle #4: How Does Transparency Make Taxation Responsive?

Tax structures should be simple, understandable, and predictable. The goal is to increase voluntary compliance, lower taxpayers' costs for obeying the rules, and lower the tax collectors' administrative costs. In turn, the overall transparency of the revenue system increases its efficiency and lowers its costs. It is easier to collect a tax that is paid voluntarily than forcing payment after an intrusive audit. Remember the tax evaders described earlier in this chapter? Each case of tax evasion raises the administrative costs of delinquencies, audits, and appeals.

When a transparent system makes clear when and to what extent a carefully defined item or activity is subject to tax, the tax is more easily managed and controlled. Translating tax legislation into practical guidance for taxpayers requires terabytes of tax rules and examples. Why does it require upwards of 70,000 pages

"Look...people are basically honest and decent. Why don't we scrap the tax laws completely and have the people pay whatever they think is fair?"

Figure 7.4. Tax Transparency and Tax Fairness Are Related

Reprinted by permission of www.cartoonstock.com

BOX 7.2

Roman Tax Collectors and City Speed Traps

In the Roman era, tax collectors were among the most unpopular people of Israel because they not only collected the empire's heavy taxes, but they overcharged, kept the profits, and got rich doing this. These tax collectors had what is termed today a "pecuniary interest," or opportunity to profit, from their job.

It is unfair to associate this past behavior with today's tax collectors, who are professionals paid for implementing without bias or personal gain the taxes approved by elected representatives.

What do you think about the following situations that involve profiting from a public duty?

- A judge receives as income a share of a court fine levied at her discretion.

- A police officer gets a good job performance rating for writing more traffic tickets.

- A county sheriff gets to personally pocket any savings from not spending the state-provided per day allowance for an inmate's food costs.

- A police department receives a larger budget allocation for generating more city revenue as a result of running a "speed trap."

---

of federal tax law now, according to CCH International, when it was *only* 26,000 pages in 1984 (CCH International, 2009)? The page count suggests that tax legislation has changed over time to better handle the complexity of economic activity. As a result, the tax system itself has become more complex. This complexity fuels anti-tax sentiment and provokes calls for a simpler tax system (see chapter 3). Regardless of the political impact, tax authorities concerned with transparency have the burden of making tax rules and forms accessible and Web-friendly (see figure 7.4).

No one likes surprises in tax policy. Without reliable rules that taxpayers can use as they plan and conduct their economic activity, taxpayers become subject to the whim of the tax collector. Even less appealing is when the tax collector profits from finding against the taxpayer (see box 7.2). Relatively stable and predictable tax structures avoid disrupting business and individual tax planning. Savvy political leaders plan for a cooling-off period after a tax change that whipped up strong political opposition. It is best to wait until the economic and political effects of past changes are known before changing the tax again.

Elected officials have an uneasy relationship with their government's tax collection agency. Congress, for example, wants tax deadbeats caught and a reduction in the **tax gap** between the overall amounts legally owed and the unpaid taxes

---

Tax Gap—the difference between the estimated amount of money government might expect from a tax and actual collections.

due to government. Congress also responds to stories about alleged aggressive behavior by IRS tax collection agents. Similar tension exists in legislative instructions at all levels of government between a hardheaded "collect-the-tax" demand and a soft-headed "be-nice-to-taxpayers" behavior. A common budget request from a tax-collection agency is justified with statements attesting that more tax agents will cover their cost through increased enforcement against tax deadbeats and a reduction in the tax gap. As an example, the Kansas Department of Revenue (2009) says that in fiscal years 2006 to 2008 it collected an average of $14.49 for every dollar spent on compliance enforcement. Such a high return on investment offers legislators a compelling case for higher budgets. At the federal level at least, all too often, efforts to crack down on those not paying taxes leads later to legislative hearings against the "abuse" by the tax collectors. Support for a U.S. Taxpayer Bill of Rights grew out of charges of abuse by IRS agents; congressional hearings started in 1981 and led to the passage of symbolic responses. (This federal response is very different from Colorado's, structured as a tax limitation and as described in chapter 3.) Today, the IRS labels as "independent" an organization within the IRS that is designed to protect taxpayers' rights and reduce the burden of paying taxes. A more forthright response of a tax agency's responsiveness to the universal concern of taxpayers is represented by Canada's adoption in 2007 of a taxpayer bill of rights that spells out the public's rights in clear language. Shown in box 7.3, the Canadian approach is designed to promote transparency and responsiveness.

Applying Tax Principle #5: What Is a Fair Tax?
Who should pay? Fairness is in the eye of the beholder, as evident by the shrill statements about taxes in political campaigns and radio call-in shows. Different from the discussion in chapter 3 that stresses political issues, here we add the perspectives of public finance and tax theory.

Benefits-Received Principle
There are ways to go beyond the rhetoric to get a handle on tax equity or fairness. Essentially, tax fairness can be based either on the benefits received from public services or the ability-to-pay principle. Under the first approach, the **benefits-received principle**, those who benefit from the service should be the ones to pay for it. This way, the tax burden is tied to the spending side of government. Complainers to call-in shows yammer about how they do not use all their city services, so why should they have to pay for them? Paying taxes is unlike buying a hamburger instead of a steak. Citizens do not get to personalize their public services, as if in a cafeteria. Rather, everyone in the nation gets the same conceptual level of national defense despite personal differences on how to define the scope of that service. You get police service even if you do not have any direct interaction with them; however, you get safer roads and safer neighborhoods and so, in fact, you do derive an indirect benefit.

Benefits-Received Principle—the idea that a person's tax burden should be based on the benefits that the person receives from the services provided.

BOX 7.3

Canada's Taxpayer Bill of Rights

1. You have the right to receive entitlements and to pay no more and no less than what is required by law.*

2. You have the right to service in both official languages.**

3. You have the right to privacy and confidentiality.

4. You have the right to a formal review and a subsequent appeal.

5. You have the right to be treated professionally, courteously, and fairly.

6. You have the right to complete, accurate, clear, and timely information.

7. You have the right, as an individual, not to pay income tax amounts in dispute before you have had an impartial review.

8. You have the right to have the law applied consistently.

9. You have the right to lodge a service complaint and to be provided with an explanation of our findings.

10. You have the right to have the costs of compliance taken into account when administering tax legislation.

11. You have the right to expect us to be accountable.

12. You have the right to relief from penalties and interest under tax legislation because of extraordinary circumstances.***

13. You have the right to expect us to publish our service standards and report annually.

14. You have the right to expect us to warn you about questionable tax schemes in a timely manner.

15. You have the right to be represented by a person of your choice.

Reproduced with permission of the Canada Revenue Agency and the Minister of Public Works and Government Services. Canada Revenue Agency, 2009.

* Entitlements defined as the benefits, credits and refunds to which one is entitled under the law.

** Canada has two official languages, English and French.

*** Canada's tax agency can consider items not under the taxpayer's control (such as natural disasters and fire) as a reason to offer relief from penalty and interest charges.

One way to link the cost of government to the benefits received is through dedicated taxes, or taxes that flow to a designated purpose, if (and this is a big "if") the purpose is related to the tax payment. In this case, public finance theory tells us that the revenue source should reveal taxpayer preference for the service (the demand) which then produces a change in the service (supply) to meet the service needs. For example, the number of vehicles paying tolls reflects the amount of demand for using the toll road, which in turn supplies the toll-road authority with

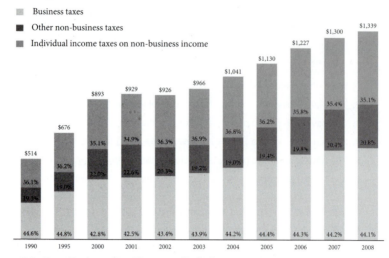

Figure 7.5. Does Business Pay Almost Half of All State and Local Taxes?
Total State and Local Business Taxes: 50-State Estimates. Fiscal Years 1990–2008.
SOURCE: Reprinted by permission of Ernst & Young, LLP and Council on State Taxation, 2009.

valuable information and resources to preserve and improve this road. A common dedicated revenue source is an **excise tax**, defined as a specific tax on units purchased (gallons of oil, packs of cigarettes, and bottles of beer) instead of price. Gas and diesel excise taxes often are dedicated to highway and transportation programs on the basis that the tax and the service are linked.

Because business does not bear the economic burden of a tax—only people pay taxes (ultimately)—the most effective argument for business taxation is to structure it to recover the costs of governmental services rendered to business in general. Figure 7.5 shows that the business community estimates that business pays almost one-half of all state and local taxes, mostly through property taxes on business property and sales taxes on supplies for the business. Do you think that businesses directly receive this share of the value of all government services? Perhaps you do, if you include the indirect benefits, such as from the contribution of public education to a productive workforce or from the contribution of the police or fire services to the safety of the business. If this estimate of the tax burden on businesses is correct (and other analysts may differ), then the benefits-received tax principal is not being followed. The lack of consistency in tax policy according to public finance theory should not come as a shock, because tax policy is a political decision and therefore subject to political pressures.

Ability-to-Pay Principle

In contrast to the benefits-received principle, the tax principle based on ability to pay considers only how wealthy the taxpayer is. Adam Smith made a passionate

---

Excise Tax—a tax levied on the volume purchased such as a gallon of gasoline or pint of liquor.

case for taxes "in proportion to…respective abilities." An example of this practice is the structure of the federal income tax, shown in table 7.4, with the marginal tax rate in the federal income tax increasing with each category to a top rate
of 35 percent. Despite this nominal rate, the average effective tax rate is less. For
example, in table 7.5 we see that the top 1 percent of taxpayers in 2008 averaged an
18 percent effective tax rate on their federal individual income tax. Once the individual income tax is combined with all other federal taxes, the federal tax system has
a progressive tilt by which tax liability increases as income increases. How does the
progressive structure of federal taxes compare to the total for state and local governments? Again, the result is a progressive tax structure overall, as shown in figure 7.6.
A progressive tax system is an example of unequal treatment of unequals.

The principle of horizontal equity calls for the equal treatment of taxpayers
in similar situations. If one individual earns a wage of $5,000 and another per-
son receives $5,000 in interest earnings from a bank account, should both have
the same tax liability? At the basic level they are equal because both receive equal
amounts of $5,000 of spendable resources. Horizontal equity would suggest
that they should get the same tax bill. Would it make a difference if the interest
is earned on savings from wages already taxed or from interest gained from an
inheritance or gift? Politicians write tax laws to make distinctions because not all
circumstances are equal, although this is subject to change in the next election! It
is no wonder that the tax laws are so complex.

Courts show great deference to the legislature in the design of taxes to serve
public interests. As shown with individual taxpayers on savings, valid arguments
for different public policies can and are made. The courts usually leave the design

Table 7.5. Average Effective Federal Tax Rates in 2008: By Type of Tax and Cash Income
Percentile

CASH INCOME PERCENTILE	INDIVIDUAL INCOME TAX	PAYROLL TAXES	CORPORATE INCOME TAX	ESTATE TAX	ALL FEDERAL TAXES
Lowest Quintile	−8.1	8.4	0.9	0	1.1
Second Quintile	−3.1	10.4	1.0	0	8.3
Middle Quintile	3.3	10.9	0.9	0	15.1
Fourth Quintile	6.6	10.7	1.2	0	18.6
Top Quintile	15.0	5.7	5.1	0.4	26.2
All	9.5	7.9	3.3	0.2	20.9
ADDENDUM					
80–90	9.8	10.2	1.7	0.1	21.8
90–95	13.1	8.6	2.2	0.1	24.0
95–99	16.8	5.3	4.1	0.4	26.5
Top 1 %	18.3	1.5	9.6	0.7	30.0
Top 0.1 %	18.0	0.7	12.2	0.8	31.6

NOTE: Each quintile contains 20 percent of the income distribution.

SOURCE: Reprinted by permission of the Tax Policy Center. Rohaly, 2009.

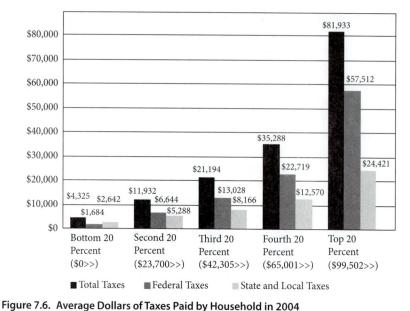

Figure 7.6. Average Dollars of Taxes Paid by Household in 2004
SOURCE: Reprinted by permission of The Tax Foundation. Chamberlain, Prante, and Scott, 2007, p. 5.

of taxes in the hands of the legislature, unless they see a constitutionally overriding principle, such as the tax violates interstate commerce.

Tax Incidence

Tax incidence refers to the ultimate economic burden of a tax or revenue system. Again, only people pay taxes, not the legal entity termed a corporation or partnership. Although the business firm may write the check, the ultimate burden rests elsewhere. The effect of taxes is that owners may pocket less profit, employees may receive lower wages than available elsewhere, suppliers may be pressed to accept lower prices, and/or customers may have to pay higher prices. Although there is no way to know precisely how this tax shifting occurs, estimates are valuable in assessing a tax system.

A tax burden is characterized as progressive if the effective tax rate rises with income, regressive if it falls as income rises, and proportional if the effective tax rate is the same for all income levels. According to figure 7.7, the individual income tax in Minnesota is highly progressive but the sales, business, and property taxes are each regressive. Figure 7.6, which gives the national picture in 2004 of the combined federal, state, and local tax burden for the *average* household across the income groups, reveals that higher income households have the higher tax burden.

Now consider the distributional impacts of the legal loopholes in tax law, the specific deductions, exclusions, exemptions, credits or deferrals from tax liability

---

Tax Incidence—the person bearing the ultimate economic burden of a tax.

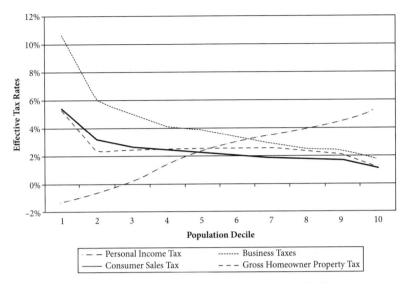

Figure 7.7. Minnesota Effective Tax Rates for 2004 by Population Decile

SOURCE: Reprinted by permission of the State of Minnesota, Department of Revenue, 2009.

Table 7.6. Comparative Tax Burdens in Industrialized Countries, 2008

COUNTRY	SINGLE, NO CHILDREN	MARRIED, 2 CHILDREN
Canada	31.3%	20.2%
France	49.3%	42.1%
Germany	52.0%	36.4%
Italy	46.5%	36.0%
Japan	29.5%	24.0%
United Kingdom	32.8%	26.9%
United States	30.1%	17.7%
Average for 30 industrialized countries	37.4%	27.3%

SOURCE: Reprinted by permission. Calculated by the authors from data provided by the OECD, 2009.

called "tax expenditures." Who benefits from tax expenditures? Three key federal personal income tax deductions illustrate the point. Two of these deductions promote home ownership (specifically, the payment of interest on mortgages on owner-occupied residences and property taxes paid on real property), and the third deduction serves as a federal offset for payment of certain state and local taxes. In each case, the largest benefits are enjoyed by higher income taxpayers who own larger houses and pay the most in state and local taxes that are deductible from federal taxable income. Those who benefit so strongly from legal loopholes in the tax base will, if they act politically in their economic self-interest, fight to keep these tax advantages. Achieving fundamental reform of the federal income tax is more difficult when tax favors and privileges give such strong incentives to certain income groups.

Taxes in the Global Economy

In a global economy, the competition for skilled workers and business activity requires attention to how domestic tax policy compares to policies in other countries. Not only can people vote with their feet by moving out of one American city to another, but individuals and business activity can move from one country to another. According to the OECD, tax burdens in 2008 on individuals and families in the United States were less than in Canada, France, Germany, Italy, Japan, the United Kingdom, and the average of thirty industrialized countries (see table 7.6). In that group, only Japan had a lower tax burden for individuals. Countries with higher tax burdens may have social programs that are more developed, so their taxpayers just get a different mix of public and private services. The trade-off between taxes and government spending is a choice the voters make.

CAN GOVERNMENTS RAISE REVENUE WITHOUT HAVING TAXES?

In addition to taxes, public service organizations depend on a variety of other sources of revenue. Consumers expect to pay for services, and so governments and other public organizations design programs that link payments to benefits received. When governments provide water service, consumers have to pay for the water used, with more usage leading to higher payments due.

Many times, however, the management imperative to maximize revenues must yield to broader public policy. For example, state universities charge tuition, but usually not at a level that covers the full cost of an education. Instead, general taxes subsidize students as a means of encouraging the development of human capital, fostering economic development by providing an educated workforce, and contributing to the educated citizenry, which is so important to a democracy. Similarly, local decision makers may opt to have children enjoy recreation programs in the summer instead of having spare time to get in trouble with the law. This type of policy often results in only a nominal charge, if any, to use public swimming pools.

Charges and fees that are imposed may not be tied directly to the service. For example, a recent proposal in one state called for residents renewing their automobile registrations to pay a fee for funding state parks. While creative, the proposal was a service fee in name only, because there was no natural link between the (relatively) few citizens who use state parks and the many who legally drive cars on the highways.

Higher levels of government may decide to share revenues with lower levels of government. The U.S. government no longer has an open-ended federal **revenue sharing program** with state and local governments; the last one was

---

Revenue Sharing—when one level of government shares its revenues with another, usually at a set rate or amount.

created in 1972 under Republican President Richard M. Nixon and ended in 1986 under Republican President Ronald Reagan. However, the government of Canada uses centrally collected revenues to raise the per capita revenues in some provinces up to the national average. Although different in design, this type of funding arrangement, an **equalization program**, is used by American states to fund primary and secondary education to meet state constitutional requirements for equality in public schools. In Texas, for example, this is referred to as the "Robin Hood" method—the property-tax-rich school districts contribute funds to the property-tax-poor districts. As you might imagine, a funding design that redistributes money is prone to produce court cases and legislation, and that is just what continues to play out in states all across the country. There is no perfect funding design, only a legal one that can balance competing interests.

More frequently, **intergovernmental aid** comes with strings attached. For example, if the federal government wants to encourage safe drinking water and effective sewage systems, as it does, it can provide funds to help local governments build these expensive utility systems. Although this federal assistance is now offered to the states for them to administer as a loan to local governments, this form of intergovernmental aid used to be provided through a grant (or grant-in-aid). Either way, it is an inducement for a specific activity or program. States can offer grants to the local governments, too.

Grant recipients must guard against skewing local priorities just to get the grant money. Ideally, there should be a local need that drives the search for grant dollars instead of the other way around. One way to ensure that the givers and receivers are on the same page is to require them to share costs. The interstate highway system was constructed with 90 percent federal revenue and 10 percent state government funds. Would you agree that getting someone else to pay for one's spending habit is generally preferable to having to find the funds oneself?

In a bipartisan show of support for getting someone else to pay, governors, mayors, and even higher education leaders approached federal policymakers in the fall of 2008 with the idea that federal government should finance "shovel-ready" public works projects. These state and local public leaders saw a natural fit with 1) a financial stimulus strategy designed to lift the economy out of recession by creating jobs; 2) helping states and other public organizations bypass the credit crunch that made borrowing for big projects too costly or even unavailable; and 3) helping repair and modernize aging roads, bridges, schools, and more.

Regardless of how governments raise the money to pay for budgeted goods and services, in the end, the financial burden rests with its taxpayers. Citizens and

---

Equalization Program—a method of distributing resources to different recipients based on a calculated amount designed to equalize benefits.

Intergovernmental Revenue—funds received by one government from another government.

taxpayers couple their responsibility with demands for accountability for the use of their tax dollars and transparency in the making of revenue policy. It is understandable, then, that tax policy looms as large as it does in electoral politics.

THUMBNAIL

People like the spending part of the budget. As taxpayers, they do not like the other side of the equation: giving up "their" money to support the spending. This frames the big question: do we tax to spend or spend to tax? What comes first? Regardless of the answer, there are certain principles that apply in raising the money. This chapter reviews tax principles to showcase the dilemmas facing a democracy founded on liberty and capitalism. A sound revenue system should foster strong economic growth, job creation, and a rising standard of living for everyone. Tax policy should minimize economic distortions, yield revenues sufficient to sustain desired public services, meet transparency standards, and impose a tax burden that is equitable in impact on households and businesses. Embedded in all tax and revenue-raising decisions are assumptions about taxpayer behavior. How will individuals respond to a particular tax and will it be the way that policymakers anticipate? Reasonable people will differ over the revenue-raising rules that "should" guide public decision-making.

CASE

Repeal the #@! Income Tax in Taxachusetts!

Question 1 on the November 2008 ballot in Massachusetts was an initiative petition for a law, "The Small Government Act to End the Income Tax." Massachusetts has had the initiative petition since the 1920s.

Summary of Question 1:

This proposed law would reduce the state personal income tax rate to 2.65 percent for all categories of taxable income for the tax year beginning on or after Jan. 1, 2009, and would eliminate the tax for all tax years beginning on or after Jan. 1, 2010.

The personal income tax applies to income received or gain realized by individuals and married couples, by estates of deceased persons, by certain trustees and other fiduciaries, by persons who are partners in and receive income from partnerships, by corporate trusts, and by persons who receive income as shareholders of "S corporations" as defined under federal tax law. The proposed law would not affect the tax due on income or gain realized in a tax year beginning before Jan. 1, 2009.

The proposed law states that if any of its parts were declared invalid, the other parts would stay in effect.

Text of Question 1:

Be it enacted by the people, and by their authority:

SECTION 1. This law, to be known as The Small Government Act to End the Income Tax, is enacted upon the following findings and declarations:

The government of the Commonwealth of Massachusetts today is Big Government, and

(1) Massachusetts Big Government programs do not work; all too often, they do not achieve their stated objectives; all too often they fail in their duties;

(2) Massachusetts Big Government programs make things worse;

(3) Massachusetts Big Government programs create new problems;

(4) Massachusetts Big Government programs squander and waste; and

(5) Massachusetts Big Government programs divert money and energy from positive and productive uses in the private sector.

Big Government has a harmful impact on those who rely upon it, and

(1) Big Government promotes irresponsibility;

(2) Big Government makes people weak and dependent; and

(3) Big Government saps personal initiative and undermines the work ethic.

Big Government cannot work. It is inherently flawed and unreformable.

High taxes feed and increase the size and scope of Massachusetts Big Government.

High taxes drive jobs out of Massachusetts.

High taxes reduce our standard of living, making more people poor and fewer able to help their friends, families, and communities in need.

Government spending rises to meet government income. To dramatically shrink government spending, we must dramatically shrink government income.

Ending the personal income tax is intended to dramatically shrink the revenue of the Commonwealth of Massachusetts. Ending the personal income tax is designed to be a bold step in making Massachusetts' government small.

Small government leaves us free and unburdened to fashion our own lives, and

(1) Small government is simple, cheap, and good;

(2) Small government is thrifty and effective;

(3) Small government is accountable and responsible;

(4) There's no place to hide waste and corruption in a small government budget; and

(5) Small government leaves us with the responsibility and the resources to manage our own lives, educate our children, protect our families, care for our neighbors, and assist those who cannot support themselves.

SECTION 2. Chapter sixty-two of the General Laws, as appearing in the 2006 Official Edition, is hereby amended by inserting at the beginning of Section 3 of said Chapter sixty-two a new paragraph to read:

"No income or other gain realized in a taxable year beginning on or after January 1, 2010 shall be taxable, or subject to tax, under the provisions of this Chapter."

Said Chapter sixty-two is hereby further amended by inserting the words "Subject to the introductory paragraph at the beginning of Section 3 of this chapter", followed by a comma, at the beginnings of each of Subsections (f), (g) and (h) of Section 2 of Chapter sixty-two.

SECTION 3. Section 4 of Chapter sixty-two of the General Laws, as appearing in the 2006 Official Edition, is hereby amended, effective January 1, 2009, first, by striking from the introductory paragraph the words "as follows" and the colon that follows them, and replacing same with the words "at the rate of 2.65 per cent", followed by a period; and second, by striking the subsections.

SECTION 4. Section 4 of Chapter sixty-two B of the General Laws, as appearing in the 2006 Official Edition, is hereby repealed, effective January 1, 2010.

SECTION 5. Chapter sixty-two C of the General Laws, as appearing in the 2006 Official Edition, is hereby amended by inserting at the beginning of Section 6 of said Chapter sixty-two C a new paragraph to read:

The term 'taxable year' as used in this Section or Section 7 of this Chapter, and applied to a natural person or to a partnership consisting only of natural persons, shall not include any period beginning on or after January 1, 2010.

SECTION 6. The Small Government Act to End the Income Tax is not intended to impair the operation of G.L. Chapter sixty-two E. Therefore, Section 2 of G.L. Chapter sixty-two E, as appearing in the 2006 Official Edition, is hereby amended by excising from the first sentence thereof the phrase "required to deduct and withhold taxes upon wages under the provisions of chapter sixty-two B" and the phrase "and any identification number such employer is required to include on a withholding tax return filed pursuant to said chapter sixty-two B".

SECTION 7. The effect of the Small Government Act to End the Income Tax is prospective, not retroactive. Notwithstanding the provisions of the foregoing sections hereof, this law shall not be construed to impair the collection of moneys due the Commonwealth for income or other gain realized by any person before the start of the taxable year described in Section 2 hereof, nor shall it be construed to affect the responsibility of any person to comply with the requirements of G.L. Chapters sixty-two B or sixty-two C as either pertains to income or other gain realized before the start of the taxable year described in Section 2 hereof or before the date of any repeal or change in the law.

SECTION 8. The provisions of this law are severable, and if any clause, sentence, paragraph or section of this chapter, or an application thereof, shall be adjudged by any court of competent jurisdiction to be invalid, such judgment shall not affect, impair, or Invalidate the remainder thereof but shall be confined in its operation to the clause, sentence, paragraph, section or application adjudged invalid.

Reprinted by permission. Office of the Attorney General, Commonwealth of Massachusetts, 2008.

Thinking It Over

1. Teachers, firefighters, and other labor groups joined social service agencies and the Massachusetts Municipal Association in the Coalition for Our Communities to defeat the ballot question. Why would *local* government employees join forces to oppose the repeal of a *state* income tax?
2. The Massachusetts Taxpayers Foundation, Greater Boston Chamber of Commerce, and other business organizations formed a coalition to oppose Question 1. Why would business organizations join forces to oppose the repeal of a state income tax?
3. A local newspaper labeled Question 1 "a catastrophe for the state." Yet, nine states have no income tax and figure 3.1 indicates that many Americans prefer smaller government with fewer services. Is repeal of the income tax a "catastrophe" for public services at the state and local level of government?

Can you identify valid arguments for the opposing view?

4. How is this proposal similar to and different from the proposals in the case (What Do *You* Think?) at the end of chapter 3?

5. The Secretary of State of the Commonwealth of Massachusetts certified the vote. More than three million votes were cast, and the initiative was defeated by more than a two-to-one margin. How would you have voted? Imagine yourself, a public official, at a press conference. How would you explain your answer?

For more information on this case, see the Web site resource, Further Resources Chapter 4.

WEB SITE RESOURCES

- Fairness and the Federal Income Tax
- Further Resources
- Internet Resources
- Using the Consumer Price Index
- Using the Gross Domestic Product to Measure the Role and Size of Government

REVIEW QUESTIONS

1. Why might paying taxes, like voting, be an important form of political participation in a democracy? What political lessons does paying taxes teach citizens and residents?

2. Why do politicians often prefer to
   a. take a "nickel-and-dime" approach to raising revenue by instituting many small taxes rather than paying for all government spending with one large tax?
   b. have tax issues be decided by the people directly through a popular referendum instead of by a vote in the legislature?

3. Why is revenue diversity important? Why is it important that the tax system be transparent?

4. Look at the most recent budget documents for your state's capital city.
   a. What two or three revenue sources does the city rely on most? Why is this information politically meaningful?
   b. Assess the three main tax sources—property, income, and retail sales—by three tax principles described in the text that you consider most important to political life. Why did you choose these three principles?

5. In *Man and Superman* the British playwright George Bernard Shaw wrote, "You should be as romantic as you please about love...but you mustn't be romantic about money."
   a. Should similar houses be taxed the same? What if one is owned by a 90-year-old widower and the other is owned by a young professional couple? Should a millionaire and a person earning only the minimum wage pay the same

tax on the purchase of $50 of food for home consumption? Should both the millionaire and the minimum-wage worker pay 10 percent of their earned income in taxes? What if the millionaire has no earned income but receives that amount yearly from the earnings of an inheritance? What principles should you use to decide? Why are these questions politically important?

b. Ask two friends what tax fairness means to them. Then ask them to answer the questions in 5a above and briefly explain their answers. Compare their responses to your own using the principles in this chapter and chapter 3.

c. In your opinion, is a progressive tax system *fair*? Why or why not?

8

⚜

Politics and Capital Budgeting

This chapter answers four questions:

- What is capital budgeting and why is it important?
- Should governments plan and if so, how?
- If not pay cash, then why and when borrow money?
- Is there such a thing as free money?

> What does Fleetwood Mac tell us not to do about the future?
>
> What happens to time in the Steve Miller Band's song, "Fly Like an Eagle?"

> You and I come by road or rail, but economists travel on infrastructure.
>
> FORMER BRITISH PRIME MINISTER MARGARET THATCHER

Politicians and the media love pictures showing the ribbon-cutting ceremony at the opening of a new road, fire station, public park, or aircraft carrier. Pictures capture the first spade of dirt turned over for the building of a major facility. These powerful images, a staple of political publicity, portray highly public events that result from the exercise of political power in the White House, Congress, the state capitol, court house, or city hall to allocate money to one expensive project, and its constituents, over many other competing projects with equally deserving interests.

The political consequences of capital project funding, or its lack, goes well beyond the public relations. Republicans lost control of Congress in 2006 in some small part because voters understood that the widely mocked "bridge to nowhere" (formally the Gravina Island Bridge project) in Alaska confirmed wasteful spending in Washington. The bridge started as a vivid example of pork barrel politics, meaning the politics surrounding spending designed to support incumbents' reelection by letting them direct spending to their districts, usually through the tacit agreement among legislators not to question public spending in each others' districts. Once this particular earmarked spending came to light, legislators, hoping to defuse public anger, gave Alaska the money to use for something other than the bridge. The offended sponsor of the bridge happened to be the sole House member from Alaska and the chairman of the transportation and infrastructure committee. Before being overruled by Congress, he was not above pointing out that the rejection of his "bringing home the bacon" project would jeopardize other legislators' projects.

Interesting research on Florida cities by Susan MacManus (2004) shows that incumbents were more likely to lose reelection because of their positions on infrastructure issues than on tax or service issues. Infrastructure decisions by public leaders reflect their choices about the projects themselves, including their financing, location, and timing. These decisions also are about local growth expectations, with some communities wanting slow growth and others favoring fast growth. These tangible, visible, and expensive decisions about allocating resources can cement a candidate's reelection image.

This chapter addresses the large, lumpy, and costly items funded by the public. Accountants call them **capital assets**. The first section provides definitions and context along with the connection between buying, building, and constructing projects and their upkeep and maintenance. Government planning got a bad name in the United States due to the communist approach to central-government master plans for all of society. As the second section conveys, planning does not have to diminish choice, the touchstone of a free society. Frankly, governments are the only organization that can plan well into the future. Well-respected, huge corporations can fail seemingly overnight. Officials face difficult decisions on capital assets, but good capital planning is possible. By definition, capital assets should last longer than one year, so the third part of the chapter explores why governments often borrow the money to fund the projects and then spread the cost over the life of the asset. We close with the proverbial question posed by all who want to spend public dollars: is there any free money?

WHAT IS CAPITAL BUDGETING AND WHY IS IT IMPORTANT?

Public capital assets include roads and highways; water and sewage systems; bridges and tunnels; canals, waterways, and levee systems; educational facilities; and other government buildings. China's Great Wall is arguably the greatest public works project of all time. The Obama Administration touts its Reinvestment and Recovery Act of 2009 as the single largest public infrastructure investment program since the creation of the interstate highway system in the 1950s. By one estimate, over $400 billion in public and private investments are spent each year on transportation, utilities, and public facilities, with

---

Capital Asset—any significant acquisition, construction, replacement, or improvement to the physical assets of an organization, including land, property, and equipment.

BOX 8.1

Current Infrastructure Spending

The most recent comprehensive data, for 2004, indicate that total capital spending from all sources on transportation, utilities, and selected other public facilities—specifically, prisons, schools, and facilities related to water and other natural resources, such as dams—was more than $400 billion that year. The federal government financed about $60 billion (including federal grants to state and local governments), or roughly 15 percent of the total. State and local governments funded (net of the federal grants) 42 percent of the investment, and the private sector provided the balance. Those funding shares have changed over time and vary greatly from one infrastructure category to another.

Federal spending on infrastructure is dominated by transportation, which accounted for nearly three-quarters of the roughly $60 billion total federal investment in infrastructure in 2004. Highways alone accounted for nearly half of the total. Capital spending by state and local governments that year was primarily for schools, highways, and water systems. Together, those categories accounted for about $135 billion in state and local government spending, which is about 80 percent of the $170 billion spent on infrastructure by state and local governments.

In contrast, private-sector investment in infrastructure is dominated by spending on energy and telecommunications, which in 2004 represented nearly 80 percent of the sector's total infrastructure spending of about $175 billion. Private entities provide most of the nation's electricity and telecommunications services (typically, under federal or state regulation) and account for nearly all capital spending on those utilities.

Reprinted from the Congressional Budget Office, 2008.

---

42 percent funded by state and local governments (see box 8.1). The federal government alone owns about 1.2 million structures with 60 percent controlled by the Department of Defense. These figures confirm that capital budgeting is a substantial fiscal issue.

Capital investments, at first shiny and new, can deteriorate through overuse or lack of maintenance and even become obsolete or under-used. Natural and human-caused disasters, when they destroy capital investments, often lead to quick shifts in the budget to accommodate large rebuilding projects.

- Reaction to the terrorist strikes on September 11, 2001 led to extensive budget allocations to protect the nation, its people, and critical public facilities.
- Highway bridges in California were retrofitted at a significant cost to handle basic earthquake risk revealed by dramatic collapses during earthquakes in 1989 and 1994.
- New Orleans, Louisiana was hit by hurricane-force winds of Hurricane Katrina on August 29, 2005, but most of the destruction occurred due to the failure of concrete-walled levees built by the U.S. Army Corps of Engineers,

which allowed water to burst into low-lying areas with enough force to blow houses off their foundations and make about 80 percent of the city's housing stock uninhabitable.

- On May 4, 2007, Greensburg, Kansas was hit by a tornado classified as F-5 (the most powerful) with winds at over 200 miles per hour; this effectively destroyed more than 95 percent of the buildings in this small (population 1,500) southwest Kansas town.
- During evening rush hour on August 1, 2007, in downtown Minneapolis, Minnesota, a 1,000 foot steel-truss span of the Interstate Highway (I-35W) bridge collapsed, plunging at least fifty vehicles and passengers over 60 feet into the Mississippi River or onto its banks.
- Wildfires in late October 2007 led to a mass evacuation of part of Southern California as public and private structures were destroyed by the wind-whipped fires.
- Flood waters inundated twenty buildings on the University of Iowa campus in June 2008 and caused an estimated $232 million in damages to campus structures and contents.

Events such as these demonstrate dramatically the vulnerability of the built environment. Each one resulted in large federal emergency allocations to restore damaged facilities and cost states and localities considerable sums. The vulnerability of urban centers has been high throughout history, punctuated most recently by the threat of terrorist attacks.

Fundamentally, it is not the sheer number or type of capital assets that matters, but how the facilities fit together to promote a livable and viable community. A **comprehensive plan** of development links the appropriate use of land with a community's long-range growth goals, in a "build-out" schedule that is affordable, doable, and commands a community's political consensus. In its comprehensive approach to planning for the state capitol area, the State of Washington (2006) noted that the "location of state government facilities and the layout of spaces within them are vital components to effective and efficient delivery of public services." Public facilities also play a key role in economic growth. A community's economy depends on safe drinking water, sanitary sewers, an adequate street network, and other infrastructure essential to modern living and commerce. Budgeting and replacing public facilities also carry political impact, even affecting public officials' approval ratings or reelection chances. President George W. Bush's approval rating plummeted when the public decided that his administration was too slow in responding to the destruction of New Orleans, despite his and Congress's success in budgeting more than $100 billion for Gulf Coast aid and reconstruction.

Comprehensive Plan—a community's plan showing how geographic, physical, social, economic and public faculties can impact local development along with public policy guidelines and funding outlines to achieve local objectives.

BOX 8.2

Infrastructure Unites the Country

"Good roads and canals will shorten distances, facilitate commercial and personal intercourse, and unite, by a still more intimate community of interests, the most remote quarters of the United States. No other single operation, within the power of government, can more effectually tend to strengthen and perpetuate that union which secures external independence, domestic peace, and internal liberty."

SOURCE: Quoted from Gallatin, 1808.

"Our unity as a nation is sustained by free communication of thought and by easy transportation of people and good....Together the unifying forces of our communication and transportation systems are dynamic elements in the very name we bear—United States. Without them, we would be a mere alliance of many separate parts."

SOURCE: Eisenhower, 1955.

EXERCISE: How do these sentiments relate to table 1.2, What Is Important in Budgetary Politics?

Infrastructure as Durable Goods and Capital Assets

Former British Prime Minister Margaret Thatcher said economists call facilities and other capital assets **infrastructure**, and they do, but the more precise term is **durable goods**, because these investments have a life span of more than several years. Accountants call them capital assets. Most of this book is about the way public organizations plan their spending for soft goods or **expendable** goods. In addition to goods, services, and equipment that are expected to be used-up in the year, expendables include payment for employees' wages and salaries because, once used, an employee's time is no longer available. An employee's time is a service purchased and consumed. In sum, the annual operating budget focuses on consumption, while the capital budget focuses on additions to capital assets.

Unless its boundary is legally changed, the geographic area of a government is permanent. Coastal erosion in Louisiana, however, is a contrary example where human decisions, such as channeling the Mississippi River, cause significant loss of land mass. Unlike fixed city boundaries, a community's civic and economic heartbeat changes. Elected officials step in and use public resources to stop decline or to stimulate growth. Providing for the common good and developing the area for the long run require trade-offs in what to buy, when, and how to pay for it. Public leaders have to engage in both consumption and investment (see box 8.2).

Durable Goods—goods that have a life span of more than several years.

Expendables—an outlay of resources for consumption in the current fiscal period.

BOX 8.3

Political Skills and Capital Projects

Robert Moses was responsible for building public works projects costing the equivalent of $166 billion in 2009 dollars. He did all this as an unelected official, but one who headed several special authorities that enjoyed monopoly services such as toll roads into Manhattan and the power to borrow against this revenue. More importantly, Moses had the insight to plan ahead and the ability to deploy quickly a battalion of engineers who could produce plans that could soak up federal financial assistance. It was his engineers who designed the basic features of our Interstate Highway system including, for example, the limited access and cloverleaf exchanges. By controlling the toll bridges and tunnels into New York City, Moses was able to claim that all streets on the island fed into his system; this gave him the leverage to expand his reach into other arenas, such as parks and public housing. He even built an overpass bridge too low over the road to an ocean park in order to prevent public buses (and their passengers) from reaching the public park. Moses "used the power of money to undermine the democratic processes of the largest city in the world, to plan and build its parks, bridges, highways and housing projects on the basis of his whim alone" (Caro, 1974, p. 19).

Doing Public Mega-Projects

In contrast to the operating budget's one-year consumption focus, public organizations also must make investment decisions that have impacts that last for many years. For example, governments buy land, install water and sewer systems, build highways and bridges, purchase fire trucks, and the federal government contracts for military hardware such as planes, ships, and tanks. There is an infrastructure legacy in all governmental jurisdictions—streets, bridges, public buildings, parks, and schools that were paid for years ago and some are being paid for still. **Mega-projects** are those that are *very* costly but, hopefully, provide long-term impacts. New York's 365-mile Erie Canal, built over eight years starting in 1817, opened the Midwest to development. One Great Depression-era construction program, the Tennessee Valley Authority, provided navigable waterways and electricity that opened the Southern Appalachian area to economic development. At this same time, the master of public works projects emerged in New York. Robert Moses was a public servant who headed the Triborough Bridge Authority and whose political skills turned this unassuming non-elected post into a powerful position reaching throughout the city and state (see box 8.3).

Another colorful infrastructure development was the extensive aqueduct system built by Los Angeles in the early 1900s. The system was to provide enough water for the growing population. The 1974 movie *Chinatown* offers a fictionalized account of the high stakes involved in this public works project.

Mega-projects—a very large public investment project.

'They never quite finished it — it was probably over budget!'

Figure 8.1. Some Capital Projects Are More Costly than Expected
Reproduced by permission of www.cartoonstock.com.

Mega-projects are often associated with cost overruns (see figure 8.1). More recently, the $15 billion "Big Dig" construction project in Boston buried a central highway through downtown, with park space above the roadway, and built a new bridge and tunnel system that eased a major traffic bottleneck. The complex Big Dig project took more time and money than expected and sparked political battles, federal earmarks, scandals, and a finding that statements made to borrow money were misleading and fraudulent. Worst still, in July 2006, a tunnel ceiling panel fell and crushed a car passenger. This event led to lawsuits and criminal investigations about shoddy work. All of these negative aspects of the Big Dig do not overshadow the huge improvements the project provided the city of Boston.

Do not underestimate the politics of capital projects. Just think about the money involved in public works and the political impact of where a new highway, sewer plant, airport, or park will be built or located. So many dollars are at stake. Projects are highly visible and also almost irreversible. Geography matters, with voters yelling "not in my backyard" (**NIMBY**) for some projects—such as the location of a new sewer plant, prison or highway—while also loudly demanding a neighborhood park or school. By contrast, some communities embrace projects, like a new state prison, for the jobs they provide.

SHOULD GOVERNMENTS PLAN AND IF SO, HOW?

Few older communities are the result of deliberate planning. Washington, D.C., based on the plan of Major Pierre Charles L'Enfant in 1791, is an example of a planned city. To this day, there are debates over how best to develop the city,

---

NIMBY (not in my back yard)—idea that conveys opposition to a change in building and development near one's property.

especially given the requirement that building heights cannot be higher than the Capitol building.

Elected officials and public managers everywhere face tough questions when they make decisions about capital facilities. Does the city hire more fire fighters or improve productivity with expensive new equipment? Should the county pave the road or continue to use a gravel road? Will a new state park in the northern part of the state be better than one in the south? Will the development and deployment of a new aircraft carrier or a new missile system better address the needs of national defense?

Yes, there are technical answers to each question, but there also are inescapable political considerations that affect the decisions. Votes are needed to allocate money for one project over another. Capital-project decisions involve high risks because of (1) the long time frame from planning to implementation, (2) the large price tag for each project compared to the smaller amounts for most items in the operating budget, (3) the almost irreversible nature of capital projects once they are built, and (4) the political coalitions necessary to get the project approved in the first place. These decisions may, or may not, be based on technical rationales. Members of Congress from Connecticut and Mississippi, two major shipbuilding states, may answer the military hardware question differently from their counterparts from the missile-construction states such as California.

Politics matters, especially when money is involved. The large sums involved in the purchase and construction of public facilities focus attention on major changes in the community and major financial commitments. Making it easier to anticipate and plan for these large sums and the trade-offs they represent is what **capital improvement planning** is all about.

Planning ahead is the key. Every organization needs a strategic plan to shape and steer its goal-focused behavior. Capital assets such as a new fire station, bridge, park, water line, or weapons system can be an integral part of achieving those strategic plans and, in this way, justify a capital planning process that identifies and prices the capital assets that can meet public needs. These needs can relate to internal government operations as well as public investments to benefit society more broadly. The current director of OMB noted that public infrastructure spending "represents an investment in the future productivity of the private sector" (Orszag, 2008). Capital planning also forces a government to systematically identify and rank competing capital projects for the government.

Identifying Capital Projects

A **capital project** is a major, one-time expenditure that is used to expand or improve public physical assets (including facilities, equipment and infrastructure), the value of which is **not** consumed in a year. Public organizations use

---

Capital Improvement Planning—creating a plan of spending for repair or replacement of existing infrastructure as well as development of new facilities to accommodate growth.

Capital Project—major construction, acquisition, or renovation activities that add value to an organization's capital assets or significantly increase their useful life.

somewhat arbitrary rules to distinguish a long-lived capital project from the recurring purchase of a shorter-lived capital asset. For example, a township with one police car might not need a new one for three years and have to save up for its purchase. By contrast, a larger city might include enough money in the operating budget to replace one-third of its police fleet every year. The monetary value and life span of an item determine its status as a capital project, such as a cost of $10,000 and a life-span of three years or longer. Capital assets above that level would be a capital project and those below would be considered an operating budget purchase. Some governments and other public organizations exclude equipment completely from the capital project definition. For example, one county government with a population of 450,000 defines capital projects as involving only: acquiring land; infrastructure projects such as roads, bridges, intersections, drainage, and sewers; new construction or additions (defined as an expanded "footprint") to public facilities exceeding $10,000; or public facility remodeling projects over $25,000.

Developing an exhaustive list of possible capital projects starts with those whose jobs are involved in planning and delivering the services. Savvy leaders go further and incorporate suggestions from citizens, users, and other interested parties. A listing of possible capital projects can emerge from using these methods:

- Apply the replacement cycle of major pieces of equipment and facilities, asking questions such as: What is the life span of the high-volume air conditioner that services the multi-story city hall?
- Compare facilities to legal or professional standards, with questions such as: Does the recreation building still meet the building code? Do we have the proper number of parks per thousand residents?
- Observe the current inventory of capital assets, with questions such as: Is the bridge deterioration so bad that it requires replacement?

Who is the constituency for a bridge? It has been said that there is no constituency for the rehabilitation of a bridge until it collapses or has to be closed. The collapse of the Minneapolis bridge in August 2007 renewed a focus on the state of America's public infrastructure (see figure 8.2). Although we depend on bridges for travel convenience and commerce that requires efficient routes, these capital projects typically lose out in the competition for current funds to advocates for education programs and senior services, among others. Maintaining the existing stock of capital assets does not offer the same visual drama and media attention as does opening a new facility. Also, the pressure in tight budget years to pay, for example, police salaries makes it very appealing for elected officials to defer the maintenance on underground pipes, road beds, roofs, and other less-visible assets. The condition of bridges in the United States dramatically illustrates this point. Of the almost 600,000 bridges, 25 percent are considered deficient by highway engineers. Over one-half of the bridges in the District of Columbia, Rhode Island, and Massachusetts fall short of standards (see table 8.1).

Figure 8.2. Sometimes the Big Story is What Is Not in the Budget
The I-35W Bridge, August 5, 2007.
Reprinted by permission. Courtesy of the City of Minneapolis.

Many assets, whether personal or public, deteriorate with wear and lose their value over time. Care must be taken to avoid the situation described in Oliver Wendell Holmes' 1858 poem: a vehicle worked perfectly well until it "went to pieces all at once…Just as bubbles do when they burst." Periodically, a national group calls for more attention to the infrastructure crisis, but is unheard in the noise of other public spending needs, until the next headline-grabbing event points to another key failure of public infrastructure (see box 8.4).

Besides compiling an inventory of capital projects from the experts and program managers, many communities rely on extensive citizen participation and meetings of neighborhood groups to identify public needs and desires. Often this is part of a city planning commission's work. Depending upon the size and scope of the public organization and its territory, there can be tens, hundreds, or even thousands of capital projects on the horizon at any point in time.

Capital Programs and Budgets

Some of these projects are so far off in the future that a precise construction schedule and price tag is of little use now. For example, building a further-out circle route around the city may be decades off, but it needs to be in the planning horizon to stay ahead of private development that will only complicate the location of

Table 8.1. Inventory of Bridges by State, as of December 2007

	NUMBER OF BRIDGES	PERCENT DEFICIENT
District of Columbia	244	62%
Rhode Island	747	53%
Massachusetts	4,986	51%
Hawaii	1,116	45%
Pennsylvania	22,221	43%
New York	17,313	38%
West Virginia	7,000	37%
Vermont	2,709	36%
New Jersey	6,407	35%
Maine	2,386	34%
Connecticut	4,167	33%
Kentucky	13,635	31%
Oklahoma	23,499	31%
Missouri	24,030	31%
New Hampshire	2,357	31%
Louisiana	13,342	30%
California	24,177	29%
North Carolina	17,783	28%
Alaska	1,229	27%
Washington	7,684	27%
Maryland	5,125	27%
Iowa	24,743	27%
Michigan	10,902	26%
Virginia	13,417	26%
Alabama	15,879	26%
Mississippi	17,002	25%
South Dakota	5,918	25%
Ohio	27,939	24%
Nebraska	15,448	23%
Arkansas	12,533	23%
Oregon	7,316	23%
South Carolina	9,221	22%
North Dakota	4,454	22%
Indiana	18,418	22%
Kansas	25,429	21%
Tennessee	19,835	21%
Wyoming	3,030	20%
Montana	4,979	20%
Georgia	14,557	20%
Texas	50,267	20%
Idaho	4,104	20%
New Mexico	3,850	18%
Florida	11,664	17%
Utah	2,850	17%
Colorado	8,371	17%
Illinois	25,957	17%
Delaware	856	15%
Wisconsin	13,793	15%
Minnesota	13,056	12%
Nevada	1,704	12%
Arizona	7,386	11%
Total	597,035	25%

SOURCE: Calculated by authors from data in Federal Highway Administration, 2008.

BOX 8.4

An Ongoing Infrastructure Crisis

1983: "The nation's public works infrastructure—defined here as including high-ways, public transit systems, wastewater treatment works, water resources, air traffic control, airports, and municipal water supply—is suffering from growing problems of deterioration, technological obsolescence, and insufficient capacity to serve future growth."

SOURCE: Congressional Budget Office, 1983.

1984: "The United States faces a serious, but manageable, problem related to the condition and adequacy of its basic infrastructure...."

SOURCE: National Infrastructure Advisory Committee, 1984.

2006: "The nation's infrastructure facilities are deteriorating at an alarming rate. For example: half of the 257 locks on the more than 12,000 miles of inland waterways operated by the Army Corps of Engineers are functionally obsolete; three-quarters of the nation's public school buildings fail to meet the basic needs of children; 27 percent of the 590,750 bridges nationwide are structurally deficient or obsolete; $11 billion annually is needed to replace aging drinking water facilities. The American Society for Civil Engineers (ASCE) estimates a five-year total investment need of $1.6 trillion, and grades the nation's overall infrastructure as a 'D'."

SOURCE: Center for Strategic and International Studies, 2006.

---

public infrastructure. Beijing, the capital city of China, recently opened its sixth ring road encircling the city, with others envisioned as the city expands further out from the center city. There are many political and technical factors that have to be considered well before such a project can be sited and priced with any precision, much less completed (see figure 8.3).

Other capital projects are needed soon. A listing of planned capital projects for the upcoming five- to ten-year period with the expected cost and financing plan for each and scheduled according to priorities and timing, is termed the **capital improvement program**. The projects in this short-term window require reasonable cost estimates and timing sequences. Surely it is better to put in the water and sewer lines before paving the street and avoid the obvious waste when the newly paved street is torn up to install the underground pipes.

Decisions on which capital project to fund and when carries political risk. For this reason, public organizations often go to great lengths to involve a wide group of

---

Capital Improvement Program—a listing of planned capital projects for the upcoming five-to ten-year period with the expected cost and financing plan for each and scheduled according to priorities and timing; updated annually.

Typical transporation project development process

Approximate Timeline (in years)

1	2	3	4	5	6	7	8	9	10

BEGIN CONSTRUCTION

Planning Studies

Environmental Studies

Preliminary Design

Final Design

Right-of-Way Engineering and Acquisition

Determine Existing Conditions	Purpose and Need	Floodplain/ Hydrologic	Geometric Design	60% Plans	Right-of-Way Setting
Traffic Forecasts	Traffic Analysis	Energy Land Use	Typical Sections	90% Plans	Right-of-Way Engineering
Analysis	Preliminary Alternatives	Economic	Grading	Specifications and Estimates	Appraisals
Needs	Public Outreach	Wetlands	Drainage	Final Plans	Purchase Offers
Conceptual Solutions	Technical Studies	Visual Effects	Structural		Counter Offers
Preliminary Coat Estimates	Air Quality	Environmental Justice	Traffic/ITS		Relocation
Coat Estimation	Noise Analysis	Cumulative & Secondary Impacts	Signing/Striping		Asbestos Clearing
Validation Process (CEVP)	Traffic Analysis	Cost-Benefit Analysis	Lighting		Demolition
	Socio/ Economic	Refine Alternatives	Utilities		Condemnation (if necessary)
	Cultural Resources	Alternative Selection	30% Plans		Federal Regulations
	Biological Resources	Section 4(f) Evaluation			
	Hazardous Materials	Record of Decision			
	Water Quality				

Figure 8.3. Typical Transportation Project Development Process
SOURCE: National Surface Transportation Policy and Revenue Policy Commission, 2008.

people in the capital project planning and selection process. One approach is to have interested parties assess proposed capital projects on a declining scale from imperative, essential, important, or desirable. The fact that such a scale is open to interpretation highlights the room for discretion in even the most technical-sounding scheme.

The **capital budget** is the first year of the capital improvement program with a detailed source of financing for each capital project to be built during the upcoming year. Tight cost estimates and precise funding arrangements are essential for capital projects in the capital budget. Then, the legislative body can vote to authorize a precise capital project instead of a concept or poorly thought-out project.

Although the distinction between the one-year capital budget and the multi-year capital improvement plan is common in most local governments, it is less so in states and does not exist in the federal government. Many municipalities develop a comprehensive plan of development and schedule projects out over a multi-year schedule. Still, it is not unusual for some cities to change their plans quickly in response to public pressure or the sudden availability of a new funding source. States are less likely to publish a comprehensive multi-year capital improvement program because of the range of state activity.

It is difficult to get a handle on the federal government's entire capital investment program because there is no federal capital budget. Congress often

================ **BOX 8.5** ================

Basic Elements of a Bill to Create a Federal Capital Budget

A. Establishes Capital and Operating Budgets:

    (1) Requires that the budget submitted by the President be a unified budget comprised of an operating budget and a capital budget;

    (2) Limits the capital budget to major activities, projects and programs that support the acquisition, construction, alteration, and rehabilitation of physical infrastructure that produces services or benefits for more than five years and has an initial cost of at least $500,000;

    (3) Restricts expenditures from the capital budget to: roadways and bridges; airports and airway facilities; mass transportation systems; waste water treatment systems; water distribution delivery and related systems; water resource projects; medical facilities; resource recovery facilities; public structures; space and communication facilities and strategic petroleum reserves and mineral stockpiles.

B. Review of capital expenditures: Requires the Comptroller General to review and report to Congress to ensure that those investments included in the capital budget adhere to the criteria set out in this act.

C. Evaluation of capital investments: Directs the Government Operations Committee to report legislation directing the Comptroller General to evaluate the value and usefulness of actual and proposed investments in the capital budget.

D. Implementation of capital budget: Directs the Rules Committee to report legislation establishing rules to enforce this act.

SOURCE: President's Commission to Study Capital Budgeting, and Wise, 1998.

Exercise. Should the federal government introduce a capital budget? What are the pros and cons? What do you think of this particular proposal?

---

appropriates in one year all the money needed for a major capital investment but the money is not all spent in one year. According to recent CBO data, three years after Congress grants new budget authority, only 84 percent of highway project money is spent, compared to 54 percent for water projects and 96 percent for new defense systems (Elmendorf, 2009). Box 8.5 outlines a bill to create a federal capital budget.

There are linkages between a capital project and future operating costs. When the new capital project—an aircraft carrier, a new highway, or a new park facility—is purchased or built with borrowed money, repayment occurs over several years. The repayment of the principal and interest or **debt service** affects the yearly operating budgets. The more money devoted to paying for debt service means that less available for operating purposes.

Debt Service—repayment of the principal and interest on debt, often through a separate debt service fund.

Project Costs and Benefits

Each proposed capital project has to be evaluated in terms of its initial cost to purchase or build and its operating cost. Ideally, the benefits to be gained from the project also are considered. Translating these benefits into dollars requires the consideration of many assumptions. Traditionally, a new bridge over the river would be evaluated by the savings in travel time from reduced congestion, savings in vehicle operating costs because of reductions in stop-and-go driving, and a reduction in traffic accidents because of overall improved travel flow. Moreover, the economic impact of the project may loom large, such as the new bridge being part of the inducement to attract a new manufacturing plant that would employ hundreds of new employees. **Cost-benefit analysis** attaches a price to these benefits to compare to the costs of building and maintaining the new bridge. On strictly economic grounds, a project would "pass" if its benefits offset its costs. However, the bridge may get built for political reasons, regardless of such technical considerations. In recent years, Congress has increased the number of federal dollars earmarked for projects that meet political needs but escape serious inquiry.

Each capital project has to be financed, with funding coming from:

- Cash, either from current revenues or from money saved from prior years;
- Borrowed money, meaning that this debt has to be repaid over time and with an interest cost;
- Receipt of money from an outside source, such as a donation from a benefactor or a grant from a higher level of government.

Each funding avenue is examined below.

IF NOT PAY CASH, THEN WHY AND WHEN BORROW MONEY?

Using government savings to fund a capital project means that the city, for example, essentially imposed a tax in one year but provided no benefits to the taxpayers who paid. Instead, the benefits are gained by the taxpayers and other users living in the city later, when the facility is up and running. Both situations violate inter-generational equity, or the idea that a government should raise enough revenue to cover all services for a given period (generally a year) and not subsidize or burden taxpayers of a future period. Besides, why should one set of elected officials bear the brunt of voter dissatisfaction for over-taxing (taxes without an offsetting benefit), and leave to future elected officials the limelight of getting to cut the ribbon at the opening of the new public facility?

In fact, today's residents gain benefits from generations of past taxpayers who have provided the current built-environment. Consider all the existing public buildings, road system, water and sewer systems, and other infrastructure facilities that you take for granted today. One might argue that it is the obligation of each generation of taxpayers to pay-forward a similar legacy in order to preserve and improve the community.

Some communities pay cash for capital projects, on a pay-as-you-go basis. Having more cash than is needed for the operating budget is difficult, particularly for less wealthy communities. An approach taken by Akron, Ohio and Oklahoma City is to set aside a share (say perhaps one-half) of a dedicated tax to the operating budget and the rest to a pay-as-you-go capital budget. This way, the cities have cash to pay for some capital projects yearly.

Not all projects provide immediate benefits; some have a later payoff. For example, a community devoted to economic growth and development has to invest for the future by laying the foundation for future private economic activity. This requires up-front public costs in pursuit of later benefits. A fundamental question arises: does the government lead or lag private investment? Which one puts in the first dollars, the public sector in hopes of attracting private investment, or the private sector making its entrepreneurial investment as a show of good faith before the public allocates scarce taxpayer dollars? Most cities have to make "lead" investments such as new streets or even downtown garages in a strategic move to spur uncertain private development in the central business district, hopefully with a positive payoff sooner rather than later.

Debt Is Not Always Bad

A second financing option is to borrow money to fund the capital project. This option makes economic sense when the loan's repayment period is no longer than the economic life of the funded project. One should not borrow to buy food or other "soft goods" that are consumed and forgotten about well before the loan is repaid. Similarly, state and local governments generally follow the practice of not borrowing to cover deficits in the operating budget. In fact, most states prohibit their local governments from doing this, although some states such as California and Connecticut borrow to replenish state coffers in the face of severe fiscal pressures. Canadian provinces are another example; they ran large operating deficits in the late 1980s and early 1990s, and borrowed money each year to cover those shortfalls. In contrast, Canadian and American cities borrow money to fund major capital projects, with the loan repayment period stretching out for twenty to thirty years in some cases because the economic life of the facility is at least this long.

Bond Ratings and Credit Quality

Have you received unsolicited letters and emails offering you credit cards and other ways to go into debt? About all that can temper your response is a sense of what you can afford and what you really need, in contrast to an uncontrolled desire to spend irrespective of the damage it might do to your overall credit quality. Poor credit quality reverberates in many ways. It determines whether you can borrow in the future and, if so, the interest rate you will have to pay. In today's computerized world, credit scores are used by employers to screen job applicants and by insurance firms to set insurance premium rates.

Nationally (and internationally) recognized statistical rating firms assess the credit quality of public organizations and private firms. It works this way. When a city wants to borrow money, it pays a fee to one (or more) of the three dominant national **credit rating firms** for an independent assessment of credit risk, meaning the probability that the city will not repay the debt. If Moody's Investors Service, one of the credit rating firms, considers the risk of default or failure to pay very low, it could assign the planned debt issuance the top rating ("Aaa"). Below this sterling "triple-A" rating are those of 'Aa', 'A', and then 'Baa'. The additional, lower ratings are considered speculative grades or worse. The credit rating matters because the lower the rating, the higher the cost of borrowing money. What this means is that the city will pay more in interest to borrow the money. Every extra penny of interest paid increases debt service, which reduces the amount of money available for other budget items.

Credit-rating decisions reverberate in the political world, providing for the current office holder "proof" of good management or, for the opposition, "evidence" of shoddy leadership. In either case, the credit rating may rest less on these governing qualities than on the government's financial condition, its debt profile, and its underlying social and economic wealth base. In politics, however, those who frame the issue often effectively define it for their own political purposes.

Debt Rules

Because it is important to maintain good credit quality, there are rules imposed by constitutions, statutes, and policy. State constitutions, for example, often limit the amount of "debt" the state and its local governments can enter into without a direct vote of the electors. Debt is put in quotation marks here because the constitutional provision may refer to a certain type of debt, and this way allow borrowing that skirts the definition. Although the Kansas constitution limits the state to no more than $1 million in debt without a vote of the electors, the state by itself chalked up almost $4 billion in debt. This difference is due in part to court rulings that carved out of the limit all debt supported by earmarked revenues, such as motor fuel taxes for the highway fund debt. Here the legal definition is different from what the market may see as a long-term obligation. For this reason, it is prudent to add up all debt to determine what amount is affordable.

State governments often define what is affordable as a percentage of the state citizens' total personal income (for example, 2 percent). After all, this is the ultimate basis for repayment. Even if a state does not have an income tax but relies on a retail sales tax, all income is either saved or spent, so estimates of state-wide personal income remains a valid indicator of state taxpayers' ability to pay. Willingness to pay is another matter all together.

State and Local Governments' Securities

American state and local governments borrow money from investors in the U.S. domestic market, unlike governments elsewhere that have to go outside their home

---

Credit Rating Firm—an independent agency that assesses the likelihood that an organization will not be able to repay its debt, and assigns a rating based on this likelihood.

country to borrow to attract money at an acceptable price. In fact, even the U.S. government itself sells its debt to foreign lenders, amounting to more than one-half of recent sales (see chapter 5). The primary reason why state and local governments borrow domestically is due to the federal tax exemption for bondholders: the interest paid by the borrowing government is exempt from the lender's federal income tax. Therefore, American state and local governments mostly issue **tax-exempt bonds** which are also known by the general term of **municipal securities**. Over 50,000 different states, local governments and nonprofit organizations issued almost 2 million separate municipal securities totaling over $2.7 trillion in value in 2008. These huge numbers indicate the importance of this **capital market** for state and local government financing.

Investors in municipal securities pay attention to the backing or source of repayment for the loan. A city can pledge its **full faith and credit** taxing power, and make the loan a **general obligation bond**. This legal pledge provides investors with a legal claim on the government's fundamental tax power to ensure that they get repaid. Alternatively, the borrowing organization can issue debt backed by a dedicated revenue stream such as a tourist tax, water fees, or a gasoline excise tax that is estimated to produce enough money to repay the loan; this type of loan is called a **revenue bond**. For decades, most municipal securities have been revenue bonds, despite the many studies showing that it is cheaper to borrow using a general obligation bond than a revenue bond. This result fits the broad backing of the general obligation bond; a revenue bond usually is backed by a narrow revenue source. For example, state governments often create a highway fund to receive gas tax receipts and other revenues related to vehicle use. A fund such as this can back debt when the state borrows money to build the road system that will, in turn, foster gasoline purchases and the related gasoline tax that will be dedicated to pay off the loan.

Have you considered one of the new hybrid cars? What will happen to the state's highway fund receipts when gasoline sales decline because of the widespread use of hybrid cars? This is one of the threats that investors or bondholders of state highway bonds face; they are repaid only out of the highway fund and, if the dedicated revenues are not sufficient to cover the amounts due, the bonds will

---

Municipal Securities—debt issued by state and local governments, usually in the form of tax-exempt bonds.

Full Faith and Credit—a legal pledge providing investors with a legal claim on the government's fundamental tax power to ensure that they get repaid.

General Obligation Bonds (G.O.)—debt secured by the full-faith and credit-guarantee; property taxes are the main revenue used to repay local government general obligation bonds but, if bondholders are not repaid, they have a legal claim against any revenue of the government.

Revenue Bond—a bond secured by the pledge of specific revenues (such as water fees, parking charges, toll receipts, stadium admission fees) to pay the principal and interest, but not secured by the full faith and credit of the debt issuer.

be in **default**. However, if the bonds were backed by the state's full faith and credit, then bondholders would be indifferent to the consumers' choice of vehicles and the impact on gasoline sales because the bondholder would have a broader base from which to get repaid. As you might expect, bondholders want to be compensated for taking on the added risk of buying a revenue bond. To the public organization that issues such bonds, this means a higher cost of borrowing: the interest rates are higher.

By entering the capital market to borrow money, the public organization is placing its future in the hands of investors who are rationally motivated by economic self-interest, not necessarily local civic pride. Figure 8.4 shows that municipal securities primarily are owned directly by households and through retail-traded tax-exempt money market funds and tax-exempt mutual funds. Households have a history of "buying and holding" municipal bonds to maturity. Institutional investors, the category for most other bond owners, can be fickle investors. While each year almost $400 billion in new municipal securities are issued, the trading among investors of old bonds is more along the lines of $6 trillion. Investors buy and sell bonds for many reasons, including revelations about the issuer's fiscal problems, concerns over natural hazards, and the opportunity to make more money by investing somewhere else. Therefore, public officials have to exercise caution in the amount and form of debt issued, or the results can strangle the borrower's finances for years without matching benefits. Debt is not the problem. The prudent use of debt is necessary for most communities to sustain the desired built environment. Some public organizations misuse their finances and compound their troubles by hiding their activity from potential

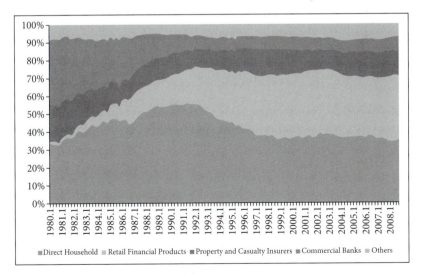

Figure 8.4. Owners of Municipal Securities

Compiled by authors from Federal Reserve Board of Governors, 2009.

BOX 8.6

Actions by the Security and Exchange Commission against Government Borrowers

A number of Commission enforcement actions have highlighted continued disclosure weaknesses, raised concerns about governmental accounting, and suggested the need for improvements to disclosure practices. These enforcement actions involved allegations that in disclosure documents used in offerings or other information provided to investors:

- the City of San Diego, California failed to disclose the gravity of its enormous pension and retiree health liabilities or that those liabilities had placed the City in serious financial jeopardy;

- the City of Miami, Florida failed to disclose an unprecedented cash flow shortage which it had eased, in part, by spending the proceeds of bonds issued for other purposes for operating costs;

- Maricopa County, Arizona failed to disclose a material decline in its financial condition and operating cash flow, the substantial deficit in its general fund, and increased deficit in another fund;

- the City of Syracuse, New York falsely claimed a surplus for its general and debt service funds, materially overstated its ending fund balances in those funds, and misled investors by describing certain financial information as audited;

- Orange County, California made misleading statements and failed to disclose material information about the County's high risk investment pool and financial condition that brought into question the County's ability to repay its securities—facts about which members of its Board of Supervisors were aware, but failed to take appropriate steps to assure were disclosed.

SOURCE: Securities and Exchange Commission, 2007.

---

investors when borrowing money, only to find themselves in trouble with securities regulators, as described in box 8.6.

IS THERE SUCH A THING AS FREE MONEY?

The third option for the financing of capital projects is to get money from a benefactor or higher level of government. There is a tendency among individuals and organizations to prefer that others pick up the bill. What is the incentive for the donor? A benefactor may want to get her name on the university building or, alternatively, to have the personal pleasure of making an anonymous donation that enables the charity to build the needed homeless shelter. An organization receiving such funds has to find a match between its needs and possible benefactors, and this is not always easy. The donor's goals can skew the programs of the receiving organization when it goes go out of its way to design a service that will receive the blessing of the soon-to-be benefactor. After the new funding dries up, the program and its constituents often remain. It is hard to terminate the program at that point, although the donor is long gone and the provider has to pay for the service out of already tight funds.

State and Local Officials Look to the Federal Government

State and local governments lust after federal aid. Look no further than the effect of a quick infusion of money by the American Recovery and Reinvestment Act of 2009. It captured the imagination of state and local officials eager to spend federal money for "shovel ready" projects. We have to go all the way back to the 1970s to find the prior peak of federal funds given to the states. What turned off the federal faucet was that members of Congress realized that they were bearing the cost in terms of voters' dislike of federal taxes while local officials got the lion's share of the good press at the ribbon-cutting ceremony. A shift to earmarks allowed federal lawmakers to target aid projects and showcase their personal success in bringing money home. Earmarks play well at home but presidents and governors generally do not like legislative earmarks because they divert resources away from executive policy priorities. Still, legislators assert their power of the purse and try to please the voters back home.

The federal share of total capital spending for highways, aviation, mass transit, rail, water transportation, water supply, and wastewater treatment and related infrastructure has declined over the past several decades. The share funded by state and local governments has increased significantly (see figure 8.5). The primary federal aid is the indirect subsidy offered by allowing state and local governments to issue municipal securities with the interest excluded from investors' federal income taxes. Congress can repeal this tax-based subsidy (a tax expenditure) but this move could increase the cost of borrowing by state and local governments and result in program cuts or tax increases.

A key source of state funds for transportation funding is the federal highway trust fund. This fund receives dedicated fuel taxes that Congress then sends to the states by formula (and earmarks). States depend upon this yearly funding stream to conduct their road and bridge construction programs. They even borrow money in advance of potential federal highway money. In June 2009, the federal government announced that the highway trust fund was running out of money earlier than expected, in part because people continued to change their driving behavior. Driving changed first in response to the increase in gasoline prices and then due to the recession. When driving slows down, gas tax receipts drop. In response to this problem, both the George W. Bush administration and now the Obama administration turned to bailing out the federal highway trust fund with general tax dollars. The alternative is the prospect of delayed road and bridge construction and repair projects across the country. A long-term solution to this problem remains to be resolved.

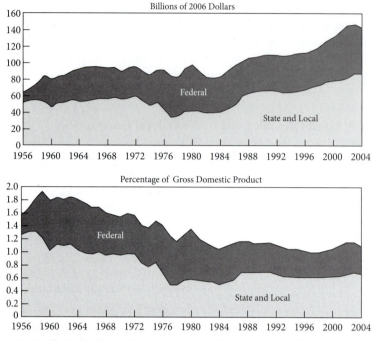

Figure 8.5. Public Capital Spending on Transportation and Water Infrastructure, 1956–2004

SOURCE: Orszag, 2008.

NOTE. Includes spending on highways, mass transit, rail, aviation, water transportation, water resources, and water supply and wastewater treatment systems.

Local Officials Look to the States

Local governments look to their state government for funding. Very much as their counterparts in the corridors of power in Washington, D.C. are treating the states, state officials are trying to wean local officials off **state aid**. The major state aid programs that persist are highway aid and shared funding for water and sewer construction projects, both prompted by federal programs. Some states help fund the construction of local public schools by directly paying some or all construction cost or sharing the cost of debt service.

There is no such a thing as "free money"; there is always a catch. Federal aid requires a plan for spending and often the plan is quite detailed. Transportation projects must be approved by a federally-sponsored, metropolitan-planning organization to ensure that the projects meet long-range coordinated planning rules. Even federal assistance after a natural disaster requires local money to be spent first. Only then can the locals request reimbursement from the federal government. This places cash-poor communities at a disadvantage as they struggle to pay for clean-up and rebuilding. For New Orleans after Hurricane Katrina, the bar was even higher. Everything hinged on a citywide comprehensive plan that included a capital improvements plan and a capital budget that provoked hot public debate over where and how to rebuild. The politics of local capital spending played out in front of an international audience, with Americans supporting the use of federal aid but somewhat dismayed at the slow pace of the rebuilding. This drama underscores the politics of capital budgeting.

THUMBNAIL

When public resources are directed to the purchase or construction of expensive, long-term capital assets, the specialized budget mechanism called the capital budget is used by most medium or large communities and by many state governments. Our built environment is the result of years, decades, and even centuries of past capital investments by public officials and voters. Their infrastructure legacy means that most Americans can take for granted clean drinking water with the turn of a faucet, the removal of sewerage away from our living and working areas, and the storm-drainage system that moves rain water away.

The operating and capital budgets are intertwined. There is only so much money that taxpayers are willing to pay. Capital projects are expensive, and so is the payment of principal and interest on the debt that often finances them. Once built, the facility has to be regularly maintained, and this cost ends up on the operating budget.

CASE

Budget Busters!

After the collapse of the I-35W bridge in downtown Minneapolis, Minnesota during the afternoon rush hour on August 1, 2007 (see figure 8.2), the state legislature appointed a joint committee to investigate all decisions "potentially relevant to the bridge collapse, within the context of MnDOT [Minnesota Department of Transportation] general practices relating to bridge inspection and repair." A law firm was hired to conduct the investigation, and their report was presented in May, 2008.

The report found that MnDOT placed the I-35W bridge work on a list of "budget buster" bridges because it would cost $75 million or more to replace. The report concluded that financial considerations played a part in the decision making (Gray Plant Mooty, 2008, pp. 11–13, notes omitted).

> In order for work to occur on a bridge, there needs to be funding to do it. The availability of funding is a very complex matter. The following description touches on the bare essentials, relevant to the maintenance, repair and replacement of the Bridge.
>
> The Bridge was part of the Minnesota Trunk Highway System. For that reason, funds for its maintenance, repair or replacement needed to come from a limited number of revenue sources including various state taxes, federal highway aid and, in recent years, state bonding. Subject to both Minnesota constitutional and statutory provisions, the Legislature appropriates this funding to MnDOT for two principal purposes: (1) maintenance of roads and bridges on the trunk highway system and (2) new construction, including expansion

projects. MnDOT, in turn, allocates a certain share of the legislative appropriation to each of its eight districts, including the Metro District. The resultant transportation programming has been described as one of the most decentralized in the country.

Within the Metro District, ordinary maintenance work on the Bridge (e.g., snowplowing and flushing) was done by MnDOT employees and paid for out of the District's annual maintenance budget. Larger or more involved projects were often out-sourced to private contractors who were paid through the District's Bridge Improvement Program ("BIP"). To become a part of the BIP, the project was by necessity of lower cost given an annual Metro District BIP budget of approximately $15 million. Projects also needed to be identified four or five years in advance of the start date, although there were exceptions made. For more costly repairs on the Bridge, the project needed to become a part of the Statewide Transportation Improvement Program ("STIP"), which meant it first needed to be proposed by the Metro District, then gain approval through the [regional planning] Metropolitan Council's review process and, finally, be submitted to MnDOT's central administration for further consideration before inclusion in the STIP. The STIP operated over a three-year funding cycle until 2007; it is now a four-year cycle.

The funding availability just described does not adequately provide for emergency repairs of a costly nature nor the major rehabilitation or replacement of what MnDOT refers to as the "Budget Buster" bridges, one of which was the I-35W Bridge. All the "Budget Buster" bridges require replacement or major renovation because of "fracture critical issues and/or deterioration". In each case, the costs involved exceed the district's funding capacity.

The report (pp. 30–31, notes omitted) concludes, "Financial considerations may have adversely influenced decision-making."

Both current and former MnDOT employees universally expressed the view that the Department would not allow the condition of a bridge to jeopardize the safety of the public; when a high risk situation becomes known, MnDOT will remove that risk without regard to cost or other implications. We found no reason to challenge the veracity of this assertion with regard to a clear and immediate danger. We did find instances, however, where cost was a factor in determining courses of action with respect to the Bridge at points in time when immediate risk was not obvious. One reason for this is that the programming and funding process for MnDOT construction projects is one of the most decentralized in the nation. This may have certain advantages, but it substantially limits the amount of funding realistically available for a major project or significant, unexpected repairs. This limitation made orphans of the so-called "budget buster" bridges.

Also, the investigation (pp. 63–64, footnotes omitted, italics deleted) found, "Funding considerations influenced decisions about the Bridge."

Funding considerations were a part of everyday life at MnDOT. Finding money, striking the proper balance among competing projects, and living within their budget were constant challenges for MnDOT administrators and staff. The following statements [from testimony] are illustrative:

[W]e have safety issues; we have capacity issues; we have aging pavement issues; we have bridge issues; we have traffic signal issues; I'm going to balance all those things out to say here's what we think are the most important projects that need to move forward....

> [I]t would be meaningless for me to contact CO [Central Office] and tell them how frequently I need more money because everybody could tell everybody how much more money we need.
>
> From an emergency response standpoint, we essentially have to live within our means. We are given appropriative authority, and that's the budget we have to work with, if you will.

The report (p. 64) notes, "In April 2004 and 2005, the I-35W Bridge was identified as one of the 'Budget Buster' bridges needing 'replacement or renovation in the next 10 years.' However, the renovation or replacement of this bridge in critical condition presented a "daunting financial challenge. This was fully acknowledged in a February 8, 2005, *Report for Commissioner's Staff Meeting* where it was noted that 'major fracture critical bridge projects continue to be postponed due to funding.' "

The report (p. 65) continues,

> On April 3, 2006, MnDOT met to discuss three investment strategies for the Bridge. They were: (1) a deck overlay scenario; (2) a deck replacement scenario; and (3) a Bridge replacement-only scenario. Replacement of the Bridge was immediately ruled out given that "MnDOT has not committed to funding this project in the next 20 years" and the $75 million or more estimated cost of a new bridge was "cost prohibitive." Concern was expressed, however, that if the Bridge needed to be closed for safety reasons in the future, the high cost of the replacement "will result in delaying many other projects to maintain our budget."

The Minnesota Department of Transportation (2008a, p. 11) responded to the report, in part, this way:

> [The investigative report] acknowledges that balancing competing project needs with available funding is part of state government....When a safety concern arises about a bridge, it is addressed. Bridge safety is a funding priority and has not been compromised because of funding considerations....[D]ecisions on priorities were, of course, made without knowledge of the fatal design flaw present in the I-35W Bridge's gusset plates [that connect steel girders].

Current Developments
Minnesota's Department of Transportation (2008b) reports that the loss of the bridge affected more than 140,000 vehicles a day at a cost of $400,000 per day "in lost revenue, increased commuter expenses, and the burden on surrounding roads." Initial federal relief funds totaled $55 million and Congress appropriated $195 million for the replacement bridge. The cost of the new bridge was estimated at $234 million and opened ahead of schedule on September 18, 2008.

For more information: Gray Plant Mooty, 2008; State of Minnesota Department of Transportation, 2008a and 2008b:

Thinking It Over
1. Should the capital project that benefits the most people be the one to fund? Why or why not?
2. What criteria should decision makers use when deciding which facility to build? To repair?
3. Is there too much "Monday morning quarterbacking" after a disaster?
4. Does your state's capital city have a capital improvements plan? A capital budget? If yes, how is capital spending financed? If not, do you think it should or should not, and why?

WEB SITE RESOURCES

- Capital Planning Principles
- Further Resources
- Internet Resources
- Selected History of Public Works and Infrastructure, 1775–2009

REVIEW QUESTIONS

1. How does the capital budget affect the operating budget and how do constraints on the operating budget affect the capital budget?
2. Should the federal government adopt a capital budget? Why, or why not?
3. Why does funding seem to chase an emergency or disaster instead of maintenance to prevent one? What significant political factors are at play?
4. When making capital planning decisions, decision makers usually consider both technical factors—projects that best satisfy a perceived need—and political factors such as projects that current voters desire most.
   a. What happens when these factors do not mesh? Should decision makers go ahead with capital projects that the voters want most, or should technical factors dominate?
   b. What role should the public play in capital project planning?
5. Who should pay for a capital project that provides benefits over several years? How would you allocate the burden of payment among citizens and users?

9

❦

How to Read a Local Budget

This chapter looks at seven dimensions:

- Budget Message
- Budget Summary
- Detailed Schedules
- Supporting Documentation
- Eight Focal Points
- Proceed with Caution!
- Go Beyond the Budget

> What does Yoda, the Jedi Master, say about doing difficult things in *The Empire Strikes Back?*

> In theory, there is no difference between theory and practice. But in practice, there is.

ATTRIBUTED TO YOGI BERRA

This chapter is different because it applies many of the ideas examined in earlier chapters. Knowing how to milk a budget for the information you need is a useful political tool and a source of political power. Being able to understand the budget is a key to wielding political power in any community and in any organization (see box 9.1).

Using any tool skillfully takes some technical know-how. Following are the technical basics needed to shift from reading about the politics of budgeting to political action. Please do not let the many tables, numbers, and terms put you off or intimidate you (see figure 9.1). After all, a budget has only four parts: the message, the summary, detailed schedules, and supporting documentation.

BOX 9.1

The Most Important Policy Document

A United Nations' issues paper explains that "the budget is the single most important policy document of governments, where complex development challenges are expressed in real budgetary terms. The...budget reflects the fundamental values underlying...policy. It outlines the government's views of the socio-economic state of a country. It is a declaration of the government's fiscal, financial and economic objectives and reflects its social and economic priorities" (United Nations, 2005).

The Organisation for Economic Co-operation and Development, with its 30 member countries, agrees: "Governments produce mountains of paper every year. But one document can reasonably claim to be more important than all the rest: the budget" (OECD, *OECD Observer*, 2003).

Figure 9.1A. Don't Let the Numbers Intimidate You
SOURCE: Reprinted by permission of www.cartoonstock.com

BUDGET MESSAGE

A good starting point is the usually understandable **budget message** or transmittal letter from the chief executive (mayor, city manager, county executive, commissioner, superintendent, etc.) to the council, legislature or board. This text is always a political statement because it is the chief executive's statement of accomplishments and priorities. The budget itself is a policy document.

Budget Message—the opening section of the budget providing a general summary of the most important aspects of the budget, changes from the current and previous fiscal years, and recommendations regarding the financial policy for the upcoming fiscal year.

Figure 9.1B. Don't Let the Numbers Intimidate You

Rosie the Riveter is a can-do symbol of the American women working in war factories during World War II.

SOURCE: National Archives and Records Administration, Still Picture Branch. Poster by J. Howard Miller, early 1940's.

Because the politics may be buried in the details, explanations, and numbers, we offer six tips for analyzing the budget message.

1. Look for finger pointing at state and federal decision makers; "stingy" aid and unfunded mandates that roll costs down to the local budget are often blamed for budget pressures.

2. Look for praise, and you may very well spot the current administration and those, including the council and the public, whose support is needed to pass the budget.

3. The chief executive sets the agenda with the budget message. What is important in this budget round? Look for sacred cows (programs or services not to be touched) and identify high- and low-priority areas.

4. How is the competition for scarce resources and trade-offs structured? Who is facing off against whom? Who and what are the winners and losers, the deeply affected parties, interests, programs, and services? How are labor costs and benefits treated?

5. Who is the audience? Look for multiple audiences. Budget messages sometimes show how chief executives are positioning themselves or other local political leaders for the next election.

6. Look for points likely to be picked up by the media (and try checking your choices against local newspaper articles). Is the budget message aimed at promoting public relations?

The budget message usually identifies major external pressures, such as changes in law or the economy, and stresses decisions over which the decision makers have some authority and discretion (such as local taxes). The message also pinpoints significant service, program, and staffing changes that should show up in the budget figures. Do they? To find out, we must turn to the more detailed parts of the budget.

BUDGET SUMMARY

This section shows major revenues and expenditures and sums up the overall budgetary picture of all budgeted resources. The examples shown later are from the budget summaries of Boston and Oklahoma City. An economic overview may be included in the budget summary.

DETAILED SCHEDULES

Schedules are simply tables showing financial data. The information provided is more detailed than in the summaries. Department-by-department information on expenditures, revenues, and staffing is shown. Often performance measures are given (see figure 9.5.). Some budgets show departmental requests along with the executive's recommendation. Although the format varies among governments and agencies, most budgets show line-item detail (see Web site resource, Budget Formats). This section shows the budget as a financial plan for the operations of programs, services, or activities during the fiscal period.

SUPPORTING DOCUMENTATION

This part may include information about employees, labor contracts, demographics, changes in state aid, economic conditions, or other factors considered directly relevant (or material) to budgetary decision making.

EIGHT FOCAL POINTS

The eight basic things you need to know when reading a budget are highlighted by the red arrows in figures 9.2 and 9.3. They are restated in different ways in the Applications at the end of this chapter. These applications give you a chance to practice working with budgets and these focal points.

1. Who/What?
Who precisely is the legal government or organization to which the budget applies and what is its legal scope? What are its missions, functions, and

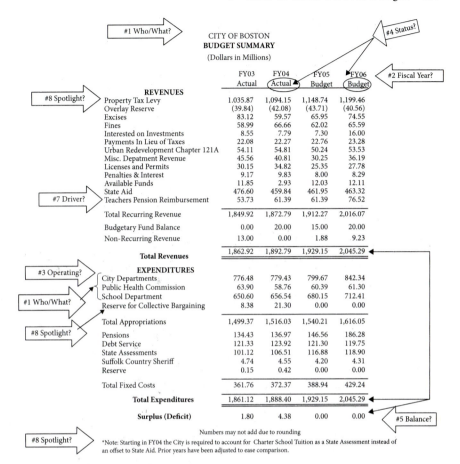

Figure 9.2. Boston, FY 2006

Recommended, Budget, FY 2006 for Boston, Massachusetts.

services, and how have these changed in the recent past? The answers are important for understanding what the budget covers and what the organization does. Beware of comparing apples to oranges when comparing one government's budget to another's and comparing this year's budget to previous budgets. For example, Boston and Oklahoma City are both cities, but while Boston's budget includes public schools (44 percent of total expenditures), public safety consumes 46 percent of Oklahoma City's total expenditures and a special district is responsible for the public schools. Also consider the organization's legal authority to raise revenue. For example, cities and towns in Oklahoma may not levy property taxes to finance routine operations and

#4
Status?

#2 Fiscal Year? → Fiscal Year 2005-2006 Proposed Budget

Departmental Budgets - General Government ← #1 Who/What?

SUMMERY OF EXPENDITURES BY FUND AND CLASSIFICATION

	FY 03-04 Actual	FY 04-05 Adopted Budget	FY 05-06 Proposed Budget	Percent Change	
General Fund #6 Fund?					#8 Spotlight?
Personal Services	421,692	420,344	448,750	6.76%	#7 Driver?
Other Services & Charges	162,940	157,747	165,069	4.64%	
Supplies	7,796	16,166	12,549	−22.37%	
Capital Outlay #3 Operating?	0	0	0	N/A	
Transfers	840	0	0	N/A	
Fund Total	593,268	594,257	626,368	5.40%	
Special Purpose Fund					
Personal Services	0	0	0	N/A	
Other Services & Charges	0	477	492	3.14%	
Supplies	0	0	0	N/A	
Capital Outlay	0	0	0	N/A	
Transfers	0	0	0	N/A	
Fund Total	0	477	492	3.14%	
Capital Improvement Fund					
Personal Services	0	0	0	N/A	
Other Services & Charges	0	0	0	N/A	
Supplies	0	0	0	N/A	
Capital Outlay	0	0	58,127	N/A	
Transfers	0	0	0	N/A	
Fund Total	0	0	58,127	N/A	

Fiscal Year 2005–2006 Proposed Budget

	Actual 2003–2004	Adopted 2004–2005	Proposed 2005–2006	
Use of Fund Balance				#5 Balance?
Beginning Fund Balance	27,075,156	30,812,642	31,440,877	
Additions/(Reductions) to Fund Balance	3,737,485	628,234	(5,000,000)	
Ending Fund Balance	30,812,641	31,440,876	26,440,877	

Figure 9.3. Oklahoma City, FY 2006

Proposed Budget, FY 2006 for Oklahoma City, Oklahoma.

Reprinted by permission. Oklahoma City, Oklahoma, 2004.

Oklahoma City relies on its two-cent sales tax, while Boston draws 60 percent of its total revenue from property taxes and does not levy a sales tax.

2. Fiscal Year?

To which fiscal year does the budget apply? Because legal authority to tax or spend often is limited to a specific fiscal year, using the budget for the correct fiscal year is critical. Many governments use a fiscal year that runs July 1–June 30, but some use other periods. The federal fiscal year runs October 1–September 30. Nonprofit agencies often use January 1–December 31. The convention is to attach the year in which the fiscal period ends to the abbreviation FY. For example, FY06 in Boston begins July 1, 2005 and ends June 30, 2006 (see Web site resource, Fiscal Year).

3. Operating or Capital Budget?

Does the operating or capital budget apply? Most governments and many other organizations use two broad types of budgets, the operating budget and the capital budget. The operating budget finances the goods and services to be consumed during the fiscal year for which the budget is adopted, while the capital budget accounts for resources devoted to long-term projects, such as bridges and buildings. Shorter-termed things that are scheduled periodically (such as replacing police cruisers) usually are in the operating budget, as the Oklahoma example illustrates. The capital budget affects the operating budget directly through debt service, meaning the payment of principal and interest on the debt, as shown under expenditures in Boston's budget. Paper for the printer belongs in the operating budget, along with the city manager or mayor's salary. The construction costs of a new school usually go in the capital budget. One important difference between the federal government and state and local governments is that the federal government does *not* have a capital budget.

4. Legal Status of the Document?
   What is the legal status of the budget document? The last column on the right-hand side answers this question. Because the next-to-the-last column in the Boston budget is labeled *budget* (often the label reads *adopted*), you know that you have the official budget as adopted for the fiscal year. Although the last column also is labeled *budget*, you know it is the proposed budget because the document is the chief executive's recommendation or proposal for fiscal 2006. The Oklahoma exhibit is the executive's proposal rather than the legally adopted budget.

   Columns to the left of the last column show earlier budgets. Sometimes the budget includes estimates for the current budget being implemented; this column usually is labeled *estimated*. A column labeled *actual* shows the audited figures or what actually happened. Also, some documents may show the departments' requests and/or the executive's recommended or proposed budget alongside the other columns.

   As the budget cycle progresses from stage to stage, the status of the budget changes. Almost three calendar years elapse to complete a full cycle from departments' requests to the audited or actual figures (see Web site resource, Fiscal Year).

5. Is the Budget Balanced?
   Because balance is a popularly and professionally accepted gauge of financial responsibility and political leadership, as well as a potent political issue, this is a critical piece of information. A balanced budget also is a core feature of professional standards and the credit rating. Chapter 5 explains that most governments and organizations are required by law and/or policy to balance the budget. A budget is in formal balance when revenues equal expenditures, as the Boston budget shows; surplus or deficit is the alternative. The Oklahoma budget is balanced using resources "left over" from prior years. Most often the proposed and adopted budgets are in balance, but many governments and nonprofit agencies are required by law or formal policy to *end* the fiscal year in balance. The federal government is not required to balance the budget and rarely has since the late 1960's.

6. What Fund Applies?
   Public budgeting and the political system it finances depend on proper stewardship of public resources. Because these resources are raised

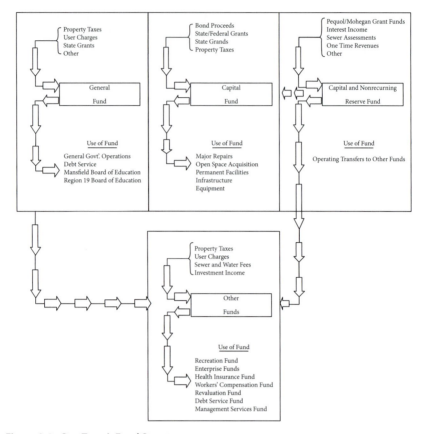

Figure 9.4. One Town's Fund Structure

Town manager's proposed budget for FY 2009–2010.

Reprinted by permission. Mansfield, Town of, Connecticut, 2009.

through public authority or donations based on tax-exempt status granted by the IRS, they are carefully controlled to limit fraud, waste, and mismanagement. One control is publication of the budget and financial report. Another control involves divvying up public resources into different pockets, or funds, as illustrated by Oklahoma City's summary by separate funds. The Boston example is a summary of all funds. Figure 9.4 shows the different funds in a small town, how they are financed, and how the resources are used. A **fund** is a self-balancing set

---

Fund—an accounting segmentation of financial transactions according to restrictions placed on their use; a self-balancing set of accounts meaning that after every financial transaction is recorded in the accounting system, assets minus liabilities must equal net assets; the three main types of funds for state and local governments are proprietary funds (to account for resources held in trust), enterprise funds (to handle business-like operations such as a city water system), and governmental funds such as the debt service fund, special revenue fund (for dedicated grants), and the general fund.

of accounts established by law and dedicated to specific purposes. What this means is that what may go into each pocket and may come out is established by law. The pocket with relatively few restrictions is the general fund. It accounts for revenues not dedicated *by law* to other purposes and services not financed through other funds. The general fund usually accounts for most general governmental activities and most routine services.

7. **What are the Budget Drivers?**
   A budget's strength is that it expresses political choices and priorities in dollars, so comparisons can be made among different organizations, programs, services and from one year to the next. Look at major items as they change across the columns, meaning as they change over time. Which spending categories or departments take most of the budget and which ones are growing the fastest? Which revenue sources are growing and which are sluggish or declining? These are the drivers of the budget and a little arithmetic locates where the action is. The Oklahoma exhibit displays percentage change as a column at the far right. The Teachers Pension Reimbursement in Boston increased about 42 percent from FY 2003 through FY 2006. Also look at dollar change because a small percentage change on a big-ticket item equals many dollars. Some budgets have a column showing dollar change.

   A budget category showing little or no dollar change over time may still mask substantial or material policy shifts. For example, the police budget may look stable in dollars but this could hide major program changes, such as a move from two-person per car patrols to one-person in each vehicle or from vehicle patrols to more officers walking the beat.

   The costs associated with employees drive local budgets. Because local governments and nonprofit service agencies are labor intensive, most of their operating costs are related to so-called **personal services**, meaning employees' pay. Oklahoma City, for example, spends two-thirds of its operating budget on pay and benefits, and only one-twentieth on supplies such as ammunition for police and paper for printers. By contrast, the federal government spends relatively little directly on personal services because so much is spent on debt service, retirement and insurance payments to individuals, and the like.

   Knowing what drives spending helps explain the budget. Different services and programs have different underlying spending patterns (see Web site resource, Analyzing the Costs of Public Programs). Not all spending may show up in the expenditures of the department or program to which it is related. For example, employees' pension or other benefits may be in a central account, with the result that a department's or program's budget does not reflect its actual total costs.

Personal Services—spending relating to compensating employees, including salaries, wages, overtime pay, shift differential and holiday pay, but excluding employee benefits.

8. Who/What Gets the Spotlight?

Budgets turn the spotlight on concerns usually selected by the chief executive (whose budget proposal sets the agenda). Oklahoma City's expenditure summary draws attention to percentage change and this affects decision making. Boston's summary draws attention to the local property tax, changes in the law, and collective bargaining over union contracts. It is typical not to budget openly the amount anticipated for future negotiated union contracts in order to avoid showing one's hand during negotiations. If a city places a plug in the budget to cover the price tag of union negotiation, then the union may treat it as a floor under union demands. When public leaders anticipate that budget transparency would produce this type of union response, they may hide the expected price tag elsewhere in the budget, to be pulled out to cover the results of collective bargaining. Be sure to flag the politically and financially hot issues in the budget message or introduction. These spotlights are important to understanding the politics of local budgeting.

Turn the spotlight off for a moment and think about what is *not* in the budget and who gains or loses by this omission. There may be more to local politics than shows up in the local budget. A budget is not a crystal ball: the budget does not show the issues, interests, and groups that are disregarded, unnoticed, or silent. In their 1962 classic article, "Two Faces of Power," Peter Bachrach and Morton Baratz suggest that "non-decisions" are critical to understanding political power in a community. What and who are overlooked today may very well affect future budgets. Perhaps more importantly, these bypassed issues may tell you a great deal about the organization's commitment to accountability, responsiveness, and more.

PROCEED WITH CAUTION!

Think of the backstory. A straight count of dollars may lead you to misleading conclusions. As you read the budget, you may discover that you need expertise and experience to distinguish between budget gimmicks and unexplained changes that make sense only when you have detailed operational knowledge. For example, what at first glance may look like a budget reduction in simple dollars actually may reflect the transfer of administrative functions that were under-funded and costly. In this example, what appears to be a budget cut is actually more program money. When an agency gets a grant that does not pay for overhead or indirect costs, "more" may actually be less.

Consider the impact of authorized but unfunded positions; a cut in authorized positions may not mean an actual reduction in staff. It is always a good idea to have some familiarity with the agency and its operations (see figure 9.5). At some point, nothing substitutes for knowing the details and this is the expertise budget analysts have. This expertise is a counterweight for budget gimmicks.

Remember, too, that professional budgeters are professionally committed to transparency, accuracy, and meeting professional standards. So, if information you want is missing, or something seems off or looks suspicious, avoid jumping to conclusions that you are up against trickery or unwillingly playing in a shell game. Understanding the budget takes more than counting the dollars.

Yet, errors are made, gimmicks are used, and games are played. Think of Sherlock Holmes's advice, "Once you eliminate the impossible, whatever remains, no matter how improbable, must be the truth."

Department of Hu | Each individual Program section starts with the goal statement

Aging and Adult Services

The goal of Aging and Adult Services is to provide re___rse and services to seniora and adult a with disabilities in order to help the maintain their highest level; of independence and remain safely in the community.

Program Totals		FY 2008 Actual	FY 2009 Approved	FY 2010 Proposed
	% of Total Budget	9.0%	9.6%	9.6%
	% of Expenditures	$5,071,307	$5,449,422	$5,431,078
	Less Revenues	$1,510,770	$1,341,879	$1,348,975
	eral Fund Expenditures	$3,560,537	$4,107,543	$4,082,103
Program Outcomes				
% effectiveness	measured by effectiveness goals	94%	97%	96%

The table immediately following the program goal contains total Program expenditures and revenues, as well as a Program outcome performance measures.

		FY 2008 Actual	FY 2009 Approved	FY 2010 Proposed
ADUL... then p... abuse.	...Data to investigate reports and ...with disabilities from			
Expend...		$625,799	$610,865	$594,253
FTE's		5.3	5.5	5.5
# of reports investigated				
Monthly average # of cases managed				
Cost per case				
% of investigations initated within 24 hours of report				
% of cases without further incidents of abuse, exploitation, or neglet within 12 months				

Each activity within a Program has its own table that contains total expenditures, FTE counts, and Activity performance measures for output, efficiency, and service quality. These tables also include the Activity goal statement.

COMPANION SERVICES–The goal of Companion Services is to Provide assessment of non-medical in home services, such as light houskeeping-personal care, etc. in on and adults with diasabilities to remain safely in their homes

	FY 2008 Actual	FY 2009 Approved	FY 2010 Proposed
Total Expenditures	$2,004,168	$2,155,818	$2,057,210
$ of Direct Service for Companion Aide Slaries	$1,223,596	$1,386,639	$1,310,711
FTE's	6.7	6.9	6.9
Monthly average # of cases managed	295	285	285
Cost per case	$6,794	$7,564	$7,218
% of clients by safely in home	100%	100%	100%

COMMUNITY Y-BASED LONG TERM CARE-The goal os Community Based Long Term Care Services is to provide resources and services to seniors aged 60 and over in order for them to maintain their highest level od independence and remain safely in the community

	FY 2008 Actual	FY 2009 Approved	FY 2010 Proposed
Expenditures	$1,362,182	$1,474,728	$1,549,117
FTE's	10.6	10.2	10.7
# of meals served	62,989	64,200	66,300
# of adultday care hours provided	19,942	24,000	20,000
% of home meals delivered on schedule	100%	98%	98%
% of day care capacity utilized	77%	93%	93%

Figure 9.5. Budget Details in One City's Budget

SOURCE: Reprinted by permission. City of Alexandria, Virginia, 2009.

NOTE: FTE refers to full-time equivalents or a way to count part-time and seasonal employees. The calculation of FTEs works this way: Start with 52 weeks a year and a standard work week of 40 hours. Two people working all year at half-time (20 hours) equal 1 FTE. A seasonal employee working full time in recreation services, for example, for one-quarter equals 1/4 FTE.

Information Technology Services

Summary of Budget Changes

Mandatory Adjustments to the Base Budget		

		FY 2010 Proposed
The summary of Budget Changes section contains descriptions of any base budget adjustments to maintain current services, supplemental adjustments, expenditure reducions, and fee increasess.	Budget ...ocol (VoIP)	($196,066)

Sotware associated with the new VoIP system in FY 2010 is ...both data and voice on the City's I-Net and will result in an overall

St Security	Network Security Tools	($56,000)

In order to improve overall IT security, three new secutiry tools are being implemented in FY 2010 through the IT Plan. One oft hese tools will enable ITS to log activity on the network, which will lead to faster detection of threats and valnerabilityes. The other two tools will enable ITS to better control network access. This $56,000 is the cost of the annual maintenance contract for these tools.

Server Maintenance	Network Management Tools	($32,560)

Two systems have been implemented through the city's IT Plan to help manage the ever-increasing amount of data on the City's network. The annual maintenance costs for these systems in $ 32.50 The first tool is symantec Enterprise Vault and will quickly and automatically store, manage, and This tool aollow for quick data retrieval while reducing data stroage tool will allow to more efficientyly identify anomalies, allocate resource expansion, even as the I-Net becomes busier and more complex.

Each adjustment to the budget contains a brief cescription and explanation. These tables also display to total value and the Activity to which the adjustment applied.

Expenditure Reducions		

Activity	Reduction Option	FTE's	FY2010 Proposed
Server Mgmt/WAN	Network Support & Maintenance		($92,786)

Effcency savings related to network support and maintenace have been identified for FY 2010. This $92,786 in efficiencies includes the following items: frewall maintenace ($8,000): Nortel wireless equipment maintenance ($4,500): Script Lofgic maintenance ($19,000): virus protection licensing ($37,000): and I-net maintenance reduction ($24,288). Due to investment in newer, more effective IT tools and systems, these support/mainteance items are no longer necessary to maintain the City's network. Overall service levels should not be impactd.

Leadership & Mgmt	Office Supplies		($115)

ITS will reduce the office supply budget by $115 in FY2010. This reduction will not impact service levels.

Wide Area Network	Decom mission VITA DS3 Line		($70, 800)

In conjunction with the migration a Voice over Interment protocol (VoIP) phone system, the City will be purchasing a new line for connectivity to the internet that will carry both voice and data traffic. This new connection will render the existing connection (VITA DS3 line) unnecessary. This option will save the City $70,800 without impacting services.

Figure 9.5. (**Continued**)

GO BEYOND THE BUDGET

How comprehensive is the budget? What is left out? What problems are ignored? Does the budget show all the organization's unpaid financial obligations? Are public facilities crumbling or being maintained and replaced? Is enough money being set aside for pension payments? A local budget may not cover all operations in which the organization has a financial interest; it may be legally required to participate in a special district or have debt obligations through another governmental unit. Is the organization facing lawsuits with potentially significant financial impacts?

BOX 9.2

Go Beyond the Budget

In a search engine, insert the name of the county, city, school district, or state that you are interested in, and the acronym "CAFR" to see if this particular government has posted its CAFR on the web. Similarly, insert the government's name, the phrase "Official Statement" and the word "debt" to see if there is a bond disclosure document (official statement) available.

To answer questions such as these, we often must go beyond the budget to an examination of the government's financial condition. The three sides to the government's financial condition are

1. financial solvency, a government's ability to generate enough cash to pay bills over 30–60 days;
2. budgetary solvency, a government's ability to generate adequate revenues over the budgetary period to meet expenditures and avoid deficits;
3. long-run solvency (or "sustainability"), the long-run balance between revenues and costs, including debt and accumulated financial obligations (termed accrued liabilities).

An analysis of the government's financial condition includes socio-economic data and uses trends over time to pinpoint the direction of change. The International City/County Management Association developed an analytic method using key financial indicators and the Government Finance Officers Association (GFOA) also uses this approach.

There is more to financial condition than the current situation. Decision makers and other users of this information really are interested in the government's future viability or sustainability over the long haul. Still, relatively few public organizations prepare reports on their financial condition and so we may have to turn elsewhere. The most useful documents for getting a handle on the financial condition are the comprehensive annual financial report (or CAFR), the credit reports issued by the credit rating firms, and the official statement (OS) issued by the organization when it borrows money (see box 9.2).

Applications
Questions to Ask When Reading a Budget
Use the Internet to access a major city's (population 100,000 or more) current operating budget, including the transmittal letter from the city manager or mayor.

City name and Web site_____

Fiscal Year_____

Choose a different piece of *strong, direct* evidence to answer each of these questions.

1. Are you sure you are using a budget developed through an executive budget process and how do you know?

2. Are you using the *current* operating budget and how do you know?
3. What is the legal status of the budget you are using and how do you know?
4. Is the current adopted budget in balance and how do you know?
5. Was the adopted budget in balance for the prior fiscal year? How do you know?
6. What is the largest fund in the operating budget? How do you know?
7. Does the city have debt? How do you know?
8. Does state or local politics affect the budget? How do you know?
9. Does competition for scarce resources and/or public demands affect the city's budget? How do you know?
10. Do economic factors (for example, changes in interest rates or inflation) affect the city's budget? How do you know?
11. Do demographic factors (for example, population growth or the age or income of residents) affect the city's budget? How do you know?
12. Do intergovernmental issues (for example, changes in federal or state aid or laws) affect the city's budget? How do you know?
13. On which particular two or three issues does the spotlight shine? How do you know?
14. How does the budget illustrate transparency?
15. How does the budget illustrate accountability?

Would You Vote for This Budget?

Use the Internet to access a major city's (population 100,000 or more) current *proposed* operating budget, including the transmittal letter from the city manager or mayor. Decide whether *you* would vote for this budget. Be prepared to defend the position you take.

City and Web site _____

Fiscal Year_____

1. What high priority areas are spotlighted?
   Short Term?   Long Term?

   _____   _____

   _____   _____

2. What drives this budget? Check off the justifications and explanations you find (and be prepared to back up your answers with evidence from the budget).

   __ electoral or partisan politics   __ administration's public commitments

   __ economic conditions   __ program or service specifics

   __ financial factors (e.g., costs)   __ general governmental mission

   __ public needs   __ intergovernmental issues

   __ public demand   __ changes in labor costs

   __ demographics   __ other

3. What is important in this budget? What values does the budget highlight? Identify the values that seem to influence strongly this budget proposal and cite your evidence.

__ efficiency or productivity (p.)   __ accountability to voters/taxpayers (p.)

__ economy or savings (p.)   __ redistributive or equity concerns (p.)

__ responsiveness to service   __ effectiveness (p.)
    recipients (p.)

__ economic concerns   __ fairness (p.)
    (development, jobs, etc.) (p.)

__ other (p.):   __ other (p.):

4. How does the budget affect interests, organizations, and groups (for example, the large taxpayers and senior citizens) that are important politically and economically?

Interests, Organizations, Groups	Proposal	Winner or Loser and Why
1.	————	————————
2.	————	————————
3.	————	————————
your comment	————	————————

5. What is held harmless or treated as sacred cows?

Agency?   ————————————————
Program or Service?   ————————————————
Groups or Interests?   ————————————————

6. What does the proposed budget mean for [select a program or agency]
Program or agency you select ————————————————
Check your overall prediction for each.

For	Excellent ☑	Moderate ☑	Poor ☑
city's economy	☐	☐	☐
city's future budget	☐	☐	☐
selected agency or program	☐	☐	☐
service recipients	☐	☐	☐
city's employees	☐	☐	☐
other concern:	☐	☐	☐

7. For a reality check on accountability and responsiveness, list the issues that you find difficult to find or budget entries that you find difficult to understand, so you (now disguised as a member of the city council) can ask for better information for decision making for the next budget round.

Issue (p.   )

Issue (p.   )

8. Cast your vote by checking one box: ☐ yes ☐ no

WEB SITE RESOURCES

- Analyzing the Costs of Public Programs
- Budget Formats
- Fiscal Year
- Further Resources
- How to Read Highlights of the Federal Budget
- Internet Resources
- Portland's Budget Process
- Tracking an Agency Budget Request

REVIEW QUESTIONS

1. Why is it important for citizens and political activists to know how to read a budget?
2. What is the point of a *budget message*?
3. Why is it important for governments to have separate capital and operating budgets?
4. What kinds of things can you learn by looking at how spending and revenue have changed over time?
5. If something is not included in the budget, what might that tell you about the program or issue?

10

⊂∞⊃

The Bottom Line

This chapter answers five questions:

- Why Does Budgeting Change and Yet So Much Stays the Same?
- How Do Today's Budget Decisions Affect Tomorrow's Democracy?
- How Are We Doing?
- Where Are We Headed?
- What Can We Do about It?

> Come senators, congressmen/Please heed the call/Don't stand
> in the doorway/Don't block up the hall/For the times they are
> a-changin'.
>
> BOB DYLAN, "THE TIMES THEY ARE A-CHANGIN," 1963
> Bob Dylan, "The Times They Are A-Changin." Copyright
> ©1963; renewed 1991 Special Rider Music. All rights reserved.
> International Copyright secured. Reprinted by permission.

> What is required of us now is a new era of responsibility...
> This is the price and the promise of citizenship.
>
> PRESIDENT BARACK OBAMA, INAUGURAL ADDRESS,
> JANUARY 20, 2009

This chapter is about how well or poorly the politics of budgeting addresses democratic concerns and policy needs. Has accountability increased? Is the process more open in meaningful ways? What big problems urgently demand the attention of citizens, voters, and taxpayers? This chapter is less a conclusion than a summing up because, in a dynamic democracy, the politics of budgeting produces temporary settlements and temporary answers to the big political questions.

Here is a key to understanding the politics of budgeting: the public sector is different and is supposed to be different. Much of what governments do and how they do it are different from the practices of large corporations, small businesses, and individuals. Something even as basic as a profit-and-loss or income statement makes little sense politically for most activities in the public sector. As the OMB (2008, p. 179) points out:

> For the federal government, there is no single number that corresponds to a business's bottom line. The government is judged by how its actions affect the country's security and well-being over time, and that cannot easily be summed up with a single statistic. Also, even though its financial condition is important, the government is not expected to earn a profit. One measure of the government's performance is the extent to which it collects the taxes that are owed to it, and another is whether it delivers value in spending the taxes that it collects.

Most activity is by no means *all* activity. At the state and local levels of government, public enterprises such as water and sewer systems, municipal electricity systems, skating rinks, parking garages, and the like are managed on a business model where the bottom line matters.

Most governments finance most of their activities through the general fund, discussed in chapter 9. These activities usually are judged on a combination of political and financial grounds. Public agencies often serve multiple missions and constituencies that push in different directions. Many public agencies are monopolies effectively insulated from competition and funded by taxes. (Public enterprises typically are financed by user charges, not taxes.) Some services are not based on a market in which customers willingly participate at market cost; the people who receive the specific service and the population that benefits are not always the same—prisons, for example. Performance criteria must be tailored to the unique purposes of public organizations. Many agencies such as nonprofit hospices and special education programs daily tackle difficult problems that cannot be solved but only eased.

In budgetary politics, the true bottom line is a political judgment about the preferred and legitimate relationship between taxes paid and benefits received, the nature and scope of the public sector, and what citizens and taxpayers want and expect from it. So we turn to political factors to assess budgetary politics today and its likely future path.

The assessment turns on democratic principles and actual practices in the politics of budgeting. Sometimes the principles and practices align but other times they do not. So how do we know where we stand on principle and practice today?

Like budgeting itself, a fair assessment is all about balance. Citizens and taxpayers do best when idealism is balanced with realism, and optimism with skepticism. As it turns out, you cannot be a purist or perfectionist and truly value democracy and budgeting in action. Certainly, democracy is untidy...and noisy.

Much of the noise and some of the mess are because budgetary politics is about links and relationships. Revenue is linked to spending and operating to capital budgets. Different levels of government, community organizations, and businesses are intertwined and interact through formal arrangements such as contracts and partnerships and informal mechanisms such as lobbying and public opinion. Financial obligations, public investments, and missed opportunities tie one generation to another. Taxes paid and services received are linked throughout a person's life cycle (discussed in chapter 3; see figure 3.3) and through benefits to the community of which the person is a member. The taxpayer demands penny-pinching, fiscally responsible, and politically accountable leaders, while the citizen demands services, solutions, and responsiveness; both are bound together in a single political system (and even within the same person). Along with institutions and rules, these links and relationships structure the politics of budgeting.

The politics of budgeting forges politically acceptable links between individual preferences and political solutions. In a sense, this chapter is all about facing-up to problems. This means that the chapter is about problem solving, and for this we need theory. As we move in and out of different problems, we knowingly shift back and forth between individual concerns and decisions on the one hand, to an organizational context and public policy arena on the other. As a result, we also shift from the rational decision-making model to an institutional setting *ordinarily* dominated by incremental decision making. When making this shift we discover that the big problems in making public policy through budgeting are (1) bridging the two theories with their different sets of concerns and (2) linking the individual's demands and the broader community's interests. What seems reasonable and fair for an individual may, multiplied across many individual actors, add up to an intolerable result in public policy. What seems reasonable and fair for an organization— such as a police department, school system, or nonprofit clinic—may run counter to the political preferences voiced and compromises struck in the hubbub and bargaining of advocacy politics and representative democracy. When it comes to the big problems, ideas about democracy are the most useful bridge and most meaningful link both for understanding and doing the politics of budgeting in America.

This chapter offers an assessment of how we are doing and where we are heading. Is the politics of budgeting changing in any significant way? If so, are the changes for the better and how do we know? Is budget reform likely and desirable? How do broad trends and current developments in budgetary politics undercut or reinforce the values and duties laid out in the first chapter in this book?

WHY DOES BUDGETING CHANGE AND YET SO MUCH STAYS THE SAME?

The reason for all the action in budgetary politics is the "Willie Sutton" effect. Explaining why he robbed banks, Willie Sutton said in 1934, "Because that's where the money is." The same can be said of public budgets today.

Change is difficult, precisely because the stakes are so high and so many powerful players have vested interests, including their political careers, in the existing process and its outcomes. Incumbent legislators use earmarks to bring home the bacon. Presidents, governors and mayors use the bully pulpit to broadcast their budget message. (President Theodore Roosevelt coined the term *bully pulpit* for a platform from which to persuasively promote a political agenda. The word bully in his day meant great or terrific.)

High stakes entice corporations, business associations and industrial coalitions, labor unions, nonprofit coalitions, professional associations, special interest and public interest organizations, and others to spend billions on lobbying and campaign contributions in order to influence budget and policy outcomes. In some cases the line-up is a who's who of political power. In 2008 to 2009, bankers, brokerage houses, insurance CEO's, giants such as Fannie Mae and Freddie Mac, automakers, public education leaders, social service coalitions, governors, and mayors along with many others tried to influence the scope, pace, and design of Washington's economic intervention. The noise of democracy that rose in state capitals across the country at times seemed to climb above legal decibel levels.

Sources of Change

Changes in budgeting often are political responses to political problems. In the 2008 presidential election, the two major-party candidates were both senators experienced in how Congress works and both advocated eliminating earmarks. Candidates for state and local office often run on promises to cut taxes, slash spending, and change the process to produce better outcomes. Of course, their "better" means a change that promotes the budget outcomes they advocate.

Not every politically motivated change is reactive. It may announce a switch in political leadership, as when President Jimmy Carter brought his idea of the ideal budget process from Georgia when he moved into the White House (see Web site resource, Budget Formats). For the same reason, his successor let zero-based budgeting die in most federal agencies. A newly elected chief executive can reach deep down into the bureaucracy and let everyone know that there is a new boss in town by changing the budget process or even just the budget forms. Federal examples are listed in the Budget of the United States, FY 2004 in which President George W. Bush introduced his performance rating initiative:

- "President Johnson launched his Planning, Programming, and Budgeting System in 1966 to 'substantially improve our ability to decide among competing proposals for funds and to evaluate actual performance.' The system was the first serious effort to link budgets to getting results, and a form of it remains in use at the Pentagon today.
- "President Nixon followed with an effort called Management By Objective. This attempted to identify the goals of federal programs so that it was easier to determine what results were expected of each program and where programs were redundant or ineffective. Nixon stated, 'By abandoning programs that have failed, we do not close our eyes to problems that exist; we shift resources to more productive use.'
- "President Carter attempted to introduce a concept known as zero-based budgeting in 1977, to force each government program to prove its value

each year. '[I]t's not enough to have created a lot of government programs. Now we must make the good programs more effective and improve or weed out those which are wasteful or unnecessary,' he told the Congress and the American people in his 1979 State of the Union Address.

• "President Clinton's Administration also offered a broad agenda to 'reinvent' government to make it cost less and do more."

OMB (2003) concluded that "the inertia of the status quo eventually limited the impact of each initiative, and we are no closer to measurable accountability than in President Johnson's day."

The historical pattern was repeated in 2009, when President Obama announced his intention to reform executive budget practices, ensure accountability in the economic stimulus spending, and veto legislation that contains earmarks.

Some budget problems are cyclical, reflecting the short-term effects of economic downturns. Yet, the responses may add up to a sea change, as they do in the financial tsunami that started in 2007 and reaches beyond 2009. Britain, France, China, Japan and other countries launched public spending programs to combat a global recession. The International Monetary Fund uncharacteristically requested nations to increase public spending by 2 percent of their GDP.

According to the National League of Cities 2008 survey, more than one-half of municipal officials in the United States reported that financing services was a major or moderate problem. A majority of city finance officers reported in 2008 that "their cities are less able to meet fiscal needs than in 2007" (Hoene and Pagano, 2008, p. 1). As figure 10.1 illustrates, the forecast is for tight budget times ahead. Moody's (2008, p. 2) predicts, "Given widespread economic distress, the

Figure 10.1. Forecast: Budget Squeeze
SOURCE: Reprinted by permission of www.cartoonstock.com.

political will to make unpopular budgetary decisions, such as increasing property tax levies, is expected to be tested."

Some problems are structural, when revenue and spending trends are out of sync. Structural problems raise questions about both financial and political sustainability. Willingness or ability to pay is out of balance with demands made on the public budget.

We now can identify six broad sources of change in budgetary politics.

1. Structural—crowding out effect of pre-existing commitments and unfunded promises (such as entitlements) on limited resources.
2. Political—responsiveness to constituents and electoral politics (lobbying, earmarks, campaign finance), electoral cycles, term limits, ideological swings, and informal influences.
3. Environmental—including natural disaster, war, the environment; new demands; and economic conditions (recession, expansion, inflation, employment, business cycles (see Figure 10.2).
4. Socio-economic change, including demographic (student count in public schools, baby boomers).
5. Technological and organizational capacity for mobilization, communication, analysis, transparency, and public scrutiny (including record keeping, disclosure, e-government).
6. Professional standards on budgeting and financial management, reporting, and auditing.

Figure 10.2A. Economic Conditions Are a Source of Change in Budgetary Politics

Figure 10.2B. Economic Conditions Are a Source of Change in Budgetary Politics
President Obama signing the American Recovery and Reinvestment Act of 2009
SOURCE: Reprinted by permission. AP Photo/Gerald Herbert

We also can identify six broad sources of stability in budgetary politics.

1. Intellectual limits and customary practices, norms, and historical precedent.
2. Core and traditional public functions such as law enforcement and national security.
3. Formal process and procedure, including constitutional arrangements (separation of powers, federalism), rules, and other legal requirements, seniority and committee assignments.
4. Structural, including entitlements, mandates, tax-and-expenditure limits, dedicated revenues, budget stabilization funds (rainy day or budget reserve funds), and accumulated assets.
5. Political, including partisan affiliation, incumbents' electoral advantage, enduring public attitudes and demands;
6. Professional budget staffs in executive and legislative branches.

These two lists highlight the continuing tension between stability and change needed in vibrant political processes and institutions. The tension produces a pattern of budgetary politics that moves and shifts, but not in a straight line of progress toward a preset endpoint. There is no endpoint in democratic politics because no set of citizens may legitimately exclude future citizens from decision making. Rather, budgetary politics pulsates around core issues and responds to changing circumstances.

In fact, some features of budgetary politics that once were politically stabilizing elements have morphed into politically destabilizing elements. For example, consider that election rules and term limits for state and local politicians may undercut decision makers' concern with the long-term effects of their decisions. Unfunded promises are another case in point. Notice that entitlements are listed as a source of both stability and change.

Entitlements such as Medicare and Social Security are designed so that people can rely on them. The entitlement mechanism protects the program and its beneficiaries by barricading the programs against changes through the yearly appropriations process. These entitlements are effective in the sense that the checks go out, the providers get paid, the services are delivered, public backing is high, and political promises are kept. True, some argue that the payments are not enough and others counter that the money is too much. Yet, programs aimed at the broad electorate are expanded (as with Medicare's prescription drug coverage in George W. Bush's administration) and more people receive Medicare and Social Security benefits.

Putting on the Squeeze

Now the very success of entitlement programs swamps public budgets and pushes a cascade of change throughout the public sector. Protected by law during economic downturns, these programs swallow a growing proportion of federal resources just as Medicaid does with state resources. Under budget pressures, federal and state governments push costs onto other governments and nonprofit agencies through conditions of aid, mandates, regulations, under-funding, and other mechanisms. States have responded in the past to financial pressures by cutting state aid and pushing costs out to nonprofits and down to local governments. Because local governments are at risk for cuts in state aid and increases in state mandates, local governments' finances are tied to states' finances. In effect, entitlements show up in local budgets as imposed costs and revenue pressures in the interconnected service and fiscal system called the public sector. Counties and cities are at the "bottom of the fiscal food chain" (Pagano and Johnston, 2000).

State and local governments have less financial wiggle room than the federal government because many are required to balance their budgets and have a narrower revenue base that is often restricted by tax limits. This statement of fact is not a justification for using the federal treasury as the public-sector version of deep pockets or an ATM. The 2009 federal recovery act was a stopgap response to widespread and deep economic distress, akin to federal responses to other serious but more localized emergencies (see figure 4.4 on 9/11 and on Hurricane Katrina, see the Web site resource, Public Spending Helps Define Us and Our Future). Although the act spawned a frenzy of advocacy politics, its intended impact and the politics surrounding its passage was different from the narrower earmarks, for example, or a broader shift in relationships and responsibilities among governments. Not everyone thinks using so many federal resources in this way and/or financed through debt is a good idea; some oppose what they fear is a permanently expanded federal role; others complain that the assistance does not go far enough, fast enough.

During economic downturns when revenue tanks, state spending on entitlements and other legal obligations is a heavy burden on state budgets. The U.S. economy officially went into recession in December 2007, according to the National Bureau of Economic Research that dates business cycles. A year later, speaking to a meeting of the National Governors Association, then President-elect Barack Obama put the intergovernmental financial effects into words: "It is in state and local government that the rubber hits the road. Of all our elected leaders, you are the ones people count on most to solve the problems in their communities and to help them get by in difficult times. And it's your state governments that bear some of the toughest burdens when an economic crisis strikes."

Government budget pressures squeeze nonprofit and for-profit service providers in communities across the country. Secular and faith-based soup kitchens, food pantries, and homeless shelters feel the pressures. Social service advocates complain that tough budget times in a weak economy are just when the services are most needed. Responding to the severe economic downturn, many state and local governments cut funding for community-based services in FY 2009 and FY 2010.

> Cuts in government funding, coupled with diminished private resources and rising costs of doing business, have left nonprofits facing significant challenges in meeting the increased demand for services.... Our nation's 1.5 million nonprofits receive roughly one-third of the funding they use to provide services to individuals and communities from government, and those that provide health and human services derive over 55 percent of their funding from government. As state and local governments have cut their budgets for these vital areas, many nonprofits have been forced to curtail programs, reduce their hours of service, or even close their doors (Aviv, 2008).

Budgetary and Political Time Bombs

Watching entitlements overwhelm public budgets, many players—on the left, right, and center—in budgetary politics are convinced that America needs fundamental changes in public policy and in public budgeting, and the sooner the better. They argue that entitlements (1) raise serious, divisive questions about intergenerational equity, (2) will undermine the capacity of American political processes to limit conflict, and (3) already curb the public sector's ability to respond creatively to new problems. In effect, entitlements' success is unsustainable financially and politically. "Unsustainable" means that change—in budgets, benefits, and politics—is inevitable. Entitlements' success at spawning advocates means that this change comes at a high political price. As President-elect Barack Obama told the governors in December 2008, "Make no mistake: these are difficult times, and we're going to have to make hard choices."

Financially, unfunded promises build in long-term structural imbalance. They set up budgetary—and political—time bombs. Public decision makers find themselves to the "right of the boom," forced to react to exploding costs instead of preparing for them (see box 10.1). Examples of "budget busters" with high growth rates are the unfunded obligations to under-funded public employees' pensions

---

BOX 10.1

Where Do You Want to Be?

To the Right/Left of the Boom refers to the time before or after a bomb explodes, as imagined on a timeline. Applied to a budget explosion, the timeline develops this way:

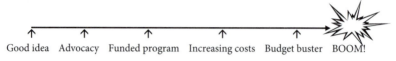

Good idea   Advocacy   Funded program   Increasing costs   Budget buster   BOOM!

Figure Box 10.3. Budgetary Time Bomb

The authors gratefully acknowledge the Summer Workshop on Teaching about Terrorism at the University of Oklahoma—Norman.

This idea seems especially fitting because at least two of the big budget problems, Medicare and Social Security, are related directly to a demographic boom, the aging the baby boomers.

---

and workers' and retiree's medical care. Another example is underfunded infrastructure. As past bills come due, responsiveness and accountability to the voters and taxpayers are reduced.

HOW DO TODAY'S BUDGET DECISIONS AFFECT TOMORROW'S DEMOCRACY?

Over time, legal, financial, and political commitments build up. Even now they seriously curtail current leaders' scope for decision making about the upcoming budget cycle. Why does this matter? After all, in order to operate on a daily basis, society needs a high level of stability and predictability in public policy and services. Business demands predictability in government rules and taxation. (Imagine showing up at each class to discover that the time and location change randomly.) In the negative column is the reduction in responsiveness and accountability in the core decision-making process in a representative democracy. If the resources are tied up, what is there to decide? Another negative is the need to short-circuit the process through, for example, emergency or supplemental appropriations in order to respond flexibly and quickly.

But are commitments made today and paid for in the future always a *bad* idea? Let us propose that locking up future resources undermines democracy. Budget commitments made in the past (1) curb the decision-making scope of future elected representatives and voters and (2) reduce responsiveness and accountability to future voters and taxpayers.

Arguments For

Although long-term contracts, debt, drawn-out projects, and accumulated but unfunded obligations may create efficiencies and cost savings, they also tie up resources for purposes selected by the elected leaders who signed off at the beginning. Future decision makers will find their ability to make choices is reduced, along with their ability to respond to future needs and demands. Cheap or efficient solutions may not be ideal when they ride roughshod over democratic concerns. In 1796, George Washington argued, "We should avoid throwing upon posterity the burden we ourselves ought to bear."

Tax and expenditure limits written into state constitutions also reduce the scope of decision making by future democratically elected officials. The very purpose of these limits is to bind future officials and make it difficult to change these limits. In effect, current voters lock in their own preferences and freeze out future voters.

For those of us concerned about democracy, the question is: "*Whose* priorities are to be in play in future budgets?" It is undemocratic for current voters to hog decision making by locking up resources and denying future elected leaders, voters, and taxpayers as much decision-making scope as the current ones enjoy. Just because legal procedures are followed does not mean that the budget outcomes foster democracy. Democratic and legal mechanisms used today can reduce tomorrow's accountability, responsiveness, and democracy (see figure 10.4).

Arguments Against

If the current politicians pay their way and fund their priorities, then they get to make some decisions, and the next generation of politicians does, too. This is democracy over time. There is also the matter of fairness over time, or intergenerational equity. If future citizens use the bridges or tunnels, then they should help foot the bill by helping to pay off the construction costs. Of course, it is unfair and financially irresponsible to shift costs to future taxpayers for goods and services consumed today.

We should not label as undemocratic all multi-year commitments that are legally agreed to by elected officials and citizens through election or referendum. A practical argument is that we cannot run government or public institutions on only yearly spending with no future commitments. If we are impractical, then how long can we expect democracy to last?

What about deficit spending? It is useful for stimulating the economy (as fiscal policy) and for meeting temporary and unexpected needs such as a sizeable crisis or war. In fact, so many state and local governments are prohibited from running a deficit that rainy day or contingency funds are the only legal alternatives to increasing taxes or cutting spending. These funds take current taxpayers' money and salt it away for a future economic or other kind of crisis. Is it undemocratic for current decision makers to take their stewardship duties seriously?

Some decisions that tie up resources represent investments for future generations and expand rather than narrow future opportunities. The purchase of

Figure 10.4. Democracy Is a Challenge
SOURCE: Library of Congress, Prints and Photographs Division, c 1936–1940.

Louisiana from France in 1803 doubled the size of the United States at the cost of less than a nickel an acre, including the cost of financing the loan from European bankers. When Secretary of State William H. Seward agreed to purchase Alaska from Russia for $7.2 million in 1867, "Seward's folly" increased the size of the United States by almost 20 percent. Although the Senate ratified the treaty with Russia relatively quickly, opposition in the House of Representatives delayed the appropriation needed to finance the transaction until July 1868. In 1959, Alaska became the 49th and largest state.

Elected officials have to make these decisions. There are trade-offs. Budgeting is about trade-offs and choices, and so is politics. Nothing is perfect in our human existence, much less our democratic processes and institutions.

HOW ARE WE DOING?

The budget is a focus of intense political activity. Governors and mayors announce budgets with fanfare; legislators scrutinize and horse-trade; advocacy groups mobilize; lobbyists tramp the corridors of Congress and state capitols; experts testify; and citizens demand explanations for small pieces of a large pie. These small pieces translate into many dollars. Many cities have budgets running to hundreds of millions of dollars, states have budgets in the many billions, and the federal government calculates in trillions. A hard look at the four factors of transparency, accountability, efficiency, and responsiveness shows how well or poorly budgetary politics makes and dodges the trade-offs and choices.

Transparency and Complexity

In some ways budgeting is more open today than a decade ago. So much information is a mouse click away. Giving rise to the expression "**e-government**," many state and local governments announce budget hearings and post budget documents, financial statements, performance reports, and even lists of registered lobbyists on official Web sites. Think tanks and public interest and special interest organizations offer data and analyses, although often these are slanted to support their political viewpoint or policy agenda. The media routinely cover budget developments and investigative reporting opens up the details of some horse-trading and back-room deals.

In fact, federal budgeting is more transparent than in the "good old days." "Although secret sessions were common in Congress's early years, they were less frequent through the 20th century. National security is the principal reason for such sessions in recent years" (Amer, 2007, p. 1).

Federal budgeting is more transparent than even a decade ago where earmarks, lobbying, and contracts are concerned. Yet, there are disturbing counter trends. In chapter 6 we see how financing national security in secrecy and military operations through supplemental or emergency appropriations reduces transparency so that even broad spending totals must be pieced together. Of course there are some good reasons for secrecy, but these reasons only explain the choice; they do not change the effect on transparency. Here again, the politics of budgeting is about trade-offs.

Unfortunately, having information available does not necessarily mean being able to make heads or tails of what is actually going on. Chapter 9 (and the Web site resource, How to Read the Highlights of the Federal Budget) makes this point pretty clear. At public budget hearings, voters and taxpayers may appear frustrated because they do not know about the links, intricacies, and legal obligations—they feel hemmed in, powerless, and voiceless. They walk away suspecting their political leaders of politically motivated trickery and budgetary "smoke and mirrors." Elected leaders and professional budgeters do not necessarily intend to scam the voters and taxpayers. Some may "dumb down" the information because they believe it is too complicated for citizens to understand, as the case concluding this chapter suggests. The revenue system supporting American governments is so fragmented and complex that it is unlikely that many citizens can actually calculate how much

---

E-government—the use of the internet (World Wide Web) in government functions, such as posting meeting minutes, making forms and budget documents available, and associated with enhancing transparency and communication with citizens, taxpayers, and residents.

they pay yearly in federal, state, and local taxes, plus the many fees and charges. The burden of informed citizenship is greater today than ever before.

The fact that each piece is more transparent does not make the whole puzzle something we can understand easily. American society and the global economy are complex, and this complexity magnifies vulnerability to outside shocks. The challenges are complex, and so are the public sector's responses.

Financing Public Higher Education

Consider the politics of financing public higher education, for example. Here the authors walk a fine line (not to be confused with walking the DUI sobriety line). The authors are not advocating a policy position but using a public policy arena familiar to many readers to illustrate the complex interconnections and interplay in the politics of budgeting.

More than 15 million undergraduates attend degree-granting institutions. Almost 80 percent of these students attend public colleges and universities, an engine of social mobility and a big part of the country's future economic muscle. The National Center for Public Policy and Higher Education "grades" states on affordability, or how much of the average family's income it costs to go to college. In December 2008, the center gave 49 of the 50 states an "F" in affordability.

In FY 2009, more than one-half the states cut funding to public higher education and/or implemented tuition increases.

Vice President Joe Biden's task force asked, "What explains the rapidly rising cost of education?" It concluded, "There are generally two major reasons for increases in tuition. Rising tuition either funds increased spending or replaces lost revenue from other sources, a process referred to as 'cost shifting.' Increases in tuition have been partly driven by each of these factors, but the majority of the rise in tuition in recent years is increasingly attributable to cost shifting." The task force observed,

> The use of increased tuition to offset lost revenue from elsewhere is particularly pronounced in public higher education, as falling state and local appropriations have forced institutions to increase tuitions in order to maintain their revenue. State and local appropriations to public higher education have failed to keep pace with enrollment and inflation since the 1980s, meaning that appropriations for public higher education have fallen over the last twenty years on an inflation-adjusted, per-student basis. These decreasing public revenues have impelled public colleges and universities to steadily increase their tuitions (Vice President of the United States, Middle Class Task Force, 2009, p. 5).

State appropriations pay for a declining share of the cost of public higher education and on the average today account for about one-quarter of the revenue of public universities. When recessions hit, they hit states hard. With the great majority of states having faced budget shortfalls in FY 2009 and even more looking at deficits in FY 2010, state support of higher education is likely to fall. In tough budget times, it is relatively easy to cut back on spending for higher education because lives are not immediately at stake and alternative revenue is available in the form of tuition (and gifts and grants). Steep cuts in state support roll out into tuition increases, enrollment caps, program cuts, layoffs, or all of these, with far-reaching economic, social, and individual effects.

It should come as no surprise, then, that many college students need some financial assistance. The student loan market runs to about $85 billion a year. The largest source of student aid is the U.S. Department of Education's programs. Undergraduate student aid comes in four different flavors.

1. Federal Pell Grants for low-income students that do not have to be repaid; the amount depends on need, educational costs, and student status; about 5,400 institutions of higher education participate in this program.
2. Federally guaranteed (subsidized) loans, some directly from the Department of Education but most through outside lenders as of 2008.
3. Private loans, a big business worth about $17 billion a year and the fastest-growing segment of the student loan market.
4. Scholarships funded through the educational institution by gifts, endowments, and some charitable and publicly financed programs (such as Georgia's Hope scholarship program).

The College Cost Reduction and Access Act of 2007, the student-loan law signed by President Bush in September 2007, provided roughly $20 billion for financial assistance to college students. The law increased Pell Grants; reduced interest rates on federally subsidized loans; and introduced an income-based repayment program, loan forgiveness for public service workers, and tuition assistance for future public school teachers. (A small student-loan reimbursement program for federal employees already existed.) To pay for the new assistance, and over Republican objections, the Democratic congressional majority reduced federal subsidies to lenders by about $20 billion. (Scandals about conflicts of interest had recently rocked the private lending industry and college financial-aid offices.)

Then the "credit crunch" spread from mortgages to other types of credit, including student loans. Private lending dried up. In April 2008, President Bush approved federal action and the Department of Education with the assistance of the Treasury Department set up emergency programs to intervene in the student credit market. The department issued federally guaranteed government loans for at least double the $14 billion issued the year before. Congress gave the Department of Education new authority to buy securities backed by private student loans.

November 2008 saw another round of intervention in higher education finance, as part of a $200 billion consumer-lending program led by the Treasury and Federal Reserve. Among other things, this program authorizes the Department of Education to buy student loans from troubled investment firms. In effect, the subsidy reduced by Congress in September 2007 was restored by executive fiat and without congressional input.

It is only by accident that the federal financing of undergraduate higher education has become more efficient. OMB reported in 2005 that government-guaranteed loans cost many times more than the cost of direct federal loans, with the difference going to the lenders in the private sector. The American Recovery and

Table 10.1. Student Aid in the 2009 American Recovery and Reinvestment Act

	FY 2009	FY 2010	FY 2011
Budget Authority	$16.50	$0.80	$0.00
Estimated Outlays	$0.90	$14.60	$1.10

In billions of dollars

SOURCE: Congressional Budget Office, 2009.

Reinvestment Act passed in February 2009 again increased the Pell Grants (see table 10.1). The increase in estimated outlays for student aid in FY 2010 reflects the issues of affordability and the part higher education plays in economic growth.

The Department of Education is taking on a bigger role in financing higher education than ever before, especially as it moves from guarantor to direct lender. Its new powers could change how millions of undergraduate students finance their college education. Add to this the credit crisis and the states' budgetary responses to the recession and we see an unplanned, largely silent transfer in the financing of public higher education from state taxpayers and lenders in the private sector to federal taxpayers and the federal government. What does this shift do to the logic and legitimacy of different tuition rates for in-state *versus* out-of-state students? What is the impact of shifting from outright state support to more loans carried by students? How will these changes affect social mobility and public perceptions of fairness? The issue of student loans slides into accountability when we ask, "How many state and congressional education and appropriation committees have deliberated over these serious changes in public policy?"

Following the Money through a Maze

Public service delivery in general in the United States today is an improvised patchwork that is growing even more complex and harder for citizens and taxpayers to map out. No GPS works here. It is difficult to hold decision makers accountable when it is a major task to pinpoint who is financing what and who decided. We find that governments are shifting more and more from directly providing services to buying them in a public-private partnership model. Governments increasingly deliver public services and respond to public problems under contract with or in collaboration with business, nonprofit agencies, and other governments.

Military and domestic programs increasingly are performed by networks, collaborators, and contractors. Many federal, state, and local agencies rely on contractors to perform a variety of functions, including running prisons and national security tasks, revenue collection, garbage collection, recreation services, health and computer services, student loans, and more. For example, the National Institutes of Health's (NIH) congressional justification for its FY 2009 budget request explains that more than 300,000 scientists and researchers affiliated with more than 3,100 non-federal research facilities form its "extramural community" that accounts for more than 80 percent of NIH appropriations.

Transparency is a political priority in the 2009 American Recovery and Reinvestment Act. Information about planned and actual spending from the $787 billion package is reported on a central Web site, recovery.gov, and on many state Web sites. Even so, because the recovery package is implemented through "network" government and "leveraging" through an intricate pattern of relationships among all levels of government, nonprofits, and the private sector, the path of money and the quality of performance will be difficult to track. Collaboration on a large scale fits the "cross-boundary" problems Americans face in health care, the food supply, public safety, homeland security, economic recovery, and more. The downside to this complexity may be its effect on the citizens' view of political legitimacy.

U.S. experience with intricate systems for public services—and even meeting what is seen today as a purely or inherently governmental function—goes back to the beginning of the Republic (see box 10.2). True, but the questions remain: Who does what, with whose taxes, and who is responsible? Whom should we hold accountable? These questions are especially important when a system shock such as the financial meltdown and recession works its historic way through the U.S. economy and society.

The public sector responds to the increasing complexity of problems with complex tools such as networks across organizations, governments, and sectors. As Albert Einstein pointed out, "The significant problems we face cannot be solved at the same level of thinking we were at when we created them." Agreed, but the result is systems—including budgeting—that are increasingly visible to the naked eye or transparent and yet so baffling to many American citizens and taxpayers as to be beyond transparency and accountability.

How can a system be transparent when it is this complex? Budget processes and procedures build up over time. Their effects unfold (usually slowly) and cut across the public and private sectors, levels of government, branches of government, and executive agencies. Is transparency a realistic political goal in a world this complex? These questions are precisely the kind best answered by the citizens, taxpayers, and elected public leaders.

Accountability, Stewardship, and the Artful Dodge
The move to executive budgeting and the development of professional staff increased accountability. Reforms to earmarks, lobbying, campaign finance, and campaign advertising coupled with freedom of information, sunshine, ethics and other laws boosted political accountability in budgeting and in politics generally. Tighter and more professional financial management improved administrative accountability, as have computerized monitoring, tracking, and record-keeping systems. Despite all these positive developments, the scorecard for accountability in budgetary politics shows mixed results across different issues and processes and across governments.

Budget Gimmicks
Like the legendary escape artist, Houdini, many public leaders around the country use tricks to get out of the tough spots in which they find themselves. They

BOX 10.2

Intricate Public-Private Systems Even for a "Purely Governmental" Function

Figure Box 10.5. Intricate Public-Private Systems Even for a "Purely Governmental" Function

SOURCE: Brasher Doubloon, 1787. American Numismatic Association http://www.money.org. Reprinted by permission.

"Before the establishment of the United States Mint in Philadelphia in 1792, several private mints operated along the Atlantic seaboard producing private copper coinage for local use. In addition, the state governments of New Hampshire, Massachusetts, Connecticut, New York, New Jersey, and Vermont all issued copper coins under the terms of the Articles of Confederation. After the ratification of the Constitution in 1789, states were no longer permitted to issue their own coinage. Meanwhile, the Federal government experimented with the use of private mints until the establishment of the United States Mint at Philadelphia in 1792."

The Brasher Doubloon

"During the period of the Confederation (from 1782 to 1789, when the US Constitution was ratified), it was unclear who was to provide the circulating money for the new United States of America. It had become clear to all that paper currency was not a viable solution—huge numbers of nearly worthless notes were still circulating at a huge discount—so private individuals and state governments began to issue copper coinage (which was legal under the Articles of Confederation) and the national Congress began to explore how to issue a national currency. One result of this confusion was this gold coin, known as the "Brasher Doubloon," which was the first gold coin to be produced in the United States. It was produced in 1787 by a goldsmith named Ephraim Brasher, a one-time neighbor of George Washington in Philadelphia, as a possible model for a national coinage. The coin was based on the Spanish American doubloons that circulated widely in international trade and has a design that incorporated elements from the ideas being discussed in Congress for the proposed national coinage. Only seven of these coins are known to exist today."

Reprinted by permission. Beeton, 2009.

may shift costs down or across the network of political and financial relationships to other governments or regions, to the future, to the private sector, or to other parts of the public sector. The tricks are politically useful, but only temporarily. Remember the boom in box 10.1?

Political gimmicks extend to misdirection, diversion, and evasion. When public leaders (or anyone else, for that matter) promise something for nothing, they fail to mention that the public usually gets what it pays for. Perhaps state and local politicians sell a favored economic development project to the voters by hyping the advantages and ignoring the downside of tax breaks, service costs, and risks. Bypassing the ordinary appropriations process, Washington funded military operations in Iraq and Afghanistan through large emergency-spending bills. This approach reduced Congress's ability to exercise the usual oversight built into the ordinary budget process and also makes it more difficult for citizens to figure out the total costs of these operations. Of course, Congress voted for the military spending and many economic development projects result in a better local economy. As it turns out, budgetary politics is less than a thing of perfection, but it is also more than a bag of tricks.

The politics of budgeting in the United States today fails to match the public's appetite for quality services with its taste for low taxes. Do you remember Wimpy the moocher? He is the character in "Popeye" who promises to pay tomorrow for the hamburgers he eats today. Rational but self-interested political leaders may respond to short-term electoral incentives that sometimes overpower other concerns. Many politicians buy some elbow room at the expense of the long-term public interest by contributing to, or at least tolerating, a structural imbalance in the budget.

Today, the internationally recognized icon of structural imbalance is the U.S. national debt. The increasing debt financed national defense and security, tax cuts, and domestic programs, but the surge in 2008–2009 most especially financed the government's CPR for an economy in recession and financial institutions and credit markets in need of resuscitation. Now add perhaps another $2 trillion of debt taken on by the 111th Congress and the Obama administration in 2009. This is not to say that debt on behalf of economic rescue is not worthy, but instead to stress that the effort is costly.

How is this mounting debt to be made manageable, fair, and affordable for future generations? Asking this question does not suggest that the economic rescue is a good or bad idea. Future generations may be better off because of this effort, but certainly they will *not* be better off if the effort is not made. The question is asked because it is central to the political concerns raised in chapters 2 and 3. That the question has become a hot-button issue in the politics of budgeting is a positive development: silence on the subject of a long-term strategy is a masterful way to dodge important political concerns now and in the future.

Why should readers of this book care? As Herbert Hoover pointed out, "Blessed are the young, for they shall inherit the national debt." The bill is in the mail.

Dodging Tough Choices

Politically motivated gimmicks help politicians of different political stripes and at different levels of government dodge many tough choices and also dodge the unpleasant chore of bringing bad news to their constituents. It is especially fitting that the Artful Dodger in Charles Dickens' *Oliver Twist* is a pickpocket. In 2007 (predating the economic stimulus packages and bailouts), the Concord Coalition urged, "Some candidates will be tempted to tell the voters what they think they want to hear, rather than what they need to hear. It's up to the voters to make each campaign a 'pander-free' zone.... We also encourage candidates to show initiative by bringing up these issues themselves, without waiting for the voters to demand answers. That is what real leadership is about."

Only the voters can put an end to the tricks and the dodging by insisting on being treated as serious players in the politics of budgeting. This is a nonpartisan challenge. The George W. Bush administration did not ask for sacrifices to pay for military operations in Iraq and Afghanistan and the economic stimulus efforts, voters did not insist on knowing the full costs, and taxpayers did not demand the privilege of paying the costs. Voters failed to insist that candidates connect the dots and fill in the blanks during the 2008 presidential campaign, when Barack Obama and John McCain pushed their broad and largely painless plans for economic recovery. Neither candidate called for true sacrifice or sharing the burden. McCain promised everyone a tax cut, while Obama promised that most would get tax cuts and only the wealthiest would pay more (plus cutting funds to the ineffective programs identified by his agency-review teams). Of course, it is not wise fiscal policy to raise taxes during a recession, but to ignore the costs—interest and principal—over the long haul is an artful dodge.

The values of accountability and transparency in a democracy require public leaders to tell the public what they are doing and why. These values are not served when some politicians obscure or hide their policy agenda or underlying political goals. These values *are* served when citizens and public leaders insist on the details of where millions or trillions of dollars go, and for what good and with what risk. A representative democracy relies on informed citizens and public stewards to ask, "If solutions are not good budgeting, how can they be good politics in the long-term?" As President Dwight D. Eisenhower pointed out in his 1953 inaugural address, "A people that values its privileges above its principles soon loses both."

Efficiency, Effectiveness, and Performance

In public agencies, poor performance is often an argument for more resources. When a community faces a skyrocketing crime rate, for example, a common response by political leaders, the public, and the police is to increase the police department's budget and hire more police. Problems "prove" that more money is needed.

On the other hand, effective responses to problems of public policy often make little noise and draw little public support. After all, effective responses are what the decision makers, taxpayers, and service recipients expect. As a result, emergencies and crises push agency budgets higher or are used as leverage in budgetary politics.

Perhaps Americans expect too much from the public sector. The different expectations listed in table 1.2 often are at odds with each other. Democratic claims and concerns show up as the costs of public participation and accountability; public notice, public hearings, competitive bidding on contracts, spending controls, and many other devices cost time and money that eat into program efficiency. Liberty and equality are basic ideals in the American democracy, but they often clash. Agencies such as Homeland Security and the Department of Education serve multiple and sometimes conflicting missions. Public policy proposals aim at bringing in as many supporters as possible under the umbrella in order to put together a supporting coalition and get the votes needed for passage, as the compromises needed for passage of the 2008 bailouts of financial institutions and the 2009 recovery act show. The result is something for everyone. We then turn around and demand efficiency.

Standards of success for program performance do not necessarily translate into standards of political success. Douglas Morgan (2002, p. 72) tells us, "The history of public budgeting is a quarrel between two different philosophical approaches: a political approach that emphasizes the importance of having budgets reflect constituency interest groups and a planning and information-driven approach that emphasizes the importance of insuring that budget allocations meet the rational planning concerns of efficiency and effectiveness." He tells us further that "public budgeting is more about successfully reconciling...competing purposes than it is about managing numbers and technical expertise" (Morgan, 2002, pp. 24–25).

Perhaps Americans get too little from the public sector. The public's dissatisfaction and expectations can drown out hard measures of performance, value, and efficiency. (Chapter 2 discusses the low levels of citizen satisfaction.) The GAO has identified fraud, waste, and abuse in Homeland Security and Defense contracts. To be fair, these departments have many resources and many contracts and so they have "program-integrity" problems.

From the federal government to small nonprofits, the public sector is measuring performance in order to increase efficiency and cost effectiveness. Leading state and local public interest associations joined together in 2008 to set up the National Performance Management Advisory Commission to create a national framework for public sector performance measurement and management. Close performance monitoring is part of the 2009 recovery act (and publicly available at www.whitehouse.gov/omb/expectmore and www.recovery.gov).

Professional associations and public interest groups include efficiency, effectiveness, and performance monitoring and measurement among their recommended best practices (see the Web site resource, Internet Resources, Financial Condition and Performance Measurement). State and local governments turned years ago to these types of measures, especially quantitative ones, as the "Total Quality Measurement" and "Reinventing Government" movements swept the country, and much of the developed world. Now outcome measurement—what difference are we making?—and measures of sustainability are in style.

The Government Performance and Results Act of 2000 requires federal agencies to submit performance reports each year. In his FY 2004 budget, President George W. Bush unveiled his Program Assessment Rating Tool (PART) to assess and improve program performance. OMB's overview of the president's proposed budget for FY 2009 says that discretionary spending (excluding security-related functions) was subjected to close review of national need and effectiveness. "Failure to meet these criteria resulted in the proposed termination or reduction of 151 programs for a savings of over $18 billion, a step that will help channel resources to more effective programs."

Of course, notions of effectiveness may change with the political leadership. Yet, if popularity is the gauge, then performance review must be a good idea. At a news conference soon after his election in November 2008, then President-elect Obama repeated his campaign pledge to go through the budget "line by line" in order to eliminate unneeded and ineffective programs and increase the cost-effectiveness of others.

Efficient performance in the public sector is (1) an ongoing concern and (2) in the eye of the beholder. The public overall says in poll after poll that it gets the most for its tax dollars from local government. The public may be on to something. A 2008 study reports that the public believes that 42 percent of federal resources are wasted because of inefficiency (Primavera, 2008). This finding comes as no surprise, given the discussion in chapter 3 about public perceptions of government waste. What is surprising is that the federal managers surveyed agree, despite eight years of performance initiatives.

Responsiveness and the Role and Size of Government

Americans' ideas about government performance and waste both mirror and also reinforce their beliefs about the proper role and size of the federal government. In caricature, these views can be summed up as (1) government as incompetent bungler and (2) government as potential tyrant. Yes, these views do contradict each other. What is there to be afraid of, if the government actually cannot do what it sets out to do? The point is that the American political culture has multiple and inconsistent strands of thought woven together into a durable whole. One strand is pragmatism, so that the practical sometimes sweeps aside the principle, as the cases ending chapters 4 and 6 illustrate.

The American political culture and Americans' deeply held beliefs continue to affect the politics of budgeting. Americans are divided about whether government should be smaller and with fewer services or larger and doing more (see figure 3.1). Many believe that government is doing too much already and "interfering" in people's lives and capitalism's market economy. They want government to improve economic conditions and jobs, but not to redistribute income or wealth. These attitudes are a part of the political culture shared by many—but not all—citizens and part of American history.

Sometimes the budget argument over who pays is disguised as an argument over principle: who is properly responsible for a particular job? This way of framing the issue can lead to big business promoting big government. By way of example, consider the security fee charged since 2002 to airlines passengers at $2.50 for every leg of a trip, to a maximum of $5 per trip. The fee captures only somewhat more than one-third the cost of passenger and baggage screening. President Obama's proposed FY 2010 budget included a fee increase starting in 2012. Predictably, the airlines industry generally opposes hikes in government fees. Representing most large airlines, an Air Transport Association of America spokesman countered, "We believe that aviation security is a U.S. government responsibility.... These costs should not be on the backs of airlines and their customers" (CNN, 2009a).

Most Americans believe that democracy and the free market need and support each other. Many believe that government must be limited if the market is to prosper and the market regulated if society is to prosper. For some, the logical result is the principle that smaller is better.

Many elected leaders appear to share this view, or at least they give lip service to what has become an American political mantra. Showing the same hands-off attitude, President George W. Bush said in July 2008, "I don't think the government ought to be involved in bailing out companies." About a dozen years earlier, in January 1996, President Clinton announced in his State of the Union Address, "We know big government does not have all the answers. We know there's not a program for every problem. We have worked to give the American people a smaller, less bureaucratic government in Washington. And we have to give the American people one that lives within its means. The era of big government is over."

The *Wall Street Journal* columnist David Wessel wrote in 2005 that "the era of small government is over. September 11 challenged it. Katrina killed it." Chapter 6 describes the impact of these events on public spending and government activity (and so does the Web site resource, Public Spending Helps Define Us and Our Future). Excluding debt, unfunded IOUs, and government guarantees and other commitments, federal spending and spending by all governments are relatively stable when compared to the size of the U.S. economy.

The federal government's response to the severe recession and credit freeze was to borrow money to (1) prevent a financial meltdown and (2) prime the economic pump. Its response to the economic turmoil greatly expanded the role and size of government. Many conservatives bitterly complain that this response locks in big government for years to come. The federal response was, in effect, the result of a risk analysis, not a stand on principle. Pragmatism prevailed. One lesson learned is that the corporate, banking, educational, nonprofit, and other communities turn to Washington's financial resources when alternatives dry up (see the Web site resource, Advocacy Politics). The people who lost their jobs or their homes turned to Washington for relief. Another lesson is that government may respond to different concerns at different times but, to loosely paraphrase Abraham Lincoln, cannot please all the people all the time.

WHERE ARE WE HEADED?

Announcing his budget director in November 2008, then President-elect Barack Obama said, "Budget reform is not an option. It's a necessity." Do you agree? Is the politics of budgeting in the United States heading toward change?

You need three things to think about budget reform. The first is some familiarity with the politics and mechanics of budgeting, which you have if you have gotten this far in this book. The second is a definition of political reform. *Reform* is a positive label for change that is used to rally support for the proposal. Reform implies a change for the better and is used so often because few public leaders would argue that their proposed change is a bad idea. The third thing you need is a crystal ball (see figure 10.6). When looking into the future, it is wise to remember that much may change and what is "true" today in the politics of budgeting may be something else entirely tomorrow or the next day.

What type of reform are you talking about—process, procedure, system, or all three? Are you thinking about federal budgeting only, all governments, or perhaps throughout the public sector? Are reforms to be short-term responses to immediate conditions or undertaken with an eye on the long term? If you think of the economic crisis in combination with budgetary unsustainability as

Figure 10.6. Polishing Up the Crystal Ball

SOURCE: Reprinted by permission of www.cartoonstock.com. Fischer, Ed, 1992.

opportunities for change, then these questions are important. This is, in fact, a perfect storm for people interested in changing the politics of budgeting. Many pundits have quipped, "A crisis is a terrible thing to waste."

In his FY 2009 budget, President Bush issued a catalog of reforms:

1. On health care he proposed "replacing the existing—and unlimited—tax exclusion for employer-sponsored insurance with a standard health insurance tax deduction," "to restructure health insurance markets," and to reduce automatically payments to health providers when a financing threshold is reached.
2. Explaining that nearly two-thirds of federal is automatic or mandatory, such as interest on the public debt and entitlements, he concluded that "the Congress and the President must enact legislation to change the path of this spending." He proposed a new statutory pay-as-you-go requirement on any legislation that affects mandatory spending.
3. A legislative line-item veto.
4. Further earmark reforms.
5. A joint budget resolution with the force of law that brings the president into the congressional budget process early on.
6. Biennial budgeting (adopting a budget every two years).
7. A budget rule to prevent government shutdowns and to substitute for continuing resolutions passed by Congress.

Nothing on this list is purely technical! Each proposal represents significant changes in the distribution of costs and benefits and the distribution of power among the branches of government. The point of budget reform is to change the decisions and outcomes and the line-up of players and their relative power in budgetary politics (see Web site resource, Power Grab or Neutral Reform?).

No reform will remove the politics and passion from budgeting. Serious people have tried for more than a century and they have failed. Hot-button issues arouse passion, polarize the public and political elites, and often trigger ideological responses or emotional reactions. Usually taxes, and especially property taxes, are hot issues. The list of today's issues includes Social Security, health insurance, national security and terrorism, quality public education and college affordability, the national debt, and immigration. You may want to add another issue or two. Or three. All of these issues have budgetary implications at all levels of government and throughout the economy and society.

Earlier efforts at budget reform teach another lesson. Budget reform, like the politics of which it is a part, rarely moves in a straight direction. The changes in the politics of budgeting probably will not be as fast or clear-cut as some readers might want. Some change will be driven by narrow self-interest. Some reformers will wrap themselves in the justification of serving the public interest, but other reformers actually will serve the public interest. Some reforms might broaden participation but reduce efficiency, while other changes would sacrifice accountability to get more simplicity and transparency. Given the many and often opposing values that are important in the politics of budgeting, the lesson is that you cannot have it all and certainly not all at once.

Reforming the Appropriations Process

The cumbersome machinery called the appropriations process evolved to defend the political power of the major players within and beyond public institutions. Today the appropriations processes at all levels of government are cramped financially by pre-existing legal commitments, intergovernmental mandates, entitlements, unfunded employee benefits, and debt service. Budget processes are cramped intellectually by routine decision making that looks too much to the past and too little to the future. The result is that innovation in public policy *usually* is *only a* small *part* of total spending and total revenues *in any single year*. What do you intend to do about this? What is at stake? Are the remedies better or worse than the problems they are supposed to cure?

The congressional budget process has not been overhauled systematically for many years. The 1974 Congressional Budget and Impoundment Control Act set up the congressional budget process and timetable, House and Senate Budget Committees, Congressional Budget Office, and several important new procedures. The division between mandatory and discretionary spending took shape in the 1980s. If wide-ranging reform and rethinking can be done once or twice, then why not yet again?

Entitlement Reform

Should any part of budgetary politics be treated as a sacred cow, too important or dangerous to touch? In 1974, the Social Security Act was amended to require automatic cost-of-living adjustments (COLAs) that account for the effect of infla-tion. The COLA for 2009 was 5.8 percent, the largest in almost three decades. Is an automatic increase coupled with the politically insulated status of an entitlement giving Americans the transparency, accountability, and political outcomes they want? The conventional wisdom for many years has been that it is political suicide to suggest changes to social security. But is it? It was done in 1974 and again under President Reagan. Is it time to change conventional wisdom?

Closure Commissions

The process used to close federal military bases and state hospitals is described in the case at the end of chapter 5. Closure commissions highlight need and cost. The fast-track, no-amendment vote bypasses regular legislative review and horse-trading. Because this model trades deliberation and coalition-building for speed and simplicity, there are strong arguments for and against using it. It has already been proposed for Congress for both spending and revenue decisions. What do you think about this idea? Should it be used in your state or hometown?

Reforming Earmarks

The new bad child of budgeting, earmarks have become for many the symbol of what is wrong in budgetary politics: special interests, waste, and hidden deals.

Although earmarks often bring to mind federal budgeting, they also turn up in state budgeting where they often are treated as issues of accountability and transparency. In April 2007, Kansas became the first state to pass—as a bill attached to the budget—the Taxpayer Transparency Act that requires a searchable Web site with budget details. In June 2007, Governor Brad Henry signed Oklahoma's Taxpayer Transparency Act that directs the Office of State Finance to build a Web site detailing state spending, including contracts, tax credits, and incentives paid. Similar efforts are underway in a number of states.

Although so many people talk about them, there is no uniform definition or standard practice for earmarks. They are popularly defined as pork barrel, an image dating to the nineteenth century that suggests publicly funded goodies brought home by politicians trying to harden their support among constituents and to thank supporters. CNN (whose many stories on earmarks are posted on YouTube, a clear sign of public enthusiasm) defines earmarks as "pet projects lawmakers use to divert money to their home districts" and "business as usual" (CNN, 2009b). OMB's definition is important in federal politics because OMB maintains the federal database on earmarks (http://earmarks.omb.gov and http://earmarks.omb.gov/earmarks_definition.html): "Earmarks are funds provided by the Congress for projects or programs where the congressional direction (in bill or report language) circumvents the merit-based or competitive allocation process, or specifies the location or recipient, or otherwise curtails the ability of the [e]xecutive [b]ranch to properly manage funds. Congress includes earmarks in appropriation bills...and also in authorization bills."

Note that OMB's definition goes right into the idea of a preference for executive dominance over public spending. Different government offices and public interest and advocacy groups have different definitions that suit their political needs. For example, Citizens against Government Waste (CAGW, http://www.cagw.org) keeps a tally in its annual *Congressional Pig Book* of projects that fit its definition.

For our purposes, a simple definition is the most useful. Earmarks are directives that individual legislators put into legislation or reports and that tell agencies to spend program money in particular geographic locations, on particular companies, for particular projects, or that grant tax breaks to pinpointed companies or individuals.

Earmarking became a growth industry: the number in federal legislation exploded from about 3,000 in the mid-1990s to more than 13,000 a decade later. The target of media coverage and public complaints, earmarks hit the national political agenda. After the 2006 elections, President George W. Bush embraced earmark reform. He said, "One important message we all should take from the elections is that people want to end the secretive process by which Washington insiders are able to get billions of dollars directed to projects, many of them pork barrel projects that have never been reviewed or voted on by the Congress." Even so, CAGW's 2008 *Pig Book* listed 11,610 projects costing $17.2 billion in the twelve appropriations acts for FY 2008.

We now know from recent experience that transparency is not enough to put the brakes on federal earmarks. Congress tried to restrain earmarking in 2006 by turning to sunlight. In the Federal Funding Accountability and Transparency Act, Congress directed OMB to establish the federal database. Next, responding to lobbying scandals such as the Abramoff affair, Congress passed the Honest Leadership and Open Government Act of 2007. This legislation amended parts of the 1995 Lobbying Disclosure Act by tightening public disclosure about lobbying activity and funding, further restricting gifts to members of Congress and their staff, imposing further rules on employment after leaving public office, and requiring mandatory disclosure of earmarks in spending bills. Since 2007, all earmarks are supposed to be identified in spending bills and members of Congress must certify that they have no financial interest in their earmark.

Both the Republican and Democratic candidates for president in 2008 pledged to end earmarks. A full-blown "blame game" erupted over the many earmarks buried in the February 2009 recovery act and in the $410 billion spending bill passed in March 2009. It turns out that it is difficult to tame this beast because earmarks touch so many important issues in the politics of budgeting.

- Executive versus legislative power. Any earmark reform tips the balance in the struggle between the executive and legislative branches over the power of the purse. Whose policy preferences will win out, the legislature or the executive's? One proposal is to give the executive the power to purge earmarks. Its simplicity is seductive, but many find its political potential less attractive. Chief executives at all levels of government have long argued for more power over the budget, and the general direction has been toward concentrating budget power in the office of the chief executive. (The governor of Texas is the weakest of all the governors when it comes to budget powers.) Supporters of more executive power over the budget argue that (1) the executive is closer to the departments and so knows what the departments really need, (2) there is only one chief executive so accountability is clearer, and (3) the chief executive can reduce or eliminate wasteful projects that are inserted in the budget by legislators trying to win voter approval in their districts. Executives with line-item veto authority already can cross-out earmarks. Those without, such as the president, would be getting the same authority but through another door. Because the president could make spending decisions without congressional approval, this route to reform seems to contradict the Constitution.
- Responsive government. The cry of responsive government counters the argument that the chief executive sits higher and so has a better view of broader priorities. Higher means distance, and an executive-driven budget may not be responsive to a district's concerns. "Bringing home the bacon" to their districts is a way for members of legislatures to respond to their voters' needs.

    Electoral support should not be played down. When it comes to elections, "all politics is local," in the words of the long-time Speaker of the

House Thomas "Tip" O'Neill. One proposal is to permit individual legislators to object to earmarks and have them stricken from the bill. The problems with this idea are (1) we need a definition of earmarks precise enough to be useful and broad enough to deal with the ingenuity of legislators and (2) objectors can expect payback when they want cooperation from thwarted legislators. Another proposal would have each earmark pass a national-interest test—meaning that it is a federal concern—or a public-interest test showing that it is a good idea. The problem is pinning down these concepts in a workable way.

- Enforcer of partisan and legislative "discipline." Although smacking of crude horse-trading to some voters, earmarks give legislative leaders a way to cajole support for legislation, reward supporters, and punish stubborn opposition. Earmarks help put together "the deal." Making the deal and lining up the votes mean that the budget includes something for everyone, now or later. This is a costly feature of representative democracy. More executive power over earmarks is no guarantee against waste, because the executive also needs legislators' votes to pass a law. An executive could use this earmark power to threaten legislators that he or she would veto their pork projects if they did not agree to pass the executive's legislative favorites or cajole them with promises of support.

- Legitimate procedure *versus* shortcut. Many object that the earmark process bypasses the regular and competitive appropriations process and that is unfair and undercuts transparency. Sometimes shortcuts are needed so using a shortcut is not itself the problem. The problem is using a shortcut for the wrong reasons. An earmark is different from supplemental appropriations and emergency legislation that are fast-tracked because speed and flexibility are needed.

- Gaming the System. Some legislators claim they oppose earmarks but use them because everyone else does and they would shortchange their constituents if they remained pure. Is this hypocrisy? Is this self-fulfilling reasoning just contributing to the problem? Or are elected leaders obligated to use the rules to help people who elected them? Senator John McCain (R-AZ) says no to the last question and has refused to get federal earmarks for his state. The database developed by Taxpayers for Common Sense reports that Arizona received less than $19 per person in FY 2008, compared to a national average of more than $51 per person. McCain's running mate in the 2008 presidential campaign, Alaska Governor Sarah Palin, a self-described reformer, "won" earmarks totaling more than $506 per person in FY 2008 (Lilly, 2008). What is the right thing to do?

- Pay to Play. Earmarks have invited corrupt behavior among some legislators and lobbyists. Bringing home the bacon may not benefit only constituents; earmarks may be aimed at campaign contributors and backers, including some unscrupulous lobbyists who deliver pork to their clients in exchange for supporting the earmarker's campaign. One of the more serious challenges that affects U.S. politics in general and budgetary decision making particularly is the pay-to-play spirit of campaign finance and lobbying. The National Institute on Money in State Politics tallies more than $2.3 billion in contributions to political candidates and committees in 2008, including more than $700 million donated on behalf of ballot measures (such as in the cases ending chapters 3 and 7). There is no denying that running a political campaign is expensive. It is also true that quiet, behind-the-scenes influence that is bought and paid for continues to undercut accountability. This corrupt and corrupting influence also lowers the public's confidence in elected leaders, who are not always seen as putting public interests ahead of their private interests and political careers.

From Florida's strict gift ban in 2005 through Louisiana's disclosure requirements adopted in 2008, at least twenty-one states have tightened their rules on lobbyists. The list also includes Alaska, Colorado, Connecticut, Georgia, Idaho, Maine, Minnesota, Missouri, Montana, New Hampshire, New York, North Carolina, Oklahoma, Oregon, Pennsylvania, Rhode Island, Tennessee, Virginia and West Virginia. The reforms include tight gift bans, stricter registration rules, fuller disclosure, and more oversight. Responding to a major scandal, in 2005 Connecticut banned lobbyists and companies going after state contracts from contributing to campaigns for legislative and statewide executive offices. "By tightening existing lobbying laws and implementing new ones, state legislatures targeted an industry that most people think, for good or bad, helps shape public policy" (Kerns, 2009).

Other Reforms

Ideas for changing federal budgeting focus on tax expenditures and simplifying the tax code (chapter 7); capital budgeting (chapter 8); constitutional amendments on debt and balancing the budget (chapter 5), and the line-item veto (chapter 4); and more, much more. States entertain ideas about sustainability (chapter 5); tax-and-expenditure limits and other hard and soft constraints (chapter 5); rainy day funds; term limits; campaign finance reform, lobbying restrictions, and increasing transparency; health care and public pension reform; property tax relief and financing public education; and more. Ideas about performance measurement, contracting out, and collaborative service arrangements cut across the whole public sector.

We certainly live in interesting times that challenge all systems, including budget systems.

Some proposals call for systematic changes, but may be targeted either broadly or more narrowly. The federal shift from relying on tariffs to an income tax affected the entire political system (see box 10.3). Fast-forward almost a century: Arizona's governor proposed budget reform in 2009 to "focus on long-term needs and resources." Some changes are impromptu or even temporary such as temporary tax hikes. When such changes are piled one on top of the other, service and financing arrangements evolve in unplanned and perhaps unwanted directions; the financing of higher education is a case in point.

BOX 10.3

Revenue Structure Is Not Carved in Stone

"After declaring its independence in 1776, the struggling young nation found itself on the brink of bankruptcy. Responding to the urgent need for revenue, the First Congress passed and President George Washington signed the Tariff Act of July 4, 1789, which authorized the collection of duties on imported goods. It was called 'the second Declaration of Independence' by the news media of that era....For nearly 125 years, Customs funded virtually the entire government, and paid for the nation's early growth and infrastructure."

SOURCE: U.S. Customs Service, n.d.

There is a role for professional associations and public interest groups to play. They could build support for more disclosure and better budget practices and work with boards setting accounting standards to help see to it that the annual audits are user friendly. They could work with the Securities and Exchange Commission to have tighter rules and regulation of state and local borrowing behavior. The groups could help make sure that professional standards for revenue and spending estimates are as sound as possible, with estimating boundaries and the risks stated openly. This way decision makers, citizens, taxpayers, and investors can make informed decisions. When central budget offices squirrel away resources by overestimating spending and underestimating revenues, they really are shifting power to themselves. Their reasons may be public spirited—removing resources from play is insurance against a deficit—but making this move should not be their call. Power, after all, is the point of politics and transparency and accountability are rules of the game.

Local governments are limited in what they can do, often by hard constraints imposed by state law. Another limit is resources that are almost always tight in local government and nonprofit agencies. Still, there is much they can do to change the politics of budgeting. For example, they can require transparent, accurate estimates.

The local public sector is standing on the front lines of democracy. By increasing participation and collaboration locally and across the region, local governments, nonprofit agencies, and community groups can stimulate deliberation, innovation, and democratic governance. The techniques include citywide and regional surveys, targeted questionnaires, community and regional forums, project workshops, citizen budget committees, advisory panels, and voter registration and get-out-the-vote drives. From Eugene, Oregon and West Hartford, Connecticut to Johannesburg and Nairobi, one or several of these techniques have been tried, and with some success. One example comes from Longmont, Colorado, by way of the National League of Cities (2006, reprinted by permission).

The Focus on Longmont project was developed by the Longmont City Council as a way to develop community-supported policies to move the city toward a sustainable future as it approached build-out within its boundaries. The Council hoped to develop policies that would achieve a balance between resources and expenditures and create a community whose economic, environmental and social needs are met. By using Appreciative Inquiry and Deliberative Dialogues, two methods of community-planning, the Council met with hundreds of community residents over the course of a year to discuss their visions for the community. From the conversations, specific planning directions were established which the council members are incorporating into their budgeting efforts and the Council Work Plan.

Techniques such as these do take some resources but remember that the upfront expense associated with democracy is less than the long-term cost of alternative forms of government. If increasing democracy in the politics of budgeting is not enough of a good idea by itself, then consider these immediate advantages: (1) getting citizens and community groups to "buy in" to budget changes such as belt-tightening or expensive new services, (2) finding imaginative approaches suitable to the community and its resources, and (3) having hard data to support reform efforts at the regional and state levels.

WHAT CAN WE DO ABOUT IT?

The decline of public confidence and trust in leading political and other institutions and in public leaders is a long-term trend that affects Americans' ability to reverse the negative developments in public budgeting and nurture the positive ones. There are vast and still growing scholarly and popular literatures about the subject. Some scholars such as Robert Putnam emphasize interpersonal trust while others stress institutions. Some analysts at the World Bank, International Monetary Fund, United Nations, Organisation for Economic Co-operation and Development, the European Union, and regional multi-national associations are concerned about the interrelationships among trust, democracy, and development. This last focus is captured in the 2002 UN Convention against Corruption that starts off by noting "the seriousness of the problems and threats posed by corruption to the stability and security of societies, undermining the institutions and values of democracy, ethical values and justice and jeopardizing sustainable development and the rule of law."

There is more to trust than the expectation that public leaders will obey the law and avoid lining their own pockets (see box 3.4). But there is a link: public service is a public trust. Basic to American political culture, this idea can be traced back at least to Thomas Jefferson in the United States and also to other times and other cultures. Benjamin Disraeli, the nineteenth-century British politician, tied together political power, trust, and accountability this way: "all power is a trust... we are accountable for its exercise." According to the OECD (2000), "Public service is a public trust. Citizens expect public servants to serve the public interest with fairness and to manage public resources properly on a daily basis. Fair and reliable public services inspire public trust."

Trust is very different from getting one's money worth, getting one's own way, or getting what one wants. Trust means being able to rely on others to do what they genuinely believe is the right thing, even if you do not agree with them, and to do it in the right way. Trust invests our shared or public life and public policy with a sense of fair play, reliability, predictability, and stability.

Trust also is fundamental to the obligation of stewardship. The Government Finance Officers Association's Code of Professional Ethics lays out the idea clearly: "Government finance officers shall demonstrate and be dedicated to the highest ideals of honor and integrity in all public and personal relationships to merit the respect, trust and confidence of governing officials, other public officials, employees, and of the public." The National Association of State Budget Officers' Budget Analyst Training Program explains, "Holding and maintaining the public trust is an absolute necessity that is judged more on what we do rather than what we say."

Trust and the Political Deficit

This book traces the build-up of short-term (and sometimes short-sighted) political deals and financial dealings. The people cutting the deals are pushed and pulled by electoral, institutional, philosophical, partisan, and public demands and financial realities. At the same time, the American public expects them to meet or at least pay attention to many different values that often contradict each other in any single budget deal. The public injects these same values into play in public affairs, which translates into often contradictory expectations for public policies, public institutions, and public leaders.

Under these circumstances, the broad political context for deal makers and for voters and taxpayers is their confidence and trust in public institutions and public leaders. Perhaps the falling level of public trust does not reflect that Americans expect less and less of their public institutions and decision-making processes. Perhaps Americans expect too much: perform efficiently, deliver the goods, value democracy, listen to me; and be fair, be just, be trustworthy, and be open about it.

American voters and taxpayers face a *political* deficit. "The main obstacle to building public support for difficult choices on our nation's finances and future is not public opposition to tax increases or to program cuts, nor is it public lack of interest; the main obstacle is a deeply felt and pervasive mistrust of government" (Rosell, Furth, and Gantwerk, 2006). In January 2009, then President-elect Barack Obama spoke to this issue: "Our problem is not just a deficit of dollars; it's a deficit of accountability and trust." He warned, "It will take time, perhaps many years, but we can rebuild that lost trust and confidence."

Participation and a Challenge to Take Two Steps

Building trust in political leaders, institutions, and processes is an ongoing challenge. Daily pressures, disappointments and dissatisfactions, and petty and great scandals chip away at public trust. Constantly building and rebuilding trust in our public life is a challenge. Meeting this challenge requires two steps. Both involve political action and both involve you, the reader. As Mahatma Gandhi taught, "You must be the change you want to see in the world."

The first step is to reconstruct a sense of shared or community purpose by asking, "What is the right thing to do and how do we do it?" Your answer defines the public interest. Whatever you answer, budgetary politics must be a part of it.

Ask yourself the question in another way. In the Preamble, the United States Constitution spells out its multiple purposes: "to form a more perfect Union; establish justice, insure domestic tranquility, provide for the common defense, promote the general welfare, and secure the blessings of liberty to ourselves and our posterity." Does the politics of budgeting damage or contribute to these purposes? How do you intend to change the negative features and expand the positive ones? What are your ideas for reforming the politics of budgeting?

The second step is to add your voice to the demand to change the conduct and content of the public's "business." How best can you go about it? The best place to intervene depends upon your immediate purpose. What level of government or network of government/nonprofit/for profit is responsible and needs to be held accountable for the decision or public policy? How is the program financed and who decides how much? Nothing substitutes for solid information and the responsible citizen must do a little homework.

The best time to intervene is *before* a decision is made. It is always easier to influence decision making in advance than to get people to change their minds. It is easier to shape programs and policy at the outset than to change them once funding is in place, people hired, contracts signed, benefits handed out, and clients are at the door.

All of this means that the concerned citizen stays on top of budget issues and stays in touch with other players and certainly with decision makers. It means getting politically active: attend public hearings, and write your council, state legislators, and senators and congressmen. The Web offers many templates for political letters and many governments, public organizations, elected leaders, and budget offices have Web sites featuring contact information and one-button email access.

To participate effectively, serious citizens must get other citizens and public leaders to listen to what they have to say. Getting people to listen is an art and can be learned (see box 10.4). Listening effectively also is an art and needs practice.

Public leaders' obligations of accountability, transparency, responsiveness, and stewardship are central to the politics of budgeting in a democracy. But without citizens meeting their responsibilities of public scrutiny and participation, the rest does not add up to very much.

THUMBNAIL

In budgetary politics, the true bottom line is a political judgment about political issues and outcomes, including concerns about democracy and specific public policies. Some budget problems are cyclical while others are structural.

BOX 10.4

Guidelines for Civic Discourse

Members of the Alexandria community, its elected officials and City staff place a high value on constructive and thoughtful debate on public issues. To this end, all who participate in meetings in the Chamber, including public officials, staff and members of the community, are expected to observe the following guidelines.

1. Treat Everyone with Respect and Courtesy

2. Do Your Homework—Be Prepared and Be Familiar with the Docket

3. Express Your Ideas and Opinions in an Open and Helpful Manner

4. Be Respectful of Others' Time by Being Clear and Concise in Your Comments and/or Questions

5. Demonstrate Honesty and Integrity in Your Comments and Actions

6. Focus on the Issues Before the Decision Making Body—Avoid Personalizing Issues

7. Listen and Let Others Express their Ideas and Opinions

8. If a Decision is Made with which You Do Not Concur, Agree to Disagree and/or Use Appropriate Means of Civil and Civic Recourse, and Move On

Adopted by the Alexandria City Council on October 12, 2004.

Reprinted by permission. Alexandria, Virginia, 2004.

Changes in budgetary politics often are political responses to political problems. Although change is difficult because high stakes and vested interests are threatened, many participants in budgetary politics believe that the United States needs key changes in public policy and in public budgeting. The rate of growth of entitlements is a destabilizing and unsustainable element in the politics of budgeting and governments' budget pressures squeeze nonprofit and for-profit service providers. Yet, commitments made today and paid for in the future are not always a bad idea.

Overly complex decision-making processes and systems of service delivery that citizens and taxpayers cannot understand lessen transparency and damage accountability. So do aspects of campaign finance, lobbying, and some political leaders' preference for dodging hard choices.

The values of accountability and transparency in a democracy require public leaders to tell the public what they are doing and why.

In public agencies, poor performance often is an argument for more resources. Divided when it comes to smaller versus larger government and fewer *versus* more services *in the abstract*, most Americans believe that democracy and the free market need and support each other. Yet, the federal government's response to the economic turmoil that began at the end of 2007 greatly expanded the role and size of government.

Is the politics of budgeting in the United States heading toward change? The purpose of budget reform is to change the decisions, outcomes, and power of participants in budgetary politics. The decline in public confidence and trust in U.S. political institutions and public leaders affects the ability to bring about meaningful reform in budgetary politics. The challenge is to foster a sense of shared purpose and to take on the citizen's responsibilities of public scrutiny and public participation.

CASE

The Gag Rule

In a particularly bitter budget battle, the chief executive officer (CEO) cuts several departments' original budget requests, then orders all municipal department heads not to discuss any budgetary matters with council members, except in formal session. The edict also orders all department heads to advocate the CEO's proposed budget before the council (the town's fiscal authority), the media, and the public.

One department head protests what he calls a *gag rule* and claims that he has the legal right and professional duty to discuss the budget under all circumstances and to address responsibly and candidly all questions from council members, whether at public hearings or not. In fact, he has just updated the spreadsheet on his office PC to submit to the CEO and prepare for the annual budget ritual.

Objecting to "blind decision making" and the "back-room politics" that cut into his doing his job, a council member requests the preliminary budget estimates that department heads routinely bring to the informal budget meetings with the CEO. The CEO, who uses these estimates to prepare the executive recommendation, responds that preliminary papers customarily are discarded after they are no longer needed.

The council member discovers that the budget, finance, and other departments' procedures for documentation and recordkeeping do not include maintaining background papers or draft worksheets. The finance head explains that too many numbers confuse the public and approvingly points to the CEO's gag rule.

Thinking It Over

1. What two or three political issues does this case raise for an elected official?
   a. _____
   b. _____
   c. _____
2. Why and how does presenting departmental requests to the council and public matter?
3. Compare this case with the OMB guidelines on budget presentations to Congress. See Web site resource, Rules of the Game in Washington. Are federal agencies' requests included in the president's budget submission to Congress? Go to budget documents via http://www.whitehouse.gov/OMB. Check one: ☐ yes ☐ no

4. Are departmental requests included in the budget recommendation to the legislature in your state?
State budget document at http://www._____
Check one: ☐ yes ☐ no

5. Are departmental requests included in the budget recommendation to the council in your state's capital?
Capital city's budget document at http://www._____
Check one: ☐ yes ☐ no

6. Is the department head correct about his "legal right and professional duty?" Yes or no, and why? See professional standards of conduct of associations for budgeting and finance such as National Association of State Budget Officers at http://www.nasbo.org/Publications/PDFs/training_modules.pdf, p. 173 and Government Finance Officers Association at http://gfoa.org/main/about.code.ethics.shtml

7. Do any laws apply in this situation? The public record is the foundation of accountability. Access a state's Freedom of Information statute and commission and your own state's laws and regulations about keeping public records.

Note. In its notice of final decision (Docket #FIC 92–105, Feb.11, 1993), the Connecticut Freedom of Information Commission noted that a mayor denied access to estimates because they were discarded. According to the Commission, "estimates are used in the…budget process to determine the operating budgets for each municipal department." The Commission found that "the estimates comprise part of the process by which governmental decisions and financial policies are formulated" and that "the estimates are public records…and subject to disclosure." The Commission warned that failing to keep copies of budget estimates might violate state statute on retaining records.

Adapted by permission from Carol W. Lewis, 2003.

WEB SITE RESOURCES

- Advocacy Politics
- Budget Formats
- Cutbacks and Priorities
- Further Resources
- How to Read the Highlights of the Federal Budget
- Internet Resources
- Power Grab or Neutral Reform?
- Public Spending Helps Define Us and Our Future: The Story of Hurricane Katrina
- Rules of the Game in Washington

REVIEW QUESTIONS

1. Why are some entitlement programs considered both a source of stability and a source of change in the politics of budgeting?

2. Why do state and local governments often have a more difficult time dealing with economic downturns than the federal government?

3. Identify several current proposals to change budgeting in your state.

   a. What are the forces pushing for change in your state's budget process and politics? What are the major political obstacles to change?

   b. What is one area of the budget that you would like to see reformed? Why is it important for this reform to take place?

   c. What are the likely political effects of your proposed change? What institutions or interests stand to gain or lose in adopting your particular budget reform?

4. What is success? Choose any big city's government with an executive budget process.

   a. Develop about one-half dozen general standards of "successful" performance for the council to use to distribute funds among competing programs. Try using as starting points table 1.2; and the Web site resources, Cutbacks and Priorities and Internet Resources, Financial Condition and Performance Measurement.

   b. How do your standards deal with the many competing interests and pressures from constituents, interests groups, legislative committees and leadership, court decisions, and the executive, all of which influence legislators' decisions? Do you think your standards would satisfy citizens, voters, taxpayers, public officials, policy experts, program administrators and service providers, contractors and suppliers, and those receiving services and benefits?

   c. Do your standards merge the purposes of efficient performance and meeting competing interests and other values? Should they, and why?

   d. Read the executive's recent budget message and summary. What goals are mentioned that might conflict with efficient performance?

   e. What should happen to programs that are unsuccessful according to the standards you developed?

5. The database required by federal law is available at http://earmarks.omb.gov. Is it accessible to citizens, as required by law? Use the database to identify two earmarks. Next, do the same using a state database. Are these earmarks in the public interest or do they serve only a narrow community or special interest?

THE BIG PICTURE: INTEGRATING QUESTIONS

Following are summary questions to help you weigh in on the politics of budgeting.

1. In what specific ways do past and current decisions affect (a) future budgets, (b) the scope of decision making in the future, (c) accountability in the future, and (c) the potential for responsiveness in the politics of budgeting? Debt service and unfunded financial promises are two examples. What others should we think about?

2. What specific mechanisms do decision makers use to dodge the hard choices? Here are a few examples: across-the-board budget cuts, tax pledges, and entitlement spending on automatic pilot. What other mechanisms and maneuvers can be added to this list?

3. In his inaugural address on January 20, 2009, President Obama spoke of "our collective failure to make hard choices." What evidence does the politics of budgeting offer to (a) support his statement and (b) contradict his statement?

    a. If yes, then consider this: Can the politics of budgeting be changed without major changes to the broader political system? In developing your answer, think about whether Americans need to forge clearer and more responsible links between responsibilities as citizen (public's appetite for services and solutions) and as taxpayer (public's resistance to paying the full bill) over one's life time. What could these links look like and what role must political leaders play?

    b. If no, then consider this: What does it mean that a budget is sustainable in the long-run and why is this politically and financially important?

4. Does public budgeting need an overhaul?

5. Do you think that the public has enough say in the budget process?

    a. What mechanisms allow the public to hold officials accountable for their budget decisions?

    b. Should we make budgeting more transparent and accountable and, if yes, then how and why?

6. Are taxes and spending fair and how do you know?

7. Should efficiency dominate our judgment about performance in the public sector? Why or why not?

8. Why are changes in public policy and the budget usually only a small part of total spending and total revenues in any single year? What are the political effects of this feature of budgeting, and would you assess this feature as overall positive or negative?

9. Marshal arguments for and against this proposition: the size and role of government in the United States in the twenty-first century should be dynamic and set more by pragmatic responses to problems than by some other criteria. What are these other criteria? In developing your answer, think about how you would measure the size and role of government (share of GDP, workforce, size and growth of budgets, number of regulations, and other measures).

10. Pick up your magic wand and wave it at one piece of the politics of budgeting that you think most seriously undercuts democracy. How would you change it? Now do the same for one piece of the politics of budgeting that supports democracy. How would you make it work better?

11. In what ways do special interests influence budgeting? Should anything and can anything be done to reduce their influence or limit advocacy politics? What are the pros and cons and where do you come down?

12. How do budgets and the politics of budgeting at one level of government affect the budgets and politics of budgeting of other levels of government, nonprofit agencies, and activities and organizations in the private sector? How does the intricate, intertwined public sector affect accountability and transparency in the politics of budgeting?

13. What features of the budgetary process reduce political conflict, how do they work, and with what political consequences?

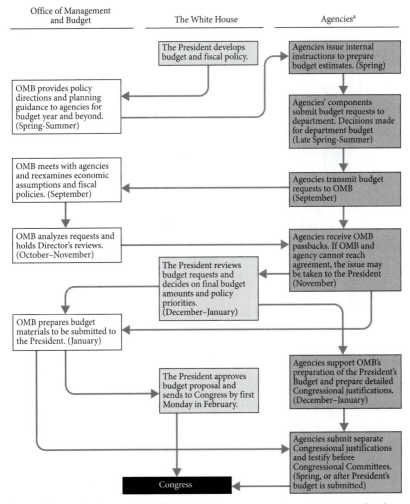

The Federal Budget Process

[a] The term "agency" refers to either the department, agency, or lower component levels, depending on the level of decision being made. The budget submitted to OMB represents the budget decisions made at the department or the highest organizational level.

Figure A.1. Federal Budget Process, Stage One

SOURCE: GAO, 2005.

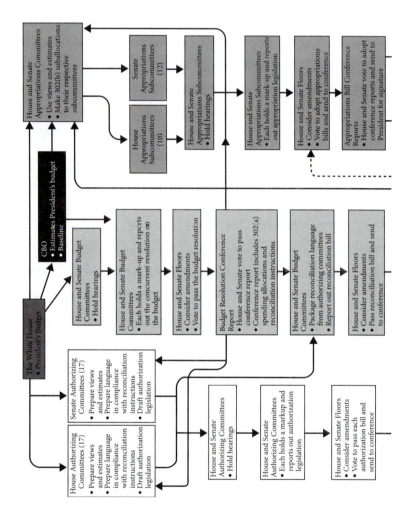

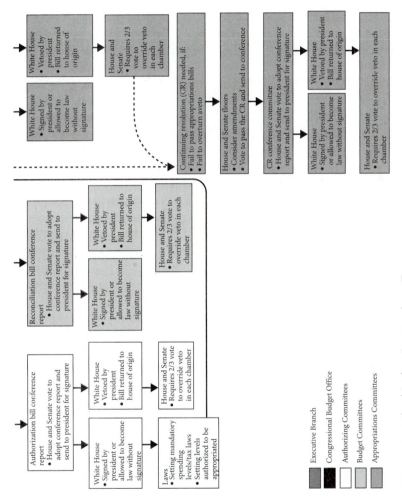

Figure A.2. Federal Budget Process, Stage Two

SOURCE: GAO, 2005.

MAJOR STEPS IN THE FORMULATION PHASE

What happens?	When?
OMB issues Spring planning guidance to Executive Branch agencies for the upcoming budget. The OMB Director issues a letter to the head of each agency providing policy guidance for the agency's budget request. Absent more specific guidance, the outyear estimates included in the previous budget serve as a starting point for the next budget. This begins the process of formulating the budget the President will submit the following February.	Spring
OMB and the Executive Branch agencies discuss budget issues and options. OMB works with the agencies to: Identify major issues for the upcoming budget; Develop and analyze options for the upcoming Fall review; and Plan for the analysis of issues that will need decisions in the future.	Spring and Summer
OMB issues Circular No. A-11 to all Federal agencies. This Circular provides detailed instructions for submitting budget data and materials.	July
Executive Branch agencies (except those not subject to Executive Branch review) make budget submissions....	September*
Fiscal year begins. The just completed budget cycle focused on this fiscal year. It was the "budget year" in that cycle and is the "current year" in this cycle.	October 1
OMB conducts its Fall review. OMB staff analyzes agency budget proposals in light of Presidential priorities, program performance, and budget constraints. They raise issues and present options to the Director and other OMB policy officials for their decisions.	October–November
OMB briefs the President and senior advisors on proposed budget policies. The OMB Director recommends a complete set of budget proposals to the President after OMB has reviewed all agency requests and considered overall budget policies.	Late November
Passback. OMB usually informs all Executive Branch agencies at the same time about the decisions on their budget requests.	Late November
All agencies, including Legislative and Judicial Branch agencies, enter MAX computer data and submit print materials and additional data. This process begins immediately after passback and continues until OMB must "lock" agencies out of the database in order to meet the printing deadline.	Late November to early January*
Executive Branch agencies may appeal to OMB and the President. An agency head may ask OMB to reverse or modify certain decisions. In most cases, OMB and the agency head resolve such issues and, if not, work together to present them to the President for a decision.	December
Agencies prepare and OMB reviews congressional budget justification materials. Agencies prepare the budget justification materials they need to explain their budget requests to the responsible congressional subcommittees.	January
President transmits the budget to the Congress.	First Monday in February

*OMB provides specific deadlines for this activity.

Table A.1 Calendar and Details of Federal Budget Formulation
SOURCE: OMB, 2008.

312

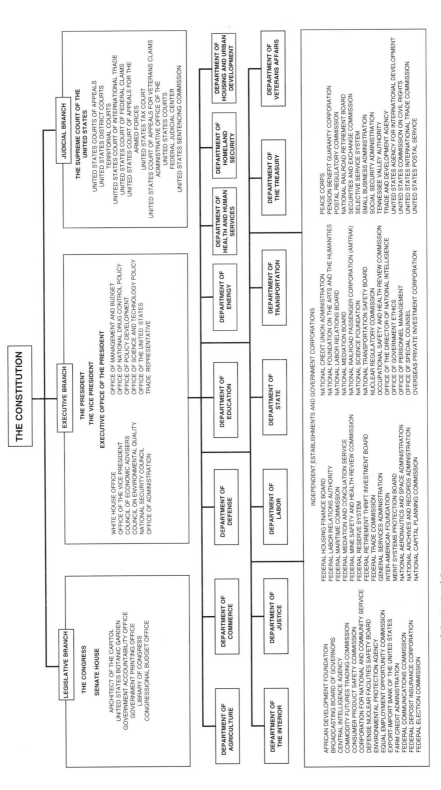

Figure A.3. Government of the United States

SOURCE: Office of the Federal Register, 2008.

Glossary of Terms in Budgetary Politics

Ability-to-Pay Principle—the idea that a person's tax burden should be based on the person's capacity to pay the taxes, with capacity usually measured as taxes paid as a percentage of the taxpayer's income.

Accountability—answering to someone (such as the legislature, chief executive, or taxpayer) for something (such as a decision, a program, or mistake); democracies hold public officials and employees accountable through elections, public records (such as accounts) and disclosure, and the chain of command in organizations.

Accounting System—the total set of records and procedures that are used to record, classify, and report information on the financial status and operations of the organization.

Across-the-board—Applied equally to all participants, such as cutting all agencies' funding by an equal percentage.

Accrual, Modified—the basis of accounting in which revenues are recognized when earned and expenditures are recorded as incurred.

Accrued Liability—benefits legally promised or bills outstanding that have not yet been paid.

Actuarial—the present value of future cash flows, as in today's value of the future payments of a pension obligation.

Adopted Budget—the financial plan of revenue and spending (or expenditures) for a fiscal year as approved by the governing unit.

Ad Valorem Tax—a tax levied on the assessed value of both real and personal property in proportion to the value of the property (also known as property taxes).

Advocate—a promoter of a particular program who pushes for funding for that program.

Agency (or department)—a sub-unit of a government or organization that provides a particular service (or services); a nonprofit organization that provides a service.

Allocation—assigning one or more items of cost or revenue to one or more segments of an organization according to benefits received, responsibilities, or
other logical measures of use; assigning expenditures or revenues to different
functions such as national defense.

Allotment—a schedule at the state and local levels by which the budget office
makes funds available to agencies (for example, quarterly).

Alternative Minimum Tax (AMT)—a parallel federal income tax structure originally enacted in 1982 that allows fewer exemptions and deductions and with
fewer rates than the standard income tax; designed to catch higher-income
individuals with little income taxed through the normal tax structure.

Amended Budget—the adopted budget, including any legal changes made during
the fiscal period.

Annual Budget—a financial plan that consists of policy and funding priorities for
the fiscal period.

Anti-Deficiency Act—law enacted in 1906 that requires a legal basis for any obligation by federal officials or employees for the federal government to spend
any money.

Appraised Value—an estimate of the market value of property established through
market sales, comparable sales or other methods; set after notification, hearing and appeals, and certification process.

Apportionment—a schedule at the federal level by which the budget office makes
funds available to agencies (for example, quarterly).

Appropriation—law passed by the legislature and signed by the chief executive
that permits the obligation for and spending of government resources.

Assessed Value—taxable value of property that may be equal to or less than market or appraised value; reduction often the result of a classification ratio or
factor (or legally allowable percent of the market value); used to determine
the basis for the tax liability of property owners.

Assessment Ratio—a legal classification that gives some types of property (especially residential) a favorable treatment compared to other (often business)
property; also termed Classification Ratio.

Asset—resources that have monetary value and are owned or held by a government.

Attrition—a method of achieving a reduction in personnel by not refilling the
positions vacated through resignation, reassignment, transfer, retirement, or
means other than layoffs.

Audit—a review of the financial and/or performance operations of a program,
agency, department, spending unit or the entire organization; see Financial
Audit; see Performance Audit.

Authorized Positions—employee positions, which are authorized in the adopted
budget, to be filled during the year.

Balance—the difference between revenues and expenditures in a fiscal period.

Balanced Budget—a balanced budget arises when the government entity estimates the same amount of money from revenue collection as it is appropriating for expenditures.

Balance Sheet—the basic financial statement that discloses the assets, liabilities, and net assets of a reporting entity as of a specific date, such as year-end; a snapshot of the financial condition.

Bankruptcy—filing under federal bankruptcy law for protection from timely payment of obligations; applies to local governments but not state governments.

Base—cost of continuing the existing levels of service under existing law in the current budget year.

Baseline—estimate of receipts, outlays, and deficit or surplus that would result from continuing current federal law into the future. (See current services.)

Benefits-Received Principle—the idea that a person's tax burden should be based on the benefits that the person receives from the services provided.

Black Budget—spending on national security that is kept a secret because the information is classified.

Block Grants—the bundling of similar grants-in-aid programs into one; to simplify administration and to provide more discretion or flexibility to the receiving government.

Bond—evidence of a debt that extends beyond a year; a written promise to pay a specified sum of money, called the face value or principal amount, at a specified date or dates in the future, called the maturity date(s), together with periodic interest at a specified rate.

Bond Rating—see Credit Rating.

Budget—the most important statement of public policies and core values of a government; identifies proposed spending for a given fiscal period and the proposed means of financing this spending.

Budgetary Politics—elements of the budget process that help to decide how and how much money is raised (revenues) and how the money gets spent (expenditures).

Budget Authority (BA)—provided in law to federal agencies to enter into legal obligations resulting in current or future government outlays.

Budget Calendar—the schedule of key dates or milestones in the preparation, adoption, and administration of the budget.

Budget Call—in an executive budget process, the chief executive's set of policies and guidelines sent to the spending units for them to follow in drafting their budget requests.

Budget Document—the official written document offering a comprehensive financial program to the governing body for its consideration and adoption.

Budgeting—a political process for making fiscally related choices among alternatives for a specific period of time.

Budget Maximizers—theory that those in charge of the budget are more interested in self-advancement than they are in achieving policy goals.

Budget Message—the opening section of the budget providing a general summary of the most important aspects of the budget, changes from the current and previous fiscal years, and recommendations regarding the financial policy for the upcoming fiscal year.

Budget Process—how choices are made about shared purposes and/or public resources through the political process.

Budget Reserve—an amount above yearly expenditures that is collected but not planned to be used in the current fiscal period.

Budget Resolution—congressional agreement that is not a law (and does not require the president's signature) that sets revenue, spending, and other budget targets; developed by House and Senate Budget Committees and their conference report produces a concurrent budget resolution.

Budget Share—a calculated percent of the total budget, often represented as a budget pie.

Budget Stabilization Fund—see Rainy Day Fund.

Bureaucracy—a generic term used to refer to complex organizations with many supervisory layers between lower-level workers and the chief executive; found in business, religious, nonprofit, and governmental organizations.

CAFR—acronym used for the Comprehensive Annual Financial Report.

Capital Asset—any significant acquisition, construction, replacement, or improvement to the physical assets of an organization, including land, property, and equipment.

Capital Budget—plan for financing long-lived projects such as bridges and buildings; the first year of the capital improvement program with a detailed source of financing for each of the specified capital projects for implementation during the upcoming fiscal year.

Capital Expenditures—spending approved in the Capital Budget related to the acquisition, construction, replacement or improvement to the physical assets of the organization.

Capital Improvement—see Capital Asset.

Capital Improvement Planning—creating a plan of spending for repair or replacement of existing infrastructure as well as development of new facilities to accommodate growth.

Capital Improvement Program—a listing of planned capital projects for the upcoming five- to ten-year period with the expected cost and financing plan for each and scheduled according to priorities and timing; updated annually.

Capital Outlay—spending related to the purchase of equipment, land and other fixed assets.

Capital Project—major construction, acquisition, or renovation activities that add value to an organization's capital assets or significantly increase their useful life.

Cash Flow—actual money (cash) coming in and going out of an organization in a fiscal period.

Charges—the payment for service rendered; often termed user fees and service charges; in contrast to a tax.

Circuit-breaker—reduction of the property tax burden on poor, disabled, or elderly households by offering a tax reduction or refund based on the proportion of income that goes to property taxes.

City Manager or **County Manager**—an official appointed and employed by an elected governing body to manage the local government's operations and services on a day-to-day basis.

Classification Ratio—a legal rule often stated in state constitutions that allow deviation from uniform treatment of property; often favors residential real property by stating that only a certain percent of the appraised value will be used to determine assessed value, and that percent is lower than the factor used for business.

Cleavage—a sociological or socio-economic category or division that cuts society into broad parts (such as gender, race, and class) with which interests are associated that may affect voting and support for budgetary issues.

COLA—see Cost of Living Adjustment.

Comprehensive Annual Financial Report (CAFR)—annual financial report prepared by state and local governments that adhere to generally accepted accounting principles (or GAAP).

Comprehensive Plan—a community's plan showing how geographic, physical, social, economic and public facilities can impact local development along with public policy guidelines and funding outlines to achieve local objectives.

Consolidated Budget—a budget that includes all resources received; at the federal level it would include Social Security as well as the ongoing operations of government. (See Unified Budget.)

Constant Dollars—the presentation of dollar amounts adjusted for inflation to reflect the real purchasing power of money as compared to a certain point in time in the past. (See Nominal Dollars and Real Dollars.)

Consumer Price Index (CPI)—a statistical description of price levels provided by the U.S. Department of Labor; the index is used as a measure of the increase in the cost of living and to convert to constant dollars.

Consumption Tax—a tax imposed on consumption instead of income; because all income is either consumed or saved, a consumption tax would not tax savings.

Contingency—a budgetary resource set aside for emergencies or spending not anticipated or known at the time the budget is adopted. (See Rainy Day Fund.)

Continuing Resolution—interim appropriations bill providing authority for federal agencies to continue operating at specified level until a specified date or until regular appropriations are passed; sometimes used to fund some or all government operations for the year; must have presidential signature.

Contracting-out—an agreement by one government with a non-governmental unit or another government to carry out a function or provide a service that would otherwise be done by the contracting government.

Cost—the monetary resources required to provide a good or service.

Cost of Living Adjustment (COLA)—an adjustment in pay or benefit levels to cover the impact of inflation.

Cost Structure—a focus on compiling, processing and using cost information; covers both pricing of services and charging for their provision; addresses the planning and implementing of a costing system and the management decisions.

Council-Manager Government—a system of local government that combines political leadership of elected officials in the form of a governing body with day-to-day management by an appointed and often professional city manager.

Council Member—elected member of the legislative body of a local government who represents the interests of the voters of a specified district or at-large.

Credit—money lent with expectation of being paid back (with interest) in the future.

Credit Crunch—the unavailability of money to be lent to borrowers.

Credit Rating—an independent assessment of risk, meaning the likelihood that an organization will not repay the debt, including principal and interest, on time.

Credit Rating Firm—an independent agency that assesses the likelihood that an organization will not be able to repay its debt, and assigns a rating based on this likelihood.

Credit Risk—the likelihood that an organization will default on its debt. (See Default.)

Current Dollars—a count of the number of dollars without paying attention to how much they are worth or their purchasing power. (See Nominal Dollars and Real Dollars)

Current Services—budget amount for continuing existing programs, allowing for changes in inflation and law.

Cutback Management—another term for budget reduction, or reducing the amount of money spent on government functions.

Cyclical Balance—an economy balanced over the business cycle.

Debt—a legal obligation to repay borrowed money.

Debt Limit—a rule limiting the amount of debt a borrower can have.

Debt Service—repayment of the principal and interest on debt, often through a separate debt service fund. (See Governmental Fund.)

Dedicated Revenue—revenue committed by law to a particular program or purpose, meaning that the money cannot legally be spent for other purposes.

Default—a failure to honor an obligation, as in not paying debt service on time.

Deficit—when total spending is greater than total revenues in a fiscal period; the result when spending (and other uses of funds) exceed revenues (and other sources of funds).

Deficit Target—a focus of federal budgeting that sets an allowable upper limit to the deficit.

Delegate—a role orientation of elected officials that places priority on voting the will of the people; in contrast to Trustee role.

Depression—an economic event with severe reductions in employment, personal income and gross domestic product that resets the economy at a lower level for an extended period.

Discretionary Spending—outlays on programs funded by annual appropriations under the jurisdiction of the House and Senate Appropriations Committees; represents about one-third of most federal spending, including most defense spending and, for example, education and housing programs. (See Mandatory Spending.)

Distributive Policy—government programs where both costs and benefits are distributed widely.

Durable Goods—goods that have a life span of more than several years.

Dynamic Scoring—where dynamic means taking into account how people respond to a tax change, and scoring means estimating the financial effects of a proposed change in law according to set definitions and rules.

Earmark—directives put into appropriations or committee reports by individual legislators that tell executive units to spend program money in particular geographic locations, on particular companies, for particular projects, or that grant tax breaks to particular companies or individuals; sometimes labeled as wasteful or corrupt. (See also Pork.)

Earned Income—includes all the income that is subject to taxation and the wages one gets as either employee or as self-employed.

Effectiveness—producing the desired outcome or results.

Effective Tax Rate—the amount of tax paid expressed as a percentage of income.

Efficiency—relates the cost to the actual output or performance.

E-government—the use of the internet (World Wide Web) in government functions, such as posting meeting minutes, making forms and budget documents available, and associated with enhancing transparency and communication with citizens, taxpayers, and residents.

Emergency Supplemental Appropriation—an addition to the regularly adopted budget that is passed in response to or under rules applicable to unusual and unanticipated circumstances. (See Supplemental Appropriation.)

Employee Benefits—contributions made or obligations for the benefit of employees beyond the employee's salary or wage; the organization's share of the costs of employee medical insurance, pension coverage, federal Social Security and Medicare programs, and payment for timed not worked (sick leave and annual leave); often called fringe benefits.

Entitlements—federal outlays funded by law other than annual appropriations and considered "mandatory" or nondiscretionary until the law is changed; includes programs such as Social Security, Medicare, Medicaid, food stamps, federal civilian and military retirement benefits, veterans' benefits, and unemployment insurance. (See Mandatory Spending.)

Equalization Program—a method of distributing resources to different recipients based on a calculated amount designed to equalize benefits.

Equity—see Horizontal Equity and Vertical Equity.

Estate Tax—a tax on the monetary value of the remaining assets after a person's death.

Excise Tax—a tax levied on the volume purchased such as a gallon of gasoline or pint of liquor.

Executive Budgeting—a budget process in which the executive formulates and submits the budget to the legislature and then implements the adopted budget.

Executive Order—an order of the president that directs executive branch activity; does not require congressional approval and is subject to change by this or another president.

Exemptions—a legal reduction in taxable income.

Expendables—an outlay of resources for consumption in the current fiscal period.

Expenditures—spending or outlays, the outflow of cash paid for assets, goods or services.

Fairness—see Equity.

Federal Offset—state and local income and property taxes are allowed as itemized deductions on the federal income tax.

Federalism—the study or operation of different levels of government. (See Fiscal Federalism.)

Feedback Loop—the method by which policies are subject to revision based on the influence and effect of prior decisions; using information about implementation and performance to adjust processes and routines.

FICA (Federal Insurance Contributions Act)—the legal name designating social security taxes.

Financial Audit—a review of the organization's accounting system, usually by an independent accounting firm, to attest that the organization's financial statements present fairly the financial results for the fiscal year; it is not designed to catch fraud, waste and abuse.

Financing—furnishing the necessary funds to operate or conduct a program or service; funds can be raised internally, borrowed, or received from a grant.

Fines—charges for compliance with laws, as with court fines.

Fiscal Capacity—ability to finance public services.

Fiscal Constraint Rule—a law, policy, practice or procedure that has financial implications.

Fiscal Federalism—issues and practices in relations among different levels of government that have financial implications.

Fiscal Gap—difference between what a government owes and what it can claim as resources, on a yearly or multi-year basis.

Fiscal Period—see Fiscal Year.

Fiscal Policy—a government's policies on revenues, spending, and debt management as these relate to government services, programs and capital investment; using government's revenues and expenditures, including its surplus and deficit positions, to influence the overall economy.

Fiscal Stimulus—see Stimulus.

Fiscal Sustainability—an ongoing ability to match what a government owes to what it can claim as resources.

Fiscal Year—the period designated by an organization for the beginning and ending of financial transactions for official budgeting and external financial reporting purposes; typically a twelve-month period.

Fixed Assets—assets of a long-term character such as land, buildings, improvements other than buildings, machinery, equipment, and furniture whose cost is in excess of a specific amount and whose life expectancy is in excess of one year.

Fixed Costs—costs that vary little regardless of amount of work performed, service levels, or units provided; examples are debt service, rent, and utilities.

Forecast—an estimate of the amount (of revenues, spending, or services) expected over a specified period.

Foreclosure—legal process through which a lender can recover the value of the loan from the debtor by forcing the sale or taking possession of the collateral used to guarantee the loan; for home mortgages, the home is the collateral.

Formula Grant—a grant program that is dispensed by a set formula such as so much per person, per unit of service, or other measure.

Franchise Fees—annual fees paid by utilities (electricity, telephone, cable TV, natural gas) for the use of the city's public rights-of-way, or that are granted a service monopoly that is regulated by the city (garbage collection); the franchise fee is typically a set percentage of gross revenue within the city.

Freedom of Information Laws (FOI)—a legally defined process for individuals and organizations (especially the press) to gain access to public records.

Fringe Benefits—see Employee Benefits.

Full Faith and Credit—a legal pledge providing investors with a legal claim on the government's fundamental tax power to ensure that they get repaid. (See General Obligation Bonds.)

Full-Time Equivalent (FTE)—a way to count part-time and seasonal employees; calculate FTEs by starting with fifty-two weeks a year and a standard work week of forty hours (for a total of 2,080 hours of work a year). Two people working all year at half-time (twenty hours) equal one FTE.

Fund—an accounting segmentation of financial transactions according to restrictions placed on their use; a self-balancing set of accounts meaning that after every financial transaction is recorded in the accounting system, assets minus liabilities must equal net assets; the three main types of funds for state and local governments are proprietary funds (to account for resources held in trust), enterprise funds (to handle business-like operations such as a city water system), and governmental funds such as the debt service fund, special revenue fund (for dedicated grants), and the general fund.

Fund Balance—the difference between assets and obligations (liabilities) in a governmental fund; a positive ending fund balance from one fiscal year is available as a resource for the following fiscal year's activities; the ending fund balance for one fiscal year is the same amount as the beginning fund balance for the following fiscal year.

Fund Structure—the financial system of all the accounting funds in the organization.

Furlough—a mandatory reduction in hours worked or unpaid time off.

GAAP—see generally accepted accounting principles.

Gaming—use of lotteries, casinos, racetracks, etc., which bring in revenues that are sometimes used for specific purposes, such as education.

Gasoline Tax—A tax on the use, sale, or delivery of all motor vehicle fuels used, sold, or delivered in this state for any purpose whatsoever.

General Fund—an accounting fund to account for all financial resources that the organization can legally engage in, except those legally required to be accounted for in a more specialized fund; usually accounts for most government programs, thereby making it the most visible and competitive avenue for funding a program.

Generally Accepted Accounting Principles (GAAP)—A uniform standard for financial accounting and recording, encompassing the conventions, rules, and procedures that define broadly-accepted accounting principles; allows ease of comparison of financial results over time and across similar organizations; GAAP for state and local governments established by the Governmental Accounting Standards Board; GAAP for private business and nonprofit organizations established by the Financial Accounting Standards Board; GAAP for the U.S. Government set by the Federal Accounting Standards Board.

General Obligation Bonds (G.O.)—debt secured by the full-faith and credit-guarantee; property taxes are the main revenue used to repay local government general obligation bonds but, if bondholders are not repaid, they have a legal claim against any revenue of the government. (See Full Faith and Credit.)

Gini Index or Coefficient—a measure of income inequity.

Governmental Fund—the set of accounting funds that includes the general fund, special revenue funds, the debt service fund, and any permanent funds.

Government-Sponsored Enterprise—quasi-independent entities created by the government for a specific purpose and run on a business or commercial basis.

Grant—see Intergovernmental Transfer.

Grant-in-aid—see Intergovernmental Transfer.

Gross Domestic Product (GDP)—a measure of the income generated by the production of goods and services on U.S. soil, including production financed by foreigners.

Growth Rate—a constant percentage rate at which a data series would grow or contract on a yearly basis to reach its current value (formally known as the compound annual growth rate).

Guardian—the budget role characterized by protecting public resource by saying "no" to spending advocates and opposing spending increases.

Hard Fiscal Constraint Rule—rule imposed by another level of government or rule that cannot be changed by government officials on their own, but rather voters have to ratify any changes or, in the states with initiatives and referendums, the voters can impose hard rules on their own. (See Soft Fiscal Constraint Rule.)

Hidden Tax—(a) a tax whose cost is not readily known by the taxpayer; (b) the impact of government regulation that dictates spending by those regulated and, although not classified as a tax, is the loss of alternative uses of the income. (See Regulatory Tax.)

Home Equity—the value of the home that the homeowner owns free and clear; the value of the home not owed to someone else (as in a mortgage).

Homeland Security—a government function defined in 2007 National Strategy for Homeland Security as "a concerted national effort to prevent terrorist attacks within the United States, reduce America's vulnerability to terrorism, and minimize the damage and recover from attacks that do occur."

Home Rule Charter—a grant of authority by a state government to designated local governments allowing these sub-state jurisdictions to operate with flexibility unless specifically mandated otherwise by state law.

Horizontal Equity—a standard of tax fairness that states that taxpayers with the same income should pay the same amount in taxes; a concept of fairness that calls for treating everyone equally by applying the same tax rate to the same economic choice.

Ideology—a systematic set of beliefs and values that shape our understanding of the world. These beliefs and values are the basis for political preferences.

Impoundment—presidential method to withhold spending authority without legislative approval; Congress prohibited the practice.

Income Statement—the basic financial statement that shows all the resources received and used during the fiscal period.

Income Tax—a tax on specific elements of income.

Incrementalism—the budget theory holding that small changes from prior decisions are to be expected due to the limits of time, resources, and ability to evaluate all options; helps describe political/organizational decision-making as influenced by the most recent past.

Independent Sector—another term for the universe of nonprofit organizations and non-governmental organizations (NGOs); not government nor private business.

Inflation—decreasing purchasing power of the dollar; the overall general upward price movement of goods and services in an economy.

Infrastructure—publicly owned fixed assets such as roads, bridges, curbs and gutters, streets and sidewalks, drainage systems, lighting systems and similar assets that are immovable and of financial value only to the government unit.

Initiative—proposal for a new law that is placed on the ballot by collecting a certain number of citizens' signatures on a petition.

Intergenerational Equity—fairness across age groups or generations; often thought of as requiring the generation enjoying the benefit to pay for it.

Intergovernmental Revenue—funds received by one government from another government.

Intergovernmental Transfer—payments made by one government and distributed to another government, usually through some predetermined formula.

Interest—the rental value of money; interest is paid to the lender of money (the investor) by the borrower, in addition to paying back the amount of money borrowed (the principal amount).

Internal Control—the system of policies, procedures and practices used by an organization to protect its financial and physical assets.

Intra-governmental Account—federal debt held by its own accounts, especially governmental trust funds such as Social Security; debt other than sold to the public investors.

Investor—the lender of money; the person or entity that has invested in or (purchased) the debt securities of the issuer or borrower.

Iron Triangle—cooperation among executive branch agency, those who receive the services, and legislative spending committees; considered a formidable team for higher spending. (See Issue Network and Guardian.)

Issue Network—fluid, temporary coalition around an issue.

Issuer—the borrower of money through the issuance of debt.

Lapse—the loss of spending authority when the appropriation runs out, often at the end of the fiscal year.

Laws—a binding custom or practice of a community; a rule of conduct or action prescribed or formally recognized as binding or enforced by a controlling authority; often enforced by the police authority of government.

Layoff—a mandatory temporary separation from a job.

Legislative Budgeting—a budget process that gives more power to the legislative branch than the executive branch; a budget process in which the units of the executive branch submit their budget requests directly to the legislature and not to the chief executive.

Legislative Call—in executive budgeting, the executive's request for departments to submit their proposals for changes in law to the executive for approval and submission to the legislature.

Liability—amounts owed.

Line Item—the smallest expenditure detail in a budget.

Line-item Budget—a budget that shows line items; when used in appropriations, a form of legislative control over spending and, therefore, the executive.

Line-item Veto—the chief elected official's authority to pick out specific items in the budget and veto them without vetoing the whole appropriation bill.

Lobbying—the direct promotion of a particular viewpoint in order to influence what government does (spends, taxes, regulates).

Local Option Tax—the grant of authority by a state that allows local citizens to vote for a new local tax.

Logrolling—an exchange of votes among legislators to pass legislation that achieves the goal of each legislator in the exchange; agreement (often unspoken) among legislators to support public spending in each other's legislative districts without questioning the need or purpose.

Long-Term Debt—debt with a maturity of more than one year after the date of issuance.

Luxury Tax—a tax levied on the purchase of an expensive item that is also considered frivolous or self-indulgent.

Mandate—a binding obligation by law or contract accepted by one organization in order to receive certain benefits or funds from another organization; can be a mandate on use and/or procedures involving the funds.

Mandatory Spending—federal budget concept meaning spending is controlled by federal laws other than appropriations acts; includes spending for entitlement programs and interest on the national debt. (See also Discretionary Spending.)

Marginal Tax Rate—the tax on the next dollar of income and the point at which economic decisions about work, consumption, and investment can be affected by tax policy.

Materiality—a matter is "material" if there is a substantial likelihood that a reasonable person would consider it important.

Means-tested Program—a distribution program based on the need of the person receiving the benefit; need is determined by a standardized method. (See Non-means-tested Program.)

Median Voter—a theory holding that contested decisions turn on the views of the voter in the middle (such that the vote becomes 51/49 instead of 50/50); a theory of electoral politics that explains the tendency of political parties to appeal to as many voters as possible by taking positions at the center of the issue(s).

Mega-projects—a very large public investment project.

Mill or **Millage**—measurement unit used in property tax assessment; one mill is equal to 1/1000 of a dollar and is multiplied by the taxable value of property to determine the total amount of property tax due; often referred to as mill or millage rate and mill or millage levy.

Monetary Policy—actions by the Federal Reserve, done as the central bank to influence the availability and cost of money and credit.

Municipality—a primarily urban political unit having corporate status and usually powers of self-government as delegated by the state.

Municipal Securities—debt issued by state and local governments, usually in the form of tax-exempt bonds.

New Deal—the name given to the programs advanced by President Franklin D. Roosevelt during the Great Depression.

New England Town Meeting—where citizens gather annually in a meeting to formally vote on the local budget.

NGO (nongovernmental organization)—term used around the world to refer to organizations that are neither public (governmental) nor private business. (See nonprofit.)

NIMBY (not in my back yard)—idea that conveys opposition to a change in building and development near one's property.

Nominal Dollars—the amount stated in current dollars. (See Current Dollars and Real Dollars.)

Nominal Tax Rate—the stated legal tax rate.

Non-governmental Organization—see NGO.

Non-means-tested Program—a distribution program in which benefits are distributed on some basis other than the need of the person receiving the benefit. (See Means-tested Program.)

Nonprofit—an organization classified by the U.S. Internal Revenue Code as a religious, charitable, or educational in purpose; activities that directly support those purposes are not subject to federal income tax (and most state income tax laws also). (See NGO.)

Non-recurring—a one-time source or use of money, instead of something that occurs over and over again.

Omnibus Appropriation Bill—a bundling of bills at the federal level authorizing spending by various agencies on various projects.

Operating Budget—finances goods and services consumed in the fiscal period.

Opportunity cost—what must be given up in order to have something else.

Other Post-Employment Benefits (OPEB)—benefits other than pensions earned by employees over their years of service that will not be received until after their employment ends; benefits provided to eligible retirees may include health insurance and dental, vision, prescription or life insurance.

Outlays—see Expenditures.

Own-Source Revenue—resources generated from sources that are under the control of the particular organization or governmental unit.

Pay-as-you-go (PAYGO)—current payment of current expenses; rule introduced into federal budgeting by the 1990 Budget Enforcement Act that required increases in mandatory spending or decreases in revenues be offset (or paid for) so that the change does not increase the deficit (is deficit neutral); used in state and local government to describe a financial policy by which the capital program is financed from current revenue rather than through borrowing.

Pecuniary Interest—having a personal financial interest in one side of a decision and the ability to make the decision.

Pension—financial resources received (usually in periodic installments) during retirement for past work performed according to prior agreements.

Pension Funds—accounts in which a portion of employees' salaries are placed and invested, so that resources will be available to pay for employees' pensions.

Pension Liability—a shortfall in pension funds to cover the employer's agreed-upon pension obligation to its current and future retirees; calculated by using assumptions about life expectancy and interest rates (actuarial assumptions).

Per Capita—a unit of measurement that indicates an amount of quantity per person.

Percent Change—change in a data series from the initial value expressed as a fraction of 100; calculated as [(newer number minus older number)/older number) times 100 to convert to a percent].

Performance Audit—an audit that focuses on performance of activities and work programs instead of strictly financial matters; can focus on economy, effectiveness, and/or outcomes.

Performance Budget—a budget with expenditures based primarily upon measurable indicators of work performed and/or quality of services produced or delivered; a budget that includes performance indicators. (See Performance Measure.)

Performance Measure—indicator of work performed and/or quality of services produced or delivered; specific, observable and measurable characteristics that show the progress a program or service is making toward achieving a specified goal.

Permanent Authority—the legal ability of a federal government program to continue in existence unless the law is changed.

Permanent Budget Authority—the legal permission to continue spending until the law is changed.

Personal Property—ownership interest in items either tangible (for example, equipment, household goods, or animals) or intangible (such as stocks, bonds, or intellectual property rights, where the tangible paper has no value because the value actually resides in the asset that is cited on the paper); state and local governments may tax one or more of these through a personal property tax.

Personal Services—spending relating to compensating employees, including salaries, wages, overtime pay, shift differential and holiday pay, but excluding employee benefits.

Political Base—the enthusiastic and reliable political supporters who are counted on to vote.

Political Thermometer Effect—public's evaluation of performance and responsiveness as influenced by people's feelings toward the party in office.

Politics—competition over public policy and priorities through the use of power and authority.

Politics of Resentment—a political orientation to look down at or feel ill will toward some other group; often associated with policies that redistribute resources.

Pork—negative label asserted to deride the specific spending or tax item by implying waste, inefficiency, and sometimes corruption.

Pork Barrel Politics—politics surrounding spending designed to support incumbents' reelection by letting them direct spending such as capital projects or grants to their districts, usually through the tacit agreement among legislators to support public spending in each others' districts.

Price Index—a statistical manner of tracking prices over time to determine the impact of inflation. (See Consumer Price Index.)

Price of Government—an estimate of the cost of government to the economy; often measured as total taxes or revenues as a share of the economy, defined nationally as gross domestic product, and for a state or city often as aggregate personal income.

Principal—the amount of money borrowed and owed, which is the basis for interest computations.

Privatization—transferring the production and delivery of a service and/or operation and administration of a function formerly performed by government to a private entity.

Professional Standards—a set of rules established by an association to guide the practice of its members.

Program Budget—a budget format in which spending is organized around the goals and objectives of an identifiable program or service; may be a part of one department/agency or cross several departments/agencies.

Progressive Tax—a tax by which higher-income earners pay a larger share of their incomes in taxes than do lower-income earners,

Property Tax—a tax levied on real and/or personal property according to the assessed valuation and the tax rate. (See Personal Property.)

Property Value—the estimated monetary value of property.

Proportional Tax—the tax rate is the same for all taxpayers without consideration of their income.

Public Enterprise—a business-type operation provided by government that may or may not be performed by government employees and may or may not be privatized.

Public Good—a shared benefit or service which is both (a) non-rival, meaning that one person's use does not prevent another person's use and (b) non-excludable, meaning that a person can receive the benefit of the good without having to pay for it because the benefit or service is delivered to the whole community.

Public Interest Group—a collection of like-minded people organized together for political action that the group claims benefits the general public. (See Special Interest.)

Quid Pro Quo—"This-for-that," receiving something in return for giving something, an exchange of benefits or favors, "I'll do this for you if you do that for me."

Rainy Day Fund—resources put aside into a particular fund now in case revenue is temporarily reduced in the future.

Rational Choice Theory—a theory derived from economics that explains political behavior by the actor's self-interest.

Real Dollars—when monetary values are adjusted for changes in the value or purchasing power of the dollar. (See Current Dollars and Nominal Dollars.)

Real Property—land and improvements to land such as buildings, paved parking lots, and landscaping.

Rebudgeting—the idea that the adopted budget is subject to amendment and modification during the fiscal year.

Recall—when electors vote to turn an elected official out of office.

Recession—a significant decline in economic activity lasting more than a few months.

Reciprocity—principle of mutual exchange or supporting behavior, such as in the *golden rule* that calls for treating others as you would like to be treated.

Reconciliation—an important political tool, instructions to congressional authorizing committees to change existing spending and revenue laws by a set date so that the targets set in the budget resolution can be met.

Redistributive Policy—costs are distributed widely and benefits are concentrated on narrow segments of the population; examples include Medicaid, food stamps, and poverty programs.

Referendum—when electors directly exercise legislative power and vote to adopt a specific law.

Reform—a change from past practice; a positive label for change that is used to rally support for the proposal.

Regressive Tax—lower-income earners pay a larger share of their incomes in taxes than do higher income earners.

Regulatory Tax—the costs of obeying government requirements and, although not classified as a tax, is the loss of alternative uses of the income. (See Hidden Tax.)

Rent-seeking—actions to increase one's income or economic returns at the expense of others, such as special interest group seeking to increase its members' income or economic returns at the expense of other taxpayers.

Rescission—reduction, often by chief executive, of spending authority during budget implementation below the amount appropriated.

Retail Sales Tax—see Sales Tax.

Return on Investment (ROI)—a calculation of an outcome's benefits compared to its costs; used to assess the economic efficiency of an investment with multiple years of benefits and costs.

Revenue—resources that the government receives in a fiscal period.

Revenue Bond—a bond secured by the pledge of specific revenues (such as water fees, parking charges, toll receipts, stadium admission fees) to pay the principal and interest, but not secured by the full faith and credit of the debt issuer.

Revenue Diversity—revenue is generated through a variety of sources.

Revenue Estimate—a formal estimate of how much revenue will be earned from a specific revenue source for some future period, typically a future fiscal year.

Revenue Forecast—an estimate of expected revenue.

Revenue Sharing—when one level of government shares its revenues with another, usually at a set rate or amount.

Revised Budget—a legal change to the adopted budget.

Right-of-Way—the right by a public utility or railroad to use land that is owned by someone else.

Right-Sizing—the term used to describe a variety of policies and practices that seek to reduce the size and scope of an organization or government.

Roll-back—the tax rate which would generate the same *ad valorem* tax revenue as was generated the previous year that usually but not always excludes changes in taxable valuation resulting from new construction, annexation or de-annexation. (See Mill Rate and Ad Valorem Tax.)

Sales Tax—a tax levied on the market price of designated items purchased; the companion tax is the "use tax."

Securities—the form of a debt instrument.

Securities Fraud—a violation of law in the selling and/or trading of securities.

Self-balancing Set of Accounts—the accounting equation, assets = liabilities + equity; alternatively stated as assets – liabilities = equity; GAAP for state and local governments modifies the equation as assets – liabilities = net assets.

Separation of Powers—each branch of government has its own set of powers, not to be infringed upon by another branch of government.

Service Charge and User Fees—a means of paying for something based on services received or paying to use something, such as a public golf course.

Sinking Fund—money put aside now, to be available to pay off (redeem) a note or bond at a specified time in the future.

Single Audit—the federal government allows recipients of its financial aid to provide it with one locally-generated audit (a single audit) of all federal dollars.

Sin Tax—a tax levied on the purchase of goods and services that are considered bad for the health or character such as taxes on alcohol, cigarettes, and gambling.

Social Capital—organizational networks, norms, and social trust that aid working together for common benefit.

Soft Fiscal Constraint Rule—a rule governing an organization's fiscal affairs that it controls and can change at will. (See Hard Fiscal Constraint Rule.)

Special Interest—an individual or organization supporting a position or program that may fail to benefit the general public or benefits a few far more than the public at large and the costs of which may outweigh the general benefit.

Starve the Beast—a political approach to check government spending by reducing revenues and increasing debt in order to squeeze discretionary spending.

State Aid—see Intergovernmental Transfer.

Statute—a written law enacted by a duly organized and constituted legislative body and signed into law by the chief executive.

Statutory Debt Limit—restriction in the law that limits how much debt a government or public organization can owe.

Stewardship—preserving the value of an asset over time; to safeguard the public's purse and also future choices and opportunities.

Stimulus—an effort by the government to spur certain economic activity.

Structural Balance—when the growth rate of revenues is equal to or greater than the growth rate of spending.

Sunset Provision—a law or program ends after a certain period of time as specified in the initiating legislation.

Sunshine Laws—or open meetings laws, to require meetings to be conducted in public session so decision-makers are accountable to the public.

Supplemental Appropriations—an authorization to spend that is adopted during the fiscal year for the current budget, usually as a timely response to unforeseen circumstances or emergencies. (See Emergency Supplemental Appropriation.)

Surplus—when revenues are greater than spending in a fiscal period.

Sustainable Budget—a budget in which current resources cover current benefits and services received by current taxpayers and residents and also any future costs associated with these current benefits and services. (See Structural Balance.)

TABOR—"Taxpayer Bill of Rights," a statutory limit on government's power to raise tax levels without the specific consent of the voters.

Tax—the compulsory confiscation of resources through the use of legal authority.

Tax and Expenditure Limit (TEL)—a curb on the taxing and spending discretion of a political jurisdiction.

Tax Avoidance—the use of legal methods including deductions, credits and allowances, to decrease the amount of taxes owed or tax liability.

Tax Base—that which is taxed, such as property, consumption, or income.

Tax Break—special, targeted exemption from general tax legislation.

Tax Burden—total tax payments divided by total income; taxes expressed as percent of income.

Tax Deduction—a reduction in the amount that is used to calculate an individual's tax liability.

Tax Elasticity—how readily the amount generated by a tax is affected by changes in economic conditions or demand.

Tax Evasion—the use of illegal methods to escape paying the amount of taxes legally owed or tax liability.

Tax Exempt Bond—see Municipal Security.

Tax Expenditures—revenue foregone by government or reductions in income tax liabilities from special tax provisions or regulations that provide tax benefits to particular taxpayers.

Tax Fairness—defining who should pay and how much. (See Horizontal Equity and Vertical Equity.)

Tax Gap—the difference between the estimated amount of money government might expect from a tax and actual collections.

Tax Impact—the initial burden of the tax on the person or firm legally obligated to pay the tax. (See Tax Incidence.)

Tax Incidence—the person bearing the ultimate economic burden of a tax. (See Tax Impact.)

Tax Liability—the dollar amount owed by taxpayer.

Taxpayers Bill of Rights—see TABOR.

Tax Rate—portion of the tax base that is taken in tax.

Tax Rebate—a refund of a portion of the amount of taxes paid.

Tax Resistance—a dislike of taxes that is expressed politically.

Tax Shift—the process by which the burden of a tax is translated from the Tax Impact to Tax Incidence, or the reverse.

Tax System—the accumulation of tax laws and their impact.

Tax Yield—the amount resulting from applying the tax rate to the tax base; the amount collected.

Three-legged Stool—the principle stating that income, property, and sales taxes should each constitute about one-third of total state and local tax revenues.

Tools of Direct Democracy—refers to Initiative, Recall and Referendum; may also include town meetings. (See New England Town Meeting.)

Transfer Payments—a form of financial assistance.

Transparency—information is readily available and understandable and decision-making processes are regular, known, open, and participatory.

Treasury Securities—the form of debt issued by the U.S. government.

Trustee—a role orientation of elected officials that places priority on their use of judgment and conscience in making decisions. (See Delegate.)

Unassigned Balance—the value of financial assets available for future purposes.

Uncontrollable—a budget item that is not subject to yearly renewal but continues until the enabling law or obligation is fundamentally changed; refers to Medicare, Medicaid, Veterans benefits, and interest on the national debt.

Unfunded Liability—see Liability.

Unfunded Mandate—see Mandate.

Unified Budget—a federal budget approach that includes all accounts in one consolidated budget, including trust funds (such as Social Security).

Unreserved Fund Balance—portion of fund balance that is available for future use and may be drawn on to balance the budget in a fiscal period.

User Charges—the payment of a fee for direct receipt of a public service by the party who benefits from the service. (See Charges.)

Use Tax—the obligation to pay the equivalent retail sales tax even if the item is not purchased locally but is purchased out-of-state, in a garage sale, or even over the Internet. (See Retail Sales Tax.)

Vertical Equity—a standard of tax fairness that calls for treating differently people in different circumstances; a tax is fair if its economic impact is related to income; the principle underlying the idea of tax burden. (See Horizontal Equity.)

Vested Interest—a concerned party with a strong preference that is related to receiving benefits or privileges.

Vesting—point at which the employee has a permanent legal right to certain employer-provided benefits even if the employee no longer works for the employer.

Veto—see Line-item Veto.

Wedge—a divisive issue such as abortion that often is associated with ideology and social values and that may be used to promote electoral support for one side and erode support for the opposing position and candidate, with consequences for budgetary politics.

Whistle Blower—a person who alerts others to a perceived wrong-doing by going outside the organization or around the usual chain of command.

Willingness to Pay—an acceptance of taxation.

Windfalls—unexpected money or resources.

Yellow Book—the compilation of generally accepted auditing guidelines for state and local governments receiving any federal funds; published by the U.S. Government Accountability Office (GAO) in a book with a yellow cover.

Zero-Based Budgeting—a budget format approach that places an emphasis on re-justifying each program anew each year.

REFERENCES

❦

INTRODUCTION

Dahl, Robert, 1982. *Dilemmas of Pluralist Democracy*. New Haven, CT: Yale University Press.

Diamond, Larry D. and Marc F. Plattner (eds.), 1996. *The Global Resurgence of Democracy*, 2nd ed. Baltimore: John Hopkins University Press.

Lippmann, Walter, 1956. *Essays in the Public Philosophy*. New York: New American Library.

Olson, Laura, 2009. In Alexandria, Virginia, weighing ethics in decisions about budget cuts. *Chicago Tribune*, January 1, 2009. At www.chicagotribune.com/news/nationworld/chi-ethics-budgets-thujan01,0, 4536195.story, accessed January 5, 2009.

Schumpeter, Joseph, 1943. *Capitalism, Socialism, and Democracy*. London: George Allen and Unwin.

Sen, Amartya, 1999. Democracy as a Universal Value. *Journal of Democracy* 10 no.3: 3–17, http://muse.jhu.edu/, accessed May 28, 2008.

Wildavsky, Aaron, 1964. *The Politics of the Budgetary Process*. Boston: Little Brown.

CHAPTER 1

American National Election Studies, 2005. "The ANES Guides to Public Opinion and Electoral Behavior." Ann Arbor, MI: University of Michigan, Center for Political Studies [producer and distributor], http://www.electionstudies.org.accessed Aug. 7, 2007.

Lewis, Carol W. and Stuart C. Gilman, 2005. *The Ethics Challenge in Public Service: A Problem-Solving Guide*. San Francisco: Jossey-Bass.

Office of Management and Budget (OMB), 2002. A Citizen's Guide to the Federal Budget, FY 2003. GPO: Washington, D.C.

Open Budget Initiative, 2009. Open Budget Index 2008 Rankings. http://www.open budgetindex.org/index.cfm?fa=rankings, accessed May 15, 2009.

Schmidt, Peter, 2007. Pennsylvania Lawmaker Schools University in Political Lesson. *Chronicle of Higher Education*, 53, 47.

U.S. Bureau of Census. *Census of Governments*. 2009 vol. 1, no. 1, Government Organization, Series GC07(1)-1, http://www.census.gov/govs/www/cog2007.html, accessed May 15, 2009.

CHAPTER 2

Alt, James E., David Dreyer Lassen, and Shanna Rose, 2006. The Causes of Fiscal Transparency: Evidence from the American States. *IMF Staff Papers* v. 53, Special Issue. International Monetary Fund, http://www.imf.org/, accessed July 16, 2008.

Birnbaum, Jeffrey H., 2007. Tax-Cut Supporters Ready for 'World Series of Lobbying.' *Washington Post*, Oct. 2, p. A17, http://www.washingtonpost.com/, accessed October 12, 2007.

Brodie, Mollyann, Lisa Ferraro Marmelee, April Brackett, and Drew E. Altman, 2001. The Will of the People. *Public Perspective*, special issue on Polling and Democracy, July/ August, pp. 10– 24.

Center for Public Integrity, 2005. State Lobbyists Near the $1 Billion Mark, Laws in flux for 19 states, August 10, http://www.publicintegrity.org/hiredguns, accessed 9–05-05. www.FireFighterCloseCalls.com, http://www.firefighterclosecalls.com/downloads.php, accessed July 1, 2007.

Frank, Thomas, 2004. *What's the Matter with Kansas? How Conservatives Won the Heart of America.* New York: Henry Holt and Company.

Gallup, 2007. The People's Priorities: Gallup's Top 10, November 2, http://www.gallup.com/poll/102526/Peoples-Priorities-Gallups-Top.aspx, accessed June 2, 2008.

Government Accountability Office (GAO), 2007. "High Risk Series, An Update." 2007, GAO-07-310, http://www.gao.gov/new.items/d07310.pdf, accessed July 10, 2008.

Harris Poll, 2005. Poll #19: National telephone survey of adults in Jan.–Dec. 2004. At http://www.harrisinteractive.com/harris_poll/index.asp?PID=548, accessed Oct. 15, 2007.

Initiative Use, 2009. Initiative and Referendum Institute, February, http://www.iandrinstitute.org/IRI%20Initiative%20Use%20(1904–2008).pdf, accessed February 19, 2009.

Kopits, George, and Jon Craig. 1998. "Transparency in Government Operations." IMF Occasional Paper 158, International Monetary Fund, http://www.imf.org/, accessed July 16, 2008.

Kranish, Michael, 2008. Obama's budget-cutting options are limited. *Boston Globe*, November 26, http://www.boston.com/news/politics/2008/articles/2008/11/26/obamas_budget_cutting_options_are_limited/.

Lewis, Carol W. and Stuart C. Gilman. 2005. *The Ethics Challenge in Public Service: A Problem-Solving Guide*, 2nd ed. San Francisco: Jossey-Bass.

National League of Cities, n.d. Davenport, Iowa, City Practice Online Database, http://www.nlc.org , accessed January 26, 2009 & May 22, 2009.

Orrick, Dwayne, undated. Maneuvering in the Political Environment. International Association of Chiefs of Police, IACP Research Best Practices Guides, pp. 1, 9–10, reprinted by permission.

Pew Research Center, 1994–2007. "Partisan Views on Government Helping the Needy." Retrieved from the iPOLL Databank, The Roper Center for Public Opinion Research, University of Connecticut, http://www.ropercenter.uconn.edu/ipoll.html, accessed September 25, 2008.

Pew Research Center for the People & the Press, 2007. "Trends in Political Values and Core Attitudes: 1987–2007." March, http://people-press.org/reports/pdf/312.pdf, accessed January 28, 2009.

Phillips, Macon, 2009. Covering kids. White House blog, Feb 5, 2009, http://www.whitehouse.gov/blog_post/covering_kids/.

Public Agenda, 2007. "The Federal Budget: People's Chief Concerns in 2006." At http://www.publicagenda.org:80/issues/pcc.cf?issue_type=federal_budget, accessed August 15, 2007.

Shaviro, Daniel N, 2007. *Taxes, Spending, and the U.S. Government's March Toward Bankruptcy.* New York: Oxford University Press.

Teichner, Martha, 2008. "Breaking through Gridlock in Washington." CBS News, October 5, http://www.cbsnews.com/stories/2008/10/05/sunday/main4502174.shtml, accessed October 5, 2008.

Usher, Dan, 1985. The Value of Life for Decision Making in the Public Sector. *Social Philosophy & Policy*, 2, 2: 168–191.

Weisman, Jonathan, 2007. As Lott Leaves the Senate, Compromise Appears to Be a Lost Art. *Washington Post*, November 28, p. A04, http://www.washingtonpost.com/, accessed Nov. 28, 2007.

Weisman, Jonathan and Christopher Lee, 2007. Showdown Looms as Child Health Bill Passes. *Washington Post*, Sept. 28, p. A01, http://www.washingtonpost.com/, accessed Sept. 28, 2007.

Williamson, Elizabeth, 2007. Obey Raises the Specter of War Tax. *Washington Post*, October 19, p. A19, http://www.washingtonpost.com, accessed October 19, 2007.

Wisconsin Government Accountability Board, State of, 2009. 2007–2008 Legislative Session Total Lobbying Expenditures (sorted by organization), September 08, p. 70, http://ethics.state.wi.us/LobbyingRegistrationReports/SLAESummary_AllOrgs_alpha0708.pdf.

World Public Opinion, 2008. "American Public Says Government Leaders Should Pay Attention to Polls." http://www.worldpublicopinion.org/pipa/articles/governance_bt/461.php?lb= btgov&pnt=461&nid=&id, accessed May 6, 2008.

CHAPTER 3

ABC News and *The Washington Post*, 1985–2006. "Divided over Size and Role of Government." Retrieved from the iPOLL Databank, The Roper Center for Public Opinion Research, University of Connecticut, http://www.ropercenter.uconn.edu/ipoll.html, accessed September 17, 2008.

Alt, James E., David Dreyer Lassen, and Shanna Rose, 2006. The Causes of Fiscal Transparency: Evidence from the American States. *IMF Staff Papers* v. 53, Special Issue. Washington D.C.: International Monetary Fund, http://www.imf.org/, accessed July 31, 2008.

Americans for Tax Reform, n.d. "The Taxpayer Protection Pledge." At http://www.atr.org, accessed May 24, 2007.

Association of Government Accountants, 2008. "Public Attitudes toward Government Accountability and Transparency." At http://www.agacgfm.org/harrispoll2008.aspx, accessed March 13, 2008.

Bernstein, Jared, Elizabeth McNichol, and Andrew Nicholas, 2008. "Pulling Apart: A State-by-State Analysis of Income Trends." Center on Budget and Policy Priorities, http://www.cbpp.org/, accessed May 26, 2008.,

Center on Budget and Policy Priorities, n.d. "What is TABOR?" At http://www.cbpp.org/ssl-series.htm, accessed May 24, 2007.

Cole, Richard L. and John Kincaid, 2006. Public Opinion on U.S. Federal and Intergovernmental Issues in 2006: Continuity and Change, *Publius* 36, 3: 443–459, http://publius.oxfordjournals.org/, accessed June 1, 2006.

Department of the U. S. Treasury, 2008.

Downs, Anthony, 1960. Why the government budget is too small in a democracy. *World Politics*, 12 (July): 541–562.

Ellis, Christopher and James A. Stimson, 2007. "On Symbolic Conservatism in America." Paper prepared for the Annual Meetings of the American Political Science Association, Chicago, August 30–September 2, 2007, http://www.unc.edu/~jstimson/apsa07F.pdf, accessed May 16, 2008.

Facing Up to the Nation's Finances, undated. At http://www.facingup.org/node/199/proscons, accessed July 31, 2008.

Money, Money, Money, *Public Perspective*, May/June 2003, pp. 48–49.

Montgomery, Lori, 2008. Big Promises Bump Into Budget Realities. *Washington Post*, June 21, p. A01, http://www.washingtonpost.com//20/AR200806200889pdf.htmlm, accessed June 21, 2008.

Newport, Frank, 2007. Americans More in Favor of Heavily Taxing Rich Now than in 1939, Half of Americans favor heavy taxes on rich to redistribute wealth. Gallup News Service, April 16, http://www.gallup.com/poll/27208/Americans-More-Favor-Heavily-Taxing-Rich-Now-Than-1939.aspx.

Newport, Frank, 2008. U.S. Satisfaction at 15%, Lowest Since 1992, Gallup, April 14, http://www.gallup.com/poll/106498/US-Satisfaction-15-Lowest-Since-1992.aspx and Jones, Jeffrey M., 2008. Trust in Government Remains Low. Gallup, Sept. 18, http://www.gallup.com/poll/110458/Trust-Government-Remains-Low.aspx.

Peter G. Peterson Foundation, 2009. "State of the Union's Finances, A Citizen's Guide." March, http://www.pgpf.org/resources/PGPF_CitizensGuide_2009.pdf, accessed April 10, 2009.

Pew Research Center for the People & the Press, 2002–2008. Retrieved from the iPOLL Databank, The Roper Center for Public Opinion Research, University of Connecticut, http://www.ropercenter.uconn.edu/ipoll.html, September 17, 2008.

Piketty, Thomas and Emmanuel Saez, 2007. How Progressive Is the U.S. Federal Tax System? A Historical and International Perspective, *Journal of Economic Perspectives*, 21(1): 3–24.

Prante, Gerald, 2007. New Census Data on Income Gives a Welcome Dose of Fact Checking to "Middle-Class" Rhetoric. Tax Foundation, Fiscal Fact No. 102, http://www.taxfoundation.org/research/show/22600.html, accessed May 20, 2008 and Money, Money, Money, Survey by the Gallup Organization, April 8–11, 2002. *Public Perspective*, May/June 2003, p. 38.

Program on International Policy Attitudes (PIPA), University of Maryland, 2008. "World Publics Say Governments Should Be More Responsive to the Will of the People." http://www.worldpublicopinion.org/pipa/articles/, accessed May 13, 2008.

Public Agenda, 2007. The Federal Budget: People's Chief Concerns in 2006. At http:// www.public agenda.org:80/issues/pcc.cf?issue_type=federal_budget.

Putnam, Robert D. 2000. Bowling Alone: The Collapse and Revival of American Community. New York: Simon & Schuster.

Rosell, Steven A., Isabella Furth, and Heidi Gantwerk, 2006. "Americans Deliberate Our Nation's Finances and Future: It's not about taxes—It's about trust." Viewpoint Learning, http://www.publicagenda.org/research/pdfs/americans_deliberate_our_nations_finances.pdf, accessed June 3, 2008.

Shapiro, Issac. 2002. Overall Tax Burden on Most Families—including Middle-income Families—at Lowest Levels in More than Two Decades, Center on Budget and Policy Priorities, http://www.cbpp.org/4-10-02tax.htm, accessed May 22, 2008.

Shrestha, Laura B. 2006. "The Changing Demographic Profile of the United States." Congressional Research Service, RL32701, updated, http://ncseonline.org/NLE/CRSreports/06Jul/RL32701.pdf, accessed May 26, 2008.

Steuerle, C. Eugene, 2004. "The Long-Run Budget Squeeze and the Short-Run Race to November." The Urban Institute, http://www.urban.org/publications/900717.html, accessed July 12, 2008.

Steuerle, C. Eugene, 2007. "Testimony before the U.S. Senate Budget Committee." http://urban.org/economy/fedbudgets.cfm, accessed February 12, 2007.

Tax Foundation, 2005–2009. "Public Opinion Surveys on Taxes." At http://www.taxfoundation.org/taxdata/topic/101.html, accessed May 21, 2009.

United Kingdom, Treasury, 2007. "How does public spending change with age?" http://csr07.treasury.gov.uk/spending-by-age, accessed August 2, 2007.

United Nations, 2007. "Vienna Declaration on Building Trust in Government. Preamble." http://unpan1.un.org/intradoc/groups/public/documents/un/unpan026677.pdf accessed August 24, 2008.

Wlezien, Christopher, 1995. The Public as Thermostat: Dynamics of Preferences for Spending. *American Journal of Political Science* 39, 4: 981–1000.

World Public Opinion, 2008. "American Public Says Government Leaders Should Pay Attention to Polls." At http://www.worldpublicopinion.org/, accessed May 6, 2008.

CHAPTER 4

Associated Press, 2008. States abstain from program. *The Oklahoman*, June 25, p. A8.

Becker, Jo and Barton Gellman, 2007. A Strong Push from Backstage. *Washington Post*, June 26, p. A01, http://blog.washingtonpost.com, accessed June 26, 2007.

Braga, Ann Hess J.D., staff director, Boston City Council, personal communication with authors, September 2007.

Cohen, Richard, 2007. Rangel's Reach. *National Journal*, Nov. 2, 2007, http://nationaljournal.com/about/njweekly/stories/2007/1102nj1.htm#, accessed Nov. 6, 2007.

Eggen, Dan and Paul Kane, 2008. Recent Bush Victories Smell of Compromise. *Washington Post*, p. A04, http://www.washingtonpost.com/wp-dyn/content/article/2008/07/2/AR2008071201 616.html?wpisrc=newsletter, accessed July 17, 2008.

Government Accountability Office, 2005. Performance and Accountability Report, p. 4, http://www.gao.gov/new.items/d061sp.pdf.

Government Accountability Office (GAO), 2008. "Supplemental Appropriations, Opportunities Exist to Increase Transparency and Provide Additional Controls,." GAO-08-314, http://www.gao.gov/new.items/d08314.pdf, accessed August 1, 2008.

Governmental Accounting Standards Board (GASB), undated, http://gasb.org.

Keith, Robert, 2001. "Suspension of Budget Enforcement Procedures during Hostilities Abroad." Congressional Research Service Report, Library of Congress, p. 1, http://digital.library.unt.edu/govdocs/crs/data/2001/meta-crs-6984.tkl, accessed August 2, 2008.

Keith, Robert and Allen Schick, 2004. "Introduction to the Federal Budget Process." Congressional Research Service Report, 98–721 GOV, Dec., http://us.gallerywatch.com/docs/ php/US/CRS/98–721.pdf, accessed July 24, 2007.

Lewis, Carol W., 2003. Budgeting in the Public Sector. In Jack Rabin, Robert F. Munzenrider and Sherrie M. Bartell (eds.). *Principles and Practices of Public Administration*. New York: Marcel Dekker.

Library of Congress, 2001. At http://thomas.loc.gov/, accessed March 25, 2009.

Moore, Stephen, 1998. Proposition 13 Then, Now and Forever. At http://www.cato.org/dailys/7–30-98.html, accessed July 26, 2007.

Morgan, Douglas, with the assistance of Kent Robinson and support of Drew Barden and Dennis Strachota, 2002. *Handbook on Public Budgeting*. Portland State University, Hatfield School of Government, State of Oregon edition.

National Association of State Budget Officers (NASBO), n.d. "Overview of State Budgeting." At http://www.nasbo.org/trainingProgramOverview.php, accessed Aug. 10, 2007.

National Association of State Budget Officers (NASBO), n.d. "Training Manual, Overview." At http://www.nasbo.org, accessed August 10, 2007.

National Conference of State Legislatures (NCSL), 2008. "Legislative Budget Procedures: A Guide to Appropriations and Budget Processes in the States, Commonwealths and Territories." At http://www.ncsl.org/programs/fiscal/lbptabls/index.htm, accessed May 22, 2009.

National Numismatic Collection, Smithsonian Institution. At http://americanhistory.si.edu/collections/object.cfm?key=35&objkey=211.

Office of Management and Budget (OMB). 2008. "Announcement." November 25, http://change.gov/newsroom/entry/president_elect_barack_obama_announces_office_of_management_and_budget_dire, accessed December 1, 2008.

Ohio, State of, Legislative Service Commission, 2005. "126th GA Budget in Detail—HB 66." February http://lbo.state.oh.us/fiscal/budget/BudgetInDetail/BID126/BudgetInDetail126_IN.pdf, accessed Aug. 10, 2007.

OMB Watch, 2007. "Understanding PAYGO: Questions and Answers." March 20, 2007, http://www.ombwatch.org/article/articleview/3763, accessed August 1, 2008.

Pazniokas, Mark, 2009. Man in the Middle. *Hartford Courant*, February 1, 2009, pp. A1, A9.

Persson, Torsten and Guido Tabellini, 2005. *The Economic Effects of Constitutions*. Cambridge, MA: MIT Press.

Texas, State of, Legislative Budget Board, 2007. Legislative Budget Estimates for the 2008–2009 Biennium, p. v-33, http://www.lbb.state.tx.us/LBE/2008–2009/LBE_2008–2009_0107.pdf, accessed August 6, 2008.

U.S. Treasury, Department of the, Office of the Curator. At http://www.ustreas.gov/education/history/brochure/history.shtml, accessed December 7, 2008 and May 15, 2009

Wildavsky, Aaron, 1964. *The Politics of the Budgetary Process*. Boston: Little Brown.

Williamson, Elizabeth, 2007. Obey Raises the Specter of War Tax. *Washington Post*, Oct. 19, http://www.washingtonpost.com/, accessed Oct. 19, 2007.

CHAPTER 5

American Recovery and Reinvestment Act of 2009, Section 1604, http://thomas.loc.gov/, accessed April 26, 2009.

Birnbaum, Jeffrey H. and Alan S. Murray, 1987. *Showdown at Gucci Gulch*. New York, Random House, Inc.

Bush, George W., 2008 "Remarks By President Bush On Summit On Financial Markets And The World Economy." November 17, http://www.america.gov/st/texttrans-english/2008/November/20081117112627xjsnommis0.6390039.html, accessed December 28, 2008.

Common Cause of New York, 2005. "Connect the Dots: Budget Reform." July, http://www.commoncause.org/, accessed December 30, 2008.

Confessore, Nicholas. Spitzer Seeks Ways to Find State Prisons He Can Close. *New York Times,* February 5, 2007.

Congressional Budget Office, 2009. "A Preliminary Analysis of the President's Budget and an Update of CBO's Budget and Economic Outlook." March, http://cbo.gov/doc.cfm?index=10014, Budget Projections (selected_tables.xls), accessed April 26, 2009.

Faust, Drew G. and Ed Forst, 2008. Financial Update, Letter to the Council of Deans. Cambridge, Mass. December 2, p. 2, http://www.president.harvard.edu/speeches/faust/081202_economy.php, accessed December 21, 2008.

Federal Accounting Standards Advisory Board, 2008. "Reporting Comprehensive Long-Term Fiscal Projections for the U.S. Government, Exposure Draft." September 2, http://www.fasab.gov/pdffiles/fsr_edfinal.pdf , accessed January 2, 2009.

Financial Accounting Foundation. 2006. Governmental Accounting Standards Board, 2006. "Project Pages: Economic Condition Reporting: Fiscal Sustainability." January, http://gasb.org/project_pages/index.html, accessed February 23, 2009.

Government Finance Officers Association, 2009. "Fiscal First Aid Techniques." http://www.gfoa.org/index.php?option=com_content&task=view&id=937, accessed April 24, 2009.

Kansas, State of, 2009. "Department of Revenue Annual Statistical Report for the Fiscal Year Ended June 30, 2008." January. Topeka, KS: State of Kansas, http://www.ksrevenue.org/pdf/forms/08arcomplete.pdf , accessed April 13, 2009.

Lockwood, David E. and George Siehl, 2004. "Military Base Closures: A Historical Review from 1988 to 1995." Washington, D.C.: Congressional Research Service, October 18.

National Association of State Budget Officers, 2008. "Budget Processes in the States." Summer, Table 11, pp. 40–42, http://www.nasbo.org/, accessed December 31, 2008.

Office of Management and Budget, 2005. "President Bush's Proposed Bill to Allow Results Commission and Sunset Commissions." http://www.whitehouse.gov/omb/legislative/grppi_act_2005.pdf, accessed January 17, 2009.

———, 2008a. Fiscal Year 2009 Federal Budget, Historical Tables, Federal Debt at the End of Year: 1940–2013, Table 7.1, http://www.gpoaccess.gov/usbudget/fy09/sheets/hist07z1.xls, accessed November 18, 2008.

———, 2008b. Statutory Limits on Federal Debt: 1940-Current (Table 7.3), Budget of the United State Government: Historical Tables, Fiscal Year 2009, www.gpoaccess.gov/usbudget/fy09/sheets/Hist07z3, accessed December 31, 2008.

Perez-Pena, Richard, 2006. State Panel Urges Broad Changes in Financing of Health Care. *New York Times*, November 21.

Ranney, Dave, 2009. "Closure Commission Appointments Announced." Kansas Health Institute, available http://www.khi.org/s/index.cfm?aid=2002, accessed May 19, 2009.

Texas Sunset Advisory Commission, http://www.sunset.state.tx.us, accessed January 17, 2009.

U.S. Treasury, Department of the, 2008. "Overview of U.S. Treasury Debt Management." June, p. 22, http://www.treas.gov/offices/domestic-finance/debt-management/Treas_DebtMgmt_Overview.ppt, accessed January 2, 2009.

———, 2009. "Debt Subject to Limit." February 18, http://www.treasurydirect.gov/govt/charts/charts_debt.htm, accessed April 26, 2009.

———, 2009b. "1768 American Bond." http://www.publicdebt.treas.gov/history/history.htm, accessed April 29, 2009.

CHAPTER 6

The 9/11 Commission Report. 2004. "Final Report of the National Commission on Terrorist Attacks Upon the United States." http://www.gpoaccess.gov/911/Index.html, accessed August 6, 2008.

Barr, Stephen, 2008. For Defense, Crunching the Numbers Is Half the Battle. *Washington Post*, May 12, p. D01, http://www.washingtonpost.com/wp-dyn/accessed May 12, 2008.

Beach, William W., 2008. "Discussion of the Costs of the Iraq War." Testimony before the U.S. Senate Finance Committee, June 16, Heritage Foundation, http://www.heritage. org/Research/Budget/tst062008a.cfm, accessed August 10, 2008.

Best, Richard A., Jr. and Elizabeth B. Bazan, 2007. "Intelligence Spending: Public Disclosure Issues." CRS Report for Congress 94–261, updated February 15. Washington D.C.: Congressional Research Service.

Broward County, Florida, 2009. "Broward County FY09 Management Report, 1st Quarter ending December 31, 2008." Quarterly Performance Measurement Report, Community Services, http://www.broward.org:80/budget/fy2009mr1qtr.htm, accessed March 30, 2009.

Bureau of Economic Analysis, U.S. Department of Commerce, 2006. Tables 1.1.5, 3.2, and 3.3, at http://www.bea.gov.

Bureau of Labor Statistics, 2006. "Cost of benefits for State and local government employees." September 2006, http://www.bls.gov/opub/ted/2006/dec/wk3/art04.htm, accessed July 11, 2007.

Bureau of Labor Statistics, 2009. "Employment, Hours, and Earnings from the Current Employment Statistics Survey (National)." http://data.bls.gov/PDQ/servlet/Survey OutputServlet, accessed May 15, 2009.

Cato Institute, 2009. Advertisement published in newspapers during the last week of January, http://www.cato.org/fiscalreality, accessed January 30, 2009.

Cole, Richard L. and John Kincaid, 2006. "Public Opinion on U.S. Federal and Intergovernmental Issues in 2006: Continuity and Change." *Publius* 36, 3: 443–459, http://publius.oxfordjournals.org/,accessed June 1, 2006.

Cooke, Alistair, 1973. *America*. New York: Alfred A. Knopf.

Davies, Glyn, 2002. *A History of Money from Ancient Times to the Present Day*, 3rd ed. Cardiff: University of Wales Press, http://www.ex.ac.uk/, accessed Feb. 11, 2007.

Council of Economic Advisors, Economic Report of the President, 2008. At http://origin. www.gpoaccess.gov/eop/2008/2008_erp.pdf, p. 54, accessed December 1, 2008.

Government Accountability Office, 2009. "The Federal Government's Financial Health: A Citizen's Guide to the 2008 Financial Report of the U.S. Government." http://www.gao. gov/financial/fy2008/citizensguide2008.pdf.

Heffley, Dennis and MaryJane, Lenon, 2009. Foreclosures and Falling Home Prices. *ConnecticutEconomy* 17, 1: 8–9.

Jefferson, Thomas, 1803. "Confidential Message to Congress." National Archives and Records Administration, http://www.ourdocuments.gov/doc.php?doc=17&page=transcript, accessed January 30, 2009.

Key, V. O., Jr., 1940. The Lack of a Budgetary Theory. *American Political Science Review* 34: 1137–1140.

Kosiak, Steven M., 2008. "Classified Funding in the FY 2009 Defense Budget Request." Center for Strategic and Budgetary Assessments, http://www.csbaonline.org/4Publications/

PubLibrary/U.20080618.Classified_Funding/U.20080618.Classified_Funding.pdf, accessed August 5, 2008.

National Association of State Budget Officers, n.d. "NASBO Training Curriculum." p. 100, http://www.nasbo.org, accessed August 27, 2007.

National Conference of State Legislatures, 2006. *Reflections, Being Ethical in Today's Legislature*. Denver, November.

National Governors Association and National Association of State Budget Officers, 2008. "The Fiscal Survey of the States, 2008." http://www.nasbo.org/, accessed August 5, 2008.

National Numismatic Collection, Smithsonian Institution, n.d. At http://americanhistory. si.edu/collections/popup.cfm?master_key=42&preview=&user=, accessed July 16, 2008.

Peter G. Peterson Foundation, 2009. "State of the Union's Finances, A Citizen's Guide." March, http://www.pgpf.org/resources/PGPF_CitizensGuide_2009.pdf, accessed April 10, 2009.

Raleigh, City of, North Carolina, n.d. "Performance Indicators, Fiscal Year 2005–2006." At http://www.raleighnc.gov/publications/, accessed September 12, 2008.

Sandler, Todd, Daniel G. Arce, and Walter Enders, 2008. "Transnational Terrorism." In Bjorn Lomborg, ed., 2009 forthcoming, *Global Crises, Global Solutions, Copenhagen Consensus 2008*. Cambridge: Cambridge University Press. (Electronic copy of unpublished manuscript.)

Shane, Scott, 2005. Official Reveals Budget for U.S. Intelligence. *New York Times*, Nov. 8, http://www.nytimes.com/, accessed August 5, 2008.

Shaw, George B., 1904. *The Common Sense of Municipal Trading*. Westminster: A. Constable & Co.

Stiglitz, Joseph E. and Linda J. Bilmes, 2008. *The Three Trillion Dollar War: The True Cost of the Iraq Conflict*. New York: W.W. Norton.

United Nations Online, n.d. "Network in Public Administration and Finance." (Table 4.b,) http://unpan1.un.org/intradoc/groups/public/documents/un/unpan014700.pdf, accessed March 27, 2009.

U.S. Census Bureau. 2007. "Statistical Abstract of the United States: 2007." Tables 1–2, p. 7, http://www.census.gov/prod/2006pubs/07statab/pop.pdf.

———, 2008. "State and Local Government Finances by Level of Government and by State: 2005–06. Table 1." At http://www.census.gov/govs/estimate/0600ussl_1.html, accessed August 22, 2008.

U.S., Homeland Security, Department of (DHS), 2004: "Budget in Brief." www.dhs.gov/ xlibrary/assets/FY_2004_BUDGET_IN_BRIEF.pdf, accessed July 1, 2008.

CHAPTER 7

Bowman, Karlyn, 2009. What Do Americans Think About Taxes? *Tax Notes*. American Enterprise Institute, pp. 99–105, http://www.aei.org/docLib/BowmanTaxNotes.pdf.

CCH International, 2009. "Federal Tax Laws Keep Piling Up," http://www.cch.com/ wbot2009/WBOT_TaxLawPileUp2009_(27)_f.pdf, accessed April 6, 2009.

Canada Revenue Agency, 2009. Taxpayer Bill of Rights, http://www.cra-arc.gc.ca/E/pub/tg/ rc17/README.html, accessed November 31, 2009.

Chamberlain, Andrew and Gerald Prante, 2007. Who Pays Taxes and Who Receives Government Spending? An Analysis of Federal, State and Local Tax and Spending Distributions, 1991–2004. *Tax Foundation Working Paper* No. 1, Figure 1, p. 22. At http://taxfoundation.org/files/wp1.pdf, accessed January 5, 2009.

Chamberlain, Andrew, Gerald Prante, and Scott A. Hodge, 2007. Who Pays America's Tax Burden, and Who Gets the Most Government Spending? *Special Report 151*,

Tax Foundation, http://taxfoundation.org/files/sr151.pdf, accessed December 18, 2008.

Congressional Budget Office, 2009. "A Preliminary Analysis of the President's Budget and an Update of CBO's Budget and Economic Outlook." At http://cbo.gov/doc.cfm?index=10014, Historical Budget Data (historicalMar09.xls), March, accessed April 26, 2009.

Conrad, Kent, 2006. Remarks by Senator Kent Conrad (D-ND) on Senator Ensign's Dynamic Scoring Amendment at Senate Budget Committee Markup of GOP Budget Process Proposal, June 20, http://budget.senate.gov/democratic/statements/2006/stmt_budget processbilldynamicscoringamendmentstat062006.pdf, accessed June 4, 2009.

Ernest & Young, LLP and Council on State Taxation, 2009.Total State and Local Business Taxes: 50 State Estimates for Fiscal Year 2008. At http://www.statetax.com, accessed April 27, 2009.

Hamilton, Billy, 2007. The Revenue Estimator's Lament. *State Tax Notes*. May 14, p. 513.

Hoene, Christopher and Michael A. Pagano, "2008. Cities and State Fiscal Structure." National League of Cities, May, http://www.nlc.org/ASSETS/121BB38D99-B4B8C9A 703AFDE4B43E/CitiesandStateFiscal.pdf, accessed January 30, 2009.

Internal Revenue Service (IRS), 1996. "1996 Individual Income Tax Returns, All Returns, by Marital Status." At http://www.irs.gov/pub/irs-soi/96in12ar.xls, accessed April 27, 2009.

——, 2000. "2000 Individual Income Tax Returns, All Returns, by Marital Status." At http://www.irs.gov/pub/irs-soi/00in12ar.xls, accessed April 27, 2009.

——, 2004. "2004 Individual Income Tax Returns, All Returns, by Marital Status." At http://www.irs.gov/pub/irs-soi/04in12ms.xls, accessed April 27, 2009.

——, 2009a. "2009 Inflation Adjustments Widen Tax Brackets and Expand Tax Benefits." At http://www.irs.gov/newsroom/article/0,,id=187825,00.html, accessed November 31, 2009.

——, 2009b. "Tax Withholding and Estimated Tax." Washington, D.C.: Department of the Treasury, Publication 505, March, p. 40, http://www.irs.gov/pub/irs-pdf/p505.pdf, accessed April 21, 2009.

Kansas, 1998. "Report of the Governor's Tax Review Committee." Wichita, Kansas: Kansas Public Finance Center, Wichita State University.

Kansas Department of Revenue, Division of Taxation, 2009. "Comprehensive Enforcement Program, Program Return on Investment (ROI), Annual Statistical Report for Fiscal Year Ended June 30, 2008." p. 67.

Minnesota Department of Revenue, 2009. 2009 Minnesota Tax Incidence Study. March, Figure 2-2, p. 32, http://www.taxes.state.mn.us/legal_policy/other_supporting_content/2009_tax_incidence_study_links.pdf, accessed April 27, 2009.

Okun, Arthur, 1969. Transcript of Oral History Interview I, 03/20/69, by David McComb, p. 9–10, Lyndon B. Johnson Library.

Organisation for Economic Co-Operation and Development (OECD), 2009. Data provided electronically to authors from Taxing Wages 2007/2008: 2008 Edition, www.oecd.org/ctp/taxingwages.

Rohaly, Jeffrey, 2008. The Distribution of Federal Taxes, 2008-11. Tax Policy Center, http://www.taxpolicycenter.org/UploadedPDF/1001189_federal_taxes.pdf, accessed June 5, 2009.

U.S. Census Bureau, 2004. "The 2004 Statistical Abstract, Resident Population by Age and Sex." http://www.census.gov/prod/2004pubs/04statab/pop.pdf,pdf, accessed April 27, 2009.

————, 2008. "The 2008 Statistical Abstract, Popular Vote Cast for President by Political Party." http://www.census.gov/prod/2007pubs/08abstract/election.pdf,pdf, accessed April 27, 2009.

————, 2009. "The 2009 Statistical Abstract, Resident Population by Age and Sex." http://www.census.gov/compendia/statab/tables/09s0007.pdf,accessed April 27, 2009.

————, n.d. "State and Local Government Finance, 2005–6, Table 1." [No page numbers and no publication date given.] At http://ftp2.census.gov/govs/estimate/06slsstab1a.xls and http://ftp2.census.gov/govs/estimate/06slsstab1b.xls, accessed December 16, 2008.

CHAPTER 8

Bush, George W. 2008. "Remarks By President Bush On Summit On Financial Markets And The World Economy." November 17, http://www.america.gov/st/texttrans-english/2008/November/20081117112627xjsnommis0.6390039.html, accessed December 28, 2008.

Caro, Robert, 1974. *The Power Broker: Robert Moses and the Fall of New York.* NYC: Alfred A. Knopf.

Center for Strategic and International Studies Commission on Public Infrastructure, 2006. "Guiding Principles for Strengthening America's Infrastructure." Washington D.C.: Center for Strategic and International Studies, March 27, p. 1, http://csis.org/files/media/csis/pubs/060327_infrastructure_principles.pdf , accessed February 27, 2009.

Congressional Budget Office, 1983. "Public Works Infrastructure: Policy Considerations for the 1980s," p. 1.

Congressional Budget Office, 2008. "Investing in Infrastructure." pp. 2–3, http://www.cbo.gov/ftpdocs/95xx/doc9534/7–10-Infrastructure.pdf, accessed September 10, 2008.

Eisenhower, Dwight D., 1955. Quote, National Surface Transportation Policy and Revenue Policy Commission Report, vol. 1, p. 2.

Elmendorf, Doug, 2009. "Implementation Lags of Fiscal Policy." Congressional Budget Office. http://www.cbo.gov/doc.cfm?index=10255, accessed June 3, 2009.

Federal Highway Administration, 2008. "Bridge by Year Built and Deficient Bridges." http://www.fhwa.dot.gov/bridge/britab.htm, accessed September 10, 2008.

Federal Reserve Board of Governors, 2009. "Municipal Securities and Loans." Flow of Funds, Table L.211.

Gallatin, Albert, 1808. *Report on Roads and Canals by Secretary of Treasury Albert Gallatin.* 1808.

Gray Plant Mooty, 2008. "Investigative Report to Joint Committee to Investigate the I-35W Bridge Collapse." May. At http://www.commissions.leg.state.mn.us/jbc/gpm.htm, accessed June 6, 2009.

MacManus, Susan A, 2004. Brick and Mortar' Politics: How Infrastructure Decisions Defeat Incumbents. *Public Budgeting & Finance,* March, vol. 24, no. 1, pp. 96–112.

Minnesota, State of, Department of Revenue, 2009. 2009 Minnesota Tax Incidence Study, March, Figure 2-2, p. 32, http://www.taxes.state.mn.us/legal_policy/other_supporting_content/2009_tax_incidence_study_links.pdf, accessed April 27, 2009.

Minnesota, State of, Department of Transportation, 2008a. "Letter from MnDOT Commissioner on Response to the Investigative Report to the Joint Committee

Investigating the I-35W Bridge Collapse." At http://www.commissions.leg.state.mn.us/jbc/mndotresponse.pdf, accessed June 6, 2009.

Minnesota, State of, Department of Transportation, 2008b. "The New Bridge." At http://projects.dot.state.mn.us/35wbridge/index.html, September 8, 2008.

National Infrastructure Advisory Committee to the Joint Economic Committee, 1984. "Hard Choices: A Report on the Increasing Gap between America's Infrastructure Needs and Our Ability to Pay for Them." Washington, D.C.: U.S. Government Printing Office for the Joint Economic Committee, 98th Congress, 2d Session, Senate Print 98–164, p. 1.

National Surface Transportation Policy and Revenue Policy Commission, 2008. "Report," p. 12, http://www.transportationfortomorrow.org/final_report/pdf/volume_1.pdf, accessed September 10, 2008.

Organisation for Economic Co-Operation and Development (OECD), 2009. Taxing Wages 2007/2008, http://www.oecd.org/ctp/taxingwages.

Orszag, Peter R., 2008. Investing in Infrastructure, Statement before the Senate Committee on Finance. "Congressional Budget Office Testimony. July 10, p. 6, http://www.cbo.gov/ftpdocs/95xx/doc9534/7–10-Infrastructure.pdf, accessed September 7, 2008.

President's Commission to Study Capital Budgeting, 1998. At http://clinton3.nara.gov/pcscb/wt_wise.html, accessed August 3, 2007.

Securities and Exchange Commission, 2007. "Disclosure and Accounting Practices in the Municipal Securities Market." At http://sec.gov/news/press/2007/2007–148wp.pdf, accessed July 27, 2007.

Washington, State of, 2006. "Master Plan for the Capitol of the State of Washington." p. 2–1, http://www.ga.wa.gov/MasterPlan/Campus-Master-Plan.pdf, accessed June 3, 2009.

Wise, Bob, 1998. Statement of Congressman Bob Wise of West Virginia before the President's Commission to Study Capital Budgeting. January 30, http://clinton3.nara.gov/pcscb/wt_wise.html, accessed August 3, 2007.

CHAPTER 9

Alexandria, City of, Virginia, 2009. "Proposed Budget, FYI 2010, Understanding the Budget." At http://alexandriava.gov/uploadedfiles/budget/info/budget2010/FY10Proposed Budget-Understanding.pdf.

Boston, City of, Massachusetts, 2005. "Recommended Budget, FY 2006." At http://www.cityofboston.gov/budget.

Mansfield, Town of, Connecticut, 2009. "Town Manager's Proposed Budget for FY 2009–2010, Fund Structure for Legally Adopted Budgets." May, p. 23, http://www.mansfieldct.org/town/departments/finance/budget/2009-2010_proposed_budget.pdf, accessed March 26, 2009.

Miller, J. Howard, early 1940's. Rosie the Riveter. National Archives and Records Administration, Still Picture Branch. Produced by Westinghouse for the War Production Coordinating Committee, NWDNS-179-WP-1563, http://www.archives.gov/exhibits/powers_of_persuasion/its_a_womans_war_too/images html/we_can_do_it.html, accessed April 22, 2009.

Organisation for Economic Co-operation and Development, 2003. Does budgeting have a future? OECD Observe, http://www/oecdobserver.org/news/printpage.php/aid/826/Does_budgeting_have_a_future_.html.

Oklahoma City, City of, Oklahoma, 2004. "Proposed Budget, Fiscal Year 2005–2006." At http://www.okc.gov.

United Nations, Economic and Social Council, Economic Commission for Africa, Committee on Human Development and Civil Society, 2005. "Participation and Partnerships for Improving Development and Governance in Africa, Issues Paper." p. 2, http://www.uneca.org/chdcs/chdcs3/Issues_Paper.pdf, accessed September 3, 2008.

CHAPTER 10

Alexandria, City of, Virginia, 2004. "Guidelines for Honest Civic Discourse for Those Participating in Meetings in the Council Chamber." City of Alexandria, Virginia. At http://alexandriava.gov/council/info/default.aspx?id=4518, accessed January 11, 2009.

Aviv, Diana, 2008. *Statement before the U.S. House of Representatives Committee on Ways and Means, Hearing on Economic Recovery, Job Creation and Investment in America.* October 30, http://waysandmeans.house.gov/hearings.asp?formmode=view&id=7492, accessed January 12, 2009.

Beeton, Jay, 2009. Electronic communication to authors. American Numismatic Association, http://www.money.org.

California, State of 2009. Governor Unveils Two May Revision Proposals to Address California's Budget Deficit." May 14, 2009, http://gov.ca.gov/images/essays/20090514_01.jpg, accessed May 21, 2009.

CNN, 2009a. *Airline passenger fee to rise.* February 26, http://www.cnn.com/, accessed February 27, 2009.

CNN, 2009b. *They're back: Representatives reveal their earmarks.* April 3, http://www.cnn.com/, accessed April 5, 2009.

Concord Coalition, 2007. "Concord Coalition Releases "Key Questions" and Encourages Voters to Test Candidates' Fiscal Rhetoric." press release, September 7, via email to author.

Congressional Budget Office, 2009. "Cost estimate for the conference agreement for H.R. 1," February 13, p. 3, http://www.cbo.gov/ftpdocs/99xx/doc9989/hr1conference.pdf, accessed February 15, 2009.

Goldman, David, 2008. *Bailouts: $7 trillion and rising.* CNNMoney, November 26, http://money.cnn.com/, accessed November 26, 2008.

Hoene, Christopher and Michael Pagano, 2008. "City Fiscal Conditions in 2008." National League of Cities, www.nlc.org, accessed January 12. 2009.

Kerns, Peggy, 2009. The Influence Business. *State Legislatures Magazine.* National Conference of State Legislatures, January, http://www.ncsl.org/, accessed April 3, 2009.

Lilly, Scott, 2008. Sarah Palin, John McCain, and Earmarks. Center for American Progress Action Fund, September 4, http://www.americanprogressaction.org/, accessed April 5, 2009.

Longmont, Colorado, c 2006. National League of Cities, City Practice Online Database, http://www.nlc.org, accessed May 22, 2009.

Moody's U.S. "Public Finance, 2008. Impact of the Credit Crisis and Recession on Local Governments, Special Comment." December.

Morgan, Douglas, with the assistance of Kent Robinson and support of Drew Barden and Dennis Strachota, 2002. *Handbook on Public Budgeting.* Portland State University, Hatfield School of Government, State of Oregon edition, http://eli.pdx.edu/erc/morgan/handbook6.doc.

National League of Cities, "Examples Database." At www.nlc.org, accessed January 26, 2009.

Office of Management and Budget, 2003. "Budget of the United States Government, FY 2004, Rating the Performance of Federal Programs." At http://www.gpoaccess.gov/, accessed December 30, 2008.

———, 2008. "Analytical Perspectives, Budget of the United States Government, Fiscal Year 2009." At http://www.whitehouse.gov/omb/budget/fy2009/, accessed July 28, 2008.

Organisation for Economic Co-operation and Development (OECD), 2000. Building Public Trust, Ethics Measures in OECD Countries. *Public Management Policy Brief no.7.* Paris: OECD, http://www.oecd.org/, accessed January 12, 2009.

Pagano, Michael, A., and Jocelyn M. Johnston, 2000. Life at the Bottom of the Fiscal Food Chain: Examining City and County Revenue Decisions. *Publius* 30(1):159–170.

Primavera, 2008. "Government 2.0 Study Makes Case for "Change" in Government—Highlights Challenges of Transition from Rhetoric to Reality." At http://www.primavera.com/, accessed December 21, 2008.

Rosell, Steven A., Isabella Furth, Heidi Gantwerk, 2006. Americans Deliberate Our Nation's Finances and Future: It's not about taxes—It's about trust. *Public Agenda*, ViewPoint Learning, http://www.publicagenda.org/, accessed January 12, 2009.

U.S. Customs Service, n.d. "Over 200 Years of History." At http://www.cbp.gov/xp/cgov/about/history/history2.xml, accessed Dec. 24, 2008.

U.S. Treasury, Department of, 2008. "President George W. Bush Signs the Emergency Economic Stabilization Act of 2008." At http://www.treasury.gov, accessed October 29, 2008.

Vice President of the United States Middle Class Task Force, 2009. "Financing the Dream: Securing College Affordability for the Middle Class." At http://www.whitehouse.gov/assets/documents/staff_report_college_affordability1.pdf, accessed April 18, 2009.

White House, 2009. Photo by Pete Souza, 2009. President Obama signing the American Recovery and Reinvestment Act of 2009. February 17, http://www.whitehouse.gov/, accessed February 18, 2009.

Works Progress Administration (WPA), *circa* 1936–1940. *Democracy…a challenge. U.S.* Library of Congress, Prints and Photographs Division, http://memory.loc.gov/, accessed Nov. 23, 2008.

APPENDIX A

Government Accountability Office (GAO), 2005. "A Glossary of Terms Used in the Federal Budget Process." (Appendix II, Federal Budget Formulation and Appropriation Processes.) GAO- 05–734SP, September, pp. 117–119, http://www.gao.gov/new.items/d05734sp.pdf, accessed March 6, 2009.

Office of Management and Budget, 2008. "OMB Circular No. A–11 (2008)." Sec.10, pp. 3–5, http://www.whitehouse.gov/pdf, accessed April 14, 2009.

Office of the Federal Register, 2008. "The United States Government Manual 2008/2009." National Archives and Records Administration, June, http://www.gpoaccess.gov/.

INDEX

‹❈›